The Life of Sir John Eliot

SIR JOHN ELIOT, 1628

From the portrait at Port Eliot
reproduced by permission of the Earl of St. Germans

THE LIFE OF
Sir John Eliot

1592 TO 1632

STRUGGLE FOR PARLIAMENTARY

FREEDOM

❦

HAROLD HULME

New York University

LONDON

GEORGE ALLEN & UNWIN LTD

RUSKIN HOUSE MUSEUM STREET

PRINTED IN GREAT BRITAIN
in 11 point Bembo type
BY SIMSON SHAND LTD
LONDON, HERTFORD AND HARLOW

To

WALLACE NOTESTEIN

An Inspiring Teacher

PREFACE

WHEN I began to work on the life of Sir John Eliot in 1930 I soon realized that the Eliot papers at Port Eliot, St. Germans, Cornwall, must be carefully examined. While in England in 1933 I obtained permission to use these papers, and I shall never forget the gracious and cordial hospitality the Hon Mr Montague Eliot, now the 8th Earl of St. Germans, showed me during the four months I worked at Port Eliot. I am deeply grateful to him for putting at my disposal all the Eliot papers and for enabling me to obtain photographs of the two Eliot portraits I have used as illustrations in this book. Many thanks are due to the officials of the British Museum, Public Record Office, South Kensington Museum and Bodleian Library for their assistance in my search for Eliot material. But above all my deepest gratitude and thanks are due to Miss C. V. Wedgwood, who not only read my manuscript and chose two portraits to serve as illustrations but also with unflagging effort finally found the right publisher for this book.

In this country I cannot thank enough my old friend and former mentor, Professor Wallace Notestein, for lending me the typescripts of numerous unpublished parliamentary diaries I have been so fortunate to be able to use. Also I must thank the Yale University Library for lending me microfilms of several of these diaries. But Professor Notestein deserves even more of my thanks for reading my manuscript in its first and longest form and for giving me much helpful criticism. Likewise I must express great thanks to my old and valued friend, Professor Ross J. S. Hoffman of Fordham University, for his careful reading of that first manuscript and his many fruitful suggestions. Finally, to my younger friends, Professor John F. Glaser of Ripon College, Mr Thomas R. Parker and Mr D. Hugh Darden of New York University, are due my thanks for reading the final manuscript and making many proposals for improving it.

I must say something about the spelling, capitalization and punctuation I have used in my quotations. As is well known, according to modern standards the spelling and punctuation of seventeenth-century men and women were bad. Sir John Eliot was no exception. If anything he was worse than many of his contemporaries. In addition his style was frequently involved and confusing to the reader. Because of these factors I have modernized the spelling and capitalization of all quotations from whatsoever source. In the case of Eliot I have also on occasion changed his punctuation to make his meaning a bit clearer to the reader. But I have never tampered with his words without indicating such an alteration. Modern dating has been used throughout this work.

HAROLD HULME

Larchmont, N.Y.
September 1956

CONTENTS

ILLUSTRATIONS

INTRODUCTION

BETWEEN March, 1603, when James I succeeded to the goodly heritage of the Tudor monarchy, and March, 1629, when Charles I decided to rule without the assistance of his Lords and Commons, seven Parliaments met. With every session, possibly excluding that of 1624, the battle of words in the House of Commons grew more intense, as it raged with increasing bitterness over the misgovernment of the early Stuarts. A minority in the House of Commons gradually grew into a majority led by some of the ablest minds in the country. The attack of this opposition, for 'opposition' it was, centred on policies and on men rather than on the Crown. But as the Crown regarded itself responsible for both its ministers and their policies, James and particularly Charles considered this attack to be directed against themselves. Thus, to curb the power of a minister, to challenge the policy of the government, meant an assault upon the sovereignty of the Crown. Under the aegis of the divine right theory both James and Charles felt that their sovereign power in the state was inviolate. Only occasionally and grudgingly would they acknowledge that their powers were limited in any way. To Charles the increasing opposition in the House of Commons was nothing less than rebellion. But the Commons did not regard their criticism as disloyal, certainly not during the debates of these seven Parliaments. They could not see that if they continued to run counter to the fixed ideas of the King the result might be rebellion. That is what happened, but not until after the Long Parliament met in November, 1640.

Among the leaders of the opposition Sir John Eliot ranked high. He sat in five of the seven Parliaments and was active in the last four. To him loyalty to the Crown was a sacred principle. To him the right of the Commons to attack a minister of the Crown without so much as scratching royal sovereignty was unquestioned. To him the House of Commons above all was sacrosanct. When it came to the government of England Sir John Eliot was an idealist. His ideal was that King and Commons should work together in perfect harmony for the good of the country. Towards this ideal he was always striving during his parliamentary career. But the tragedy of Eliot's last years was the growing conflict between King Charles and the House of Commons. Blind to this struggle for most of that time because he could always blame a minister for the troubles of the nation, Sir John naturally leaned more and more to the side of the Commons. But he was never given the opportunity to witness the consequences of the attack he and others were pushing so relentlessly. He died too soon. While his colleagues Pym and Hampden became famous as leaders of a rebellion, Eliot died in the Tower a decade before it commenced. He died a martyr to freedom of speech in the House of Commons. There, gifted as a speaker above all others of his day, he defended it. In the royal courts he fought for it. That is the basis of his fame, that and his oratory which at times stirred the lower House to its depths.

In 1865 John Forster published his *Sir John Eliot* in two volumes. Seven years later he issued a second edition somewhat revised and reduced in size. Ever since, this work has been considered the standard life, in fact an outstanding biography, by students of the seventeenth century. It has been cited by all who have written during the last seventy-five years on the men and times of the early decades of that century. But John Forster was not a good historian as measured by the standards of the twentieth century. He was a Whig with such a strong bias that it was reflected in every page of his book. He could not see both sides of any question where his sympathies were involved. He read the controversial history of his country with the belief that only one side was right. He depicted the life of a man as being so perfect that not a flaw was apparent in his character, mind, and actions. Such a man was Sir John Eliot peering from the pages of John Forster's biography.

The Eliot presented by Forster has been revised and redrawn by S. R. Gardiner in his ten-volume *History of England, 1603–1642*, and in his article in the *Dictionary of National Biography*. Gardiner, employing a few sources Forster never saw but depending chiefly on his two-volume *Eliot*, has toned down the man, made him more plausible, more historical, and more of an idealist. While the main lines of Eliot's personality and contributions have been correctly drawn by Gardiner, few readers are willing or have the time or opportunity to follow Eliot in the scattered pages and volumes of that great historian's detailed account of men and events during the first half of the seventeenth century. A new full-length biography has long been needed. The purpose of this book is to fill that need and present as complete and as accurate a picture of Sir John Eliot as the surviving sources permit.

For over twenty years I have been engaged on this work. I have visited Port Eliot in Cornwall. There through the kindness and courtesy of The Rt Hon Sir Montague Eliot, 8th Earl of St. Germans, I worked over the papers of Sir John. Though these Port Eliot papers disclosed few new facts to be added to those presented by Forster in his biography, to me they revealed an Eliot totally different from Forster's hero and an Eliot different in many respects from Gardiner's delineation of him. Also at Port Eliot I found in the muniment room a box of deeds and papers which Forster either never saw or never bothered to investigate.[1] These papers contained a number of new facts on the early history of the Eliot family, on its economic status shortly before and after the birth of Sir John, and on some of the events of the life of that man. The manuscripts of the Bodleian Library, British Museum, and Public Record Office brought to light little that was new on Eliot, but enabled me to use in their original form all the letters, papers, and documents which Forster cites in his biography.

Apart from the above, the most important contribution of new source material to be found in my life of Eliot comes from a dozen or so unpublished parliamentary diaries. They were compiled in the last Parliament of James and in the second and third of Charles. It was through the kindness of Professor Wallace Notestein and the library of Yale University that I was able to make use of copies of these diaries. Taken together with those printed in *Commons Debates for 1629* by Wallace Notestein and Frances H. Relf these unpublished diaries help to complete the picture of Sir John Eliot in the House of Commons. Not having had the use of such diaries Forster was confronted with numerous gaps in his story. Some he fills by means of his own coloured imagination, others he leaves for the reader to fill. Gardiner has employed two or three of these diaries with the result that he has been able to change several lines in Forster's portrait of Eliot.

My own conception of Eliot, based on these varied sources, is a man of moderate ability but ample means, a brilliant orator but a slovenly thinker, an ambitious man touched with vanity, selfishness, and opportunism, a man of little spiritual depth to whom Protestantism was none the less sacred, and an idealist in government who was so loyal to his

---

[1] Of invaluable assistance to me in examining the contents of this box was an excellent manuscript catalogue compiled by Charles Henderson, dated 1928. He was a young don at Corpus Christi College, Oxford, whose interest in local history, particularly that of Cornwall, resulted in the posthumous publication in 1935 of his *Essays in Cornish History*.

convictions that he was eager to fight and willing to die for them. Sir John Eliot's story is an integral part of the early, and to my mind the determining, years of the great constitutional drama of the seventeenth century. It is my hope that this biography will not only prove to be an unprejudiced and comprehensive reinterpretation of a significant historical figure, but also that it will make for a clearer understanding of the development of parliamentary freedom and supremacy in England.

ABBREVIATIONS

⁊⟨ᚾ⟩ᚷ

A.P.C.	*Acts of the Privy Council*
C.S.P.D.	*Calendar of State Papers, Domestic*
C.J.	*Journals of the House of Commons*
C.J. 1625	*Journals of the House of Commons from June 21 to July 5, 1625*
C. and T. Chas. I	Birch, Thomas: *The Court and Times of Charles the First*
D.N.B.	*Dictionary of National Biography*
'Eliot and Vice-Admir.'	Hulme, Harold: 'Sir John Eliot and The Vice-Admiralty of Devon'. *Camden Miscellany*, Vol. XVII
E.H.R.	*English Historical Review*
Eph. Parl.	Fuller, Thomas: *Ephemeris Parliamentaria or A Faithfull Register of the Transactions in Parliament, in the 3rd and 4th years of the reign of . . . King Charles*
Forster, *Eliot*	Forster, John: *Sir John Eliot*
Gardiner	Gardiner, S. R.: *The History of England, 1603–1642*
G.E.C.	Cokayne, G. E., editor of *The Complete Peerage of England* and *The Complete Baronetage*
H.M.C.	*Historical Manuscripts Commission*
'Inventory'	Hulme, Harold: 'A Probate Inventory of Goods and Chattels of Sir John Eliot'. *Camden Miscellany*, Vol. XVI
J.M.H.	*Journal of Modern History*
L.J.	*Journals of the House of Lords*
O.R.	*The Official Return of Members of Parliament*
Rushworth	Rushworth, John: *Historical Collections*
H.C.A.	High Court of Admiralty
S.P.D.	State Papers, Domestic Series

For abbreviations of Port Eliot manuscripts and parliamentary diaries see Bibliography.

CHAPTER I

John Eliot

1592 to 1618

SIR JOHN ELIOT, Cornish squire and hero of parliamentary freedom, was
born into a family of means, Tudor *nouveaux riches*,[1] whose roots were
barely covered by Cornish soil. For nearly two hundred years the Eliots
had lived in Devon, where they were not important people, small freeholders at best. The founder of the family's fortunes and the first to attain prominence was John Eliot, gentleman, merchant, and mayor of
Plymouth.[2] In 1544 when England was at war with France, Henry VIII
assisted Eliot to equip four ships and eight barques with which 'to an-
noy our enemies and defend our realm'.[3] Soon after the death of King
Henry, John Eliot leased the manor of Cuddenbeak in St. Germans,
Cornwall, from the Bishop of Exeter.[4] He was the first of the family to
cross the Tamar into Cornwall.

Cuddenbeak was an old episcopal palace originally built in the tenth
century for the Bishop of Cornwall.[5] Situated on a hilltop overlooking

---

[1] A. L. Rowse, *Tudor Cornwall* (London, 1941), p. 202, speaking of John Eliot, the uncle
of Richard and great uncle of Sir John, says he was not rich and that the total value of his
estate was £34 5s. a year. This figure is substantiated by P.E. Title Deeds, no. 20a. But as a
measure of the real wealth of the Eliots it is misleading. Its source is a valuation for the
Court of Wards and Liveries presented in 1578 to enable Richard Eliot to obtain livery of
his uncle's estate. Such a valuation was notoriously low in comparison with the actual return from the properties involved. For example, in 1578 and again in 1635 under the same
conditions (*ibid.*, no. 29) Port Eliot was valued at £7 per annum. But in 1632 Port Eliot
actually produced an income of £66 15s. 10d. P.E. Munim. Room, Manor of Cuddenbeak
Title Deeds, Bundle LXIX. Consequently, it can safely be said that the actual annual value
of the estate inherited by Richard Eliot from his uncle John must have amounted at least
to £300, if not a good deal more.

[2] R. N. Worth, *History of Plymouth* (Plymouth, 1871), p. 127. He was mayor in 1534–5,
1547–8, and 1560–1.

[3] J. A. Williamson, *Sir John Hawkins, The Times and the Man* (Oxford, 1927), pp. 20–3,
26.

[4] At least by 1554. P.E. Munim. Room, P.E. Title Deeds, no. 7b.

[5] William Hunt, *The English Church from its Foundation to the Norman Conquest* (London,

the Tiddy, a tidal tributary of the Tamar, it was about six miles from Plymouth. Looking down from Cuddenbeak John Eliot must have been entranced by the old Norman church and Augustinian priory[1] flanked on two sides by copses of beach and meadow lands rolling to the river bank. He must have looked with yearning at these buildings and broad acres which a short time ago had fallen into the hands of the Champernown family in consequence of the monastic depredations of Henry VIII.[2] In 1565 Henry Champernown sold to John Eliot of Cuddenbeak for £500 the priory of St. Germans and nearly two hundred acres.[3] In consequence Eliot became a vassal of Queen Elizabeth. He held this Cornish property in fee simple of the Crown by service of one-fiftieth of a knight's fee.[4]

John Eliot made the former home of the priors his residence, but not until he had completely rebuilt it and had turned it into an attractive and extensive Tudor dwelling which he called Port Eliot.[5] Though he married twice, he does not seem to have had any legitimate issue. When he died on April 29, 1577, at the ripe age of seventy-four, he left his wife Grace and his nephew Richard as his executors and residuary legatees.[6]

Richard Eliot inherited most of his uncle's Cornish and extensive Devonshire properties. Among them was the lease of Cuddenbeak in St. Germans. But the mansion house of Port Eliot, orchards, gardens, and about fifty acres of land had been given by John Eliot to his wife Grace as her jointure. Eventually this estate reverted to Richard and his heirs. From 1577 to about 1598 he was living at Cuddenbeak, while from the latter date to his death in 1609 he made Port Eliot his residence.

Richard Eliot married Bridget, daughter of Nicholas Carswell of Hatch Arundell in Devonshire. Their son and only child, John Eliot,

---

1899), p. 300. Thomas Tanner, *Notitia Monastica* (London, 1744), p. 66. John Whitaker, *The Ancient Cathedral of Cornwall Historically Surveyed* (London, 1804), II, 181–3.

[1] Tanner, *op. cit.*, p. 66. Charles Henderson, *Essays in Cornish History* (Oxford, 1935), p. 24. Whitaker, *op. cit.*, II, 217, 225.

[2] Browne Willis, *Notitia Parliamentaria* (London, 1716–50), II, 143, 152–3. Rowse, *op. cit.*, p. 201. P.E. Munim. Room, P.E. Title Deeds, nos. 2 and 3.

[3] *Ibid.*, no. 11.   [4] *Ibid.*, no. 25.

[5] Browne Willis tells the story of how Port Eliot was named in Bodleian MS. Willis 2, f. 135v. This early eighteenth century antiquary relates in his *Notitia Parliamentaria*, II, 146, how he married Katherine, the sole heir of Daniel Eliot, last of the line of Sir John Eliot through his eldest son. Port Eliot was bequeathed by Daniel to Edward Eliot, grandson of Nicholas who was the fourth son of Sir John. The Eliot family of today is descended from Nicholas. See also Bodleian MS. Willis 41, f. 267.

[6] P.E. Title Deeds, nos. 18 and 19.

the future knight, was born at Cuddenbeak on April 11, 1592.[1] The middle-aged father must have been overjoyed at the birth of a son and heir. When, on April 20, the child was baptized[2] in the old Norman church festivities were the order of the day at Cuddenbeak. Richard Eliot invited his neighbours to drink to the health and prosperity of his son and feast upon the bounty of his lands. It is said that the lord of Cuddenbeak and Port Eliot 'by his ancient hospitality and generous living [had] attracted the acquaintance of most of the gentlemen in his neighbourhood who frequently visited him at his house at St. Germans'.[3]

During the first eleven years of John Eliot's life Englishmen looked with growing veneration upon their ageing Queen. A new patriotism flowed through the nation which must have touched the boy. From some such source there developed in him a loyalty and affection for his sovereign which remained a powerful force throughout his life. Similarly Elizabethan Anglicanism imbibed at home and in the parish church of St. Germans gave John a lasting religious faith, gave him another loyalty which could be shaken only by momentous events.

That John Eliot was a normal or ordinary youth as measured by the standards of his day is doubtful. He was too sensitive, too intelligent a lad to be put in that category. His impulsive nature could flare at a moment's notice into an ungovernable temper and subside just as rapidly. His intelligence coupled with a vivid imagination gave promise of a man of exceptional ability. On occasion he took himself and life in general too seriously. On the other hand, he frequently displayed a gay and ardent temperament. As has already been indicated, there developed in this impetuous child a strong strain of loyalty which first manifested itself with family and friends and later was extended to principles and institutions. This loyalty had as a partial basis a streak of obstinacy which cropped up now and then to the dismay of friend and foe alike. It is doubtful that John Eliot's interests and pursuits were the same as those of the youth of his class, hunting, riding, and chivalric sports. He was too much of an individualist to fit into the pattern on which so many scions of the gentry were reared. As the child grew into a youth he became very much of a person. He must have been a puzzle to his parents, particularly to his father whose spirited sociability un-

---

[1] J. L. Vivian and H. H. Drake, *The Visitation of the County of Cornwall in the Year 1620* (Harleian Society, 1874), p. 67. P.E. Munim. Room, P.E. Title Deeds, no. 23.

[2] St. Germans, Parish Register.

[3] Bodleian MS. Willis 2, f. 135v.

doubtedly clashed with an increasing aloofness in his son. Possibly he
was better understood by his mother, but of her we know nothing.
Clearly he was spoiled, and badly spoiled, by his parents. To those who
understood and knew him in his youth he must have presented an intensely interesting personality.

That personality, so intractable at times, is perfectly illustrated by an
undated incident which involved young John Eliot.[1] It seems that he
was making a name for himself by living too gay and extravagant a
life. A neighbour, Mr John Moyle of Bake, a well-to-do squire living
two miles from Port Eliot, thought it his duty to acquaint Richard
Eliot with his son's excesses. That was a neighbourly act, to be sure,
but not exactly tactful or to the liking of young John. When the youth
was given the report accompanied by some exaggerated details from an
irate father, his temper got the best of him. With wrath in his heart he
picked up a sword and hurried to Bake. There he found Mr Moyle
drinking a glass of wine. Without a word of explanation John rushed
at him and struck him in the side with his sword. On seeing that he had
wounded Mr Moyle he fled. Fortunately, the wound was not serious
and John Moyle soon recovered. As the two families had always been
on excellent terms, a formal apology from John Eliot restored complete
harmony.[2] That such harmony existed in later years is attested by the
friendly correspondence between Sir John Eliot and Mr Moyle.[3] The
apology is of particular interest in that two of its seven witnessing signatures are those of William Coryton and Bevil Grenville.[4] In later
life they will be known as two of Eliot's staunchest friends. In his youth
they must have been more than acquaintances.

The most important person in the family circle of John Eliot, youth
and man, was Richard Gedy. He was to become his father-in-law and
in many respects was to take the place of John's father. Richard Gedy,
gentleman, of South Petherwin in Cornwall, entered the life of the boy
in 1605 when he paid £80 to Sir William Ward of Middlesex, for the
wardship of John Eliot.[5] The fiscal aspects of feudalism were still very

[1] This incident is based largely on Lucy Aikin, *Memoirs of the Court of King Charles the
First* (London, 1833), I, 264–5. Another version, not as reliable, is to be found in Laurence
Echard, *The History of England* (London, 1720), p. 424. See also Lord Nugent, *Some
Memorials of John Hampden, his Party and his Times* (London, 1832), I, 148–55.

[2] I found the apology in a modern filing box in the bookery at Port Eliot. It is an undated nineteenth century copy of the original.

[3] In 1630 while Eliot was a prisoner in the Tower. *Letter Book*, pp. 109, 143, 147.

[4] The other five names are entirely unknown and do not appear again in the life of Eliot.

[5] P.E. Mun. Room, P.E. Title Deeds, no. 23c.

much alive in England. Richard Eliot, no doubt involved in this trans-action, was conducting a clever piece of business. By that time the two fathers must have decided that John Eliot and Radigund Gedy should become husband and wife as soon as they had reached a suitable age. Richard Eliot was getting old; he was fifty-seven in 1603 when James I succeeded Queen Elizabeth on the throne. The Court of Wards and Liveries might cause John Eliot no end of trouble and expense if he should find himself on the death of his father a minor, unmarried, and a ward of the King. But now all was different. If affairs were properly handled, and if his father died before he came of age, John Eliot would find himself the ward of his father-in-law and virtually out of the cluches of that hated institution, the Court of Wards.

Just when the Eliots and Gedys began to draw together is difficult to say. Already by March 16, 1603, Gedy, according to the will of Richard Eliot, was named one of the four trustees of his lands.[1] That was good business, as was choosing him to be the father-in-law of his son. In eastern and northern Cornwall Richard Gedy was one of the coming men. Eliot seems to have been fully aware of this. Before his death in 1629 Gedy was to be sheriff of his shire[2] and one of the wealthiest of its country gentry.[3] Solely through his own efforts he climbed the ladder of material success, buying more and more land in successive years. Richard Eliot must have seen great possibilities in Gedy, twenty years more or less his junior, to have been willing to join his family to one without lineage or social standing before much of its wealth was ap-parent. Richard Gedy had only recently styled himself yeoman, now he was gentleman, and soon he was to write esquire after his name. That Radigund Gedy was the sole heiress of her father[4] made her a most desirable candidate for the hand of John Eliot.

But John was a bit too young either in 1603 or 1605 to be married. First he must be sent to school. Of his primary education nothing is known. We can only surmise that his early studies were guided by a tutor or some member of the family. In all likelihood it was a tutor, and that tutor was the parish priest, Mr Thomas Dix, to whom Eliot in later life showed more than usual favour.[5] On reaching the age of twelve in 1604 the presumption is that John was sent in the autumn of that year to

[1] P.E. Mun. Room, P.E. Title Deeds, no. 21a.
[2] Quietus roll of Richard Gedy esq., high sheriff of Cornwall, 1623–24. *Ibid.*, no. 68.
[3] Will of Richard Gedy esq. *Ibid.*, no. 65.
[4] Vivian and Drake, *op. cit.*, p. 67.
[5] See below, p. 386.

Blundell's grammar school. This school was just being opened at Tiverton in Devon and soon became the most important educational institution in the south-west of England. A generation later the two eldest sons of Sir John Eliot were probably educated there.[1]

Like so many sons of the seventeenth-century gentry John was sent to Oxford. On December 4, 1607, he matriculated in Exeter College.[2] No record of his student days has survived. That great gossip of his time, Anthony à Wood, says that John was at Exeter for three years but failed to obtain a degree.[3] It is much more likely that officially he remained at Oxford for only a year and a half, and that, excluding the holidays, he was in actual residence no more than ten months. As will shortly be seen, he was married in the late spring, and his father died in the early summer of 1609. Under the circumstances it is hardly likely that after that date Eliot returned to Oxford.

The days that John Eliot spent at Exeter College, though none too numerous, must have left their mark on the man. In fact, there should be sign posts in later life which point back to the Oxford days. But there were virtually none. To be sure, when twenty years later Richard Eliot, Sir John's second son, began sowing his wild oats at the University, his father could not understand his son's temperament or his indulgences. Possibly the natures of the man and boy were too much alike. The man had forgotten his youth, had been checked by life, and now condemned the licence in his son.

The deduction from this comparison, coupled with the known temperament of the boy who attacked John Moyle, leads to the belief that John Eliot did not take his studies at Oxford too seriously. On the other hand, the mature man displayed such a love, understanding, and knowledge of the literature of ancient Greece and Rome as would imply a firm grounding in the classics acquired at school and the University which was followed in succeeding years by intensive reading of the works of his favourite authors. In many of his speeches in the House of Commons Eliot, like other members, could quote his Latin favourites with the greatest of ease. In writing history and philosophy in the Tower he could smother his pages with citations from the works of his friends in ancient Greece and Rome. Undoubtedly Oxford had played

[1] William Harding, *The History of Tiverton in the County of Devon* (Tiverton and London, 1845–47), I, 43. See also below, p. 345.

[2] Joseph Foster, *Alumni Oxonienses, 1500–1714* (Oxford, 1891–2), II, 456. Andrew Clark, *Register of the University of Oxford* (Oxford Historical Society, 1887), II, Pt. II, 299.

[3] *Athenae Oxonienses* (London, 1813–20), II, 478.

its part in making it possible for the man to make such use and display of his learning. It also played a part in preparing a capable young man to perform the tasks and duties with which he would be burdened in life.

John Eliot must have made friends during his year and a half at Exeter College. He was far from being a recluse. Yet he did not have the gregarious instincts of his father. Within his circle he must have discussed the events of the day, on which Oxford was much better informed than St. Germans in that distant and secluded corner of southwestern England. But the events of 1608 and 1609 were far from exciting. Peace and prosperity reigned in the land. Though the extravagance of King James was beginning to be felt by a few in the nation, it had not yet become a topic common to the conversation of intelligent men. Oxford would hardly be touched by such reports; nor was it likely that more than a few rumours of the autocratic tendencies of the new King reached the portals of the University. Consequently Eliot's inherent loyalty to his sovereign could flourish and grow in the sympathetic atmosphere of his surroundings. But repercussions of the Gunpowder Plot were still being felt throughout the country. Anti-papist and puritan feeling was increasing. To Eliot and most of Oxford the latter sentiment had little appeal. But he must have been as eager as any of his undergraduate friends to harry the papists out of the land.

The year 1609 was to be momentous for John Eliot. As winter was turning into spring and the Hilary term at Oxford was getting well under way, John may have received disquieting news about the health of his father. The young man was probably recalled to Port Eliot where he quietly celebrated on April 11 his seventeenth birthday. His father, an old man of sixty-three, was failing so rapidly that it was decided to marry John Eliot and Radigund Gedy immediately.[1] Already in the previous year the manor house of Cuddenbeak had been settled on the two with the knowledge that the wedding would soon take place.[2] The ceremony was performed some time in the spring. Now Richard could rest in peace knowing that the future of his son was secure and that his lord, King James, through the Court of Wards, would be unable to collect a marriage fee from the Eliot estate. On June 22 the old gentleman died.

[1] P.E. Title Deeds, no. 23.
[2] In a modern filing box in the bookery at Port Eliot there is a sheet of parchment without heading and written in a seventeenth century hand. Among several items is to be found the following: 'Richard Eliot's settlement of Cuddenbeak on the intended marriage of his son John with Radigund Gedy, 1608.'

Richard Eliot left two-thirds of his property in the hands of four good Cornish neighbours, one of whom was Richard Gedy, as trustees to be administered by them until his son came of age.[1] The other third, consisting of lands chiefly in Devon, he had already bequeathed to his wife Bridget. The property he left to his wife and son was considerable. But not until the summer of 1617, four years after he had reached the age of twenty-one, was John Eliot able to obtain livery of his lands.[2] At that time the annual value of only those lands held of the King by him and his mother was between forty and fifty pounds on the basis of the extremely low formal rating of the seventeenth century.[3] In addition to this property the family deeds show that during the second decade of the century Eliot and Gedy, or Gedy alone, were buying more lands chiefly in Cornwall.

The most interesting of these deeds concerns itself with a lease rather than a purchase.[4] It was dated two weeks before John Eliot received livery of the lands he held of the King. On July 1, 1617, John Eliot of Port Eliot esq. signed a lease with Arthur Copleston gent. whereby Copleston received Port Eliot and all the land attached to it for sixteen years from the 10th of October ensuing on the payment of a fine of £1,500 and an annual rent of £6 15s. 11d. Copleston was to maintain Port Eliot in good condition. But he was protected against legal actions involving this property and was not required to perform any suits and services demanded by its overlord. Unless the lease was annulled or changed before it expired, it indicates that Port Eliot was not the residence of Sir John during the most active part of his life. The lease, to be sure, did not prevent him from being styled 'of Port Eliot'. In his correspondence there are only two letters dated from this manor.[5] Cuddenbeak was obviously the residence of the Eliots during the early seventeenth century. There young John and Radigund began their married life. There a child was born every two years from the birth of John in 1612 to that of Nicholas in 1628.[6] There the great orator sought peace and quiet after hectic days in the House of Commons. Who inhabited

[1] P.E. Title Deeds, no. 21a.   [2] Ibid., no. 26.   [3] Ibid., no. 25.   [4] Ibid., no. 33.

[5] One was written to the Duke of Buckingham on Feb. 28, 1625, and the other to Henry Waller on Aug. 11, 1628. S.P.D. Jas. I, CLXXXIV, no. 56, and Letter Book, p. 18.

[6] According to the Parish Register of St. Germans the Eliot children were baptized as follows: John, Oct. 18, 1612; Elizabeth, Dec. 29, 1616; Edward, July 9, 1618; Bridget, April 26, 1620; Radigund, Oct. 11, 1622; Susan, Oct. 14, 1624; Thomas, Sept. 7, 1626; Nicholas, June 15, 1628. There is no record at St. Germans of the baptism of Richard, the second son. According to Vivian and Drake, op. cit., p. 67, Richard was two years younger than John, so he must have been born in 1614.

Port Eliot before Copleston signed his lease is difficult to say. Possibly that mansion lay idle for many a year. Possibly Bridget Eliot, the mother of John, moved into its spacious grandeur after the death of her husband. But Arthur Copleston was unable to infuse life into that monument of the first John Eliot of St. Germans. From an inventory of the personal property of Sir John Eliot,[1] carefully written on a long parchment roll on April 6, 1633, less than a year after his death, it is clear that Cuddenbeak[2] still was the residence of the Eliots and that Port Eliot was neglected and unused. According to this record the furnishings of the dining room and parlour at Port Eliot are listed as beds, featherbeds, and trunks. It was just a storehouse. Copleston was its caretaker and, we assume, farmed its acres as a tenant farmer.[3] Such is the picture one gets of Port Eliot at the time of Sir John's death. Probably it was little different fifteen years earlier.

In following the fortunes of his property we left the youthful John Eliot suddenly thrust into the role of a grown man. He was married, the head of a family, and yet only seventeen. Of course he had his mother and a clever father-in-law at his elbow. With trustees managing his estate he could not have had too many financial worries. How his marriage affected him is difficult to say. We know nothing of his wife Radigund except that she was about the same age as her husband. The least that can be said is that if Oxford had had a sobering and maturing effect on John Eliot, his marriage and the death of his father continued the process. It is unlikely, however, that the husband of Radigund and the master of Cuddenbeak returned to Exeter College. Nor did he attend one of the Inns of Court for a few years to obtain a smattering of law, as was the custom among the sons of the gentry of that day. Anthony à Wood declares that he did, and even became a barrister.[4] But an incident later in the life of Eliot demonstrates that Wood was wrong in calling him a barrister. In a speech delivered in the last Parliament of James I Sir John dissociated himself from the lawyer clan.[5] In fact, Wood, the only authority to give him a legal education of any

---

[1] 'Inventory', pp. 1–14.

[2] Browne Willis writing at the beginning of the eighteenth century says that Cuddenbeak at that time was 'only a farm house'. *Op. cit.*, II, 148. Today 'the site of Cuddenbeak is . . . occupied by the goods station of the Great Western Railway at St. Germans'. 'Inventory', p v, note 4.

[3] If Copleston was only a tenant farmer, it seems improbable that he was able to pay the fine of £1,500. He is a mystery. His name has been found only in the lease and the inventory.

[4] *Op. cit.*, II, 478.   [5] See below, p. 58.

kind, is discredited even on this point. No Inn of Court records the admission of John Eliot. He never exhibited an extensive knowledge of law and always remained on the side-lines in the great legal debates of the House of Commons. Naturally, an intelligent man, who had long officiated in fields of government requiring judicial action, who was involved in a number of lawsuits, and who was the close associate of several of the most prominent lawyers of his day, was bound to pick up a great deal of legal knowledge without ever having listened to a reading at one of the Inns of Court.

What Eliot did during the four years between the death of his father and his twenty-first birthday, when he could assume the management of his estates, is uncertain. The report is that he went abroad and spent a year or two travelling on the Continent. On his travels he is said to have met young George Villiers,[1] later the King's favourite and Duke of Buckingham, from whose friendship he gained much to his future profit.[2] That Villiers was sent to France by his mother in 1610 is certain. He remained abroad for three years and travelled in various countries of Europe. If Eliot and Villiers met, John must have been on the continent in 1610 and the greater part of 1611. The strong supposition is, of course, that the young Cornishman was travelling without his wife, otherwise he was breaking the custom of his day. After a sojourn abroad for a year or two Eliot returned to the halls of Cuddenbeak by the end of 1611. His eldest son John was born in October, 1612.

Unfortunately John Eliot's impressions of the continent, if he had any, were not immediately recorded for posterity. No hint of what might be called travel recollections is to be found in any of his letters or speeches until he wrote his eldest son from the Tower a little over a year before he died.[3] But the information and advice he gives his son about various countries, especially the strong but natural prejudice he expresses against Rome and Spain, might readily have been acquired by Sir John Eliot without ever having visited these countries. In addition there is no evidence in the writings or speeches of Sir John that he ever acquired a speaking knowledge of any of the modern languages. Though there is little corroborative evidence available that John Eliot

[1] George Villiers was a few months younger than Eliot. He was born Aug. 28, 1592. Sir Henry Wotton, 'A short View of the Life and Death of George Villiers, Duke of Buckingham' in *Harleian Miscellany* (London, 1810), VIII, 613–14.
[2] The original and sole source for this statement is Echard, *op. cit.*, p. 424, who gives no source. All other authorities have accepted him without further investigation.
[3] See below, p. 353.

travelled abroad in 1610 and 1611 and met George Villiers, we must accept it as an episode in his life. It fits the pattern set by his class. It accounts for his later friendship with the King's favourite and the honours he bestowed on him.

While Eliot in distant Cornwall was growing to manhood, James I in London with the help of incompetent ministers, was depleting the financial resources of the Crown. The situation became so desperate that the King finally agreed to summon a Parliament. He ordered it to meet him at Westminster on April 5, 1614. When proceedings began John Eliot, barely twenty-two years old, was sitting in the House of Commons as a member for St. Germans.[1] It was probably through the influence of the Bishop of Exeter that the young man was given an opportunity to represent his home constituency.[2] What the member for St. Germans did or said in that talkative House of Commons during the two months the King was able to stand its criticism and invective is a question impossible to answer. The records are so brief and the man was so young and inexperienced that it is questionable whether the records or the man are to blame for this silence. But as a listener John Eliot must have learned a good deal. He heard that outstanding opponent of the government, Sir Edwin Sandys, lead the attack on impositions, those customs duties over and above what had been sanctioned by the law. He heard Sandys ably supported by Oxford's Thomas Wentworth and by that clever politician, Sir Dudley Digges. Digges twelve years later was to be Eliot's chief lieutenant in hunting down George Villiers, Duke of Buckingham. He heard denunciations of monopolies and undertakers, those agents who supposedly prepared many a constituency to choose a candidate for the House who would be friendly to the King. And then Eliot witnessed and possibly participated in a protracted scene which illustrated the youthful nature of a House in which

[1] *O.R.*, I, App., p. xxxvii. On Feb. 27, 1624, Eliot in his speech to the House of Commons says: '. . . but in the last two Conventions, at one of which I was present, and to the other a wellwisher'. And again he says: 'In the last meeting it were presumption in me that have nothing thence but on credit'. See below, p. 47.

[2] In 1614 William Cotton was Bishop of Exeter. He was succeeded in 1621 by Valentine Carey. On Jan. 22, 1626, Carey wrote to his brother-in-law, Sir John Coke, the King's Principal Secretary, about election possibilities for the Parliament of 1626. He said: 'I sent a direct messenger to St. Germans in Cornwall requesting the like favour of that Corporation as my predecessors and myself had formerly found. I requested of them their election to be made with a blank and left to my nomination, but if that could not be obtained then I commended unto them your name.' *H.M.C. 12 Rept.*, App. Pt. I, 251.

the majority were new and 'divers young'.[1] This was the uproar caused by the words spoken by Bishop Neile in the House of Lords. He had insulted the Commons on May 24 when he advised the peers against consulting with the lower House on impositions. The outcry of the Commons was so great and the demands for Neile's punishment were so insistent that it was not in the least surprising for King James to send these headstrong boys home to their constituencies after two weeks of such verbosity. So John Eliot went back to Cornwall on June 7 with much to think about and little to show for his two months at Westminster.

As his opinions of this Parliament which Eliot expressed ten years later are coloured by intervening events, it is best to leave them for future discussion. But the mental picture of his first Parliament which he carried back to Cornwall must have been a conglomeration of good and bad, with the bad, no doubt, predominating. Paramount must have been disgust at the futility and incompetence displayed in the debates of the Commons. But that tempest of words provoked by Bishop Neile, though it could not have produced respect in Eliot for the conduct of the House, may have aroused in him an interest in the principle which was to become the lodestar of his life—the defence of the liberties and privileges of the House of Commons. That, like the perfection of monarchy, appealed to an idealism which was to become more and more manifest in the man. Throughout the Parliament of 1614 minor incidents involving the privileges of the House were brought to the attention of the Commons. All these together with the Neile episode gave the young man food for intensive thought on his return to Cuddenbeak and prepared him for the battles he was to lead and direct in future Parliaments.

Within a few years of his return to Cornwall John Eliot was to receive new responsibilities and obligations. On June 28, 1617, his mother completed her will.[2] Bridget made her son her sole executor to administer numerous money bequests. There is no mention of lands. They had apparently been transferred to John at an earlier date. About two weeks later, as we have seen, Eliot finally obtained livery of the lands he held of the King. And then on March 4, 1618, Bridget Eliot died and was buried at St. Germans on the next day.[3] Not until May 14 was her

---

[1] C.J., I, 467.
[2] P.E. Title Deeds, no. 23d.
[3] St. Germans, Parish Register.

will proved and John Eliot esq. given its administration.[1] Four days later he was knighted at Whitehall by King James.[2]

[1] P.E. Title Deeds, no. 23d.

[2] W. A. Shaw, *The Knights of England* (London, 1906), II, 168. Shaw gives the 10th and 13th as alternatives to the 18th. But as Eliot is called esq. in the administration of his mother's will on May 14, he could not have been knighted before that date.

CHAPTER II

Sir John Eliot, Vice-Admiral of Devon

1618 to 1623

ELIOT's friendship with George Villiers explains why the young Cornishman was knighted in 1618. By that year Villiers had risen with electric rapidity to become the all-powerful favourite of King James with the title of Marquis of Buckingham.[1]

But why should Buckingham extend a helping hand to a young man of undistinguished family? There was more behind this act than friendship. As always, the court at London was divided into factions. In recent years, however, similar factions, or parties, were manifesting themselves in Parliament and were spreading through the upper classes of the nation. The opposition party in the House of Commons, opposed more and more to the policies of the government, was growing stronger. In a few years it was to be called the 'country', in contrast to the 'court', party. Buckingham must have understood this political trend and realized that the 'court' needed recruits. In Eliot he had a friend as well as a young man of ability, good family, and growing influence in Cornwall. To attach him to his side by means of a knighthood and an office or two might be of considerable political value in a county with many small parliamentary boroughs whose electors were frequently influenced by the gentry of the shire. Knowing Eliot, Buckingham must have been aware of his intense loyalty to the Crown. Hence the advancement of Sir John Eliot during the early years of Buckingham's power cannot be accounted for solely by his friendship with George Villiers. It made what followed possible but not inevitable.

Though 1618 witnessed an honour bestowed upon Eliot by King

---

[1] George Villiers was knighted April 24, 1615; installed K.G. July 7, 1616; created Baron Whaddon of Whaddon, Bucks, and Viscount Villiers Aug. 27, 1616; created Earl of Buckingham Jan. 5, 1617; admitted to the Privy Council Feb. 4, 1617, and created Marquis of Buckingham Jan. 1, 1618. G.E.C., II, 392–93, and Gardiner, III, 30, 58, 101.

James, it also witnessed a far greater dishonour reserved by that same King for Sir Walter Raleigh. On October 29, 1618, in Palace Yard the head of the great Elizabethan fell from the block, a sacrifice to Spanish vengeance. That Eliot knew Raleigh personally is unauthenticated; that he admired him is certain.[1] It has been said that Sir John witnessed the execution.[2] Over a dozen years later writing his *Monarchy of Man* while a prisoner in the Tower Eliot penned a graphic account of the death of Raleigh.[3] Only a man whose imagination was made vivid by suffering anticipation of a similar fate or one who had actually seen what he is describing could have written, 'guards and officers about him, fetters and chains upon him, the scaffold and executioner before him, and then the ax'. It is useless to speculate what Eliot felt for those who were responsible for this death. At most we can say that his dislike of Spain must have turned into bitter hatred.

In the year of Raleigh's death the fortunes of Buckingham had not reached their zenith. And under his patronage those of Eliot were on the rise. In January, 1619, the Marquis was made Lord Admiral. The office gave him the right to fill dozens of subordinate positions with his nominees. But Sir John was not immediately taken into the service of the Lord Admiral. First he was appointed on January 10, 1621, to the commission of the peace for Cornwall,[4] on which he served for four years. In 1624 he was placed upon the commission for piracy in his county and was made a commissioner of *oyer et terminer* to function in the six south-western shires.[5] Acting as a royal justice in criminal cases and helping in many different ways to run local government, the young knight was becoming prominent in his section of the country. Buckingham, no doubt, had a hand in guiding his friend into these paths of honour and service.

In the very month Sir John was receiving his first appointment to the commission of the peace for Cornwall, James I was meeting his third Parliament at Westminster. But Eliot was not returned to the House of Commons. It is difficult to understand why he did not represent St.

---

[1] A copy in Eliot's hand of Raleigh's *Prerogative of Parliaments*, not published until 1628 in Holland, is among the Port Eliot papers.

[2] Forster, *Eliot*, I, 34.

[3] II, 158.

[4] Patent Roll, 15—2234.

[5] He was reappointed to both commissions several times. His last appointment as commissioner of piracy for Cornwall was June, 1626; and his last appointment as commissioner of *oyer et terminer* was June, 1625. Crown Office Entry Books, Chancery C.181, no. 3, ff. 113, 118v, 130, 137, *passim*.

Germans or some other nomination borough at the disposal of the Crown in the Parliament of 1621.

Not for a year after James tore the famous Protestation on freedom of speech from the journals of the Commons[1] did Eliot enter the service of the Lord Admiral. On December 8, 1622, Sir Henry Marten, judge of the High Court of Admiralty, received a warrant from Buckingham ordering Sir Edward Seymour, vice-admiral of Devon, to surrender his office to Sir John Eliot.[2] As vice-admiral Eliot would have numerous judicial, administrative, and executive functions to perform. Of course, fees and payments went with these duties, of which the administrative were the most lucrative. A half or moiety of the value of all property seized, condemned, or found by the vice-admiral and his officers went into his pocket. The other half was to be transmitted to the Lord Admiral. Every Michaelmas the vice-admiral had to make a financial report to the High Court of Admiralty.[3]

Sir John Eliot began his duties in January, 1623. He was occupied during the early months of that year at Plymouth and Dartmouth salvaging ships for their owners, seizing some for the Lord Admiral, confiscating silver bullion and ordnance, and, with the assistance of several gentry and officials, pressing seamen into the service of the royal navy. In the last assignment he did his best to please the Privy Council, from whom he had received this order, but found it impossible to secure the required number of men. Most mariners preferred to go fishing on the Newfoundland banks rather than serve with little or no pay on his Majesty's ships which were being prepared for a peaceful trip to Spain. James was about to bring his son and favourite[4] back to England after the Prince had failed to win the Infanta on his secret journey to her home.[5]

By May, 1623, these routine duties of the vice-admiral of Devon were overshadowed by the appearance of a pirate off the coast under his jurisdiction. Before the end of the month Captain John Nutt established his headquarters at Torbay, just around the corner from Dartmouth.

---

[1] See 'The Winning of Freedom of Speech by the House of Commons' by Harold Hulme. *American Historical Review*, 1956, XLI, pp. 825-53.

[2] H.C.A. 30, Misc., Warrants for Appointments, Bundle 820, no. 11.

[3] For the duties and functions of a vice-admiral see S.P.D. Chas. I, CCVIII, no. 11, pp. 456-69. R. G. Marsden, 'The Vice-Admirals of the Coast'. *E.H.R.* XXII, 474.

[4] Buckingham was created Duke on May 18, 1623, during his absence in Spain. G.E.C., II, 393.

[5] For this paragraph see 'Eliot and Vice-Admir.', pp. 1, 3, 13; *A.P.C. 1621–1623*, pp. 433, 436, 496; S.P.D. Jas. I, CXLII, no. 42.

Nutt was comparatively new in the business of piracy. On the New-foundland fishing banks in the summer of 1621 he and a number of other rascals had mutinied and seized several ships. But what is most important for our story, Nutt had also been helpful in Newfoundland. He had protected, presumably from the French, a new settlement in the province of Avalon which was sponsored by the King's Secretary, Sir George Calvert, soon to be created Lord Baltimore. The good in this pirate seemed to predominate, for by the summer of 1622 he was thinking of renouncing his precarious career provided he could obtain a pardon. That should not be difficult, as he had a strong friend at court. The machinery was set in motion, the pardon was issued dated Febru-ary 1, 1623, with an extension of three months, but it arrived in New-foundland after Nutt had sailed for England. So the pirate continued to ply his 'trade', first off Land's End and then off the coast of Devon.

Sir John Eliot soon learned through Richard Randall, his deputy vice-admiral for Dartmouth, that Nutt was still looking for a pardon and would forsake his profession if he were permitted to keep the prizes he had taken. They were already numerous and were growing day by day. While Randall with the assistance of John Norber, Eliot's mar-shal, were paying several visits to Nutt's ship the *Defiance* to negotiate with the crafty pirate, Sir John was taking steps to obtain a pardon. Eliot's object was to keep Nutt in Torbay and prevent him from seizing any more ships before the pardon arrived. On one of the visits of the two officials to the *Defiance* Randall inadvertently gave the pirate valu-able information about some richly laden ships anchored at Dart-mouth. Though no attack was made on them Eliot's plan of keeping Nutt in Torbay was not successful. Early in June he captured the *Edward and John* of Colchester, a rich prize with a cargo valued at £4,000. But a few days after this piece of luck befell Nutt, Sir John was rewarded for his efforts. Somehow, somewhere, but not from the Privy Council, he obtained a copy of Nutt's old pardon. It was invalid, out of date since the first of May. Somehow, in some way, the vice-admiral fooled the not-too-clever pirate into believing that the pardon was good. Nutt even agreed to give a bond of £500 to Eliot in ex-change for what was actually a worthless document. On June 7 Captain Nutt sailed into Dartmouth harbour accompanied by all his prizes. He surrendered himself, crew, goods, and ships into the hands of the elated vice-admiral of Devon. Well done, Sir John Eliot![1]

[1] The story of the capture of Nutt is to be found in the essay of Mary B. Fuller entitled

B

The adage, to the victor belong the spoils, did not, I am afraid, apply to Eliot. He was confronted with the problem of what to do with Nutt, his crew, and his prizes. Naturally he wrote to the Privy Council for instructions. The trouble was that the Council was divided at this time. The main group to which Secretary Calvert was attached sat in London. A smaller group was with the King at Oatlands where the other Secretary, Sir Edward Conway, carried on the correspondence. It seems that the two groups, particularly the two Secretaries, were not in close touch with each other. Frequently days intervened before one was informed of what the other had done. In addition it has been shown that Calvert was partial to Nutt, while from later evidence we know that Conway was friendly to Eliot.[1]

During the rest of June the poor vice-admiral of Devon found himself receiving instructions from London and a few days later a somewhat different set from Conway at Oatlands. Conway was always late in getting his news, much of it from Eliot, therefore his orders were usually late or were slightly different from those issued by the Council in London. This group seemed not too enthusiastic over the trick Eliot had played on Nutt. And yet the Lords of the Council told Sir John that 'we are very glad and do commend your diligence in being so careful to discharge that which belongeth unto your part to do'. On the other hand Conway and King James were delighted with Eliot's success, so much so that he was given the honour of kissing the hands of his Majesty as a reward for his service. It is more than doubtful that Sir John ever had the opportunity to perform this ceremony.

One of the concrete results of this double correspondence Sir John Eliot was conducting was that on June 13 he was ordered to send Nutt to London. He did this immediately, and the pirate in the custody of Randall arrived there on June 20th. The Council in London also ordered Eliot to sequester Nutt's ships and goods. But it was not until

'Sir John Eliot and John Nutt, The Pirate'. It is one of three under the title *In the Time of Sir John Eliot—Three Studies in English History of the Seventeenth Century*, Smith College *Studies in History*, IV, no. 2. I have also employed D. W. Prowse, *The History of Newfoundland* (London, 1896), pp. 128–32, 136. H.C.A., 1, *Oyer et Terminer* 49, ff. 19–25v, and *ibid.*, Misc. 30, Bundle 857. S.P.D. Jas. I, CXLVI, no. 63 and CL, no. 82. 'Eliot and Vice-Admir.', pp. 13–16.

[1] The correspondence between Eliot, the Lords of the Council, and Conway is to be found in S.P.D. Jas. I, CXLVI, nos. 52, 62, 107, and CXLVII, nos. 22, 58. *A.P.C. 1623–1625*, pp. 13, 17.

late in June, on hearing from Conway, that he received the order to put Nutt's crew in 'safe custody'.

When John Nutt arrived in London it is known that he was put in the custody of John Foster, one of the messengers of his Majesty's chamber, that he was questioned by the Council on June 21, and that he was remanded to the custody of the messenger. It is not known what he was asked or what his answers were. It is significant, however, that on June 30th Sir John Eliot was ordered to appear before the Lords of the Council to speak with them on some matters of business. Did he, while travelling to London, have premonitions of trouble ahead? He knew that Nutt was no fool and would profit by blackening Eliot. He also knew by now that Calvert had considerable interest in the pirate. Sir John arrived in London on July 7. The communication issued by the Privy Council on that day speaks for itself.[1]

'Whereas Sir John Eliot . . . was this day convented before their Lordships to answer some indirect and unjustifiable dealings and practices with one Captain John Nutt, a pirate, touching his Majesty's pardon granted unto him, was committed prisoner to the Marshalsea, and upon his answer to the matters objected, being very suspicious, their Lordships desiring to know all the particular passages and whole truth of this business do think fit and accordingly order that Sir Henry Marten, knight, Judge of his Majesty's Court of Admiralty, shall take a strict examination thereof, calling before him the said Sir John Eliot, Captain Nutt, and any other whom he shall find cause to convent for that purpose, and that having taken the said examination he make report of the same unto the board.'[2]

Such was the plight of the hero of June 7. A month after he had 'captured' the pirate, the pirate had his captor in jail.

Before examining the records of the inquest held before Sir Henry Marten, brief mention must be made of the difficulties Sir John Eliot encountered in handling Nutt's chief prize, the *Edward and John* of Colchester. A number of interlocking law suits in the Court of Admiralty, orders of the Council, and private agreements between the litigants

---

[1] For this paragraph see *ibid.*, pp. 21, 23, 43. Hereafter the sources listed in a footnote placed at the end of a paragraph usually cover all the pertinent information in that paragraph.

[2] *Ibid.*, p. 51.

soon became entangled and had to be unravelled before the ship was permitted to sail to its home port. Of course, Sir John Eliot was in the midst of it all. What caused the trouble was that when the first suit was started on June 17 in the Court of Admiralty by the merchants of Colchester to recover their ship, an agreement was made between the plaintiffs and the defendant. It was that they were 'to pay him the said Sir John all such sums of money as shall be adjudged by this court to have been laid out by the said Sir John or his officers about the saving and preserving of the said ship and goods'. Eliot never forgot this agreement and refused to restore the ship, regardless of who ordered him to do so, until he had been paid. Not until May 24, 1624, was a settlement reached, and that out of court. The ship and her cargo were restored, while the vice-admiral of Devon received £90 for his trouble in saving this property by inducing John Nutt to surrender. It would, indeed, be interesting to know what all this litigation cost Sir John. Though money was important to him, his rights as vice-admiral as well as those of the Lord Admiral played a part in this episode. Sir John Eliot showed that he could be a hardheaded, conscientious administrator.[1]

In the inquest held before Sir Henry Marten on July 9, 22, and 23, Nutt, Randall, and Eliot testified in that order.[2] It seems that when Randall gave his testimony he knew little about the accusations made by Nutt, and that when Eliot deposed he knew nothing of Randall's statements but had been told of the charges made by the pirate.

The crucial point in the evidence presented by John Nutt concerned itself with the agreement he had made with the vice-admiral to pay him £500 and expenses for a pardon. Marten was told by the pirate that when he, Nutt, informed Eliot that he had no cash, he was told by Sir John that he must produce either money or goods. Nutt also asserted that the vice-admiral hinted broadly to him that he should continue his piracy until he had obtained the requisite amount of money or goods. To strengthen this accusation the pirate declared that Richard Randall had told him that at Dartmouth there were several richly laden ships from Spain, one of which had in her cargo cash to the value of £1,500.

---

[1] H.C.A., Act Book, 30, ff. 138, *passim*, and 38, Warrant Book, no. 14. S.P.D. Jas I, CXLVII, nos. 55–57, CXLVIII, no. 27, CL, no. 25. *A.P.C. 1623–1625*, pp. 24–5. 'Eliot and Vice-Admir.', pp. ix, 6, 10, 14. In June, 1624, Eliot paid Marten £90. This may represent his court expenses. If that is the case, he just broke even in this business.

[2] H.C.A., I, *Oyer et Terminer* 49, ff. 19–25v. Another copy in S.P.D. Jas. I, CXLIX, no. 45, I, II, III.

Nutt testified that Randall had suggested that if this ship could be seized, Sir John Eliot 'would work for all'.

If true, this was damaging evidence against the vice-admiral of Devon. The picture became really black for him, however, as a result of Randall's testimony. He denied every charge against Eliot made by the pirate. But he admitted that, when being questioned by Nutt and his crew on board the *Defiance*, he had told them 'that at Dartmouth there were eighteen sail of great ships reported to be rich, and told amongst Nutt's company then aboard . . . that one of those ships . . . had received fifteen hundred pounds for freight'. Of course Randall asserted that he had in no way encouraged the pirate to try to capture this ship or had ever said that Sir John 'would work for all'. He had said enough, however, to get the vice-admiral into serious trouble. Honesty and complete naïvety seems to be the only explanation for the deputy vice-admiral's damaging statements.

Not knowing what Randall had said made it doubly difficult for Eliot to defend himself against the charges of John Nutt. Naturally he denied emphatically every accusation Nutt had made against him. He insisted that he had been most anxious to keep the pirate in Torbay where it would be much easier to induce him to surrender than if he were cruising along the coast. Of course he had not sent word to Nutt about the Dartmouth ships. But Sir John freely admitted that the pirate had promised him money, though he made no mention of the £500 bond. To have offered something for nothing would have made Nutt suspicious. Whatever Sir John Eliot might say, it would have little worth in the face of Randall's admission.[1] The cards were stacked against the vice-admiral of Devon.

Sir Henry Marten quickly reported to the Privy Council. On July 25 he sent a summary of the evidence presented to him to the board.[2] In the eyes of the judge, Randall's testimony was bad. He wrote that the deputy vice-admiral 'confesseth some words spoken by himself to Nutt's company, which in my opinion imply a very dishonest and wicked sense'. By implication Marten involved Eliot, but he never openly blamed or accused him. He seemed to expect the Lords of the Council to read between the lines. It must be realized that Sir Henry

[1] Eliot's marshal, John Norber, was not examined until August 9 when he appeared before William Kifte, judge of the Admiralty in Devon. His testimony produced nothing new. It strengthened Eliot's statements without materially weakening the force of Randall's deposition. H.C.A., 30 Misc., Bundle 857.

[2] S.P.D. Jas. I, CXLIX, no. 45.

Marten and Sir John Eliot were good friends, as is evident from their later correspondence. Obviously Marten found himself in a difficult position.

This report, of course, did not help Sir John who continued to languish in the Marshalsea. At the same time the business of the admiralty in Devonshire was being neglected. During the last week of July and the first in August a considerable correspondence was passing between Eliot and Thomas Aylesbury, secretary to the Lord Admiral, between Sir John and Secretary Conway, and between Sir Henry Marten and Conway.[1] The letters to and from these men disclose that others besides Eliot were worrying about the losses the Admiralty was suffering in Devon. They disclose in particular that Sir John was and remained completely ignorant of Randall's testimony. Consequently he believed himself entirely innocent of any of the charges brought against him. And Conway, his friend, did not enlighten him except to inform him that some member or members of the Privy Council had given the King a rather unfavourable picture of the steps he had taken against Nutt. At least Sir John showed that he had a correct understanding of one of the causes of his troubles. That was that he had offended Secretary Calvert because he had tricked Nutt, one of his henchmen, into surrendering by means of an outdated pardon.

In the letter Marten wrote to Conway on August 4 he showed himself to be an excellent fence straddler. Obviously he did not want to antagonize either Secretary for fear that King James or the Lord Admiral, when he returned to England, might be turned against him. At the same time he was anxious to prevent the Lord Admiral from losing any profits from the Devonshire vice-admiralty because of the imprisonment of his officials. Finally, he hoped to be able to help his friend Eliot without hurting himself. In this letter Marten gave a number of good reasons from the point of view of profit to the vice-admiralty of Devon for liberating Sir John. He suggested that Eliot be released pending the return of the Lord Admiral and that he be 'cautiously bailed'. Marten admitted that he 'must do Sir John Eliot this right to say, this bringing in of Nutt was *factum bonum*, if not, *bene*'. All this was to no avail. James decided to keep Sir John in prison.

While the vice-admiral of Devon lay discouraged and disconsolate in prison, on occasion writing an obscure and verbose letter to Sir Edward Conway, activity on behalf of John Nutt was taking place. Sir George

[1] S.P.D. Jas. I, CXLIX, nos. 78, 89; CL, nos. 14, 22–25, 50, 76.

Calvert wrote to his fellow Secretary and asked him to obtain a pardon for the pirate. Giving a touching picture of Nutt and enlarging on the favours the pirate and the Secretary had shown each other, but not making a single reference to Eliot, Calvert presented John Nutt in the most favourable possible light to Conway. King James must have been impressed, for on August 22 Conway sent Nutt's pardon fully signed and attested to Sir George Calvert. It absolved the pirate and his crew for all their depredations committed before June 25 last. It permitted Nutt and his company to retain all the ships and goods in their possession except those which had been seized since February 1, 1623. To all appearances by September 1 of that year John Nutt and his crew were once again free to sail the seas on their good ship *Defiance*.[1]

The pirate captain was not set at liberty, however, for some time to come. He had not been confined to a prison but had been in the custody of a messenger of the King's chamber, first John Foster then Nicholas Stott. Stott had supplied food and lodging to Nutt, and therefore would not release his prisoner until he had been paid £100 for these necessities of life. At the order of the Council and on the command of the judge of the Admiralty Eliot was released on September 22 from the Marshalsea to go to Dartmouth and sell some of the ex-pirate's property so that the King's messenger could be paid his £100. Unfortunately for Nutt, Eliot refused to do this, as it would jeopardize the rights of the Lord Admiral who was returning to England from Spain. Sir John would act only if ordered by his superior. Neither Council nor judge could budge him. So the vice-admiral was 'committed to the custody of a messenger of the Chamber until further direction given by their Lordships concerning him'.[2]

Somehow Stott was induced to release John Nutt before the end of October.[3] But Eliot was not so fortunate. In the meantime, on October 5, 1623, the Lord Admiral and Prince Charles had returned to England. The mass of Englishmen with their strong dislike of Spain were overjoyed that the two travellers had returned without the Spanish Infanta as the bride of their future King. Had men known of the Duke's newly acquired hatred of Spain, which guided all his actions from now on, their joy would have been even greater. It took some weeks after the

---

[1] Letters and documents mentioned in this paragraph are to be found in *ibid.*, nos. 82, 90; CLI, nos. 9, 38. The pardon itself is dated August 28 and is found in *ibid.*, Docquet 1623–25, no. 12, f. 161.

[2] *A.P.C. 1623–1625*, pp. 85–6, 88. S.P.D. Jas. I, CLII, no. 90.

[3] *A.P.C. 1623–1625*, pp. 322–23.

favourite's return before his latest antipathy and warlike ambitions against Spain became common knowledge. Sir John Eliot, still guarded by his messenger, must have rejoiced at his chief's complete change of front. But that was a minor consideration to Eliot. His interest was centred on his liberation. All reason pointed to his being free to perform his duties in Devon within a few weeks after Buckingham's return. But as the weeks passed and no action was taken, hope was displaced by despair. He was neglected and forgotten.

It is idle to speculate why the Lord Admiral took so long to free his official. Sir John wrote to him at least twice to inform him of his sad plight.[1] But not until December 23 did Buckingham act. It is recorded that 'upon motion this day made on behalf of the Lord Admiral the board did give order that Sir John Eliot . . . should be discharged out of the custody of the messenger to whom he had been formerly committed'.[2] An act of justice long overdue had been done.

Of his first year as vice-admiral Eliot had spent nearly six months as a prisoner because he had been too zealous in performing his duty and had completely disregarded politics and politicians. He was being taught the hard way. His initial imprisonment was caused solely by his ignorance and bad luck. But when he was offered his freedom on condition that he raised £100 for Nutt, his obstinacy combined with his devotion to the Lord Admiral made him refuse to take such a step.[3] It cannot be said that a reason for his refusal was to save for himself part of the loot of the pirate. The small value involved[4] was not worth the sacrifice of freedom, especially as his personal fortune was suffering severely by his continued detention. His refusal to act was based upon his sense of duty as vice-admiral and his fidelity to his superior. This loyalty to persons and causes will bring Eliot trouble enough in the future. It made it difficult for him to play politics, as did his inherent

[1] In his letter of Nov. 8 he makes reference to an earlier communication he had sent Buckingham. *Cabala, sive Scrina Sacra* (London, 1691), p. 377.

[2] *A.P.C. 1623–1625*, p. 156.

[3] For nearly a year Nicholas Stott with the help of the Privy Council endeavoured to collect the £100 due him from John Nutt. Late in September, 1624, the Council tried to induce Eliot and the Colchester merchants to pay £50 each to Stott because they had benefited by the fact that Nutt had been in the custody of the messenger for four months. Similar weak and worthless arguments were used by the Lords of the Council to induce payment. But there is not a shred of evidence surviving to show that Stott ever received his £100. *A.P.C. 1623–1625*, pp. 322–23, 331.

[4] According to the figures in 'Eliot and Vice-Admir.', p. 14, Nutt's ship and goods were eventually sold, when is not recorded, for a net profit to the Admiralty (including Eliot's moiety) of only £84. The £500 bond Nutt had given Eliot was worthless.

frankness which frequently displayed itself during this incident of his vice-admiralty.

But the year 1623 had borne fruit, though slightly bitter, for Sir John Eliot. His faith in the ministers of the King was severely shaken. With Calvert as a glaring example, he saw them as a group of politicians devoid of patriotism working for their own selfish ends. Even his supposed friends Conway and Marten, afraid or unable to speak for him, were a disappointment. But what did he think about the Lord Admiral? Fortunately, Buckingham's absence during the greater part of this affair made it impossible for him to display to Eliot characteristics similar to those the vice-admiral had discovered in the Duke's inferiors. That he neglected his imprisoned officer for so many weeks after his return to England Sir John could, and probably did, explain away. Though Eliot was dismayed at the inaction of his chief, he had not begun to lose faith in him.

CHAPTER III

The Birth of an Orator

January to May, 1624

ON his release from custody Sir John Eliot returned to his family in Cornwall and to his duties in Devon. He must have reached his native heath about the same time the sheriff of Cornwall received a writ, issued by the Lord Keeper on December 28, 1623, for the election of members to a Parliament.

King James had finally been persuaded by the Duke of Buckingham and the Prince to summon the Lords and Commons. They were to be consulted in general on the relations of England with the continent and in particular on peace or war with Spain. That the Commons would be asked for money was self-evident. For months the Duke and the Prince had been urging the King to substitute revenge and war for a royal marriage and peace between England and Spain. But James remained deaf to these pleas and retained the vain hope that negotiations between the two countries would produce the results he desired. They were the restoration of the Palatinate, lost to the Catholics at the beginning of the Thirty Years War, to Frederick, his son-in-law, and the marriage of Prince Charles to the Spanish Infanta. With each dispatch from London the Earl of Bristol, English Ambassador to the court of Madrid, was put in a more difficult position. Though popular in Spain and endowed with a sound understanding of Anglo-Spanish and Anglo-German relations, the ambassador found himself unable to secure any of the demands of his master. Finding neither Spain, Frederick, nor the Austrian Hapsburgs willing to co-operate, James finally succumbed to the wishes of his son and his favourite and summoned a Parliament.

During the early weeks of January, 1624, the constituencies were humming with activity. Eliot was returned on January 19th for Newport in Cornwall with Richard Escott, a London barrister, as his colleague.[1] This constituency, composed of sixty householders, was one of those pocket boroughs which had been created during the reign of Edward VI. During the reigns of Elizabeth and James, one or both of its seats were at the disposal of the Crown or court.[2] Why Eliot did not sit for his home constituency is difficult to say. He may have thought that he had had enough of life in London but in the end decided or was persuaded to stand for Parliament. By that time it was too late for him to represent St. Germans. So Buckingham found him a seat at Newport.

Whatever his reasons may have been for accepting this seat, Sir John Eliot was back in London early in February to be present in the House of Commons when proceedings were begun on the 19th of that month. Though almost a stranger to the benches of the House, Eliot saw about him many familiar faces. Among them were his old friends William Coryton and Bevil Grenville. There were his business associates James Bagg, vice-admiral of south Cornwall, and John Coke, one of the commissioners of the navy, for both of whom he had little love. These four sat for Cornish constituencies. From neighbouring Devon came Sir Edward Giles with whom Sir John had been working in his vice-admiralty.

Ten years had passed since Eliot had listened for two brief months in the House to the harangues of one outraged member after another. Young and inexperienced he had been, only twenty-two; eager to learn and willing to listen he had sat in silence while others talked. But now it was different. He was ready to test his voice among the echoes of the House, to bring himself to the attention of his colleagues. But he was not yet ready to stand above the many and lead them. Experience was lacking as well as a cause. The last ten years had furnished excellent training for a young man growing to maturity. And the last year had been particularly rough on him. Fortunately, his recent hardships had not spoiled his enthusiasm, his zest for life and work.

In the Parliament of 1624 Sir John Eliot was to display far greater feeling for and interest in the House of Commons than his short, silent novitiate in 1614 had promised. On leaving his seat in June of that year he may have suspected that all men in the government were not as perfect as the King. At the same time his colleagues had displayed to him

[1] O.R. I, 456.

[2] For a view of how this and other constituencies controlled by the Crown fitted into the political picture of that day see J. E. Neale, *The Elizabethan House of Commons* (London, 1949), pp. 282–300; Rowse, *op. cit.*, p. 94; Browne Willis, *op. cit.*, II, 162; and Edward Porritt, *The Unreformed House of Commons* (Cambridge, 1903), I, 374.

more folly and weakness than wisdom and strength. But he must have felt the potential power and importance of this body of men gathered to advise its Sovereign. During the next ten years he became acquainted with the evil ways of some of his Majesty's ministers and officials. In this period also he was told about the power and ability displayed by the Commons in the third Parliament of King James. His respect for that institution undoubtedly grew. Now in 1624 he was once again a member of a House of Commons which he knew had become a place of importance. If he was to play a prominent part in its deliberations, he must first become known to the majority of the members. Such seems to have been the task he set himself in the fourth and last Parliament of James I.

On February 19 the King addressed the two Houses of Parliament. He asked for advice on the proposed marriage of his son, on the policy England should follow towards Spain and the Palatinate, and on how religion should be furthered in the country. Such requests sent a thrill through those Commons who had been present in the last session and remembered how James had checked them when they had broached these very same matters. Undoubtedly Sir John Eliot was surprised, as were most of the Commons, at this sudden change in the royal policy. Undoubtedly he accepted enthusiastically Buckingham's explanations, made on February 24, of the journey he and Prince Charles had taken to Spain. But he was not as yet prepared to speak.[1]

Two days later in completely different circumstances Eliot addressed his colleagues for the first time.[2] In committee of the whole House for trade, not in the formal House, he replied to Sir Edwin Sandys. As chairman of the committee, Sandys had declared that the causes for the decline of trade should constitute the business for that day. There were three causes in Eliot's opinion: monopolies, pirates, and impositions. And the last he considered the most important. Many members saw other reasons for the decline of commerce. But no decision was reached, for the committee was to discuss that subject at least once a week throughout the session. Monopolies and particularly impositions received the greatest blame in these debates.

An attack on these two evils is the theme of a lengthy speech written

[1] Rushworth, I, 115-6, 119-25, and *L.J.*, III, 220-32.
[2] Nicholas. As the folios are not always clearly indicated in the transcripts of this diary and others to be used, all folio references will be omitted. References to the diaries may be easily found from the day cited.

by Eliot but undelivered according to the journals and diaries of this Parliament.[1] As the speech is undated, and as its contents would fit it into half a dozen different debates of the committee of the whole House for trade, it would be futile to speculate on the day when Eliot intended to present it. What he wrote is of importance, for it is one of the few times he expressed himself on the difficult subject of economics.

One may wonder where Sir John got his information on this subject, particularly on impositions.[2] It must be remembered that as a member of the Parliament of 1614 he listened to long and learned debates on impositions and monopolies. As vice-admiral he probably came into contact with collectors of the customs at Plymouth and was told by them about impositions. Friends who had attended the Parliament of 1621 must have told him or written to him about monopolies and the stir they caused in this Parliament. That he would have enough knowledge to talk about these two subjects in the House is obvious. But also he might not have enough to prevent him from confusing economic terms or from understanding the true nature of the economic difficulties confronting King and people.

In his written speech Eliot elaborated on the evil of impositions as the leading cause for the decline of trade. He continually confused them with monopolies, and on occasion made the two words appear to be synonymous. To Sir John the most damaging impositions were those put upon exported cloth by the Merchant Adventurers and the Crown. This company had a monopoly to export woollen cloth to certain parts of the continent and at this time was forcing its own members to pay an

[1] Forster, *Eliot*, I, 164–72. This is the only place where this speech is to be found. There is no trace of it either at Port Eliot or among Forster's own papers in the Dyce-Forster Collection at South Kensington. See Gardiner, V, 233, note 2, for his comment on the whereabout of the speech. It seems that the original of this speech was somehow mislaid or lost. Here Eliot, like other members, displayed a habit which he carried throughout his Parliamentary career. That was to prepare in advance a speech on a subject which he thought would be discussed in the House. At times the opportunity never presented itself to deliver such a speech. On other occasions the speech as prepared did not fit the temper of the House and remained undelivered. Frequently, of course, it was spoken. But one wonders whether the delivered speech was always the same as the prepared one. Naturally on many occasions Eliot spoke extemporaneously.

[2] Impositions were import and export duties levied by the government or a company either on goods which paid no duty at all or on goods which already paid a duty that had been approved by Parliament or sanctioned by tradition. The levying of import and export duties at certain *ad valorem* rates, known as tonnage and poundage, had been approved by Parliament at the beginning of a sovereign's reign for over a hundred years. Therefore, impositions might be duties paid in addition to tonnage and poundage or at a rate higher than that prescribed by tonnage and poundage.

imposition on their exports.[1] Concurrently the government was levying additional duties on exported cloth.[2] Such levies Eliot denounced.
At the same time he admitted that impositions were an important
source of royal revenue. All could not be abolished; only those which
bore too heavily on the trade and pockets of Englishmen. In conclusion
he advocated the preparation of a bill which would include only those
impositions which were 'judged less dangerous in their consequences'.
The bill should revoke all other levies and declare 'that no impositions
more be laid but by the general consent of Parliament'.

What Sir John Eliot proposed was nothing new; actually it was
much the same as the bill on impositions introduced in 1610 which
never became law.[3] By 1624 impositions had become so complicated
and had grown into such an evil that the simple solution of fourteen
years earlier would not have appealed to the members of the House of
Commons. Possibly Sir John made inquiries as to how his proposal
would be accepted by the committee of the whole House for trade. When
he found no support he decided to abandon it. Hence the speech survived
only on paper.

Eliot's diagnosis of the economic ills of England would have produced no protest from his contemporaries. Like other members of the
House of Commons he was ignorant of the real causes of the sudden
decline in the trade of the commodity on which most of England's
wealth at that time was based, of the causes of the depression which had
hit the country a few years before the opening of this Parliament. Now
we know that they were occasioned in part by the New Company of
Merchant Adventurers which exported only poorly dyed and finished
cloth and thereby lost most of the customers for this product, by the
damaging effect of the Thirty Years War on the sale of English cloth in
central Europe, and by the currency crisis which was partially caused by
the government's lack of knowledge of the proper ratio at which to
coin gold and silver.[4]

Though Sir John made his first speech in committee of the whole
House on the economic evils of the day, his name was first brought before the formal House on a matter of privilege. On February 27 Sir Ed-

---

[1] E. Lipson, *The Economic History of England* (London, 1934), II, 247.

[2] F. C. Dietz, *English Public Finance, 1558–1641* (New York, 1932), p. 373. Astrid Friis,
Alderman Cockayne's Project and the Cloth Trade (Oxford, 1927), pp. 218–9.

[3] Gardiner, II, 82–3.

[4] Lipson, *op. cit.*, III, 374–82. W. A. Shaw, *The History of Currency* (New York, 1896),
pp. 144–5.

ward Giles moved the stay of two trials at the Exeter assize. In one of them Eliot was a party and in the other his servant was involved. The motion was passed and was confirmed on March 2, when it was ordered that a letter from the Speaker be sent to the judge requesting that the trials be adjourned until Sir John was freed from his parliamentary duties.[1]

The motion of Sir Edward Giles on behalf of his friend was the cue for Sir John to deliver his maiden address to the formal House of Commons.[2] The body of his speech consisted of a long exposition of the relationship of English kings and their Parliaments. Sometimes he dealt with the distant past; at other times he talked about the last two Parliaments, 'at one of which I was present and the other a well-wisher'. His object was to prevent a repetition of the troubles which had arisen in the Parliament of 1621 over the privilege of freedom of speech.[3] Eliot, the historian, painted in most rosy hues and with complete disregard for historical truth the co-operation that existed between medieval kings and their parliaments. But he was no worse as an historian than many others on both sides of the House. Eliot, the interpreter of the present, supported both King James and the Commons. The trouble in 1614 had been caused by evil ministers of the King seeking their own dark ends. The trouble in 1621 had been that the two sides had been misrepresented to each other.

As Sir John saw it, the King had his prerogative and the Commons their privileges, and they should not conflict. Refusing to define his terms he declared that 'no man may dispute' the royal prerogative, and with almost the same breath praised the Great Protestation of 1621 in which the Commons had defended their right to speak on virtually any subject. Once again laying emphasis on the power of the King over the Lords and Commons, Eliot finally came to his point and placed the blame for the trouble in 1621 on misrepresentation. If the Commons in any way had harmed the King, he said, it was not done deliberately; misreport of their activities was responsible. This was an old complaint. It had been the closing plea of the Protestation of 1621. Sir John ended his speech with the request that the King 'reject the whispers of our enemies or not believe them', and that the Commons petition his Majesty

[1] *C.J.*, I, 719, 724. Nicholas. Holland. Holles (misdated Feb. 26 and March 3).
[2] *Neg. Post.* I, Supp., pp. 130–9. P.E. MSS, 'Eliot, Speeches, etc.', ff. 2–6. Brief accounts in *C.J.*, I, 719, Nicholas, Holland, Holles, Earle, Pym.
[3] Rushworth, I, 53–4.

on the same subject. By implication he suggested that the Commons include in their petition a statement of their privileges and an appeal that they be preserved.

Without specifically mentioning it Sir John Eliot wanted the Protestation of December 18, 1621, which James had torn from the journals with his own hands, replaced by a petition on the privileges of the Commons, in which the right of freedom of speech was to be stated as clearly as it had been in the previous Parliament. Throughout his speech he had tried to be impartial. But he could not, or would not, see that the royal prerogative, as it had been defined by James up to that time, was bound to clash with the privileges of the lower House which daily were being extended and more clearly defined by their defenders.

At the moment Eliot made his plea the situation had changed and his plea fell on deaf ears. The majority of the Commons, that is, their leaders, were no longer interested in obtaining the privilege of freedom of speech in theory when they had it in practice. In his opening plea to Parliament King James had given the Commons permission to talk about everything they had been prohibited from discussing in the previous session. Anglo-Spanish relations, the Prince's marriage, religion, and related subjects which the King had snatched from their tongues in 1621 were now presented to them for debate without limitations. The door of freedom of speech had been opened wide. A petition, such as Eliot suggested, might make it swing back and forth to the discomfort of both sides. In his proposal he was either ignoring the present or was ignorant of the changed situation in the House and was thinking only of its future safety. But his colleagues were opportunists, were satisfied with the gain of the moment, and were anxious to let sleeping dogs lie.

As one diarist expressed it, 'divers were afraid this motion would have put the House into some such heat as to disturb the greater business'.[1] Edward Alford, wise in the ways of that body, agreed with Eliot but felt the time inopportune for such a petition. Better to appoint a select committee to prepare a bill for the preservation of their liberties was his suggestion. Only the fiery Sir Francis Seymour gave frank support to Sir John's proposal and even advocated the revival of the old Protestation. Sane and able Sir Robert Phelips, the great Sir Edward Coke, and Sir James Perrot all spoke in favour of Alford's suggestion. It was natural to expect bitterness and a demand for some retribution from the first two of the three, for they had suffered imprisonment in

[1] Pym.

December, 1621, as a result of the Protestation. Instead they counselled moderation. That also was the feeling of the majority in the House. A select committee of fifteen was ordered to be named to discuss what might be done with the privileges of the Commons. Though Eliot was named one of the fifteen, the subject was not again brought before the Commons in this session.[1]

With privileges sidetracked the Commons could turn their attention to the all-important subject of Anglo-Spanish affairs. The debate was opened on March 1 by Sir Benjamin Rudyerd. A good speaker, great enemy of Spain, and known to be in touch with the inner circle at court, Rudyerd was the ideal member to be the first in the House to advocate a breach of the treaties pending with Spain. He made it clear that this step would lead to war and advocated a war near at home which would revive the broken hopes of the Protestants in Germany and recover the Palatinate for Frederick. The storm against Spain then broke from all sides of the House. The cry for war and denunciation of the Spaniards came from Phelips, Seymour, and several others before Sir John Eliot got an opportunity to express his hostility to the murderers of Raleigh. He began by reminding his listeners that King James had been in a dilemma as to what to do about Spain and was now seeking the advice of his faithful Commons. Eliot was in favour of war. Action now seemed more important than words. He had heard the rumour that a Spanish armada was being prepared, therefore Sir John wanted the English fleet sent to sea to defend Ireland. To him the best way to defray the expense of such a fleet was to fine heavily all Roman Catholics in England. These words against Spain were a spontaneous outburst produced by the temper of the House. Eliot was beginning to find his place among the more vocal members. Soon after this speech a message from the Lords put a temporary halt to the debate. When it was later resumed in committee of the whole House, the member for Newport remained silent while the anti-Spanish storm continued to rage.[2]

Obviously it was not going to take the Commons long to decide what should be done about Spain. All negotiations for treaties with that country must be broken off immediately; the only difficulty was to persuade James to take this step. On March 3 a committee of 48, of

[1] The speeches in this paragraph are to be found in *C.J.*, I, 719–20, Nicholas, and Pym. There is no evidence supporting the statement of Forster, *Eliot*, I, 143, that the language employed by Alford and Phelips suggests 'that Buckingham had privately communicated with them'. See also Gardiner, IV, 188, note 1 on this point. *A.H.R.*, LXI, 851-52.

[2] *C.J.*, I, 675–76 and 722–23, Nicholas, Holland, and Gurney.

which Eliot was a member, was appointed to confer with the Lords on how to word the advice to the King for the breach of the Spanish treaties. The will of the two Houses was soon properly worded and sent to King James, who replied on March 5 with gracious thanks for the advice given him. He accepted the four points which Rudyerd had originally made in the Commons and which had been incorporated in the advice, namely: to mobilize the fleet, to repair fortresses, to strengthen the defences of Ireland, and to give aid to the Dutch. But the King made it clear that he wanted little war against Spain and much in Germany to recover the Palatinate. He went on to say that he needed money to conduct this war as well as to pay off his debts. The tone of his reply, however, was cordial throughout and carried no shafts which might injure the tender susceptibilities of the Commons.[1]

After the reply was reported to the Commons by Sir Heneage Finch, Recorder of London, the only person to make any comment, as recorded in the sources, was Sir John Eliot.[2] He said he had heard rumours that his Majesty had given a most unsatisfactory answer to the humble advice of the Houses. But as he had been one of the delegation which had gone to Theobalds to receive the King's words, he could testify that these rumours were false. Now that the House was in possession of the reply Sir John proposed that copies be made of it for all members so that they could study it carefully. He concluded with the suggestion that the time be set for a discussion of the reply. These proposals were carried at the order of the House and Wednesday, the 10th, fixed for the debate. Thus we see the House of Commons already following suggestions made by Sir John Eliot. A minor point it was, to be sure, but even so it has value in his training for leadership.

Not until March 11 did the Commons consider the answer of James to the humble advice. Little enthusiasm was shown for a war in Germany; and no progress was made towards settling the financial needs of the nation and King. It was obvious that a direct attack on Spain was close to the heart of every member. The only benefit James could glean from a long discussion was a resolution to assist him in a parliamentary way as soon as the negotiations with Spain were stopped.[3]

In the Lords, on the other hand, the King's request for money to pay his debts was not as readily overlooked as in the Commons. To ease the

---

[1] *C.J.*, I, 676, 726. Rushworth, I, 128–31, and *L.J.*, III, 246–7, 250–1.
[2] On March 8. *C.J.*, I, 678, 731, Nicholas, and Holland.
[3] *C.J.*, I, 683 and 733.

situation and assure a grant for war with Spain Prince Charles explained his father's request to the great satisfaction of all who heard him.[1] When the Prince's words were reported to the Commons on March 12 by Secretary Calvert, much enthusiasm was exhibited for this timely intervention. In the ensuing debate the other Secretary, Conway, requested the House to reach an agreement on a particular sum to be voted as soon as the King had cancelled all diplomatic activity with Spain. To this proposal Eliot was opposed, for he felt that a parliamentary promise to help finance the war was of greater value than a fixed number of subsidies which might be exhausted long before the war was over. Sir John wanted the Commons to abide by their original resolution to give financial assistance for a war as soon as James had abandoned the Spaniards. Almost immediately after Eliot had spoken the subject was dropped, and the impression is left that his words carried greater weight than those of Mr Secretary. At conclusion of the debate a committee was appointed, with Sir John a member, to frame a message of thanks to the Prince.[2]

Two days later, on Sunday, March 14, a 'humble Address' from both Houses embodying the leading views of the Commons was presented to King James by the Archbishop of Canterbury, who headed a delegation of Lords and Commons. That same day the King replied to this delegation and unfortunately said the wrong thing in the wrong way. First he showed some of his old rancour over the terms employed against Spain. Then in a more friendly tone he made it clear that he was looking towards a great continental alliance to recover the Palatinate and said virtually nothing about a war directly against Spain. Finally, to add to the discomfort of his audience, he requested six subsidies and twelve fifteenths, close to £800,000, and earmarked the last subsidy and two-fifteenths for his debts. All who heard him, including the Duke and the Prince, were filled with dismay. But before the bad impression King James had created could take full effect the favourite had persuaded his pliable master to permit Prince Charles to elucidate his father's words. Consequently on March 15 Charles told the Lords and a committee of the Commons that the King really meant to go to war with Spain and that he would devote all the subsidies he had requested to that war. The report of the royal words and princely explanations was made to the Commons on March 17 by Sir Robert Heath, the

[1] Gardiner, V, 195–6.
[2] *C.J.*, I, 684, 734; Holland, Holles, and particularly Gurney.

Solicitor General. But there was no debate; instead Friday, March 19, was set for a full-dress discussion of the proposed wars and supply.[1]

Once again Sir Benjamin Rudyerd set the ball in motion on that Friday when he declared that, as the King had now promised to break the negotiations and unleash the dogs of war against Spain, it was up to Parliament to decide how much financial assistance should be given. He enumerated some of the projects which needed financing, urged a speedy vote of a definite sum, and then gave way to Sir John Eliot. The second speaker was staggered by the demands of the King. The country was poor and so huge a sum would be difficult to raise, he felt. On the other hand, if not enough money could be found, all would be lost, their hopes and desires in vain. They were, indeed, on the horns of a painful dilemma. Eliot continued by saying that he had been dejected over the reply of King James to their address. Misinterpreting one part of the reply he had disliked the whole. But with the explanation of Prince Charles he was well satisfied and now would gladly accept the answer of his Majesty. Next he turned to the proposed treaties with Spain and declared that they were responsible for all their troubles, for the ruin of the nation through loss of friends abroad, for the destruction of wealth at home, and for the threat to English Protestantism. Spain grows '*non tam potentia sua, quam negligentia nostra*' insisted Sir John, working himself to oratorical heights. However much the immediate needs of the nation cry against granting too much money, we must make ourselves safe for all times, he maintained. Are we poor, he asked. 'Spain is rich! Let her be our Indies, our storehouse of treasure. Let us quickly give the King an answer to his request, so that there may be as little delay as possible in declaring his intentions against Spain'.[2] This was no time for oratory. There was no need of arousing the House; it was already thoroughly aroused. Concrete proposals, not vague generalities were the order of the day. Eliot, still inexperienced in the ways of Parliament, let his enthusiasm carry him away. As frequently was to be the case, that same spirit blinded him to the temper of the House of Commons.

He was followed by Sir Thomas Edmondes, Treasurer of the Household and Privy Councillor, who did not care for Eliot's oratorical out-

---

[1] Gardiner, V, 196; *L.J.*, III, 259, 261, 265–6; Rushworth, I, 136–8; *C.J.*, I, 738. Eliot expressed opinions on some minor points of discussion on March 16 and 17. *Ibid.*, 687, 738–9; Holland, and Holles.

[2] *C.J.*, I, 740, Holland, Holles, Harl. 159, and Gurney.

burst. He felt sure the members realized what an important situation confronted them and that they needed no further stimulation. Then he turned to the proposed supply of six subsidies and corresponding fifteenths which staggered him by its size. He thought half the amount enough for a beginning. The debate continued at great length all morning with the trend towards granting a smaller sum than that requested by the King. It was resumed the next day in committee of the whole House, but Sir John neither presented more suggestions nor gave vent again to his eloquence. He must have been satisfied with the final decision of the Commons to vote three subsidies and three fifteenths to be paid to treasurers, appointed by Parliament, within a year after James had broken with Spain. Finally, on March 23, the King declared that he would end the Spanish negotiations, and the way was left open for the subsidy bill.[1]

James had assured Parliament on that day that he would carry out its wishes, but not until April 6 did he dispatch messengers to Madrid to announce the new English policy. In the meantime Parliament had been adjourned for a week over Easter. When it reassembled the Commons had several conferences with the Lords on the dissolution of the treaties. At one of these on April 1, just after the Houses had returned from their brief holiday, the Duke declared he had seen the dispatches to Spain which announced the cessation of all friendly negotiations with that country. Moreover, he had had word from Spain of a great fleet being prepared to attack England. Buckingham felt, therefore, that money should be found immediately to put the English fleet into fighting trim. He suggested that such funds be raised on the credit of the subsidies promised by Parliament.[2]

These facts and suggestions were reported to the House of Commons on that same Thursday, the first of the month, by Sir Edwin Sandys. In the debate following the report Phelips and others said that the matter was too important and the House too thin to discuss it at this time. Some suggested postponement to the next morning, others to the following Monday. Eliot was one who favoured Friday, as the subject was of importance and should be settled at once. He informed the Commons that he had seen the letters from Spain to the Duke which told of the armada preparing against England.[3] Here we can see the vice-

---

[1] *C.J.*, I, 744, Rushworth, I, 138-40.
[2] Gardiner, V, 211, *L.J.*, III, 284-5.
[3] *C.J.*, I, 751-52 and Holles.

admiral of Devon on intimate terms with his superior. He was being shown the Lord Admiral's correspondence dealing with the affairs of the navy. In spite of the advice of Sir John and others, the House decided that Monday, April 5, was soon enough for a discussion of this subject. But neither on that day nor on any subsequent one is there recorded a word about Buckingham's proposal. Either the news of the Spanish preparations was shown to be false, or else the startling charge, presented for the first time on that Monday, that the Lord Treasurer, the Earl of Middlesex, had been accepting bribes, completely distracted the attention of the Commons from their planned debate.

Postponing the predicament of the Lord Treasurer for the moment, we must deal with another subject which interested both the Lords and the Commons during the first three weeks of April. It was the preparation of a petition against English Roman Catholics for presentation by both Houses to King James. Little has been said of the part Protestantism played in the life of Sir John Eliot. But little is known of his religious views until he began to explain them with increasing clarity and force in later sessions of Parliament. All that is necessary to say here is that there was no stauncher defender of Elizabethan Anglicanism in the House of Commons at this time than Eliot. Any variations in doctrine or ceremony from the 39 Articles and the Prayer Book of the Queen were anathema to him. Consequently, it is natural to find him denouncing recusants in language not a whit less emphatic than came from any of his colleagues in the House. In this session, however, Sir John had little need to take the initiative or little opportunity to display any independence in attacking the papists. It was being done by member after member; and terms to be included in the petition for religion were being suggested from all sides. He could do little more than support or criticize the suggestions of others, as may be seen by his remarks on April 2, 7, and 8.[1]

When the petition had been completed by the middle of the month and had obtained the Lords' assent, there arose the difficulty of securing an audience from the King for its presentation. Finally, through the efforts of Prince Charles,[2] James set April 23 as the day on which he would receive the delegation from both Houses with their petition.

---

[1] Holland, Holles, Gurney, and *C.J.*, I, 758.

[2] He had to make two requests and was successful only when he told his father that the Commons were about to give the subsidy bill its first reading. *C.J.*, I, 772 and Pym. The subsidy bill was read for the first time on April 22. *C.J.*, I, 772.

The favourable answer of the King[1] was reported to the Commons on the next day. It gave great pleasure, particularly to Sir John Eliot. So delighted was he that again he allowed his enthusiasm to get the better of him. He delivered a stirring speech in which he moved 'for thanks to the Prince, King, and God' and 'a message of thanks to the Prince to desire him to be our mouth of thanks to the King, and to entreat him there may be a general thanksgiving to God throughout the kingdom'. For this message of thanks to the Prince, he believed, there was 'much more reason to do it now than before'. The House did not think so. It was unimpressed by this outburst. Sir Francis Seymour directed it upon a saner course by declaring that it was better 'to express thankfulness rather in action than words' and by moving that the House rise immediately in order to meet the sooner that afternoon to discuss the subsidy bill. The Commons passed Seymour's motion and ignored Eliot's.[2]

Sir John had spoken extemporaneously. He has left no copy of the speech and had no opportunity to prepare it. That it was long we know, for Pym has recorded in his diary that it was 'of some length and curiosity'. What did he mean by 'curiosity'? A partial explanation may be found in a letter Sir Francis Nethersole, MP and courtier, wrote to Sir Dudley Carleton, English ambassador at the Hague. In this letter dated April 25 Nethersole says:

'There is one Sir John Eliot of our House, a spruce young man and as spruce a speaker, who had provided a wondrous fine speech for this time fraught with quaint words and no less with extolling praise of the King, Prince, and Duke, tending to have solemn thanks conveyed to them and to God in the third place, which was a motion generally misliked. And one observing it moved instead thereof that we might rise and meet the hour after dinner about the bill of subsidy committed that morning and appointed then to be debated. This was the hatchet cut Sir John very short then . . .'.[3]

Eliot was an eloquent speaker at times, in fact he might already be called an orator. Though his manner of speaking and the language he used intrigued his listeners, what he said had no influence on them. Experience

[1] Rushworth, I, 143–44.
[2] C.J., I, 690 and 774, also Pym.
[3] S.P.D., Jas. I, CLXIII, no. 50.

would eliminate those 'quaint words'. Greater knowledge of opinion in the House of Commons would bring the speaker into tune with the members. Then matter as well as manner would be pleasing to all. But if Eliot was to have a maximum effect upon the Commons, he must learn to control his impetuous nature.

Returning to the troubles of Lionel Cranfield, Earl of Middlesex, we find that the attack upon him begun on April 5 eventually resulted in his impeachment and fall. Of all those in authority in the government this most able Lord Treasurer with his London mercantile background had been almost alone in opposing persistently the anti-Spanish policy of the Duke of Buckingham.[1] When, therefore, hailstones began pelting the Earl out of a clear blue sky, it is not necessary to look far for the storm cloud with its bolt of lightning. Thus it was on that April Monday that Middlesex was charged in the House of Commons with accepting bribes.[2] Actually a capable man doing his job well, he had to a lesser extent than most public men of the time indulged in a few practices which would be called shady today.

Whatever the morals of the case may be, the Commons spent ten days debating the accusations against the Lord Treasurer. From April 5 to 15 discussion of this subject took up most of the time of the committee of the whole for grievances. Already by Saturday afternoon, April 10, many felt that the charges against the Earl should be reported to the House so that they might be transmitted to the Lords. One of those who was anxious that the Speaker take the chair and that the chairman of the committee, Sir Edward Coke, make his report, was Sir John Eliot.[3] This move, however, was prevented for that day by others, particularly by that able speaker, Sir Humphrey May, the Chancellor of the Duchy of Lancaster.

On Monday, April 12, the case of the Earl of Middlesex was brought before the committee again. This time, after he had been thoroughly denounced by several speakers, it was decided that the Commons were ready to hand him over to the Lords. Among these denunciatory speakers was Eliot.[4] His speech is typical of the man, typical of many of his compositions, whether to be read or heard. Speaking in generalities at first he bewildered his audience, but before he reached his end his

---

[1] Gardiner, V, 228–29.
[2] C.J., I, 755.
[3] Holland and Holles.
[4] P.E. MSS., 'Eliot, Speeches, etc.', ff. 9, 9v, Nicholas, Holland, Harl. 159, Gurney.

oratory rang true. Better if Sir John had used a few well-chosen words to tell the House what he wanted done to the Earl of Middlesex. Instead he first compared him to a strange meteor 'of which the effects may sooner be discovered then the reasons'. After playing with this metaphor at considerable length Eliot came back to reality and praised the justice of the House of Commons which 'declines to no favour or respect'. Turning to the defendant he declared that when a great man sins he sins not only against himself but also against those 'whose acts their great examples have misled'. Next he contrasted the blessings and curses which will be heaped upon good and bad officials in a state. Finally he came to the case before the House and told the Commons that he was not going to repeat the charges against the Earl or speak of his weak defence. But on the basis of these charges and this defence 'to give you the sentence of a true English heart . . . I shall be bold to say of that great lord. . . . I hold him unworthy the favour of his country, unworthy the favour of his Prince, unworthy the employments of either, and so I would have him transmitted to the Lords'.

Such words with their oratorical flashes did not always captivate the Commons. But they kept Sir John before the House. He was making a place for himself in that body which raised him well above the ordinary member. Though he could interest and hold an audience, he could rarely guide or lead it.

This speech and more factual denunciations ruined all the chances of the Lord Treasurer in the House of Commons. On April 15 impeachment proceedings were begun against him when Coke and Sandys laid the charges of the Commons before the Lords. By May 13 the Peers had decided he was guilty and sentenced him to imprisonment in the Tower, loss of all his offices and payment of a fine of £50,000.[1] For the next two weeks Parliament drifted towards a close, as measures approved by both Houses began to pile up. The subsidy bill received its final passage in the Commons on May 21, and was sent to the upper House three days later.[2] And then King James felt the time had come for work to cease and for him to send his faithful members to their homes.

Before considering the prorogation of Parliament we must glance at another speech of Eliot's. It was written for this Parliament, but there is

[1] Gardiner, V, 231. For mitigation of sentence by James see *ibid.*, V, 308.
[2] *C.J.*, I, 708, 710 and 792, 794.

no evidence that it was delivered.[1] The speech was in support of a private bill to disinherit a son who was born theoretically in wedlock. Actually the alleged father had not had access to the mother for more than two years previous to the birth of the child. The courts had upheld the legitimacy of the son and his right to inherit. Now an attempt was to be made to invalidate this decision by an act of Parliament. The bill appealed to the common sense of Sir John. It shows him not afraid to mince words when he could not see eye to eye with the law and the lawyers. Whatever the law might say, it made no sense to Eliot that a man who had not seen his wife for two years could be judged the father of the child born at the end of that period to the woman in question. He had always believed, he declared, that the law was based on reason. But to believe something to be true because a lawyer said so, 'or to believe that law which is not reason', he could not do and begged their pardon for his ignorance. Clearly Sir John Eliot did not worship at the feet of the common law.

A function of Parliament was to make law, Statute Law. Here the session of 1624 led the three preceding Parliaments by a wide margin. On May 29 when James prorogued the Houses to November 2, he gave his assent to seventy-three public and private bills[2] and thereby placed upon the statute book more laws than ever before in his reign. Eliot was fortunate indeed to be active for the first time in the happiest Parliament faced by the first two Stuarts. Except for a harsh word, misunderstanding, or ominous rumble now and then the three and a half months of the session produced so little bad feeling and so much good work that the term happy is most appropriate. In such an atmosphere Sir John began to build his reputation and erase from his mind the bad impression made by the Parliament of 1614. Some who heard him may have admired him, many were bored by his verbosity and annoyed by his misplaced zeal, but all were made aware of his personality. Sir John Eliot was becoming known as a young man of promise with an enviable gift of speech and an ardour which his friends hoped would be

---

[1] P.E. MSS., 'Eliot, Speeches, etc.', ff. 7, 7v. The speech is labelled in Eliot's hand 'in parl. 21 Ja.'. Forster, *Eliot*, I, 151–3, giving his usual garbled version, says it was delivered on March 17. Neither in the diaries or in *C.J.* on this day or on any other is there a mention of a subject to which this speech could be attached. There is no reference, which I could find, in the records of this Parliament to 'Duncombe's case', as Forster calls it, or any similar case to which the speech could be related. Possibly Eliot prepared it when he heard that such a private bill was to be introduced. But for some reason the bill was never brought before the House, and the speech never delivered.

[2] Rushworth, I, 148–51.

properly directed by experience. As has been seen, his advice and proposals, when made independently of wiser and saner minds, were rarely
accepted and occasionally openly spurned. But he had ideas, ideas on
many subjects, which he was not afraid to put before the House. In
fact, he, like others, did all that could be expected of an inexperienced
young man of spirit seeking a place in the sun.[1]

In the coming years Eliot was to recall with pleasure the temper of
this Parliament. But it is doubtful that he ever realized what seeds of
discontent and distress were sown in those bright spring days of 1624.
The cry for war against Spain had thrilled all except King James. But in
the end he yielded to pressure and, with eyes closed, took a leap in the
dark. Then the question, secondary at first, became prominent. Where
and against whom was the war to be waged? Directly against Spain,
against Spain and all the Catholics in Europe, or only in Germany to
recover the Palatinate? These questions had not been answered when
the Commons departed at the end of May. With James in his grave less
than a year later there was bound to be a direct conflict between the
Commons, controlling the purse strings and advocating a limited war
against Spain, and the new King, hampered by poverty and debts and
insisting with Buckingham on an unlimited attack against all Catholics
of western Europe. Such a picture was hardly envisaged by Sir John or
anybody else in 1624.

Similarly, at this time there was no more than rumour in the ears of
these Protestant and puritan legislators of the newly contemplated match
between Prince Charles and the French Catholic Princess, Henrietta
Maria.[2] As yet the King's reply to their petition, that he would grant no
favours to Catholics in England through any treaty of marriage, held a
prominent place in their minds. These Commons, still trusting their
sovereign, had yet to meet with the duplicity of a King.

Finally, restrictions on free speech had been removed, and that was
bound to lead to trouble with a Stuart of the calibre of Charles I on the
throne. True, no formal privilege had been granted, as had been desired
by Eliot. But the Commons were given permission to talk freely on
subjects which in 1621 James had labelled with 'prerogative royal' and
'unfit things to be handled in Parliament'. Once the bars were down,

---

[1] Eliot was named to sit on 21 committees of which 5 were joint committees of both
Houses. Of the 16 remaining committees only four were of any importance. The rest were
appointed to handle chiefly private bills. He was not named to the most important standing
committee of the House, the committee of privileges.

[2] Gardiner, V, 199.

freedom of discussion was bound to extend to all subjects whether the King willed it or not. Of this King James had been unaware, while the Commons, sensing it, had been too busy with their new freedom to grasp its significance. Charles, however, was to learn to his sorrow what the licence his father had permitted was to mean.

Most assuredly, the storm clouds were gathering when Sir John Eliot, elated over the proceedings at Westminster and at least encouraged by the part he had played in them, returned in June to his family in Cornwall and his vice-admiralty in Devon.

CHAPTER IV

Loyalty to the Lord Admiral

June, 1624, to May, 1625

IN June, 1624, Sir John Eliot resumed his duties as vice-admiral of Devon. For nearly a year he had been absent from his post. Between his release from prison and his return to London for the opening of Parliament at Westminster he had been unable to devote more than a day or two early in January, 1624, to his vice-admiralty business at Plymouth.[1]

Eliot's accounts, both personal and in the Admiralty records, substantiate this absence from his duties. Had any of his deputies performed his functions for him while he was away, there would be no blank for ten months in his accounts. But it is highly improbable that there was no income or expenditure in the vice-admiralty of Devon for all this time. Who took Sir John's place, if anybody, poses a problem. It is possible that James Bagg, jr., vice-admiral of south Cornwall, served also as vice-admiral of Devon during the latter half of 1623 when Eliot was in prison.[2] Bagg would probably have reported the accounts of the vice-admiralty of Devon for this period with his own for southern Cornwall. Unfortunately, his accounts are not available. Those of Eliot for this period, which will be mentioned later, appear to be slim indeed.[3] One suspects that James Bagg may have had something to do with the vice-admiralty of Sir John Eliot between July, 1623, and June, 1624.

As will be seen, Bagg and Eliot were not only to become rivals for the favour of the Duke of Buckingham but also to grow into bitter enemies. Possibly the beginning of the trouble between the two men is to be found during this interlude in the vice-admiralty of Sir John. In

---

[1] 'Eliot and Vice-Admir.', p. 10.

[2] On Sept. 25, 1623, Conway in a letter to James Bagg, jr., of Plymouth, addressed him as vice-admiral of Devon. S.P.D. Jas I, CLII, no. 66. Of course this may be an error for south Cornwall.

[3] See below, p. 62, note 5.

any case, that Bagg was comptroller of the customs at Plymouth[1] as well as vice-admiral of southern Cornwall should have furnished numerous occasions for friction to develop between the two men.

As vice-admiral of Devon from June, 1624, Eliot was active again salvaging wine from a wreck, confiscating bags of sumac found floating on the sea, and receiving a barrel of sugar and a Holland cheese from a Dutch warship in payment for some service he had performed for it. Now at Exeter for the assizes, then at Plymouth, or at Appledore and Bideford in the northern part of his district, Sir John was busy in his vice-admiralty all summer and well into the autumn.[2]

During October he was occupied for a number of days at home in Cornwall. On the 14th of the month he was present at the baptism of Susanna, his third daughter and sixth child. Six days later he purchased the borough of St. Germans from Richard Danyell, a London draper and merchant of Truro in Cornwall, for £100. In 1622 Sir John had bought certain houses in the borough for £100 from John Smith, esq. of Tregonecke. The presumption, therefore, is that with the second purchase Eliot owned the entire borough. By the end of James I's reign we see that he had consolidated and firmly established his landed possessions on the bank of the Tiddy.[3]

With the approach of winter it was time for the vice-admiral of Devon to make his first official report to the Court of Admiralty. As a prisoner during the early winter of 1623 it was impossible for him to make a return on the first year of his vice-admiralty. Consequently when he brought in his accounts on December 10, 1624, they were officially for two years.[4] With Sir Henry Marten, Eliot left a copy of his official accounts as well as £224 16s. 11d. for the Duke of Buckingham.[5] This was the moiety of the profits of the vice-admiralty of Devon for

---

[1] S.P.D. Jas. I, LXXVII, no. 30.

[2] 'Eliot and Vice-Admir.', pp. 3, 11.

[3] For this paragraph see above p. 24, note 6; P.E. Munim. Room, P.E. Title Deeds, no. 24; ibid., St. Germans Borough Title Deeds, Bundle LIV. His purchase of the borough did not necessarily carry with it its political control.

[4] 'Eliot and Vice-Admir.', p. 13.

[5] Ibid., p. 12. On March 21, 1625, James Bagg writing to Buckingham said that his 'year's service will bring to your Lordship's coffers better than twelve hundred pounds'. S.P.D., Jas. I, CLXXXV, no. 89. That is a huge sum when compared with Eliot's. What it contains, whether it includes income from the vice-admiralty of Devon, and why the report was made at this time of the year are impossible to say and raise a wealth of speculation.

two years due to the Lord Admiral. Was this all that Eliot owed?[1] In comparing his official with his private accounts it appears that he had not paid the full amount due to his chief. Unfortunately the two records were not kept on the same basis and so they cannot be compared as a whole; indeed their totals have no relation to each other. Certain items from both accounts, however, can be compared. In 1623 according to his private accounts he seized from pirates and other sources silver bullion which he sold for over £250. But in the figures he gave to the Admiralty the total value of the silver he had taken amounted to only £175 10s. That left more than £75 in the vice-admiral's hands which he should have divided with Buckingham. In 1624 Eliot's official accounts give Nutt's ship as appraised at £77 and sold for £100. But in his private reckoning he gives £113 as the sum he received for Nutt's ship.[2] Again Sir John pocketed £13 which he should have divided with the Lord Admiral.

These discrepancies are difficult to understand in the light of a letter Eliot wrote to Buckingham three months after he had visited London. Replying to the complaint of his chief against the low valuation of a certain ship, Sir John declared that this was only the appraised value used for the 'benefit' (use) of the owners, while 'the overplus . . . [or] advantage of the sale . . . [was] thereby reserved wholly to your Grace's use'. He went on to explain that this practice was not usually followed in Admiralty business and declared that some of his 'fellow officers' had objected to it. But he was pleased to set a precedent for the benefit of the Lord Admiral.[3] This statement and the figures just quoted do not agree. On the other hand there are items in Eliot's accounts which show that he gave the Lord Admiral the benefit of the sale rather than the appraised value of properties. Why didn't he do it every time? In his letter to Buckingham he declared that he was more honest than most vice-admirals. In practice he showed that sometimes he was only a little more honest than most vice-admirals. To appraise the degree of honesty displayed here is impossible. Morality in the seventeenth century

---

[1] Among the papers of Sir John Coke, commissioner of the navy, Master of Requests, and soon to be one of the Secretaries of State, there is a copy of the official accounts of Eliot for the first two years of his vice-admiralty to which is attached the following note in Coke's hand: 'A ship of corn and wines in his hands (£1,035) not accounted for'. *H.M.C. 12Rept.*, App., Pt. I, 177. This ship cannot be identified in Sir John's private accounts. It may have been restored to its owners resulting in no profit, without Coke knowing about it. Coke may have heard of this ship from Bagg.

[2] 'Eliot and Vice-Admir.', pp. 1, 3, 4, 7, 13–4.

[3] *Ibid.*, p. xii. S.P.D., Jas. I, CLXXXV, no. 45.

differed from that in the twentieth. Similarly, what appeared to be honest to James Bagg might be considered dishonest to Sir John Eliot. That he was human with the faults and weaknesses of a normal man nobody can doubt. At the same time he seems by comparison more honest than the average reliable official of his day, when the corruption known to have existed in the early seventeenth century is taken into consideration.

At the time when the vice-admiral of Devon was paying the Lord Admiral his moiety there began a period of harmony between the two men greater than had existed since the rise of the favourite to power. In the winter of 1624–25 negotiations were being conducted between England and France for the marriage of Prince Charles to Henrietta Maria. During the first half of December word was received in London that a dispensation for the marriage had been granted in Rome. At the same time King James signed the marriage treaty. The Duke of Buckingham was given the proxy of the Prince for the marriage ceremony in Paris. Consequently he was making preparations for his journey before the Christmas holidays. But troubles over the papal dispensation were not removed until March 21, 1625, six days before the death of King James, when the French government announced that it was ready to have the marriage performed. With the death of the King it was obvious to Buckingham that he was much too busy at home to go to Paris. So the proxy for Charles was put in the hands of the new King's distant relative, the Duke of Chevreuse.[1] It was this proposed journey of the Duke of Buckingham to France which brought him and Sir John Eliot into closer relationship. Presumably while Eliot was in London in December, 1624, he was invited by the Duke to accompany him to Paris.[2] Of course, Sir John was delighted to go. Possibly Buckingham was rewarding the faithful services of a friend, or he felt that the vice-admiral of Devon had not been adequately compensated for the inconveniences and losses he had suffered through John Nutt and therefore decided to request Eliot's company on his visit to France.

Though the journey never took place, it throws an interesting light on the political and religious opinions of Sir John Eliot at this time. He must have known the general purpose of the visit to Paris and in prin-

---

[1] Gardiner, V, 249–79, 306–7, 326.

[2] For mention and hints of this journey see Eliot's letters to Buckingham of Feb. 21, March 11, and April 1, 1625. S.P.D., Jas. I, CLXXXIV, no. 16, CLXXXV, no. 45, and Chas. I, I, no. 25.

ciple, at least, have approved it. This does not agree with Sir John's oft-disclosed hatred of Roman Catholics. Presumably his love for France dampened any dislike he had of the religion of the future Queen of England. Papists, bad in England in the eyes of Eliot, were to him at their worst in Spain. But in France they wore a coat of a different colour, particularly if that country was to be allied with England. In all his parliamentary utterances he never denounced France and always felt her to be England's natural ally. The well-being of the state was para-mount with him. Therefore, a marriage and political alliance with France, even though it meant a Catholic Queen for England's Protest-ant King, was to be encouraged and assisted. Of course, Sir John could not have had the slightest inkling of the letter granting protection to English Catholics which James and Charles had signed. That was still a closely guarded secret and would have aroused Eliot's opposition to the French match had he known about it.

During the winter of 1624–25 Eliot was doing his best to ingratiate himself with his chief. He even employed circuitous methods in curry-ing favour with the Duke. Valentine Carey, Bishop of Exeter, was Sir John Eliot's landlord and patron. He was also brother-in-law of Sir John Coke[1], who was rising in prominence at court under the tutelage of Buckingham. Late in 1624 or early in 1625 the Bishop wrote to Coke as follows:

'I am become a suitor unto you in the behalf of Sir John Eliot, who hath divers ways merited this office at my hands, that you would afford him your favour and friendship in his just and honest causes, which may fall within your cognizance and power. I pray you let him taste of your friendship at my request and mediation that thereby he may both find me ready to requite his former courtesies as also be obliged to me in the like hereafter'.[2]

Carey did not write this letter without Eliot's solicitation. Sir John knew the powerful position Coke was in at this time. As commissioner of the navy he could help or harm him in his relations with the Lord Admiral. A good word from a man so close to Buckingham might be of great assistance in advancing Eliot both with the favourite and at court. There is no evidence that during this winter Sir John as yet disliked

---

[1] Dorothea Coke, *The Last Elizabethan, Sir John Coke* (London, 1937), *1563–1644*, p. 5.
[2] *H.M.C. 12th Rept.*, App. Pt. I, 177. See also Coke, *op. cit.*, p. 110.

Coke. Nor can Coke and Bagg be suspected of working against Eliot, except when the commissioner of the navy questioned the accounts of the vice-admiral of Devon.[1] That the Bishop of Exeter's request to his brother-in-law was fulfilled is impossible to say. But Valentine Carey saw the growing influence of Sir John Eliot and realized that one good turn deserved another both in the past and in the future.

While contemplating the prospect of visiting France in the company of the all-powerful Duke of Buckingham, Eliot returned to his vice-admiralty duties in Devon. During the next three months his correspondence with the Duke shows the relationship of the two men. A number of letters were exchanged in which Eliot told his chief how he was safeguarding the Lord Admiral's interests in handling a derelict laden with rye which had fallen into his hands, while the Duke sent him requested instructions and was liberal in his praise of work well done. In another series of letters, in which, as in the previous one, those of Eliot are the only ones surviving, he kept Buckingham informed of his attempts with other commissioners to induce Plymouth and Saltash to co-operate in clearing a wreck out of that part of the harbour of Plymouth in which Saltash had commercial rights. Again instructions were sought, and presumably given, though none seem to have been authoritative enough to settle the dispute.[2]

From the national point of view the most important service Sir John Eliot was performing as vice-admiral at this time was to act as a listening post and keep his government informed of the course of events in Spain, as a state of war between England and that country was slowly developing. With the gossip and reports of seamen in Plymouth and other Devonshire ports filling his ears, he was in an excellent position to receive much news, true and false, from Spain and other countries. On January 10 he wrote the Lord Admiral from Dartmouth that he had heard of great preparations in Spain 'for the seas' without any destination mentioned. At the same time Englishmen in Spain were being treated with 'extraordinary respect' and 'unusual courtesy'. To many it looked like the calm before the storm, he declared, so that English merchants were glad to be leaving that country.[3]

At the same time the Duke was planning to send a great fleet to seize

---

[1] See above, p. 63, note 1.

[2] 'Eliot and Vice-Admir.', p. 17, and S.P.D., Jas. I, CLXXXI, nos. 7, 32, CLXXXII, no. 52, CLXXXIII, nos. 6, 7, 51, CLXXXIV, no. 16, CLXXXV, no. 45.

[3] *Ibid.*, CLXXXI, no. 32.

a Spanish port. In laying the groundwork for this action the vice-admiral of Devon and other officials of the western coasts had been ordered to stop the sale of all fish so that the navy would have ample supply, to prevent ships from sailing to Spain, and to make a survey of all provisions in their districts which could be used on such an expedition. In several letters written late in January and in February Eliot protested to the Lord Admiral that the prohibition to sell fish might be disastrous for the fishermen of Devon, might cause their ruin. But these repeated protests seem to have remained unanswered. In one of the above letters, that of February 2nd, Sir John reported that a brand new Pomeranian ship, mounting a dozen guns with room for many more and sailing virtually in ballast, had put into Plymouth on her way to Spain. Having ordered the ship detained, he requested instructions as to what to do with her as several more were said to be due in Plymouth soon. On February 13 the vice-admiral had more news from Spain for his chief. The Spaniards were now said to be doing great harm to English merchants, seizing their goods and stopping their ships on the high seas, he wrote. The placid picture of the previous month had changed. Both nations were becoming openly hostile to each other.[1]

There are two more surviving letters of Sir John Eliot which display his great affection for the Duke of Buckingham. The first, written on February 28,[2] disclosed that Sir John had heard by report and rumour that the northern division of his vice-admiralty had been taken from him and given to the Earl of Bath. He was worried. With honeyed words and in language that today has the ring of insincerity he professed his subservience and loyalty to the Duke. At the same time Eliot reminded him of his rights in that part of his vice-admiralty, saying he need not recall 'how your Lordship passed it to me in my patent; how I have used it since the death of the old Lord of Bath, for whose time only there was a particular exception'.[3] Sir John had been hurt by the report of this loss. His language shows that his friendship and affection for the Duke of Buckingham were fundamental as far as he was con-

---

[1] *A.P.C., 1623-25*, pp. 403-4, 423, and *S.P.D.*, Jas. I, CLXXXII, no. 52, CLXXXIII, nos. 8, 51. He mentioned France only once and that was to say that he had heard that the Duke of Soubise, one of the Huguenot leaders, had begun 'some new troubles' around Rochelle. *Ibid.*, CLXXXII, no. 52.

[2] *Ibid.*, CLXXXIV, no. 56.

[3] William Bourchier, 3rd Earl of Bath, was vice-admiral of Devon in 1586 and Lord Lieutenant of Devon in 1587. He died July 12, 1623. Edward Bourchier, the 4th Earl, was born in 1599 and had nothing to do with the vice-admiralty of Devon. G.E.C.

cerned. But it seems there was no basis for Eliot's fear. Buckingham must quickly have informed him that he was entirely mistaken, for the subject was never mentioned again.

The second letter was written on April 1 and is the last of Sir John's to the Duke that has survived.[1] Writing from Exeter he began in his usual saccharine style and told Buckingham that he was on his way to London to attend his Grace when in some letters from the Lords of the Council he learned of the death of King James. That news

'hath imposed not only a sorrow but an astonishment on all my faculties, that of myself I have not power to move in any thing without new direction. The apprehension of so great a loss and the particular sense which, I know, remains in your Grace, whose affections I must bear, makes me doubt a general indisposition until the grief may somewhat be digested, upon which I dare not presume further but as I shall be warranted by your commands . . .'

Knowing Eliot and knowing his common use of extravagant language, his sincerity cannot be impugned. Buckingham, James, and Charles were men to be revered, respected, and obeyed.

In the letters from the Lords of the Council mentioned by Sir John when writing to Buckingham, the vice-admiral of Devon was warned against proceeding with a press of mariners which had been previously ordered. Here we have the first indication of an episode which was to lead Eliot into serious trouble.

Let us see what lay behind the order of the Lords of the Council. Issuing several behests in February and March which were to lay the foundations for the raising and equipping of a fleet with which to attack Spain, the Privy Council on March 18 gave instructions for impressing seamen in western and southern England. Devonshire was divided into two. Three hundred men were to be raised in the eastern half of that county by Sir John Eliot and Sir Edward Giles. In the western section three hundred and fifty were to be impressed by John Drake and the mayor of Plymouth. For all of Devon as well as Cornwall James Bagg was appointed 'prester'. In other words, Eliot was to report to him.[2]

As King James had died on March 27th, it was necessary to obtain

---

[1] S.P.D., Chas. I, I, no. 25.
[2] *A.P.C., 1623–25*, pp. 486–7, 498–500; *H.M.C. 9th Rept.*, App., Pt. I, 269b.

the formal approval of the new King to the policy initiated by his father. It was a mere formality, of course. Even so, it was the reason why Eliot in his letter of April 1 to the Duke said that he had been ordered to delay pressing mariners in Devonshire. The point was substantiated and approached from a somewhat different point of view in a letter also written on April 1 by Thomas Bridgeman, mayor of Exeter and an assistant commissioner for all of Devon, to James Bagg. He said that he could not induce Sir John Eliot and the other commissioners to proceed with pressing of men on the basis of his 'Majesty's late commission under the Great Seal'. They showed 'a new command under the hands of the Lords of the Privy Council that no proclamation was come from the new King', Bridgeman wrote. Reading between the lines of this letter it can be seen that the trouble was that Eliot, a stickler for form, supported by most of his fellow commissioners, refused to proceed. Bridgeman, on the other hand, saw the need of obtaining mariners as quickly as possible and wanted to ignore such a minor formality as a warrant from the new King, which he knew would arrive shortly. But Bagg arriving at Exeter on the next day immediately took advantage of Sir John's stand. Writing to Sir John Coke on that day he said he found that 'Sir John Eliot came to the commissioners, resolved not to proceed, which took off the rest. Be assured whatever are his ways he shall not more than he hath hinder the business, but what is in the power of a diligent and careful man, I will perform'.[1]

Here is the first evidence of a feud which was to darken most of the rest of Eliot's life. It may have been in existence for some time, but there has been no indication of it up to now. Bagg had an excellent opportunity to get his rival into trouble and was taking full advantage of it. Disregarding the Council's order and possibly supplied with a mandate from the Lord Admiral to continue the forced recruiting of seamen, he persisted with his assignment and denounced Sir John to the commissioner of the navy with the hope that his words would reach the ears of the Duke. At first Eliot had the support of most of the other commissioners, but soon he was isolated and the vice-admiral of Cornwall was in full command. On April 18 James Bagg wrote from Fowey to his friend Coke and told him of his progress as 'prester', in which he had the support of all the commissioners except Eliot.[2] He alone opposed him.

[1] *H.M.C. 12th Rept.*, App., Pt. I, 190.
[2] *Ibid.*

Why Sir John should stand alone in opposition and put himself in the wrong is difficult to say. Already on March 31 King Charles had signed a proclamation for the pressing of mariners.[1] Surely, nearly three weeks later Eliot should have had notice of this and should have turned himself into an obedient servant of the state. The trouble now seems to be that this impressionable man had had his feelings hurt. And they were getting the better of his judgment and sense of duty. Writing to Buckingham on April 18 Bagg gives a clue to what was troubling Sir John Eliot. That gentleman, he said, 'is displeased he was not solely employed [to press men] and therefore could not be invited to assist'.[2] It sounds as though Sir John felt that he should have been made 'prester' instead of Bagg, that he was jealous of his rival, and that, therefore, he would not co-operate in pressing mariners for his Majesty's navy. Consequently he had been excluded from the commission working under Bagg. Unquestionably Eliot was harming himself in the eyes of the Lord Admiral and the Privy Council. Presumably early in April that body directed 'the Lord Russell only' to press men 'for the east part of Devon'.[3] Why Sir Edward Giles, who appears to have been willing to work with Bagg, was also excluded is impossible to say.

The vice-admiral of southern Cornwall was beginning to reap the reward of his loyal, though probably unscrupulous, service to the Duke of Buckingham. Joint victualler of the fleet preparing for Spain with Sir Allen Apsley and collector for Cornwall of the Lord Admiral's tenths due on all prizes of war, Sir James Bagg, recently knighted, was gaining profit and honour between the spring and autumn of 1625. Sir John Eliot, on the other hand, was able only to hold his own. At every opportunity Bagg denounced his rival in stronger and stronger terms and attempted to push him down as he went up. It must be admitted, however, that Eliot on at least one occasion left himself open to attack.[4]

By the opening of the first Parliament of the new reign Bagg and Eliot hated each other intensely; no longer were they merely rivals

---

[1] *A.P.C.*, *1625–26*, p. 7.   [2] S.P.D., Chas. I, I, no. 69.

[3] In a form letter dated March 18 (cited above, p. 68) giving instructions for pressing seamen, the Privy Council added at the end, 'Directed afterwards to the Lord Russell only for the east part of Devon'. The 'afterwards' cannot be identified by any particular date, but most likely it was some time in April. Russell was Lord-Lieutenant of the county of Devon and in 1627 succeeded his cousin as 4th Earl of Bedford. D.N.B.

[4] S.P.D., Jas. I, CLXXXIII, no. 47, CLXXXV, no. 89, and *C.S.P.D.*, *Chas. I, 1625–26*, pp. 79, 116, 182.

but enemies, with Sir John Coke closely allied to Bagg. The Duke of Buckingham could with difficulty have played an impartial role between the two men. That he was veering to the side of Bagg can readily be seen. But it did not mean he was openly turning against Eliot. His advancement in the Admiralty might be slowed or even brought to a stop; but the Lord Admiral still considered his vice-admiral of Devon as an obedient and devoted servant. At the same time it is doubtful that Sir John even harboured a grudge against Buckingham when he attended Parliament in June, 1625. As will be seen, he vented most of his spleen on Coke and wished to remain on good terms with his chief.[1] Intense loyalty to a man is liable to take a severe buffeting before it succumbs. The events of that Parliament and those immediately following it finally opened the eyes of Sir John Eliot.

[1] Bagg was not prominent enough for Eliot to attack him in Parliament.

CHAPTER V

Prelude to the Breach

June to August, 1625

THE death of James I on March 27, 1625, closed the first ominous chapter of government by a King who was attempting to establish an absolutism based on divine right. A suppressed sigh of relief arose from Englishmen, as they turned a new page with hope of better days to come. Charles as King was still riding the wave of popularity which had been set in motion by his return as Prince from that fruitless Spanish escapade. Not enough was known as yet about his prospective marriage to Henrietta Maria to cause more than a qualm in stout puritan hearts. It was a bit too early to link the King's name with the Mansfeld disaster abroad.[1] There is little question that Sir John Eliot expressed the accepted view of the time when he wrote that 'with the new King a new spirit of life and comfort possessed all men'.[2]

With these words Eliot began his *Negotium Posterorum*, historically the most important of his works. It was written during the last years of his life while a prisoner in the Tower. Just when the treatise was begun and surviving segment completed is impossible to say.[3] According to his preface Sir John intended to write a history of Parliament during the reigns of James I and Charles I to 1630. His object was to show how the nation had fallen from the heights it had attained at the end of the reign of Queen Elizabeth to the depths it had reached by the sixth year of the reign of King Charles. Unfortunately only enough time was allotted him to write an account of the first Parliament of Charles.[4]

---

[1] See below, p. 95.   [2] *Neg. Post.*, I, 41.

[3] I cannot accept Forster's unsubstantiated statement in *Eliot*, I, 210, that 'at the close of the first stormy session of the great Parliament of 1628 . . . it appears to have been begun; though not likely to have been brought into the state in which we find it, until the author's later imprisonment'. There is no evidence, internal or otherwise, which supports this view.

[4] On the title page he wrote *Tomus Secundus, Liber Primus* and headed the description of the second session at Oxford with *Liber Secundus*. It appears that he intended to

CHARLES I by Daniel Mytens
From the portrait at Hatfield House
reproduced by permission of the Marquess of Salisbury

As the title indicates, Eliot was recording the events of these trouble-some times for posterity, so that it might learn the truth from one who was active then. Unfortunately, a participant is rarely able later in life to report events as they actually took place. After more than six years much had happened to influence and change his impressionable mind. The events of 1625 he saw in the light of 1631 through spectacles darkened by the intervening years. His great quarrel with Buckingham had not begun in the summer of 1625, but by 1631 it was becoming his-tory. Whenever the name of the Duke came to the tongue of the prisoner in the Tower it must have produced a bitter taste in his mouth. But in the first Parliament of the new reign Eliot was still the loyal servant of the Lord Admiral. It is unhistorical, therefore, to accept the *Negotium Posterorum* at its face value.[1]

There is much in this work, however, which is of importance and cannot be found in any other source. Nowhere else have we such an in-timate personal account of an early seventeenth century Parliament. Opinions about members and their speeches are liberally scattered throughout Sir John's story. Some are obviously his own, but many ex-press the views of this or that party. The terms 'country' and 'courtiers' are used so frequently as party names that there is no doubt of their common usage at the time. Unable to recapture the thoughts and feel-ings he had had during this Parliament and blinded by intervening events, Eliot hurls most of his poisoned shafts at the Duke of Bucking-ham. On the other hand Sir John's sarcastic and contemptuous por-trayal of Sir John Coke was more like the image he had of him in 1625. What he thought of Coke's 'great abilities' is seen when he writes that 'his conversation being with books, and that to teach, not study them, men and business were subjects which he knew not'.[2]

---

devote his first volume to the Parliaments of James. But after he had completed the preface to the whole work, he decided to write first about those Parliaments which were still fresh in his mind. Then death overtook him with not more than a third of his second volume completed and his first not even begun. I canot agree with Grosart in *Neg. Post.*, I, xxi, where he believes that the first volume has been lost. Internal evidence disproves such a belief.

[1] It must be compared with such sources at *C.J. C.D.* and E.P.N. In the appendix of *C.D.*, pp. 129–51, there is an additional diary or account of the Oxford session. And then there is also Calthorpe which is brief for the first session but fuller and practically the same for the Oxford session as the last-mentioned account. E.P.N. is Eliot's notes for this Parlia-ment of which there are two sets. The first is practically the same as *C.J.*, and like *C.J.* contains a gap from June 22 to July 4. The second set of Eliot's notes, brief though they may be, help to fill this gap, chiefly with proceedings in committee of the whole House.

[2] *Neg. Post.*, I, 114. Between 1583 and 1591 Coke was a Fellow at Trinity College, Cam-

Of the men of his own party Eliot had the highest opinion of 'that master of expression Sir Robert Phelips'. He says of him: 'There was in this gentleman a natural grace of oratory, a moving and Nestorian way of rhetoric, a choice store he had and elegance of words, readiness and dexterity in fancy and conception, a voice and pronunciation of much sweetness.' But Phelips was not perfect, for 'a redundancy and exuberance he had and an affected cadence and delivery'. What impressed Sir John particularly was that Phelips 'upon all occasions, at all times' spoke extemporaneously.[1]

The most interesting sketch Sir John Eliot has left to posterity is that of his great rival in the House of Commons, Sir Thomas Wentworth. Much of what he had to say of him was as true in 1631 as in 1625. This is how he described Sir Thomas:

'There was in that gentleman a good choice of parts, natural and acquisit, and no less opinion of them. A strong eloquence he had and a comprehension of much reason. His arguments were weighty and acute and his descriptions exquisite. . . . His abilities were great both in judgment and persuasion, and as great a reputation did attend them.'

These virtues, Eliot said, were opposed by great vices. In fact, he believed that the virtues

'seldom were directed to good ends, and when they had that colour some other secret moved them. His covetousness and ambition were both violent, as were his ways to serve them . . . and those affections raised him to so much pride and choler, as any opposition did transport him'.[2]

This appraisal of Wentworth is excellent. Its criticism is not highly coloured by personal antipathy. Though too severe, it is essentially sound. But, like most of his contemporaries, Sir John had no understanding of the nature of his rival's objective. Both Eliot and Wentworth developed the same political ideal, good government.[3] Where they differed was in the composition of that ideal. To Sir John, the peo-

bridge, and public lecturer in rhetoric at that university. He did not return to academic life after 1591. Coke, *The Last Elizabethan*, pp. 6–7.

[1] *Neg. Post.*, I, 118.   [2] *Ibid.*, 104.

[3] C. V. Wedgwood, *Strafford* (London, 1935), p. 73, gives Wentworth's ideal.

ple working through Parliament in complete harmony with their Sovereign constituted good government. To Sir Thomas, the King acting through his prerogative and sparingly using Parliament for domestic reform meant the same.[1] This ideal with its differences and similarities was to be endangered for both men when they saw the incompetent Duke of Buckingham gaining complete control of both King and government. Consequently, the favourite became the enemy of both Eliot and Wentworth and had to be removed at all costs. Temporarily their paths were the same. After the Duke's hands were supposedly tied by the Petition of Right and his life taken by John Felton, their paths separated again, as the two men worked for the same end with totally different means.

Besides Wentworth and Phelips, Sir John Eliot gives glimpses in his *Negotium Posterorum* of other worthies, both 'courtiers' and 'of the country'. 'That great artist', Sir Benjamin Rudyerd, received more than his due when it was said of him 'a great reputation was implied both in learning and wisdom of the man'. As a speaker the author considered him good, but he 'did speak never but premeditated, which had more show of memory than affection and made his words less powerful than observed'.[2] But a man of such reputation as Sir Edward Coke received little comment beyond 'that great father of the law',[3] though his speeches were by no means neglected.

Now we must examine from all available sources the part played by Sir John Eliot in the Parliament of 1625. It is logical to suppose that the recognition he had received in the last Parliament might turn into prominence in this. That must be kept in mind in following his parliamentary career during these summer months. Sir John was returned for a second time for Newport on April 21,[4] presumably with the influence of Buckingham and the court again behind him.

It was nearly two months, however, before he took his seat in the House of Commons. The attendance of the Commons on their King in his first Parliament awaited the arrival of the new Queen from France.

[1] For Wentworth's early lack of respect for Parliament see William Knowler, *The Earl of Strafford's Letters and Despatches* (London, 1739), I, 9, 24, Lady Burghclere, *Strafford* (London, 1931), I, 115.

[2] *Neg. Post.*, I, 69, 75.   [3] *Ibid.*, II, 39.

[4] *O.R.*, I, 463. St. Germans chose Sir John Coke and Sir Henry Marten. Coke sat through the influence of the Bishop of Exeter, while Marten probably had the backing of Eliot. *H.M.C. 12 Rept.*, App. Pt. I, 251, and David H. Willson, *Privy Councillors in the House of Commons* (Minneapolis, 1940), p. 78.

She did not reach Dover until June 12. In the meantime English troops under Mansfeld, protected by Dutch fortresses from the forces of the Holy Roman Emperor across the border, were being decimated by idleness and disease.[1] English Roman Catholics were filled with new hope at the royal order relieving them from further persecution[2] and were enthusiastic at the prospect of a queen of their own faith sharing the throne with Charles. To cap all this the plague had again appeared and was sweeping its devastating way through the populous centres of the country.

Fortunately most of these evils were unknown to the majority of the land and to Eliot in particular when he reached London early that summer. But like others who had come to attend Parliament, he quickly realized the danger from the pestilence which, by the middle of June, was taking a weekly toll of nearly two hundred lives in the metropolis alone. It was under such conditions that on June 18 King Charles addressed the two Houses at the opening of Parliament.

Of the speech Sir John wrote: 'Both the sense and shortness of this expression were well liked as meeting with the inclination of the time, which wearied with the long orations of King James that did inherit but the wind, was much moved at this brevity and plainness'. During the preliminary activities of the Commons, in which Eliot was named for the first time to the standing committee of privileges, a motion was made to ask the King to adjourn Parliament until Michaelmas because of danger from the plague. After some debate it was defeated and the House was ready for business. At least the Commons had been made very conscious of the danger surrounding them.[3]

When on the next day discussion centred on the appointment of the committee of grievances both Sir Edward Coke and Sir John Eliot were opposed for different reasons to naming this committee. Furthermore, Sir John wanted no private bills presented to the House, so that its business could be expedited. Like Coke and others, he was anxious to cut the work of the Commons to a minimum to enable them to leave London as soon as possible. Through the efforts of Sir Francis Seymour, who ignored Eliot's suggestion, the debate was diverted to the subject of religion to which supply was shortly added. But it was

---

Gardiner, V, 335–6.

[2] Issued on May 1, 1625.

[3] *Neg. Post.*, I, 44–5, and *C.J.*, I, 799. Eliot took no part in the brief debate contrary to the statement of Forster in *Eliot*, I, 240, 241. See E.P.N., f. 1v, *C.J.*, I, 800, and *C.D.*, p. 7.

brought to a speedy close with the decision to consider the two subjects on the next day in committee of the whole House.[1]

When it met on the afternoon of June 23 the discussion was opened by a speech on religion from Sir John Eliot.[2] It is one of the best he ever delivered. Not too long and beautifully organized it displays his oratory ripening to perfection. 'Religion', he begins, 'is the touchstone of all actions, the trial by which they are known, upon which all policy, all wisdom, all excellence must be grounded. And what rests not on this centre can have no perfection or assurance.' He continues by expounding at some length the importance of religion in the relation of men to each other and in the operation of a government. Turning to the nature of his subject he says that 'two things are considerable therein, the purity, the unity thereof'. As to purity of religion, he says he need not speak in Parliament of that subject, 'seeing how beautiful the memories of our fathers are therein made by their endeavours'.[3] But with unity it was a different matter. 'What divisions, what factions, nay what fractions in religion this kingdom does now suffer', Eliot cries. And here he points a sharp, accusing finger at the papists, though he never calls them by any name. In conclusion he seeks a remedy for this disunity, 'this sickness'. The trouble lies, he believes, either in the laws or in their execution. 'If the laws be perfect, how can division enter but by a breach of them?' he asks. Therefore, his motion is that there be made

'a review of the laws . . . that if the division have got in by imperfection of the laws they may be amended; . . . if, as I most do fear it, through neglect and want of execution, the power may be enforced with some great mulct and penalty on the ministers, who for that will be more vigilant and we thereby secure.'

The Elizabethan Anglican, hating Roman Catholicism as much as he loved true Protestantism, had spoken. The supporter of the government, the 'courtier', found trouble right at home. He put the blame, if blame there was, on the ministers of the Crown but never on the King, that perfect partner of the people in ideal government.

The debate, begun on so high a plane, quickly came down to earth,

[1] C.J., I, 800–1 and E.P.N., f. 2.

[2] Neg. Post., I, 70–3, E.P.N., f. 20 and C.J. 1625, p. 4. It is not mentioned in C.D.

[3] He is, of course, referring to the Church of England as established in the reign of Queen Elizabeth. W. H. Frere, The English Church in the Reigns of Elizabeth and James I (London, 1904), pp. 30, 32, 97, 163.

as member after member pointed to this or that cause for the spread of
popery in England.[1] But Eliot's motion received no support. Unfortunately it was made by the wrong person. A 'courtier' was suggesting
that ministers of state be watched and even punished. An Anglican
midst many puritans was denouncing Roman Catholics. The 'country'
did not trust him, the 'court' was displeased with him. Speaking at such
a level Sir John Eliot could make little headway in a House of Commons daily becoming more divided, more suspicious of the government.

Coming to no conclusion, the debate was adjourned to the following
day with the final result that on June 30 a petition against recusants was
sent to the Lords on its way to be presented to the King.[2] From the
meagre surviving records of these discussions it appears that Eliot remained silent after his magnificent opening address.[3] Possibly it sounds
more magnificent now than it did in 1625. His facile pen in 1631 may
have improved and elaborated it.

For nearly two weeks, during which the House decided to vote the
King two subsidies and denounced Richard Montague, the Arminian
author of *A New Gag for an Old Goose*, no word spoken by Sir John has
survived. But he tells the whole story in his *Negotium*, possibly more
than the whole. He is the sole authority for the statement 'that his
Majesty received great satisfaction and contentment in their [the Commons'] gift', as reported on July 4 by the Lord Keeper.[4]

On that day the disputed election involving Sir Thomas Wentworth received a thorough airing in the House. On the next day,
while it was being settled, Sir John Eliot was heard again by the Commons. This Yorkshire election dispute had been referred to the committee of privileges on the opening day when Sir John Savile, the defeated candidate, presented, through Sir Edward Giles, a petition to the
House. The first report from the committee of privileges, followed by
a brief debate, was made on June 22. It was not until July 4 that the
case was seriously considered. Briefly the trouble was that the sheriff of
Yorkshire, according to Savile, had closed the poll illegally and had
declared Wentworth and his colleague, Sir Thomas Fairfax, elected.[5]

---

[1] *C.J. 1625*, p. 4.   [2] *C.D.*, p. 30.

[3] The only other time Eliot spoke according to the records at my disposal was on
June 28 when he presented a petition for Mr Arthur Basset, MP for Fowey, Cornwall.
C.J. 1625, p. 7.

[4] *C.D.*, pp. 30–5, *Neg. Post.*, I, 92, 105–9, and Gardiner, V, 348, note 3.

[5] *C.J.*, I, 799–802, *C.D.*, pp. 36–7, E.P.N., ff. 2v–3. There is no evidence that Eliot spoke
in the committee of privileges on July 4, as Forster, *Eliot*, I, 271, asserts.

When on July 5 the case again was receiving the careful attention of the Commons, a motion was made and defeated that Sir Thomas be heard by counsel. Thereupon it was moved that he be heard in his own defence. This motion Eliot was discussing[1] when, contrary to the rules of the House, Wentworth entered. Sir John stopped immediately. After a moment's hesitation he launched a bitter attack on the offender. The violation of the rights of the Commons by strangers, he declared, can be pardoned when members of the House, displaying scorn and contempt, abuse them. 'A greater dishonour and contempt this House has no time suffered than what does now affront it.' What can be worse, he asked, than to be excluded by a fundamental order of the House, only to have that order broken by the man who recently urged it be observed.[2] This member, Eliot asserted, enters our House to ruin it, to destroy its privilege. Here he corrected himself and declared the man was not a member, not worthy of the name. And so, he closed, 'let us from hence expel him'.[3] He was so enraged that he could not even call him by his parliamentary name.

On such a plea against the breach of such a privilege Wentworth was forced to leave the floor. But as the motion that he be heard was passed immediately, he returned to defend his seat in the House. In his plea he contemptuously ignored his breach of privilege and Eliot's attack and devoted himself to defending the actions of the Yorkshire sheriff. His efforts were, however, of no avail, for shortly afterwards the House, without a division, declared void the election of Sir Thomas Wentworth and Sir Thomas Fairfax and ordered a new writ issued.[4]

It was indeed unfortunate for Wentworth that he entered the House just as Sir John Eliot was speaking. Of all the members, he would take most seriously this obvious infringement of the rules. The incident shows the two men standing at opposite poles. The one, disdainful of

[1] From no source, not even *Neg. Post.*, can we learn what Eliot was saying here.

[2] Probably refers to Wentworth's remarks on March 22, 1624, in the Pomfrett election discussion when he said: 'To have both parties suspended till the cause be determined.' *C.J.*, I, 745.

[3] This speech is found only in *Neg. Post.*, I, 101–2. All *C.J.* says is 'Sir John Eliot against it', meaning against the motion that Wentworth be heard. But E.P.N. says: 'debate proceeds, Wentworth comes in. He that was arguing the point stays his speech and turned to the privilege of the House. Wentworth sent out again. After, the motion being renewed.' Obviously Eliot spoke extemporaneously. But it is more than likely that the words he wrote in his *Neg. Post.* on this occasion are an embellishment of what he said at the time. It seems improbable that he wrote out the speech after he had delivered it. To remember after six years just what he had said at a particular time would be extremely difficult.

[4] *C.J.*, I, 804, C.D., p. 45, E.P.N., f. 5v.

all regulations which obstructed his own purposes; the other, venerating every convention of an institution which he regarded with awe and admiration. It would be difficult to find common ground for two such antithetic personalities who insisted on fighting for their ideas.

During these proceedings at Westminster the plague had been increasing in London. The King had retired to Hampton Court; and many members had departed to the greater safety of the open country. Realizing how serious the situation had become, Charles sent word on July 4 that as soon as he heard the Commons were ready he would put an end to the session.[1] That afternoon the subsidy bill had its first reading and passed its second on the next day. In a division on July 5 barely half the House voted. The number which finally passed the subsidy bill on July 8 must have been small indeed. Hardly had the bill been sent to the Lords when Sir John Coke arose and said 'that his Majesty graciously accepts the gift, which is already resolved of, as a welcome and pledge of the love not only of this representative body but of the whole kingdom'. Before continuing with this speech we must examine a most significant preliminary episode.[2]

The two subsidies which had been voted by the Commons were far from enough in the eyes of both Charles and Buckingham, the King's gracious thanks notwithstanding. This small amount had not been proposed by a Privy Councillor or 'courtier' but by Sir Francis Seymour, a rabid leader of the 'country'.[3] In the debate on the subsidy signs were appearing that the Commons were far from pleased with the policies of the government and were exhibiting little faith in the Duke of Buckingham.

Disappointed over the two subsidies and resolved to do something about it, the Duke, late on the night of July 7, hurried from the King at Hampton Court to York House, his London residence.[4] There he summoned his henchmen. The few who were able to attend at midnight received his order that the Commons must be induced to vote further supply. As none of the more intelligent members of the 'court' party were present, none opposed Buckingham's request, and all gave it hearty support. But early the next morning the plan reached the ears of the more able of his followers. Among them was Sir Humphrey May,

[1] See above, p. 78, for the addition to this message as Eliot gives it in *Neg. Post.*, I, 92.
[2] *C.J.*, I, 802, 803, 806; *C.D.*, pp. 41, 56; *L.J.*, III, 454; E.P.N., ff. 4, 7.
[3] *C.D.*, p. 30. Actually he proposed one subsidy and a fifteenth.
[4] The following incident is based entirely on *Neg. Post.*, I, 110–13.

Chancellor of the Duchy. He with others tried in vain to change the will of the favourite. Then May hurried 'to a gentleman whom he thought more powerful with the Duke and knew to be affectionate to the public'.

This gentleman was Sir John Eliot who was still on excellent terms with his chief. There was little, if any, occasion as yet for him to have turned against the Lord Admiral. He may have had his doubts about the man in more than one way. But his loyalty to his superior was not yet jeopardized by definite knowledge of Buckingham's incompetence and inability to direct King Charles towards Eliot's ideal of good government. On the other hand it is doubtful that the Duke had a high regard for the opinion of Sir John at this time. The subterranean burrowing of Sir James Bagg, probably assisted already by Sir John Coke and others, may have begun to weaken the repute of the vice-admiral of Devon with Buckingham. In the House of Commons Eliot had demonstrated that he was not a pawn to be moved about the board at the will of the leaders of the government. Though by no means an opponent of those in power, his speech on privilege in the previous Parliament and his two recent speeches in this one had shown which way his mind was tending.

In spite of these possibilities May was entirely justified in picking Sir John Eliot to make the final attempt to alter the plan of the favourite. But the time was short. Sir Humphrey met Eliot at Westminster early on the morning of the 8th before the opening of proceedings in Parliament. Sir John was afraid that before he could get back to the House the proposal to vote additional supply would have been presented to the Commons. But the Chancellor of the Duchy promised to delay the presentation of the measure until Eliot had returned. That he must do as quickly as possible, and in his conversation he must make the Duke realize that his plan was being shelved in the House until the interview was completed.

On arriving at his destination Sir John found the Duke and Duchess still in bed. When she had withdrawn into her own chamber, he was admitted and explained to his Grace the reason for this early morning visit. Eliot's argument that the intended request to be made of the Commons would harm the honour of the King and would make both his Majesty and his Grace unpopular, had no effect on Buckingham. Nor did the favourite feel that it was unfair to present such a proposal in so thin a House, as Sir John believed it would be. Nothing Eliot could say would change Buckingham's mind. In fact, it appeared to the emissary that the favourite wanted the plan carried out 'merely to be denied', that is, to have it defeated. His Grace's visitor finally left to return to the House of Commons. Eliot's last comment in the narrative of the episode was that 'no respect of persons' would make 'him desert his country'.

Sir John's impression of the Duke's motive and his final remark on his visit were written when he was lodged in the Tower in 1631 consumed by bitter memories of his former chief. Did he believe on the morning of July 8, 1625, that Buckingham wanted his plan defeated?[1] That is more than doubtful. He had no way of telling at the time that the motion would be defeated, that many of the courtiers, not advised of their leader's plan, would desert him in the House of Commons. On the contrary, it looked as though in the poorly attended House the 'court' had a comfortable majority for any measure it wished to pass. To be sure, Eliot knew already that May and a few others were not in favour of the project, but he could not have been certain how far they would go in their opposition.

In this first Parliament of King Charles the favourite's intention was not to be denied. He felt that in so thin a House the courtiers could easily carry the motion against the opposition and had not counted on the defection of most of his followers. Just what that motion was is uncertain. The *Negotium* says that it contained an alternative. The Commons were either to vote more money immediately or promise to do it in the next session. The only other source to record it says that Coke moved that the House agree to vote further supply when it reassembled.[2] It is not likely that Buckingham permitted his henchman to give the Commons a choice. That would have led to protracted debate and the probable death of the measure. Whatever the request, the whole affair was a stupid tactical blunder. Probably at that time, Sir John Eliot, unwilling to believe his chief guilty of such a crass political error, felt there must have been a deeper meaning behind it. But what that meaning was for Eliot in July, 1625, it is impossible to say. 'Merely to be denied' it could not have been.

In concluding this episode our historian's final phrase, 'that no re-

---

[1] I do not agree with the remarks in support of this argument in Gardiner, V, 389. Why should the Duke ask the Commons for more money in July 'merely to be denied', and then induce the King to summon Parliament in August to be denied again?

[2] *C.D.*, p. 59.

spect of persons made him desert his country', must not be forgotten. If it could only be discovered just when these words came to his mind, in 1625 or in 1631. They indicate that his ideal, the good of the country, had now been placed above his loyalty to the Lord Admiral of England. But they do not mean that he had forsaken his chief and had turned from fidelity to enmity. He may have realized for the first time that Buckingham was not working towards the same objective which motivated Sir John's public actions. But in July, 1625, he could not have known how completely at variance he was with the Duke. Only gradually during the next six months was the vice-admiral of Devon made conscious of the existence of a wide chasm between himself and his chief. But there was hardly more than a crack visible when the second session opened at Oxford.

At York House the favourite, slowly dressing for that day, probably realized that the vice-admiral of Devon was lost as one of his close adherents. A 'privado' he could never make of him; better to listen more closely to the strictures of Sir James Bagg and others who had seen for some time the weakness of the man as measured by their standards. But the Duke did not realize as yet how dangerous this Cornishman could become, what latent power there was in his words when inspired by idealism. True, he had had a taste of the force of Eliot's spoken word, yet he could not have believed in the summer of 1625 that his protégé would be so ungrateful as to turn his strength against his friend and benefactor. In any case, Buckingham must now have realized that Sir John Eliot would not let friendship and personal loyalty blot out completely his own ideas of right and wrong.

Bewildered, unhappy, and disturbed Eliot himself hurried to Westminster on that morning of July 8. Sir Humphrey May had been successful in holding back that proposition which was so distasteful to some of the few who knew about it. But the delay had been of no avail. Sir John Coke was now free to do his master's bidding. We have seen how he began by expressing his Majesty's acceptance of the two subsidies voted by the Commons.[1] Then he launched into a long exposition of the expenditure on the war, the alliances made, and the further financial needs for the naval and military projects of the government. The plan of the war was so broad and the sums of money required were so huge that the handful of members remaining must have been aghast. Consequently when Coke moved in closing that 'we should express

[1] See above, p. 80.

our own affection to the business now in hand, and that when we return again we are willing to relieve his Majesty in some farther proportion', there was not the slightest inclination to approve his motion. In
fact, it found a seconder with difficulty and caused so little spoken
comment that it can hardly be called a debate. In a House of barely
sixty members where the majority were courtiers, it should have passed
with ease. But, as Eliot says, 'the courtiers much disliking it, some as it
came not in particular by them, or that they were not preconsulted for
the work, others for the danger and prejudice it imported', the motion
'vanished through its own lightness and futility'.

On Saturday, July 9, it was decided by the Commons that adjournment should be on Monday, the 11th. When the two Houses met to
hear the royal assent to their bills and to present his Majesty with two
subsidies, the members were much dismayed to hear from the Lord
Keeper that they were to meet shortly again at Oxford. And the
'shortly' was explained to mean August 1, just three weeks away. They
had hoped it would be autumn at least, if not winter, before they would
gather again at Westminster. But an interval of only three weeks and
then a return to Oxford would give the plague time to spread to that
town where report said it had already made its appearance. Those three
weeks would permit Sir John Eliot only the briefest visit to his home in
Cornwall, hardly enough time to attend to private affairs, not to mention his vice-admiralty duties.[1]

In this first session of the Parliament of 1625 Eliot had not played the
role his growing prestige in the previous Parliament had foreshadowed.
His appointment to the committee of privileges in 1625 was a good beginning. But he received little further recognition. His speech on religion, however excellent it may have been as a speech, did him more
harm than good. A 'courtier', as he could only have been labelled at the
time, was attacking the government. That was not good politics. Party
lines were hardening in this Parliament as never before. But Eliot, the
individualist and poor politician, could not yet be completely identified
with either group. As a 'courtier' he saw that blind allegiance to the
government and the Duke of Buckingham was becoming the order of
the day. That was too much to expect of him. His loyalty to the Duke
and his inability to see him as he really was prevented Sir John from
siding with the 'country'. A man whose affiliations were so confused
could have little influence. Unless the surviving records have seriously

[1] C.J., I, 807–8; C.D., p. 67; Neg. Post., I, 119, 124.

neglected him, his speeches and remarks in the House were far less numerous than in the previous Parliament. No, Eliot had slipped in his climb towards parliamentary leadership. His censorious loyalty to Buckingham and the government made him unwanted in the inner ranks of either party.

In July of 1625 Sir John Eliot returned to Plymouth where his vice-admiralty engrossed his attention. He has left to posterity a terrible tale of the depredations of Turkish pirates on the south-west coast of England during the summer of 1625.[1] Sir John declared that he reported this sad state of affairs directly to the King who immediately ordered him to attend the Privy Council. In spite of the orders of the Lords of the Council on hearing Eliot's report that ships be sent to drive off the pirates, no action whatsoever was taken, Sir John asserted, by Sir John Coke and the commissioners of the navy on receiving the commands of the Council. This is the story, wrong in details but right in its main contention,[2] with which Sir John Eliot introduces his account of the Oxford session of King Charles's first Parliament.

No wonder Eliot was in not too pleasant a mood when he took his seat in the Divinity School on August 1. Commissioner Coke was his *bête noire* against whom he was liable to vent his wrath at any moment.

Shortly after business began Sir Edward Giles presented to the Commons a pardon for a Jesuit and other Catholic priests who had been imprisoned by the city of Exeter. The anger of the members was immediately aroused, for the pardon was dated July 12. That was a day after the Lord Keeper had given the King's brief but favourable answer to the petition for religion by which he promised to enforce the laws against papists. Protests against this breach of a promise, weak excuses from government supporters, and a prolonged silence were the procedure of the moment. That silence was broken by Sir John Eliot.[3]

He began by expressing the wish that necessity had not forced him to speak. But the consideration of religion, the honour of the King, and service to the House had induced him to break his silence. He did not believe that the King was responsible for this pardon. In fact, Eliot was

---

[1] C.J., I, 807-8; C.D., p. 67; Neg. Post., II, 3-7.

[2] I have been unable to find any official evidence that Eliot either wrote to the King or appeared before the Privy Council. That protests were made to the Council by somebody, that the Council ordered ships sent to drive off the pirates, and that Coke and his fellow commissioners failed to carry out the order can be seen from A.P.C. 1625-1626, pp. 59, 79-80, 139-40.

[3] C.J., I, 809; C.D., pp. 67, 68; Neg. Post., II, 9; E.P.N., f. 9.

sure that his Majesty was far too busy to have time to read every document he was asked to sign. With other weak excuses he exonerated the
King and put the blame on unknown ministers. They might be discovered by an examination of the warrant used by the Lord Keeper in
issuing the pardon. The King, he felt, would recall this document when
he knew the truth. He closed with the request for a careful examination of the case. When the truth was known his Majesty should be informed and presented 'with our petition for some help and redress in
this particular and for a general prevention of the like'.[1] Such a weak
speech was bound to have little, if any, effect. The basic point of blaming the royal minsters was much the same as in his speech on religion in
the first session. As was to be his wont for some years to come, Eliot
displayed here his implicit and childlike faith in his Sovereign. The subject of the Exeter pardon was temporarily shelved when Sir Robert
Phelips moved to refer it to a committee of the whole House meeting
that afternoon.[2]

During a violent attack made on the next day by the Commons on
Richard Montague, the Arminian divine, Eliot displayed a sense of
moderation which was to characterize his attitude towards men in
trouble on several occasions in the future. What aroused the anger of
the members was that the prelate, in the custody of the serjeant-at-
arms, sent word that he was too ill to appear before them. In the midst
of the debate Sir John reminded his colleagues that the serjeant must be
given time to present his prisoner to the House.[3] In the end that officer
was ordered to produce Mr Montague 'with all convenient speed'.
Such in part was the effect of Eliot's moderating words. They also were
responsible for his being added with others to the committee previously
appointed to investigate the writings of that troublesome cleric.[4]

A far more important subject was brought to the attention of the
Commons when they and the Lords assembled on August 4 in Christ
Church to listen to a brief plea by King Charles for a further grant of
supply to enable the fleet to depart. His Majesty was followed by Secretary Conway who told of the alliances with Protestant countries on the
continent and what funds were necessary to maintain them. But what
required their immediate attention, he informed the Lords and Com-

---

[1] *Neg. Post.*, II, 9–10. This speech is to be found in no other source, nor have I found
another copy of it, as Forster, *Eliot*, I, 332, claims to be at Port Eliot. The possibility that it
was never delivered is overshadowed by the likelihood that it appeared to be so ineffective
that nobody thought it worth recording.

[2] *C.J.*, I, 809.   [3] *Ibid.*; *C.D.*, p. 69; E.P.N., f. 10.   [4] *C.J.*, I, 810.

mons, was the fleet. All the money which had been appropriated for its equipment had been spent. To send it out to sea 'there wanted some thirty or forty thousand pounds', he said. Finally, Sir John Coke gave a still more detailed summary of the accomplishments and needs of the government. He too declared that the King's coffers were empty, that the fleet was almost ready to sail, and that financial assistance should be granted to complete what had been begun.[1]

According to Eliot's comment in his *Negotium*, made of course six years later, the Commons were not at all impressed by these pleas. They did not seem to trust the government's secret plans and advocated the dispersion of the fleet. Furthermore, they felt that the money requested was a ridiculously small amount.[2]

The great debate on supply did not take place in the House of Commons until the next day.[3] A stirring battle of words was witnessed by the silent Eliot. On the side of the 'country' the more radical leaders, Phelips, Seymour, and Sir Edward Coke, bore the brunt of the burden. They were ably opposed by May, Weston, and Heath for the 'court'. Of course the 'country' leaders expressed their strong opposition to any further grant of supply. Insinuating that incompetence in all departments of the government was to blame for an empty treasury, they hinted that one all-powerful minister was the chief culprit. In reply the 'courtiers' placed the blame on the bankruptcy of the government of James I and argued that the new King should not be made to suffer for the errors of his father. Two subsidies and two fifteenths, considerably more than forty thousand pounds, was finally proposed by May as sufficient for the moment. But no decision was reached in this debate.

Supply continued to be discussed on Saturday, August 6, when more moderate supporters of the government tried their arguments against the opposition. In general they favoured granting additional funds provided certain important conditions were met. Of these more intelligent followers of the Duke,[4] William Coryton,[5] Sir John Eliot, and Sir Nathaniel Rich were prominent in the debate on this day.

---

[1] *C.D.*, p. 73–7; *Neg. Post.*, II, 16–21.

[2] *Ibid.*, 22.   [3] *Ibid.*, 22–48; *C.D.*, pp. 77–89; *C.J.*, I, 810–1; *E.P.N.*, ff. 11–12.

[4] On Aug. 14, 1625, Lord Keeper Williams wrote the King a defence of his activities during the last Parliament. In this paper he says: 'Sir John Eliot . . . the Lord-Viscount Saye . . . Sir William Strode and Sir Nathaniel Rich . . . were never out of my Lord-Duke's chamber and bosom'. John Hacket, *Scrina Reserata* (London, 1693), II, 18. As Gardiner, V, 415, note 3, suggests, Williams had a tendency to exaggerate. Even so, there must have been considerable truth in the above.

[5] Though nothing definite is known of a connection between Coryton and Buckingham

After the ball had been set in motion by Sir Henry Mildmay, Master of the Jewel-house, Coryton, friend of Eliot and eventually to be as opposed to the government as any in the House, declared that he was willing to assist the King financially if it was really necessary. First he desired a committee appointed to investigate all his Majesty's affairs, such as his revenue, impositions, and particularly religion.[1]

Coryton was followed by Eliot. His speech is one of the most difficult to understand of all he ever delivered. At the same time it is one of the most important, for it is the first to indicate with some degree of clarity his relationship to the government and the Duke of Buckingham. The trouble is that the speech has not survived in Eliot's own words but in those of an unknown diarist.[2]

Sir John began by professing that he was speaking for the public good and that no private interest had any influence over him. Thus he implied that he was not speaking as a follower of Buckingham. That England was at war he admitted. This war, extending over most of western Europe, had brought nothing but shame and dishonour to English arms in the eyes of Eliot. The naval expedition under preparation, he hoped, would have better success. But there was really no reason for it to sail; therefore, the Commons need vote no more money. Men, equipment, and food for this expedition had been assembled since April and May. Why had it not sailed during the best season of the year? Sir John forgot that the Commons had recently been told by Conway that the fleet could not sail because it was not fully equipped due to lack of funds. And then Eliot declared that if there had been any mismanagement of the fleet 'I dare in my conscience clear and vindicate that noble Lord who hath some aspersions laid upon him'. By these words he meant that Buckingham was in no way responsible. But the commissioners of the navy were to blame, he declared.[3] Becoming a bit more constructive Sir John believed that if the King told the Commons why the fleet was being prepared, what its objective was, then they should vote the necessary funds. In closing he asserted that as his Majesty had given

at this time, his attitude during this Parliament points to some association with the Duke. At least Coryton was on the best of terms with Sir James Bagg during the winter of 1625–26. *C.S.P.D., Addenda, 1625–499*, pp. 112–3.

[1] E.P.N., f. 12v. *C.D.*, p. 137. *C.J.*, I, 811.

[2] *C.D.*, pp. 137–8. Calthorpe.

[3] All *C.D.*, p. 90, reports is: 'Sir John Eliot to take off all faults from my Lord-Admiral. That the matters of the navy were executed by commission.'

them the choice of sitting now or in the winter,[1] they should petition
him to be allowed to discuss this subject in a winter session.[2]

The speech shows that Sir John Eliot was not in sympathy with the
government. He gives the impression of turning the Duke of Buckingham into two people. Openly he defended the Lord Admiral. But
without realizing what he was saying, he attacked the favourite whom
he probably considered responsible for governing the country. It is
possible that had Eliot been accused at the time of attacking Buckingham in this fashion, he would have honestly denied it. Sir John was in
the process of learning how the government of his country was functioning. To blame the government was easy, particularly the commissioners of the navy. To blame the Duke was a severe wrench to his
loyalty. That was soon to come, but he was not ready for it in August,
1625. Of course, to blame the King was unthinkable. Why this speech
was omitted from the *Negotium* is obvious. To the author in 1631 it was
much too friendly to his bitter enemy, the late Duke of Buckingham.

As long as Eliot was sitting on the fence neither side would respect his
words. Both the motion, whatever it was, and the speech had no influence on the Commons except to arouse Sir John Coke to answer, with
little effect, the slur on the commissioners of the navy. Little further
progress had been made in the debate when Rich took the floor. He
named five conditions which should be fulfilled before supply was
granted. They sought information and advocated reform in religion,
finance, war, and government policy. Such demands were a bit too
much to make at this time from the point of view of the government
and could not have improved relations between Buckingham and Rich.
But before the end of the day Phelips rose to sponsor the five demands
made by Sir Nathaniel.[3]

Over Sunday, August 7, the abler and more conservative friends of
the favourite did their best to induce him to make concessions which
would produce harmony between the Commons and the government.
What part Sir John Eliot played in this attempt is impossible to say. But
he must have been present and participated in the discussion, for his
account has the ring of first-hand knowledge and fortunately is not
coloured too much by his later prejudices.[4] The Duke was told that his

---

[1] I have found no evidence that Charles ever made such an offer. Compare Mr Whistler's
remarks of Aug. 5, *C.D.*, p. 77, with those of the King, *L.J.*, III, 470–1.

[2] *C.J.*, I, 811, and E.P.N., f. 12v, say just the opposite. E.P.N. says: 'Sir J.E. to resolve
in the first place whether to petition the King for a recess or to sit, opinion to sit'.

[3] *C.D.*, pp. 90–91, 138–40, and *C.J.*, I, 811.   [4] *Neg. Post.*, II, 53–4.

errors, if he retracted them, were excusable. The disorders in the navy might be imputed to the officers. And his failure to seek advice would be pardoned by obtaining it now from the Council. The greatest difficulties, however, concerned religion and the fleet. In the first place fear had been aroused by the protection he had given Montague. This should be withdrawn and that cleric left to his punishment. A public declaration on this matter would help the situation. As to the fleet, it should be sent to sea with somebody else in command.[1] There should be no necessity to disclose its objective. That point would be forgotten when it returned victorious. In any event, if the Lord Admiral did not accompany it, he could shift the blame. Buckingham was told that Parliament would not change its attitude and no assistance could be expected from that source. Such advice 'wrought an inclination [in the Duke] for the instant that gave his friends some hope'. But, Eliot asserted, Buckingham's parasites gained his ear and undid much of the good work of his friends. Such false friends, he says, resorting to his prejudices, induced the favourite 'to shoot in person some new arrows'. Here Sir John is referring to the events of Monday, August 8, when the Duke of Buckingham addressed both Houses of Parliament.

Lord Keeper Williams opened proceedings before this assembly by informing it that the King's detailed answer to the petition for religion was ready.[2] His Majesty had asked the Lord Admiral to read the answer and also 'to deliver some other matters of great importance'. After a favourable answer to each article of the petition had been read, Buckingham launched into a justification of his policy. He told of the recent preparations for the war and gave a careful exposition of the needs of the fleet. Without openly stating it, he made it clear that the enemy was Spain and explained why the government had refused officially to declare war. But he did not tell his audience what the objective of the fleet was and kept them in the dark on several other points.[3]

From the unprejudiced point of view the speech itself was not bad. And yet in no way did it satisfy the 'country'. Eliot's profuse and thorough denunciation of both speech and speaker is of no value, as it is obviously tainted by his hatred of later months and years.[4] What troubled him more than anything else was the favourite's arrogance,

---

[1] Later in *Neg. Post.*, II, 107, Eliot ridiculed the Duke for staying at home when he says: 'the Duke was held too precious to be adventured in the voyage'. Sir John had forgotten that the Lord Admiral took the advice given him by Eliot and other friends on Aug. 7, 1625.

[2] *Ibid.*, II, 56. *C.D.*, p. 94.

[3] *Ibid.*, pp. 95–102. *Neg. Post.*, II, 61–71.   [4] *Ibid.*, 76–9.

which he found in his words, his manner, and the way the whole scene was enacted. What really may have disturbed Eliot was that the Duke's exposition of policy sounded as though the policy was his rather than the King's. There is nothing in the Lord Admiral's address, however, which could have turned Sir John at the time from a doubting friend into a bitter enemy. It may have opened the breach between them just a little more.

After listening to the Duke, the humour of the Commons was not improved by the gloomy picture the Lord Treasurer painted of the country's financial status. These two speeches cast their shadow over the Commons on Tuesday, the 9th, when most of the session was devoted to reports of the previous day. A brief debate on supply produced nothing more than a motion by Phelips, accepted by the House, to refer this subject to a committee of the whole House on the next morning.[1]

But before the Commons could be turned into a committee on that morning of August 10, Sir Richard Weston delivered a message from his Majesty in which Charles urged an immediate grant for the fleet and promised that they should meet again in the winter. If they refused to vote supply, the Chancellor of the Exchequer said that his Majesty would take better care of their safety, with the plague spreading in Oxford, than they could do themselves. In such an extremity the King would take care of his own affairs as best he could, Weston declared. After the presentation of such threats and promises from King Charles, Sir Robert Naunton, Master of the Court of Wards, marshalled many reasons why the Commons should do the King's bidding. Before the debate really began, however, a resolution was passed that, because of the royal message, supply should be discussed in the House rather than in committee, as had been resolved on the previous day.

Once again the two parties clashed and made the walls of the Divinity School resound with cries of give and not give. Phelips quoted precedents against giving. May warned against venerating them. Fiery Seymour affirmed that large sums of money had fallen into 'particular men's purses'. Weston argued that the King's credit was so low that he could not borrow even forty thousand pounds. Re-elected to the House, Wentworth, like the moderate courtiers, was in favour of giving when certain abuses had been remedied. Many others used their strongest arguments for or against supply. Again there were fingers pointing in the direction of the Duke of Buckingham, but as yet no-

---

[1] For this paragraph see *Neg. Post.*, II, 72–5; *C.D.*, pp. 102–5; *C.J.*, I, 813.

body dared to name him as being to blame for the evils complained of.[1]

Eliot, Rich, and Coryton sat silent during this long debate. They had had their say on August 6 and were not yet willing to break with the favourite. It was probably at this time that Sir John refused to deliver a speech written by his friend, the great antiquary and member of the House, Sir Robert Cotton. It was a long speech full of precedents. Each one concerned a royal favourite whose acts and advice had brought the country to the verge of ruin. There was no need to accuse the Duke of Buckingham. The precedents, like spears, pointed directly at his heart. Such an attack Eliot could not make now upon the Lord Admiral.[2] Six years later, overpowered by hatred for his former patron, he accepted the speech as his own. He incorporated it in his *Negotium*, indicated that he had delivered it, and even provided the proper setting for it in the debate.[3] But on August 10, if not earlier, the manuscript of this speech was probably circulated among many members of the House. They knew that Cotton had written it and that Eliot had refused the request of his friend to deliver it.[4]

Emboldened by hints coming from every corner of the House that the Duke was to blame for the troubles of the nation, some of the radi-

---

[1] *C.J.*, 813–14. *C.D.*, pp. 105–16.

[2] Gardiner in *C.D.*, p. xx, says that the speech was 'prepared by Eliot in conjunction with Cotton'. This is conjecture. Gardiner may be right, but my belief is that Cotton wrote the speech and that Eliot did not see it until it was finished. Cotton had turned against Buckingham by this time. The style of the speech is Cotton's rather than Eliot's.

[3] *Neg. Post.*, II, 85–91.

[4] This speech is to be found in *Neg. Post.*, I, Sup. 140–8, II, 85–91; John Howell, *Cottoni Posthuma* (London, 1679), pp. 273–82; *Parl. Hist.*, II, 14–17; Forster, *Eliot*, I, 412–14; P.E. MSS., 'Eliot, speeches, etc'., ff. 19–23v; P.E. MSS., 'Eliot and Bucks.', ff. 19–20v; Lands. MS. 491, ff. 138–40v; S.P.D., Chas. I, DXXIX, no. 71. See Gardiner, V, 425, note 1 or *C.D.*, pp. xx–xxiv for Gardiner's careful exposition why Eliot did not deliver this speech.

Gardiner fails to mention what to my mind is the most conclusive bit of negative evidence to prove that Eliot did not deliver the speech. Six men, Phelips, Seymour, Sir Edward Coke, Alford, Palmes, and Wentworth, were prevented from sitting in the next Parliament. Wentworth was excluded because Buckingham feared him. The other five could not sit because of speeches they had delivered, or because of opposition they had displayed, in this session. All six were appointed sheriffs. (Gardiner, VI, 33. *J.M.H.*, I, 367) Three of the six so singled out said little in comparison with the strong language attributed to Sir John Eliot on August 10. Had he spoken such words Charles and Buckingham would surely have prevented him from sitting in the second Parliament of the reign. But Sir Robert Cotton was excluded from that Parliament. See J. N. Ball, 'Sir John Eliot at the Oxford Parliament, 1625', *Bulletin of the Institute of Historical Research*, November, 1955, XXVIII, 113–27. This excellent article appeared after I had sent my manuscript to the publisher. It gives the detailed arguments, most of which I have had to omit through lack of space, as to why Eliot had virtually nothing to do with the Cotton speech. Dr Ball's conclusions are practically identical with mine.

cals spoke frankly on the next day. While discussing the menace of pirates Seymour, supported by Phelips, openly accused Buckingham of incompetence.[1] Later that morning in committee of the whole House for supply the much-needed funds came no nearer the pockets of the King than on the previous day. Uncertain what to believe Sir John Eliot could not speak. Love of his country and loyalty to the Lord Admiral were in direct conflict. In a few months Eliot would see clearly what he must do.

The plague was increasing in Oxford; the Commons, more hostile than ever to the favourite, remained adamant against supply; Charles finally gave up in disgust. On August 12 he dissolved Parliament.

[1] C.D., p. 118.

CHAPTER VI

Leading the Attack

September, 1625, to April 17, 1626

I. THE CADIZ EXPEDITION

BEFORE following the fortunes of Sir John Eliot through the second Parliament of the reign of King Charles, it is necessary to present a brief summary of the foreign and domestic affairs of the nation.

We have seen how the breach with Spain in 1624, so enthusiastically sponsored by Buckingham and Prince Charles, was heartily supported by the Commons. For the first time they had been given *carte blanche* by King James to discuss their country's foreign affairs; and they had enjoyed themselves thoroughly. The trouble was that the Duke and the Prince had a different view of the scope of the prospective war than the Commons had. For the former it meant a far-flung attack upon Spain and all her Catholic allies by a great Protestant, anti-Catholic league under the leadership of England. For the latter such a war was to be chiefly naval, directed against Spain and her American colonies, in which some assistance might be given to the revolting Dutch Netherlands. But that was all. Even the recovery of the Palatinate for the elector, a less publicized part of Buckingham's scheme, was hardly visible in the war the Commons proposed their country wage. They dreamt of the glories of Elizabethan seamanship, already highly exaggerated, which they felt could be easily emulated. Such a war, the Commons believed, could pay for itself by the capture of the Spanish treasure fleets. On this point too the favourite set much store. For him Spanish gold was to finance his grandiose schemes of alliances and campaigns. The trouble was that he went ahead with the latter before he had an opportunity of obtaining the former. And he dared to do all this with the knowledge that the government was virtually bankrupt from the extravagance of James I. But Buckingham realized that France, though Catholic, was vital as an ally against Spain, if he was to achieve his ambitions on the continent. Hence there was negotiated the Anglo-French marriage treaty with its political alliance, its secret clause of assistance to English Catholics, and its Catholic bride for Charles I. That alliance, however, was so flimsy that the crafty Richelieu was able to use England to further his own interests against Spain; and his interests did not coincide with those of Buckingham.

Although the Commons now were allowed to discuss foreign affairs the trouble was that they rarely were informed of what was taking place. They had no means of securing plentiful and accurate news of the King's plans and activities or of occurrences abroad. They were always at the mercy of the government which told them little and much of that inaccurate. Consequently, half truths, rumours, belated news, or complete ignorance confused a House of Commons where determined and intelligent men with ideas of their own did their best to settle problems about which at times they knew virtually nothing. Such chaos might have been avoided had the government provided real leadership. But that was lacking. During the first twelve months of the new reign the Commons gradually lost faith in the man at the helm. That man in the eyes of all was the Duke of Buckingham and not King Charles.

In 1624 only a few of the Commons were suspicious that the Duke had more in mind than a war against the inhabitants of the Iberian peninsula. By the beginning of the Parliament of 1625 that suspicion began to spread among many. But it could in no way be confirmed. The favourite did not dare to disclose to Parliament what far-flung operations he had set in motion. No wonder the Commons left to themselves became aroused over religion. No wonder they voted a miserable two subsidies as their first tribute of the reign. When at the end of the session Sir John Coke for the first time disclosed the stupendous plans of the Duke, it was much too late and the plans aroused only intense hostility. Throughout this session rumours of the miserable failure of the Mansfeld expedition were being wafted back to England with every cross-Channel breeze. During the second session vague reports were heard in the House about seven English ships which had been loaned to France by the Lord Admiral and which that country was about to use against the Protestants of Rochelle. That the House of Commons should refuse further supply and openly attack the favourite was no surprise. At the time the King was dissolving his first Parliament Buckingham's hopes that the ships loaned to France would not be used against

England's co-religionists began to soar. He had received word the French government was about to make peace with the Rochellese. But these hopes were quickly dashed when war was resumed. Despair filled his heart at the news that the Huguenot admiral, the Duke of Soubise, had been defeated on September 5 and forced to flee to an English port of refuge. Unquestionably the French had used the seven borrowed ships in this battle.[1]

In the meantime the fleet at Plymouth was being given its finishing touches. More unwilling sailors and soldiers were pressed into service. More rotten equipment and supplies were carried on the ships under the none too watchful eyes of the victuallers, Sir James Bagg and Sir Allen Apsley. But where did the government find the forty thousand pounds for which it had been clamouring during the abortive Oxford session? The Commons had been told that the ships would be unable to sail without these additional funds. They had not been told that a considerable part of the Queen's dowry of £120,000 was available for this purpose. From this fast diminishing reserve and from certain economies, the money necessary to send the fleet on its way was found.[2] Even so, privy seals were issued about the middle of September for a loan from the wealthy men of the country. They were informed this money was required to complete equipping the ships at Plymouth.[3] Money, and much of it, was needed for many purposes; but the fleet was well on its way to Spain before the King saw a shilling of this loan.

Shortly before these final stages of the expedition were reached, Charles negotiated a close defensive and offensive alliance with the Dutch States-General. The treaty was signed at Southampton on September 8. By its terms the Dutch agreed to send twenty ships to join the fleet at Plymouth as well as to keep the Flemish ports in a continuous state of blockade. But the schemes of Buckingham had gone farther afield. Christian of Denmark and the north German princes were being held in line against the Catholics. By the autumn of 1625 Charles had kept the Danish King in the war with the promise of a subsidy of thirty thousand pounds a month. That was a tidy sum indeed when figured on an annual basis. How the King and Buckingham were to raise it did not seem to trouble them at the moment. Finally, it was decided that the Duke was to go to The Hague for a conference with the representa-

---

[1] For the story of the ships loaned to France see Gardiner, V, 305–6, 378–96, and VI, 2.
[2] Dietz, *English Public Finance*, pp. 223, 227.   [3] *Ibid.*, pp. 227–28.

tives of Protestantism in northern Germany and Denmark. He was to take with him the crown jewels and plate and pawn them for as much as the credit of England's King would bring. With these funds Buckingham hoped to bind securely the alliances so vital to his great schemes. Obviously he could not be with the fleet and at The Hague at the same time. Consequently, he secured the appointment of Sir Edward Cecil to command the expedition to Spain. Cecil was a good soldier but had had no experience at sea, while many of the officers under him had only the backing of the favourite to recommend them.[1]

During the early weeks of September pirates and Flemish privateers, in spite of the Dutch blockade, were harassing the south-west coast of England. On two occasions a squadron of the royal navy was employed to put an end to this menace, but each time nothing of value was accomplished. The second of these excursions under the command of Sir Samuel Argall returned with a number of Dutch and French prizes captured because they were said to be trading with the Spanish Netherlands. Among the ships brought in by Argall was the *St. Peter* of Havre de Grace. In the coming Parliament a storm was to rage around this vessel. In fomenting that storm Sir John Eliot was to take a leading part.

In the midst of the bustling activity at Plymouth the vice-admiral of Devon must have been a busy man. No doubt he witnessed on September 15 the visit of the King accompanied by the Duke of Buckingham,[2] for while the Lord Admiral and Eliot were no longer intimate, they were still friends. It is not recorded that any particular favour was shown the vice-admiral of Devon during this visit. There is no doubt, however, that he was co-operating loyally with his chief and his sovereign. On the other hand, it is difficult to picture Sir John Eliot hobnobbing with the officious vice-admiral of south Cornwall. Sir James Bagg, knighted on September 19 at Salcombe near Plymouth,[3] was truly basking in the sun of ducal and royal approval. As victualler of the fleet he must have been conspicuous in and about its rendezvous during the latter weeks of that month. The feelings of Eliot for his rival can easily be imagined; and they were not eased when he heard the news of the appointment early in September of Sir John Coke as Secretary of State on the death of Sir Albertus Morton. The vice-admiral's enemies were being advanced while he remained stationary. But he still

---

[1] Gardiner, VI, 6–10. [2] *Ibid.*, VI, 12. [3] Shaw, *The Knights of England*, II, 189.

had some standing at court and could boast of the friendship of the other Secretary of State, Lord Conway.[1]

Not until October 3 did part of the fleet set sail for Falmouth with final instructions that the ultimate destination of the whole was to be the Spanish coast around Cadiz. The remaining squadrons awaited the arrival of the Dutch, who made their appearance on the next day. On the 5th the combined squadrons departed but were driven back in confusion by a storm on the following morning and found that the open harbour of Plymouth offered them little protection. Sir John was in the midst of all this excitement. He was particularly interested in this expedition because he had had as his guest and under his charge Lord Conway's son, who sailed for Spain in the first division of the fleet. Writing to the Secretary on October 6 Eliot gave him news of the departure of the fleet bearing his son and an account of the misfortune which befell the second flotilla.[2] The damage to the ships, though considerable, was not enough to prevent their final departure for Spain on October 8. Standing on the Hoe Sir John Eliot wished them God-speed. But having some knowledge of the corruption which had played havoc with the equipment of those ships, and troubled by omens, personal and national, which boded no good, he must have been apprehensive of the fate in store for this proud venture. How it failed miserably before Cadiz is a well-known story,[3] but Englishmen at home were completely in the dark for two months to come.

In the meantime the Duke of Buckingham was preparing for his visit to the Low Countries. He crossed the Channel early in November and was at The Hague on the 9th. In the absence of representatives from Sweden and the north German princes Buckingham had to be content with negotiating a treaty between Denmark, the States-General and England by which King Christian was again assured that he would receive the £30,000 a month from Charles I. At the same time the pawning of the crown jewels was not as easy and lucrative as the Duke had expected. The £58,000 which these trinkets eventually yielded was far below the £300,000 which Charles and his favourite had hoped they would produce.[4] Of course such a small sum reached England much too late to be of any assistance in defraying the monthly subsidy

---

[1] Sir Edward Conway had been raised to the peerage, March 23, 1625, with the title of viscount. Gardiner, V, 310.

[2] S.P.D., Chas. I, VII, no. 31.

[3] Gardiner, VI, 15–21.

[4] Dietz, *op. cit.*, p. 234.

to be paid the Danish King. Actually Christian IV was held in line for a time by a personal loan of £70,000 to the English government in October, 1625, from Philip Burlamachi, the great merchant and government financier.[1] Buckingham, having concluded his negotiations on November 29, intended to return to England by way of Paris where he hoped to obtain the signature of Louis XIII to the Treaty of The Hague. But the French King had no use for this flirtatious dandy and prohibited him from setting foot on the soil of France.[2] Consequently Charles's favourite had to return as he had come. He arrived in England early in December just as the first ships came staggering home from Spain.

Shortly before these negotiations were completed in Holland the Cornish coast was confronted with an unusual spectacle. Two hostile fleets of a foreign country were about to attack each other in an English harbour. It is impossible to say whether Sir James Bagg was troubling himself about his vice-admiralty of south Cornwall. But a letter from the vice-admiral of Devon to Secretary Conway gives the impression that he was not on the job. Eliot told the Secretary that the Duke of Soubise and his ships were at Fowey where a royalist squadron, anchored at Falmouth, intended 'shortly to visit them'. He protested that the harbour of Fowey was so weak and indefensible that a fight between the two forces would result in much damage to the town. The situation was so serious that the inhabitants of Fowey begged that his Majesty be informed and that something be done about it.[3] Eliot not Bagg did the informing. But fortunately for Fowey, Soubise was not attacked and remained for a time in that port with his own ships and a prize, the *St. John*, a fine French man-of-war he had captured the previous year.[4] It is impossible to tell whether the letter of the vice-admiral of Devon played a part in preventing bloodshed.

Hardly had this flurry subsided when two ships of the Cadiz fleet returned to Plymouth bearing abundant evidence and much news of the disaster that had been suffered in Spain. Informed of their arrival by Lord Conway, the Council appointed commissioners, among whom was Sir John Eliot, to receive and provide for the remnants of the fleet as they limped back into this south-western port with their sickening

---

[1] Dietz, *op. cit.*, p. 228. For an account of Burlamachi see *Economica* (1926), VI, 285–300, 'Philip Burlamachi: A Financier of the Thirty Years War' by A. J. Judges.

[2] He had made love to Anne of Austria, Queen of France, when he was in that country to escort Henrietta Maria to England. Gardiner, V, 332, VI, 25–26.

[3] S.P.D. Chas. I, X, no. 35.

[4] Gardiner, VI, 28.

cargoes.[1] Frequent and lengthy instructions were issued to the commissioners. But, as the bleak December days disclosed to the inhabitants of Plymouth nothing but misery, disease, and starvation, it was money and supplies rather than instructions which the commissioners desperately needed. A vivid picture of this scene has been left by Eliot in a letter to Lord Conway written on December 22. At least the Secretary could take pleasure in the news of the safe return of his son. 'The miseries before us are great', he wrote. The worst complaints were against the rotten food or its total absence. Captain Bolles, 'a landman', who had died since his arrival in port, declared that he had become ill because of insufficient food 'and corruption of the provisions'. Every day a large number of bodies were being thrown from the ships into the harbour of Plymouth. 'Yesterday fell down here seven in the streets', presumably dead. Most of the rest of the soldiers were so weak that unless they were immediately supplied with clothing there was little hope of their recovery in the country districts where they were lodged.[2] Such was the sad tale Sir John Eliot wrote to Conway. Other complaints of the desperate conditions prevailing in south-western England were sent by the commissioners to the Council. In addition the inhabitants on whom the soldiers had been billeted were complaining of insufficient pay for their services.

Viewing such ghastly sights Eliot must have been deeply moved, moved to blame and condemn. The totally inadequate supplies, the rotten food, the badly equipped ships, and the absence of almost everything that is vital in the success of any naval expedition Sir John could have blamed in general on the government and in particular on the Lord Admiral and his underlings, such as Bagg, Apsley, and Sir John Coke. It is apparent that at the time he did not have sufficient evidence to lay this disaster at the door of the Duke of Buckingham. But his suspicions must have been so strong that he was induced to keep an overcareful eye on all the activities of the government with the hope of catching the right fish in the net he was spreading.

An undated paper of instructions to his agent in London,[3] which, from internal evidence, must have been composed late in December, 1625, seeks far too much detailed information to be a mere matter of

---

[1] *A.P.C. 1625–1626*, pp. 266–67, dated Dec. 12, 1625.
[2] S.P.D., Chas. I, XII, no. 38.
[3] I have been unable to find a single fact which might identify his agent.

routine for a vice-admiral of the coast.[1] Eliot requested his agent to remain in London but particularly at court. He was to ask news 'from all
parts'. While in London he was to frequent the Royal Exchange as well
as the establishments of Burlamachi and Philip Jacobson,[2] 'from whom
news may be had out of all parts'. The agent was to attend the Council
chamber where he was to take note 'of all special and public acts, com-
mitments, questions, letters of direction'. Daily he was to note carefully
all that happened. And if extraordinary acts or preparations took place,
he was to acquaint him of them as quickly as possible. At court he was
to glean all the news he could of events which had taken place at home,
and particularly abroad. He was to notify Sir John of all changes, plans,
preparations of ships, impressments of men, arrivals and duties of ambassadors, 'Parliaments, privy seals, favours or disfavours, and what
opinion or reports are entertained upon the return of the fleet'. He continued with minute instructions as to how the agent should send his
news to ensure speed and secrecy. For the purpose of speed and safety
of conveyance he was to make use of Conway and others prominent
at court and in London. Obviously these inquiries were not directed
against anyone in particular and do not necessarily imply that Sir John
was seeking to discover malevolence and corruption in the government
and its officers. But they do show that he was extremely interested in all
the activities of those in authority. Undoubtedly he might obtain much
of value from news sent by his agent, were his aim the indictment of
the government or any member of it.

   This is the time, after the Cadiz disaster, that Sir John Eliot turned
against the Duke of Buckingham. As the full extent of that catastrophe
unrolled itself before his eyes at Plymouth, Eliot's fervid, idealistic
nature made it impossible for him to disregard and forget what he had
seen. He knew that a perfunctory protest would do no good and would
only hurt him. He realized that he must do all in his power to prevent
the recurrence of such a crime against the nation. The only way to accomplish this was to secure the removal from office of those who were
responsible. But that, he knew, would be a difficult task, even with
much direct evidence of mismanagement and corruption. Against the
government as a whole it would be comparatively easy to direct such

---

[1] S.P.D. Chas. I, XVIII, no. 70. This is an undated paper in spite of the editor of the
C.S.P.D. and Forster, Eliot, I, 469, to the contrary.
[2] He was the King's jeweller, merchant stranger, and financier. C.S.P.D., 1623–1625,
pp. 153, 266, 280, 403; 1625–1626, pp. 422, 569.

an attack but with little hope of concrete results. Against an individual of the importance of the Duke of Buckingham it would be much harder. The charges would have to be explicit and incriminating, if there was to be any chance of securing his dismissal and punishment. Whether against one or the other, or against both, such an assault could be conducted only in Parliament. On December 16, when Eliot may already have been laying his plans, the Lord Keeper ordered writs issued for elections of members of Parliament. Now it was necessary to secure as much evidence as possible with absolute secrecy maintained at all costs. The Duke of Buckingham, Lord Conway, and others must have no suspicion of what was in the mind of Sir John Eliot.

With these two leaders of the government he remained on good, though not intimate, terms during the weeks before Parliament met in February. In a letter written to the Secretary on the last day of the year Eliot gave ample evidence of the friendship which continued to exist between them.[1] He solicited a favour; and favours can be solicited only from friends. Sir John desired Conway to secure the recall of the privy seal, requesting the loan of forty pounds, which had been sent to Richard Gedy, his father-in-law. In the previous year Gedy had been sheriff of Cornwall and as a result had run heavily into debt, Eliot declared. While he had been out of the county on business of the Lord Admiral, he believed the deputy-lieutenants had reported Gedy's name in place of another because they bore him a grudge. This point rankled Sir John and his father-in-law more than the amount he had been asked to lend. But the writer then did just what he had been complaining about. He said that in an accompanying note he was giving the name of another to whom Gedy's privy seal could be sent. He was a rich man and a 'usurer (which I believe made him a passage out of the first certificate) and one that has neither borne public endeavour or charge'.[2] In closing his letter Eliot gave Conway news of his son who was spending the holidays at Port Eliot.

The result of this plea to the Secretary was an order from the Privy Council, dated six days later, to reduce Gedy's privy seal to thirty pounds.[3] Eliot's request, though considered, was not fulfilled. His relations with the court could not have been of the best. Buckingham, if he

---

[1] S.P.D., Chas. I, XII, no. 95.

[2] It may have been Lord Robartes of whom Eliot borrowed money and for whom he had no love in 1631. P.E. MSS., 'Letter Book', Sept. 5, 1631.

[3] *A.P.C. 1625–1626*, p. 305. It says that the original privy seal was for fifty pounds, not forty, as Eliot claimed in his letter.

had a hand in this, may have said that the vice-admiral was not one of his intimates; therefore little should be done to satisfy him. But Conway, who was Eliot's particular friend, may have induced the Council to reduce the amount requested of Gedy. There is no doubt that outward harmony existed between Sir John Eliot and the leaders of the government at the beginning of 1626.

A few weeks after this incident had taken place Eliot gave an example of that impulsive nature which frequently got the best of him in the House of Commons. He wrote to his agent in London that as a result of the death of Sir Richard Edgcombe the position of colonel in the militia and that of deputy lieutenant of Cornwall were vacant. He asked his agent to do all in his power to obtain these posts for him from the Earl of Pembroke, Lord Chamberlain and Lord Lieutenant of that county.[1] Hardly had he despatched the letter when he learned that Edgcombe had not died. Filled with chagrin he wrote his agent the next morning a second letter to inform him of his error.[2] In this note Eliot said that his first had been despatched to him 'by a packet . . . to my Lord Duke'. Were only a few of the letters of this period to the Lord Admiral preserved, we might glean from them a slight change in attitude of the subordinate towards his superior. But undoubtedly the vice-admiral of Devon was scrupulously correct in these communications. He must at all costs prevent Buckingham from having any suspicion of his complete change and future plans.

While Sir John was settling his vice-admiralty business and the electoral campaigns for the new Parliament were being conducted throughout the country, England and France were drifting into war. This trend was set in motion by various forces, one of which was the friction between Charles I and his wife, particularly over her Catholic attendants. At the same time the capture of French merchant ships by English men-of-war on the basis that they were carrying Spanish goods was not conducive to keeping the peace. It could be preserved only if a speedy settlement were reached by the Court of Admiralty declaring that few of the goods so seized were contraband. But the English government, hard pressed for money and uncertain what policy to follow, in the end usually sold all the cargoes that had been seized. Naturally

---

[1] S.P.D., Chas. I, XVIII, no. 68. See below, p. 111, note 2, for an interesting letter Bagg wrote to Buckingham early in March, 1626, in which he gives a slightly different slant to this episode.

[2] *Ibid.*, no. 69.

the French would not tolerate such actions and retaliated by confiscating English goods and ships in the ports of France. Such practices by themselves were enough to lead to war. Furthermore, Charles, through his ambassadors, the Earl of Holland and Sir Dudley Carleton, was interfering with great arrogance in the internal affairs of France. He was trying to dictate terms of peace between the French government and the Huguenots of Rochelle. Such intervention merely served to increase the antipathy of the French government for the English and failed to give the Rochellese any assistance. At the same time Holland and Carleton attempted to secure the return of the English ship loaned to France. But they were told that the *Vanguard*, the only ship of the royal navy in the squadron, would be returned to King Charles when Soubise had restored the *St. John*[1] to the French King. As to the others, six merchantmen, the government of Louis XIII made it clear that they would be retained until the eighteen months, the duration of their lease, had expired. Thus neither Charles alone, Charles and Buckingham, nor the English ambassadors could make any progress with the clever Richelieu guiding the hand of Louis. When the second Parliament of the reign opened on February 6, 1626, the two countries were on the verge of war. The recall of the French ambassador, Blainville, had been requested; and on the 7th of that month he was prohibited from appearing at court.[2]

2. THE MEETING OF PARLIAMENT

In this Parliament, which Charles and Buckingham expected to find more tractable because the leaders of the opposition in the last session had been safely sequestered as sheriffs,[3] Sir John Eliot sat for his home constituency of St. Germans. He had been returned on January 16 with Sir Henry Marten as his colleague. It is impossible to say whether they sat for this constituency through court influence or through the growing political power of Eliot, who prevented Sir John Coke, the nominee of the Bishop of Exeter, from obtaining a seat here.[4] But it does not matter much, for there was no reason why in January, 1626, the King or Buckingham should oppose the vice-admiral of Devon's standing

[1] See above, p. 99.
[2] Gardiner, VI, 38–57.
[3] See above, p. 92, note 7.
[4] *H.M.C. 12 Rept.*, App. Pt. I, 251.

for any constituency under their control. As far as they knew he was still their supporter.

The speech of Charles which inaugurated the session and that of the new Lord Keeper, Sir Thomas Coventry,[1] gave the members of the two Houses so little information and made so few requests that the appearance of a lull before a storm was created. A storm did break, but from a most unexpected quarter. On February 10, five days after the opening of Parliament, Sir John Eliot disclosed his true colours in the sharpest denunciation of the government that had ever been heard in the House of Commons.[2] Of course, he in no way attacked the King in this speech but placed the blame within the government, now on a group and then on an unnamed individual. He worded his attack so cleverly that any officer who wished could take cover behind the back of one or more of his colleagues.

With his opening thrust Eliot reminded the Commons that the accomplishments of recent Parliaments had been far from good. In part he blamed the Commons themselves for such poor results. Still talking in generalities he focused the attention of the members on the affairs of the King and kingdom during the past year. Losses had been sustained, he declared, losses at home and abroad, losses to the revenues of the King, losses to the reputation of the country. Becoming more specific he suggested that the King's revenues had been reduced to such an extent that it had been necessary for him to 'resort to his subjects for supplies'. And then he turned to the medieval idea of government, not quite dead in his day, that the King should live of his own and that his subjects should not be taxed except under unusual circumstances such as war.

With his next suggestion Sir John became even more concrete and opened wide his attack. He requested an accounting of the subsidies voted in the last Parliament of King James. To some slight extent that had been done during the last two sessions, he admitted. But not enough had been learned as to how the money had been spent. He denounced the government for not fulfilling its promise and insisted that the military and naval actions made possible by these subsidies should be explained to Parliament.

Playing on the patriotism and loyalty of his audience Eliot, with a

[1] Rushworth, I, 202–3.
[2] *Neg. Post.*, I, Supp., pp. 148–56; P.E. MSS., 'Eliot speeches, etc.', ff. 24–27v; Whitelocke; Rich; *C.J.*, I, 817.

tremendous burst of eloquence, lamented the failures, the losses, 'the wrecked and ruined honour of our nation', 'the incomparable hopes of our most excellent Sovereign checked in their first design'. He asked the Commons to discover who was to blame, 'to discern the fault'. But he gave them no assistance. At most he offered them a clue when he declared:

'Our honour is ruined, our ships are sunk, our men perished, not by the sword, not by an enemy, not by chance, but apparently discerned beforehand out of strong predictions, by those we trust, by that pretended care and thrift that ushers all our misfortunes.'

It was the 'miseries' and 'calamities' that had taken place in western England, Sir John asserted, which had opened his eyes and aroused his fears. Without naming the expedition to Cadiz, he showed that it was a proper subject for the consideration of the House. It fell under the expenditure of funds voted in 1624; and it also was covered by the resolution of that Parliament calling for 'the setting forth of the navy'. The Commons, he felt, always had a right to discuss and to have explained to them any action which was taken as a result of their deliberations. Such has been the modern trend of parliamentary thought, but in the early seventeenth century it was revolutionary.

Eliot concluded his speech with the motion that the recent naval expedition and the 'King's estate' should be carefully investigated by various committees. With these subjects having precedence over all others, definite action should be taken on them by the House of Commons.

In this forceful speech, which proclaimed Sir John Eliot an orator of first rank, he defined a conception of the state which was finding favour with an increasing number of men during the early seventeenth century. This state was ruled by a faultless sovereign surrounded by his good and bad advisers. Whenever Parliament met it was the duty and privilege of the members to denounce and attack those counsellors and their policies which they believed were harmful to King and kingdom. The King was never to blame for such policies, it was always his ministers. This critical attitude of the Commons towards the government, particularly when it concerned itself with foreign affairs, was a novelty in 1625 and 1626. Never had Elizabeth heard such criticism; and James had put a stop to it until in his last Parliament he had invited opinion on the relations between England and Spain. And now in his first two

Parliaments Charles I was harvesting bitter fruit from the seeds sown by his father in 1624. The trouble was that the strictures grew worse from week to week and session to session as failure dogged the steps of King and favourite. In these attacks, moreover, the Commons rarely presented positive, concrete proposals. The members were too uninformed, too ignorant of conditions existing at home and abroad to be able to give sound advice. In fact, their ignorance permeated their negative criticism to such an extent that it served only to arouse the wrath of the King and Buckingham. Doubtless the failure of English projects was due in the main to incompetence and corruption. But past conditions over which the existing government had no control, luck, and the lack of support at home also played their part in the disasters abroad which encompassed England during the first years of the reign. One failure led to another, and they became so entangled that it was impossible for the most enlightened contemporary to place the blame where it was due. No wonder Sir John Eliot in his speech of February 10 could indicate only a faint trail to be followed in attacking the government.

That Eliot had the Duke of Buckingham in mind when he wrote this speech is indicated by the heading he gave it,[1] and that was what those who heard him understood. But his assault was so general and could be interpreted as directed at so many different people that the Lord Admiral gave no sign that he had felt Sir John's arrows. Why did he deliver this speech so early in the session? Because his ardour got the best of him. He had obviously written the speech before the opening of Parliament, certainly before the day it was delivered. To postpone that delivery until the right time had come was impossible for a man of such undisciplined nature and deficiency in political insight.[2] In the opinion of Christopher Wandesford, and probably most of the House, Sir John should have delayed for some time the introduction of such a vital subject.[3] There were still too many vacancies in the membership of the House of Commons, after only four days of preliminary business, for a debate on so important an issue or even for the appointment of a com-

[1] 'Sr. J. E. upon the first quest. of the D. parl. 2 Car.'
[2] The Rev Joseph Mead wrote to Sir Martin Stuteville on Feb. 18: 'I hear of a speech [in Parliament] also made that week [first week of the session] somewhat eagerly aiming at, but not naming, the Duke of Buckingham; but it was not applauded, nor seemingly liked by the House; some thought because unseasonable.' *C. and T. Char. I*, I, 82. See also another letter of same to same, Feb. 25. *Ibid.*
[3] Rich.

mittee to investigate it. This subject should have been introduced in the committee of the whole for grievances. But a motion for the establishment of that committee with its bi-weekly meetings was only passed a short time after Eliot had delivered his philippic.[1] And when it met five days later none of Sir John's proposals was considered. The attacks of pirates on English shipping were discussed without the participation of the vice-admiral of Devon, who had an intense interest in this subject.

On February 17th the committee for grievances debated the seizure of English goods and ships in France; and on the following day Mr Whitby reported its meagre conclusions to the House.[2] As a result of this report a select committee of ten, of which Eliot was both a member and its reporter, was named to investigate the whole business.

3. THE CASE OF THE 'ST. PETER'[3]

That business quickly centred itself on one ship, the *St. Peter* of Havre de Grace. The contention of Sir John Eliot and his committee was that the arrest of this French ship was the reason for the seizure of English ships and goods in France.

Let us briefly survey the facts concerning the *St. Peter*. She was captured in the Channel in September, 1625, by Capt Argall and brought into Plymouth because her cargo was under suspicion of being Spanish. After she had been sent to London in November English merchants petitioned for her release in order to secure the return of their ships and goods held in France. As a result King Charles in December ordered the discharge of the *St. Peter* and her cargo as well as the restoration of all the property belonging to her crew. In January the case of the French ship was tried in the Court of Admiralty. Sir Henry Marten, its judge, ordered her release as no proof had been presented that her cargo or any of the property of her crew were Spanish. Detained by adverse winds at Gravesend this ship was seized a second time at the order of the Lord Admiral on February 4. Buckingham issued this order because Sir Allen Apsley, Lieutenant of the Tower, and Sir John Hippesly, Lieutenant of

---

[1] *C.J.*, I, 817.   [2] *Ibid.*, I, 820.

[3] This is based essentially on Rich, Whitelocke, and P.E. MSS., 'Eliot and Bucks', ff. 3–4v. The last-named are detailed notes in Eliot's hand which were used in making his reports to the House of Commons. He made them on Feb. 22, March 1 and 11. See also J.M.H., IV, 367–69, and Gardiner VI, 43, 45, 46, 65, 66.

Dover Castle and member of the House of Commons, had asserted that the cargo of the *St. Peter* must be Spanish because at the time of her sailing from Spain there existed in that country an embargo on all French goods.

To Sir John Eliot and his committee the second arrest of this ship was vital. That had been the cause of all the trouble. That was the reason why the French were retaliating, why more and more English ships and their cargoes were being seized. In the debate in the House Sir John ignored the denial of this assumption by his friend, Sir Henry Marten, and disputed the same denial by his enemy, Sir John Coke. He refused to recognize the truth when Sir Robert Heath, speaking for the Duke,[1] told the Commons that French seizures were due to the sale in England of many French prize goods far below their actual value. On top of it all Eliot refused to blame the Lord Admiral for the second arrest of the *St. Peter*. First he placed the blame on Apsley and Hippesly. And eventually he declared that the second arrest of the ship should be proclaimed a grievance against the government. These are the points that emerge from the reports, debates, and examinations in the House of Commons between February 22 and March 11. In the midst of it all was Sir John Eliot, reporting, denouncing, and directing his plan of attack.

What plan, what attack did Sir John have in mind? Of course it was against the Duke of Buckingham. But why did he refuse to blame him for the second arrest of the *St. Peter* when he had such a perfect opportunity? Because a major part of Eliot's plan was to develop opinion in the House against the favourite. He and the leaders of the 'country' party knew that the 'court' had a majority in the House at the beginning of this Parliament. Some of the lukewarm supporters of the government and as many as possible of the neutral back-benchers would have to be won over to the 'country'. This meant that opinion in the House would have to be turned against Buckingham by craft and cleverness. By openly denouncing him too soon, by blaming him for the second arrest of the *St. Peter* as early as February 22, Eliot would have brought the support of the majority of the Commons to the favourite. The feeling against Buckingham must be developed by re-

---

[1] On March 4 the Commons desired the Duke of Buckingham to inform the House why he had ordered the arrest of the French ship. Eliot seems in no way to have been responsible for bringing the Lord Admiral into this investigation. On March 6, Heath, the Attorney General, gave the Duke's reasons for the arrest. He said that the Lord Admiral had ordered the stay of the ship at the 'express direction' of the King which was based on the information given by Apsley and Hippesly.

lentless denunciation of government policies, by bitter attacks on lesser officials, and by stealthy suggestions that one man was really to blame for all of England's troubles. The *St. Peter* incident, if properly handled, Sir John Eliot believed, would most certainly contribute to the downfall of the Duke of Buckingham. The French ship had been arrested a second time on the advice of Apsley and Hippesly. This arrest was solely to blame for the extensive retaliations in France. Therefore it was a grievance against the government which would eventually be turned against the Duke. So argued Sir John; and nothing could change his opinion. He could not accept any other reasons for the seizure of English ships and goods in France without destroying the plan of his attack.

Already on March 1 Eliot moved that the second arrest of the *St. Peter* be declared a grievance against the government. The House ignored his motion. Ten days later he introduced the same motion. By that time the thoughts of most members were centred on the favourite whenever government policies were being attacked. That attack, as we shall see, was becoming broader, stronger, and more bitter with every day. It was indeed difficult not to name the Duke. But on this day after a long debate on Eliot's motion a division was taken, and the House failed by six votes to support Sir John. The opposition leaders still had work to do. Opinion still needed pounding and moulding.

With his accustomed perseverance the member for St. Germans introduced his motion on the *St. Peter* five days later. English merchants were petitioning Parliament for relief from their troubles in France. That gave the vice-admiral of Devon the opportunity to try again to induce the House to declare the arrest of the French ship a grievance. But when several members, including Sir Dudley Digges and Christopher Wandesford, thought that the subject had better be dropped, Eliot was thwarted a third time. His estimate of opinion in the House was again mistaken. Feeling in the nation, particularly among the merchants, as well as in the House of Commons, was becoming anti-French. To censure the government on the arrest of the *St. Peter* would appear pro-French. In such an atmosphere Digges and Wandesford, gifted with far more political insight than Eliot ever had, were trying to shove this incident into the background for the time being. Working with Sir John towards the same goal but with their ears closer to the ground, they realized by this time the inherent weakness of the *St. Peter* case as a means to arouse feeling against the government and the Duke of Buckingham.

At the time they were right; but ultimately Eliot had his way. The case was dropped and no action was taken until May 1 when, as will be seen, the Duke of Buckingham had been charged and condemned on many counts in the House of Commons. The tide of opinion had turned strongly against him. By a majority of thirty-eight the House approved Sir John's motion which declared the Duke responsible for the arrest of the *St. Peter* of Havre de Grace. Undoubtedly Eliot's earlier handling of this case had helped to turn some members against the King's favourite. But by May 1 it could be taken for granted that the House would pass Sir John's motion.

4. ATTACK ON THE GOVERNMENT: EVILS AND CAUSES[1]

Shortly after the *St. Peter* case was initiated the Commons began a general attack on the government. As the dispute over the fate of the French ship gradually pointed in the direction of one man, so the general attack, once it had gotten under way, rapidly focused itself on that same man.

Sir John Eliot and the leaders of the 'country' at first had no plan. His premature attack of February 10 was wholly unexpected by both sides of the House. There seem to have been no consultations, no preparations during the next two weeks. That is understandable when it is realized that Sir John was considered to be a 'courtier'.[2] Besides the leadership of the 'country' party had been disrupted by the exclusion from this Parliament of such men as Phelips, Seymour, and Sir Edward

---

[1] Unless otherwise indicated this section is based on Whitelocke, Rich, and E.P.N. 1626. For the Parliament of 1626 there are two sets of notes in Eliot's hand among the P.E. MSS. The first set, to be designated as E.P.N. 1626 (1), deals to a considerable extent with proceedings in committee of the whole. The second set, to be designated E.P.N. 1626 (2), is essentially the same as *C.J.*

[2] Nearly a month later his worst enemy was not certain of his disloyalty to the Duke. In *Notes and Queries*, 4th Ser., X, 325–26, S. R. Gardiner has edited an interesting letter from Bagg to Buckingham which is undated but which Gardiner, from internal evidence, puts early in March, 'not long after March 3, 1626'. I have examined this letter in S.P.D., Chas. I, DXXIII, no. 77, and find it mutilated in the part of greatest interest to us. That part of the letter which refers to Eliot with Gardiner's bracketed additions and its spelling modernized is as follows:

'For Sir John Eliot, your officer, I wonder not at his ways when I consider he ca[n nei-] ther pay you your dues or deserve your past favours; and . . . I think him easily be gotten. Another Lord, [whose] I perceive he is, viz., the Earl of Pembroke's, who, [as Eliot] himself reported to Sir Edward Seymour si[nce Christ]mas last, upon knowledge of Sir Richard Edgcom[be an]d a deputy lieutenant of Cornwall his sickness, w[rote a le]tter

Coke. Men who might fill their shoes did not appear immediately. The 'country' must be sure of Eliot; and Digges and Wandesford as well as Rich, Sandys, Pym, and others must step to the fore.

Consequently when the attack really got under way on February 24 it was a confused and disorderly affair at first. But from the very beginning it was obvious that there were a great many members of the House who were thoroughly displeased with the past actions of the government. Direction and planning were necessary, however, to focus this dissatisfaction on one man, the Duke, induce enough of the Commons to swallow their fears and publicly oppose him and make others realize that he was the culprit. Along these lines opinion was being fashioned in the House of Commons during the next six weeks. Sir John Eliot, as we shall see, played an outstanding role in directing the mind of the House and in the process became an (if not, the) accepted leader of the 'country' party.

The attack on that February morning began when Wandesford, supported by Eliot and Digges, proposed that the finances of the King be examined in committee of the whole. In the ensuing debate little was said about royal finances, but one grievance after another was presented. Sir John was incensed over the totally inadequate defences of the coasts. Of course nothing was accomplished.

The results were not much better on the next day when, among many others, Eliot again insisted on a discussion of the security of the coasts. But order suddenly began to assert itself when he suggested that they first discover the evils besetting the nation, then the causes of those evils, and finally a remedy for the evils. Eliot's plan of attack was immediately accepted. When debate in committee was resumed on Monday, February 27, the evils poured forth in a flood. It was stopped by Sir Edwin Sandys who induced his colleagues to accept two evils: 'The diminution of the kingdom in reputation, honour, and strength' and 'the stopping of trade at home and abroad'. Organization was taking

and sent his deputation to Eliot, inviting and maki[ng hi]m his deputy lieutenant of Cornwall, if Edgcombe [died] and that with so much complement, (as Eliot told [Sir] Edward Seymour) he was in a distraction how to divide himself, between your Grace and the Earl of Pembroke. But to whom he hath wholly given himself your Lordship can judge. Of Eliot's proceedings I could observe somewhat, which I hope is discovered to you more perfectly by others. And indeed, if I be not by my judgment deceived, his carriage as much tends to the depraving of the present government and crossing his most sacred Majesty's princely and just demands, commands, and desires, as your Lordship's ruin'. See also Willson, *Privy Councillors in the House of Commons*, pp. 183–88, for an excellent analysis of this letter.

shape and was advanced even further when on the next day it was decided in committee to turn the numerous evils already mentioned into causes of the two evils just accepted.

For several days the attention of the Commons was diverted from the causes by other topics such as the *St. Peter* case. But it had taken only four days to turn chaos into order and to formulate a plan of attack on the government. No names were mentioned, least of all that of the Duke of Buckingham. But many of the evils (as they were at first called) or causes could be blamed only on the favourite. Undoubtedly members began to realize what was in the wind. At the same time they must have seen that this plan of attack had not been concocted in the lobbies but was being fashioned in committee of the whole simply by the trial and error method. Here Sir John Eliot had shown ability, had taken the lead. But he was not alone. At the same time he had his own pet grievance. But many others also had their evils or causes to air.

When debate on the causes was resumed in committee on March 6 only a single cause was discussed. One gets the impression now that direction from behind the scenes was playing an ever greater role. That first cause to be thoroughly aired was the failure of the government to provide adequate defence of the coasts. It was Eliot's cause. Of course he took a prominent part in the debate. He worsted Sir John Coke in an argument over why fully equipped ships lying in the Thames had not been employed for so vital a purpose. In the end it was resolved that 'the coasts have not been sufficiently guarded nor the seas secured since the dissolution of the treaties with Spain'.

Once again nearly a week was devoted to other issues. Prominent among them was a request for supply from the King and a futile questioning of the Council of War. Not until March 11 were the causes of the evils again debated by the Commons. That afternoon Eliot had just failed to secure the support of the House in declaring the arrest of the *St. Peter* a grievance when in committee of the whole the members were surprised to hear Dr Samuel Turner[1] declare that now a general cause of all causes should be stated. On the basis of common fame, that is, report or rumour, he maintained the Duke of Buckingham was that general cause. He presented six charges against him.[2] Most of them in a

[1] M.P. for Shaftesbury and follower of the Earl of Pembroke. *E.H.R.* (1935), L, 248.
[2] The Duke was responsible for the loss of the control of the Channel.
The Duke had depleted the King's finances by making huge gifts from royal resources to his relatives.

modified form had already been levelled at the government. This sudden and unexpected denunciation of the favourite by a man of no
prominence in the House left the members dumbfounded.

It has been suggested that this attack on Buckingham was a trial bal-
loon sent up by the leaders of the opposition.[1] They wanted to see
what would happen and needed a dupe for this purpose, so they told
Dr Turner what to say. But all the evidence is opposed to this theory.
A bit of such evidence is that had Eliot desired to test the effect of a
direct attack on the favourite, he had an excellent opportunity in the
St. Peter case. This he refused to do on the very day of Turner's denunciation. Even stronger evidence are the tactics of delay employed by the
leaders of the 'country' party. Either by postponing the discussion, by
debating the common fame basis of the charges, or because of the absence of Turner due to illness (possibly diplomatic) the attack was
pushed into the background for nearly two weeks. By the end of that
time Eliot had charged the Duke openly and Turner's accusations no
longer were a danger to the 'country' leaders. The situation had been
dangerous. The attack of the doctor might easily have been forced into
the limelight. The result might have been the premature disclosure of
the plans taking shape against Buckingham. First the majority of the
members must be persuaded to oppose the Duke. Opinion in the House
against him must be built on the firm foundation of the evils and their
causes. No, Turner was responsible for his words. He hated the Duke,
had heard much against him, and believed the time ripe to bring him to
justice. It is a possibility that the Earl of Pembroke, out of touch with
the leaders of the opposition in the House of Commons, was behind
that attack of Dr Samuel Turner.[2]

In the meantime the Commons were unable to discuss the causes of
the evils until March 16 when little progress was made. But the next
day brought results. The committee of the whole decided upon four
more causes of the evils. It appears that Sir John Eliot was now labour-

---

The Duke was responsible for taking over many offices and giving them to his friends,
relatives, and servants, most of whom were incompetent.

The Duke was secretly supporting papists, for his mother and father-in-law were
recusants.

The Duke had been selling offices, honours, and preferments in the Church.

The Duke was responsible for the Cadiz disaster because he had stayed at home and had
not planned it properly.

[1] Gardiner, VI, 77. There is no evidence to support the contention of Forster, *Eliot*, I,
499, that Eliot, not Turner, delivered this attack.

[2] See above, p. 111, note 2.

ing much harder behind the scenes than in the House itself.[1] On several occasions he had taken no part in the discussion of the causes. Yet there are signs that he was one of the busiest members of the House. When, however, the sixth cause was brought before the committee of the whole on March 18 Sir John was in the thick of it again. This cause was of particular interest to the vice-admiral of Devon, for it concerned the loan of the seven ships to France and their use against Rochelle. Weston and Secretary Coke did their best to excuse the government and avert the censure of the Commons. Sir John pounded them with weighty words and, in this case, unanswerable arguments. Again it was resolved 'that the sending of our ships into foreign parts, delivering them into the hands of Frenchmen strangers, which were employed against Rochelle' was a cause of the evils.

On Monday the 20th two more causes were approved without the help of Eliot. By splitting one of the causes already approved into three it turned the eight into ten. These ten and the two evils the committee of the whole approved by resolution. One gets the impression now of hurry in the debates of the Commons. The leaders of the 'country' seem to be pushing matters. Finally the end, the object of this whole attack, is clearly indicated when Eliot's proposal was upheld in committee that a primary cause, or 'causing cause', be discovered and that a sub-committee be named for that purpose.[2]

5. BUCKINGHAM BLAMED AND SUPPLY DEMANDED[3]

While Sir John's sub-committee was deliberating on the cause of causes, the attention of the House on March 23 was concentrated on supply. This subject had been brought to life again by a message from King Charles. But on the next day there was no opportunity to continue

[1] Sir Arthur Brett writing to his brother-in-law, the Earl of Middlesex on March 19 said: 'The fire in the lower House groweth into a greater flame and every day shows others against my lord Duke. . . . There are other things against the Duke, as Sir John Eliot told me, which are not yet in the House, but shall be very shortly.' H.M.C. 4th Rept., App., p. 289a.

[2] P.E. MSS., 'Eliot and Bucks', ff. 5–12v. These are all notes in Eliot's hand dealing with the proceedings of his sub-committee. Its membership, though not necessarily complete, can be compiled from them. It was composed of Digges, Wandesford, Pym, Selden, Sir John Strangways, Coryton, Edward Kirton, Henry Sherfield, Sir Thomas Lake, Sir Walter Erle, Sir Francis Barnham, Sir Thomas Hoby, Emanuel Gifford, Sir John Hippesly, Sir Robert Mansell, and Walter Long.

[3] Unless otherwise indicated this section is based on Whitelocke and E.P.N. 1626(1).

with supply or to consider the scheduled Turner business. The entire day was devoted to a session of the committee of the whole presided over by Wandesford. Its business was the report of Sir John Eliot from the sub-committee on the cause of causes. Without softening the blow in any way he asserted that the Duke of Buckingham was the 'causing cause', was responsible for the causes of the evils which beset the kingdom.

Eliot reported first that he and his colleagues believed the Duke responsible for the increase of popery in England. This charge was debated until noon with many members defending the favourite. It was finally rejected by deciding not to put it to the question. In the afternoon Sir John continued his report and demonstrated with some proof how the Lord Admiral was responsible for four causes of the evils: failing to guard the English Channel, acquiring too many offices in his own hands, selling honours in general, and conferring honours on poor men so that it was necessary to use the King's revenues to maintain them. These four the committee of the whole accepted without serious opposition. At the close of the day Eliot's motion to report the work in committee to the House was passed.

The two evils and ten causes[1] approved in committee were reported the next morning by Wandesford to the House. But in no way did he connect the Duke with them. Next he reported the four causes associated with the Lord Admiral. The House approved the two evils and ten causes but refused to blame the favourite for the four causes. The attack was not running smoothly. Impatient of delay Eliot moved that they proceed to judgment on Tuesday, March 28, if the Duke had given no satisfaction in the meantime. But the House would not be hurried. The most the Commons would agree to do was to set March 29 as the day on which to consider Wandesford's report as it touched the favourite. Of course he was to be given notice of the charges the

---

[1] The ten causes according to *C.J.*, I, 841–42 were: 1. 'The increase of papists and countenancing of them'. 2. 'The not sufficiently guarding of the narrow seas sithence the dissolution of the treaties with Spain'. 3. 'The plurality of offices in one man's hand'. 4. 'Sales of honour in general'. 5. 'The conferring of honours upon such for maintenance of whom the King's revenue exhausted'. 6. 'The intercepting and unnecessary exhausting and misemploying of the King's revenue'. 7. 'The putting to sale of offices and places of judicature'. 8. 'The delivery of our ships to the French which were employed against Rochelle'. 9. 'The impositions upon commodities, native and foreign, without assent in Parliament'. 10. 'The misemployment of the three subsidies and three fifteenths, or the not employing of it to the four ends mentioned in the act'.

House was to consider on that day.[1] Dr Turner's accusations pale into insignificance when compared with this attack by the House of Commons under the leadership of Sir John Eliot. At the same time, it was already hinted in the debates of the last two days that, as with Turner, common fame would be the legal foundation of the charges to be brought against the Duke of Buckingham. No inquiry against him by petition had been instituted by a person outside of Parliament; therefore the House could inaugurate such an inquiry itself with common fame, or public opinion, as the basis for its charges.

With the attack launched and preparations made for its speedy renewal, it is surprising to find that more than three weeks intervened before further steps were taken against the Duke. For this delay the Commons were not solely to blame, rather a combination of circumstances in which the King played a significant role.

The House of Commons had been in session only a short time on Monday, March 27, when it was turned into committee of the whole to consider supply with Glanville in the chair. This subject had been popping up for over two weeks but had not yet been seriously considered by the Commons. On this occasion events were different. Sir Benjamin Rudyerd opened proceedings by recapitulating the calamities England had suffered in the immediate past. Without mentioning a definite sum he demonstrated the urgent need of the King for supply. The amount, three subsidies and three fifteenths, was proposed by Sir John Strangways. But not a penny should be voted, he declared, until certain grievances had been redressed.

Shortly after this proposal had been made Sir John Eliot arose. He delivered one of his most famous speeches,[2] a philippic which aroused the wrath of the 'courtiers', particularly the close friends of Buckingham and the great man himself. Beginning with a diplomatic reference

---

[1] By Sir James Bagg and Mr Fotherby. *C.J.*, I, 842.

[2] P.E. MSS., 'Eliot, speeches, etc.', ff. 28–33v and 46–46v. The last two folios contain an insertion which, with clear indications, should be substituted for 19 lines that have been crossed out in the main speech. In *Neg. Post.*, I, Supp., 156–64, and II, Supp., 123–5, the speech is given plus a fragment, supposedly having no connection with each other. Rushworth, I, 220–1, prints a briefer version of the speech which is much the same in eight separates I have found in S.P.D., Chas. I, XXIII, no. 37; *H.M.C. 6th Rept.*, Pt. I, App. 351b; and in mss. in the Bodleian library and the British Museum. The opening sentence in Rushworth and the separates is: 'We have had a representation of great fear, but I hope [it] shall not darken our understandings'. The opening sentence in the P.E. MS. begins: 'This day was begun with a happy auspice, and I hope we shall give it as happy a conclusion'. A diarist's full report of the speech is to be found in Whitelocke, Rich, and E.P.N. 1626(1).

to the first anniversary of Charles I's accession, Sir John believed that, though they might express 'some variety of opinions', in the end they would agree for the good of the King and Kingdom. Then he turned to Rudyerd's speech and praised it for its 'fine insinuations' on the state of affairs in Christendom. But he did not want the dangers mentioned by Sir Benjamin to arouse such a panic in the minds of the members that they would become too hasty and fail to 'retain the . . . dignity and wisdom of our ancestors'.

At this point Eliot introduced the main theme of his discourse. It dealt with the capacity of the subject to pay, to supply the King. He divided it into 'estate' and 'will'. By the former he meant actual ability or means to pay. Quickly he dismissed it with, 'I am confident there shall never want ability in England and Englishmen to supply their King with aids necessary or fit for the advantage and support of all his just occasions'.

But the question of will to pay was a different matter. 'How the people stand disposed, how they are affected, there are many things observable for our affairs abroad, for our affairs at home', he said. Turning first to foreign affairs he minced no words in speaking of the Cadiz expedition and put the Lord Admiral into the centre of the picture when he denounced him for putting himself in command and in the end sending a deputy. Mentioning briefly other foreign fiascos Sir John lunged again at the favourite who was responsible that 'they return but loss and dishonour to our nation'.

In dealing with domestic affairs the orator got into his stride. 'The oppressions, the corruptions, the exactions, the extortions are so infinite as almost no part is free', he cried. There was not a man in the country, he believed, who had not suffered from such abuses. Citing one of Cicero's orations where great corruption was laid bare before the Senate, he compared the situation in Rome to that in England. Then he lashed out again at the Duke and his clan. The King's 'treasure', Eliot declared,

'are exhausted, his revenues are consumed as well as the treasures and faculties of the subject, wherein many hands are exercised, divers have their gleanings. But the harvest and great gathering comes to one who must protect the rest and for his countenance draws all others to him as his tributaries, who are enforced by that not only to pillage for themselves but [for] him, and to the proportion of his avarice and ambition, which makes the abuse and injury the greater.'

In order to strengthen his denunciation Sir John introduced two precedents. The first he drew from the sixteenth year of Henry III when 'Parliament' forced the dismissal of Hugh de Burgh before it would vote supply. The second was taken from the tenth year of Richard II when the supply demanded was refused until the Duke of Suffolk was dismissed and a commission issued by the King for a careful investigation of the financial status of the nation. The application of these precedents was obvious. But Eliot wished that an investigation similar to that ordered by Richard II could be instituted now and that a search could be made for crown jewels, particularly those of Queen Elizabeth. Of course he had in mind the recent pawning of the royal gems by Buckingham.

Having presented his sharply pointed precedents the orator drew his speech to a close. What should they do, he asked, refuse supply until their grievance had been redressed? No, he asserted, they should have confidence in his Majesty so that he might have more confidence in them.

'Let us now . . . present our grievances and complaints that the satisfaction given in them may prepare the affections of the people, and in the meantime so far yield to the proposition for supply that we make a promise of the aid which is urged for by the King.'[1]

As for the act itself Eliot wanted them first 'to attend the despatch of the rest of our affairs'. In other words, first settle with the Duke of Buckingham, attend to that grievance of grievances, and then vote the money bill. Was not that the same as refusing supply until the Commons' grievances had been redressed? From now on the condition which Sir John refused to state but clearly implied, that no money would be voted until the Duke was dismissed, was adhered to by the Commons without the slightest thought of compromise.

Looked at from another angle this speech shows Eliot using the subject of supply as a further means to vilify the Duke. His report of March 24 was greatly strengthened by his unsparing denunciation of the man he now hated more than anybody in the world. King and kingdom were being ruined by the grasping and incompetent hands of the Duke of Buckingham. That was Sir John Eliot's conviction which

[1] He openly supported the three subsidies and three fifteenths suggested by Strangways according to E.P.N. 1626(1), f. 29, Whitelocke, and Rich.

was also held by an ever-growing number of his colleagues in the House of Commons. Whether the speech of March 27 was to serve as a guide for the rest of the session or was an attempt to strengthen the opposition to the favourite, it is a notable contribution to seventeenth-century parliamentary oratory.

As soon as Sir John had resumed his seat Sir Robert Harley took exception to part of the speech. He did not like the paralleling of the times. While questioning whether the King had ever listened to only one man's advice, Harley 'was interrupted and they cried to the point. But upon Sir John Eliot's motion he proceeded'.[1] Sir Robert came to the point immediately. He felt that Eliot's precedents might reflect unfavourably on King Charles. Richard II was not the best of English kings; therefore it was unfortunate to compare Charles I to him, Harley implied. Sir John responded at once to say, 'that in his parallels he made no instance that might reflect upon the King but upon his instruments'. He hoped the House would clear him, which it did with one voice. He continued by saying: 'I would not put conditions to the King as if we should buy his justice by contract, but as soon as the country be enabled by reformation of our grievances we will then pass the act, and in the meantime give him assurance of it'.[2] Eliot sounds naïve in his interpretation of the intended agreement with Charles. In spite of his denial the proposal was simply a bargain between King and Commons, a *quid pro quo*, which had been a practice indulged in by the Commons for centuries.

The debate on supply, how much to give, under what conditions, and when, was a long one. On three more occasions Sir John Eliot spoke. The first was to insist that no supply bill be passed until grievances had been redressed. The second was to move a point of order to which he attached some advice on how to treat the King. 'Let your counsels and advice anchor at the King's heart not at his necessities which are sandy grounds. Make no expression to the King that we have any distrust, any fear of him', he said.[3] The third was just a suggestion as to the times when the subsidies should be paid once the act was passed. Finally, the committee of the whole resolved that three subsidies and three fifteenths should be granted Charles and that the bill should be introduced into the House as soon as the grievances presented to his Majesty had received his answer. This resolution was reported back to the House and immediately passed. The question of sup-

---

[1] Whitelocke, also Rich and E.P.N. 1626(1), f. 29v.   [2] Whitelocke.   [3] *Ibid.*

ply was settled for the time being by the Commons, but by no means in a way agreeable to Charles and Buckingham.

On Tuesday, March 28, proceedings in the House had hardly begun when the Commons received a message from the King. It asked them to meet him and the Lords on the next day at nine o'clock in the palace of Whitehall and requested them to put a temporary stop to all business. Complying with this request the members immediately adjourned themselves until Thursday morning.[1]

On Wednesday at Whitehall the King began proceedings by addressing a few words to the two Houses assembled before him.[2] He made it clear that the Lords had not been at fault and that it was solely the Commons who must be shown the error of their ways. This task he had entrusted to Lord Keeper Coventry who took up the cudgels as soon as the King had spoken.[3] Coventry reprimanded the Commons first for having neglected to punish Clement Coke[4] for his insolent words and then for their similar failure in the case of Dr Turner. In fact, he said, they had followed in the footsteps of Turner and 'proceeded in an unparliamentary inquisition' of the Duke of Buckingham. His Majesty, Coventry asserted, knew better than any other person 'the sincerity of the Duke's proceedings', the dangers and enemies he had encountered, the sacrifices he had made, and the good work he had done for the country. Consequently the King felt that this attack was directed at himself and his father rather than at the Duke. The Commons were ordered to stop their denunciations and let his Majesty reform 'these things which you suppose to be otherwise than they should be'. And then the Lord Keeper struck directly at those who had been causing trouble. The great 'Council of State' had been criticized and slandered by 'men whose years and education cannot attain to that depth'. His Majesty's handling of foreign affairs had been denounced and the activities of his government compared 'with times of most exception'. Becoming even more specific Coventry asserted that committees of the Commons had ordered the examination of letters of Secretaries of State and had commanded royal officials to produce their records, books, and even private notes. Turning to supply the royal spokesman told the Commons that the King considered the figures dis-

---

[1]. C.J., I, 843. [2] Rushworth, I, 221. [3] Ibid., 221–25.

[4] The son of Sir Edward Coke and member for Aylesbury, Bucks, who on March 10 had said in the House it was 'better to suffer by a foreign hand than at home'. Whitelocke and C.J., I, 835.

cussed to be insufficient and that he understood that the grant was to be made on condition of redress of grievances. The members of the lower House were informed that by next Saturday they should add to the grant already agreed upon and that it should be without any conditions. If they did not do this, they were told, his Majesty would not promise to let them sit any longer. Such undiplomatic commands and threats were capped with an appeal to the 'wise and well tempered' members to direct the policy of the House in the interests of the King. Not satisfied with this 'gracious admonition' Charles himself closed the session with some pointed words of his own. He told his audience 'that Parliaments are altogether in my power for their calling, sitting and dissolution; therefore, as I find the fruits of them good or evil, they are to continue or not to be'.

Such was a typical Stuart reprimand of Parliament. It contained the authoritative Tudor manner but substituted haughty arrogance for that subtly gracious tact which had frequently brought an angered House to heel. To be sure, the Commons had gone much further, said much more, and threatened more serious action than they had ever thought of doing fifty years earlier. At that time Peter Wentworth was talking about the importance of freedom of speech. Now Sir John Eliot was speaking freely, so freely that royal reprimands and dire threats were in order. But times had changed to such an extent that strong language from a King was now completely ignored except to produce anger and more words from the Commons.

No wonder that on the next day the House immediately turned itself into a committee of the whole and gave that committee power to call for the key and prevent any member from leaving without permission. No wonder that as soon as Herbert had taken the chair Sir John Eliot arose to reply to the royal rebuke and vindicate himself.[1] He began by desiring his listeners to give his words as favourable an interpretation as he would give to those of others. 'The matter now to be handled', he said, 'is of the greatest weight that ever came within these walls, tending to the satisfaction of the King and the immunities of the subject to be preserved'. He said his Majesty's speech, not the Lord Keeper's, contained three 'generals'. The first 'I know not whether I may call . . . a rebuff or censure, but it is a touch at our proceedings that they have been unparliamentary'. Secondly the words of the King were 'a retrenching of the privileges by which we sit here'. Thirdly, Eliot said,

[1] Whitelocke. Also Rich. Brief in E.P.N. 1626(1), f. 30 and (2), ff. 58v-59.

the demand for an increase in supply 'argueth a neglect of us in that which we ought to have done'. Turning to the first 'general' Sir John asserted 'that we should give the King satisfaction that we have not gone from the course of Parliament; concerning the Duke of Buckingham, ours an examination upon good and just grounds'. As to paralleling the times, there might always be an exception, he maintained, but in this instance nothing was intended 'but for the honour and safety of the King'. And then Eliot launched into a defence of their privileges which had been violated by the King's command not to touch the great. As to supply he advised the committee against considering the subject, 'for if our privileges be denied we can debate neither this nor anything else'. Finally he moved that a sub-committee be appointed to prepare a remonstrance to the King which would deal with the infraction of their privileges.[1] But no action could be taken on this motion because of the appearance of messengers from the Lords necessitating the return of the Speaker to the chair.

In this speech Sir John Eliot was walking on eggs. His idol, the King, had attacked his other idol, the House of Commons. Not to condemn one in defence of the other was a most difficult task. To which he owed greater loyalty by this time is manifest. But from the unsatisfactory report of this speech it appears that Eliot was able to avoid the pitfalls confronting him and remain true to both King and Commons.

The message from the Lords requested an immediate meeting in the Painted Chamber where both Houses were to sit as committees of the whole to listen to an explanation of the previous day's speeches by a member of the upper House.[2] King Charles and the Lord Keeper had spoken too harshly and said too much for the temper of the House of Commons. Of that they were quickly informed by 'courtiers' in the lower House. And now the Duke of Buckingham, of all people, was to pour oil on those troubled waters.[3]

First he withdrew the request for further supply by next Saturday with the remark 'that as his Majesty would not have you condition with him directly or indirectly, so he will not lie to a day for giving further supply'. He had been instructed to say, he continued, that the King had no intention of interrupting their discussion of grievances but hoped that they would not look so much for faults as 'the means to re-

[1] For a general comment on this speech see *C. and T., Chas. I*, I, 93.
[2] *C.J.*, I, 843.
[3] Rushworth, I, 225–31.

dress them'. Finally Charles through the mouth of his favourite informed the Lords and Commons that he intended to choose a committee of both Houses which would 'take the view of his estate'. He
hoped this would satisfy the Commons and would prevent their 'casting any ill odour on his government'. These concessions, so different
from the commands of the previous day, were interspersed by the Duke
with requests for additional supply. Having completed his instructions
from the King, Buckingham changed the subject to a lengthy defence
of his own past actions. It was humble enough in tone and had the ear-
marks of sincerity. The Duke tried to show that he alone had never advised the King to take this or that action, but action was always taken
either at the King's own request or with the advice of his Council. The
story the favourite had to relate was not exactly pleasant, for failure,
however justified, never sounds well. Even the truth about the ships
loaned to France could not materially lessen the complaints of the Commons on this score. The incident simply showed Buckingham to be as
tricky as any Frenchman without being half as clever.

What the Commons thought of these explanations of royal words
and ducal actions has never been recorded.[1] As they ignored them, the
implication is that they felt the King had not retracted enough and the
Duke was not to be believed.

On the last of March much of the day was devoted to hearing the report of the previous day's joint meeting. But the Commons tired of
listening to it, so they postponed its conclusion to the next day. Before
this decision was reached and as soon as a break in the report occurred
Eliot jumped up to revive the remonstrance he had proposed on the
previous day. He moved that a select committee be named to give 'a
satisfactory answer to his Majesty that our proceedings have been parliamentary and [to compose] a remonstrance to his Majesty of our
privileges'.[2] But the House was not in such a hurry. His motion was
ignored and proceedings for the day were closed with the above-
mentioned decision to conclude the report on the next day.

When Pym had completed the report on April 1, the House turned
itself into a committee in order to discuss the speeches of the King and
the Lord Keeper. As a result of a lengthy debate, in which no words of

[1] Except in a letter from Mead to Stuteville of April 8 where he called the speech 'fair
and submissive' and said that some members had written that those who were indifferent,
or were not the Duke's enemies, seemed to be well satisfied with the speech. *C. and T.*,
Chas. I, I, 93.

[2] *C.J.*, I, 843, also Whitelocke.

Sir John Eliot have been recorded, the Commons decided to frame a remonstrance to the King in which they would vindicate their privileges. To draft this document a sub-committee of twelve including Eliot was named.[1] Not until the afternoon of April 4 did Glanville report the completed remonstrance to the committee of the whole. It was approved and formally presented to the House by Edward Herbert. As was frequently the case, Eliot's hasty sowing was bearing fruit. Either his timing was wrong and his ideas right, or his perseverence induced the Commons to accept his views.

The remonstrance,[2] when compared with the Apology of 1604 and the Protestation of 1621, shows what strides towards independence the Commons had taken in less than a quarter of a century. They no longer claimed the right to talk on this or that subject. Now they asserted the right to take whatever action they pleased on any matter presented to them. The remonstrance of April, 1626, justified the failure of the House to take severe measures against Clement Coke and Dr Turner. It cleared Sir John Eliot of casting any stigma on the King in his speech of March 27. It insisted on the right of the House to attack the Duke of Buckingham or any other minister. And it refused to commit the Commons in any way to voting additional supply. Here was revolution as measured by the standards of the two previous reigns. But that they were engaged in revolution never occurred to the Commons.

On the afternoon of Wednesday, April 5, a committee of thirty from the House of Commons (from which discretion probably dictated the absence of Eliot) presented the remonstrance to Charles at Whitehall. The King informed the committee that he would not give his answer at present and requested the Commons to adjourn immediately for a week in order to celebrate Easter. When the members assembled again that afternoon a motion to adjourn was carried by only thirty out of a total of 270 votes.[3] Sir John Eliot and his friends had indeed stirred up a hornets' nest for Charles and his favourite when 120 members in a thin House were so anxious to continue the attack against the Duke that they were opposed to adjournment even over Easter. That attack, sidetracked for a time by the subject of supply, was brought to the fore again by the remonstrance. Now it was laid on the table for the Commons to pick up when they returned on April 13 from their recess.

[1] Whitelocke and E.P.N. 1626(1), f. 30v.
[2] Rushworth, I, 243–46.
[3] C.J., I, 843–44.

But it was not immediately resumed. For five days nothing was said against the Duke of Buckingham. Without doubt Eliot's sub-committee on the cause of causes was not idle during these days. Charles, however, did not improve the temper of the House when he told it on that first day he could give no answer to the remonstrance as there was too much to be done. He requested the Commons to fulfil their promise in the remonstrance to make him safe at home and feared abroad.[1] As usual the King's chief interest was in money.

Religion was the subject before the House on Monday, the 17th. Pym delivered a long report in which he condemned Richard Montague for his Arminian writings. He was strongly supported by Eliot and others.[2] On the next morning Sir Dudley Carleton, the Vice-Chamberlain, gave the Commons the story of his embassy to France.[3] They were informed that the English ships loaned to France were soon to be returned, that peace for the French Protestants was anticipated in the near future, and that France might be drawn into the league against Spain. Such was the pleasant but rather uncertain prospect painted by Carleton. But Eliot spoiled much of its good effect when he called to the attention of the Vice-Chamberlain that France had promised the return of the ships at this very time. If they were not back in English waters within a few days it would mean that the French had broken faith. Furthermore, Sir John reminded the House that in the last Parliament at Oxford they had been told that peace had been established with the Huguenots and that France had declared war against Spain.[4] Sir John Eliot might simply have said there was no use in believing any statements by his Majesty's servants. A little later in the day the temper of the members was given another jolt when Charles again prodded his faithful Commons to get down to the subject of supply. The only result of a lengthy debate was to decide that no day should be set aside for considering the needs of the King. These episodes were working into the hands of the leaders of the opposition. Opinion against the government, particularly against Buckingham, now considered by most men to be the government, was rapidly developing again. By this time many more of the doubtful back-benchers must have been opposed to the Duke.

[1] Whitelocke.   [2] *Ibid.*   [3] *C.J.*, I, 845–46.
[4] Rich (misdated April 16). Also Whitelocke.

CHAPTER VII

Impeachment of the
Duke of Buckingham

April 18 to June 20, 1626

I. PREPARATION OF THE CHARGES

THE attack against the Duke of Buckingham, which was resumed on Tuesday, April 18, 1626, was still in the hands of Sir John Eliot. He was reporting more charges[1] from his sub-committee on the cause of causes to the committee of the whole for evils, causes, and remedies, as it was being called. And as soon as the committee had approved them they were reported to the House. By Monday, April 24, Eliot's sub-committee had completed its work and was disbanded.

In the meantime a significant step was taken. On April 21 Sir Dudley Digges moved and the House approved that a select committee of twelve be named to put the 'great business' into shape and present it to the House.[2] It was time that the House itself take the charges against the Duke in hand. The spade-work had been done,[3] and opinion against the favourite had been developed. Now formal steps were in order, and impeachment of the Duke was undoubtedly in the minds of the leaders of the 'country' party.

In this new stage of the attack Sir John Eliot was not to be in as prominent a position as he had been as reporter of his sub-committee.

---

[1] Buckingham's assessment on the East India Co. (Gardiner, V, 237–40), his responsibility for loaning the ships to France, his selling offices and places of judicature, and his misemploying the King's revenue.

[2] C.J., I, 847, mistakenly called a sub-committee. The twelve were: Sir Dudley Digges, Sir Walter Erle, Sir John Eliot, John Glanville, Edward Herbert, Sir Thomas Hoby, Sir Thomas Lake, John Pym, John Selden, Christopher Sherland, Christopher Wandesford, and Edward Whitby.

[3] According to P.E. MSS., 'Eliot and Bucks', ff. 13–18v; Bodleian MS., Rawl C. 674, ff. 22–24; and S.P.D., Chas. I, XXVI, no. 72, many charges against the Duke were discussed which were never reported to the committee of the whole or the House.

It was Digges who had moved the naming of the select committee. And it was to be Digges and Glanville, not Sir John,[1] who would be reporters from the committee of twelve, as it is to be called. To be sure, Eliot was one of the twelve and, if necessary, could spur it on to its goal. The struggle against the Duke of Buckingham had reached a critical stage. Mistakes caused by over-enthusiasm or by misjudgment of the will of the majority could be easily erased in committee of the whole. But in the formal House that would be more difficult and lasting damage to the great cause might result. Men with steady hands and heads, who had a feeling for the temper of the House, now must guide the attack through its final stages. Digges, Glanville, and others were better fitted for this task than Sir John Eliot.

On the afternoon of the day the committee of twelve was named, it took charge of proceedings against the Lord Admiral. John Glanville, at the request of his colleagues on the committee, moved that on the next day the House decide as to whether to proceed against the Duke with common fame as a legal basis. The debate, which took place as requested, was far too technically legal for opinion to be expressed by Eliot and other laymen. The lawyers in the House were the sole participants. Men like Edward Littleton, John Selden, William Noy, and Henry Rolle induced the majority of the Commons to accept the will of the 'country' party and make common fame the ground on which to proceed against the Duke.[2]

Additional powers were given the committee of twelve on April 24. These men might entertain any new charge against the Duke of Buckingham.[3] That gentleman, replying to a message of the Commons that he defend himself against their accusations, sent word that he was unable to do so as the Lords refused to give him permission. The House then passed eight resolutions against him. Of these, seven charges were taken from the ten causes of the evils which had been approved on March 25, though not associated with the Duke at the time.[4] They added an eighth, the extortion of money from the East India Company.

---

[1] According to third-hand information he was at least on one occasion chairman of this committee. Nicholas Herman writing to the Earl of Middlesex on May 3 gives this bit and also that Eliot had turned into a staunch supporter of the former Lord Treasurer whom he had thoroughly denounced in 1624. *H.M.C. 4th Rept.*, p. 289b.

[2] *C.J.*, I, 847–8, Whitelocke.

[3] *C.J.*, I, 849. This matter was decided only after a vote in which the 'country' had a majority of 60.

[4] *Ibid.*, The 1st, 9th, and 10th were omitted. See list above, p. 116, note 1.

There was no turning back now, the die was cast, the House of Commons had committed itself.

During the proceedings of the past week King Charles had sent word to the Commons urging them to hasten with supply.[1] The message was immediately debated by the Commons in committee. But the discussion centred solely on the day when supply should be considered. The feeling of the House was that the charges against the Duke of Buckingham should be completed before so vital a subject could be entertained. Eliot, like others, felt that not enough had been voted the King, that the charges should first be disposed of, but that no day should be fixed for the debate on supply. He believed that now they would complete their indictment rather quickly. Therefore, by not setting a day, they might get to a discussion of supply sooner than was expected. But the majority of the Commons backed a resolution of Digges that Tuesday, April 25, be set on which to consider the financial needs of his Majesty. In the end Eliot was right. By April 24, as we have seen, the Commons had condemned Buckingham under eight heads and were ready to discuss supply. It was debated at length on that day and the next two. Finally it was decided to grant an additional subsidy. This decision, made in committee of the whole, was not reported to the House until May 3 with the stipulation that no subsidy bill was to be introduced until the Duke of Buckingham had been dismissed.[2]

Meanwhile the committee of twelve had been discussing a new charge against the favourite: namely that he was to blame for the death of King James. It was maintained that the Duke had administered a plaster and a drink which had caused the death of the late King. When the new charge was presented to the committee of the whole on April 27 Eliot participated in the debate and proffered evidence which showed that the King's physicians had disapproved of the plaster.[3] The committee of the whole decided to make the incident of the plaster and the drink another charge against the Duke; and on the next day the House accepted it.[4]

Charles, realizing how futile his attempt to stem the tide had become and believing that the accusations would do his omnipotent friend no lasting harm, sent a message on April 28 to the Commons. They were told he had 'given way to the inquiry about the Duke of Buckingham'.

[1] April 20.
[2] C.J., I, 847, 854; Whitelocke; Grosvenor; E.P.N. 1626(1), ff. 33v, 34v–36v.
[3] Whitelocke.   [4] C.J., I, 851.

E

He asked them to make all possible speed in presenting their charges either to him or to the Lords.[1] 'Go ahead and do your worst,' his Majesty might have said, 'but hurry up and be done with it so that I can have my money.' With this message both sides believed that the road ahead had been cleared for them. But the 'country' leaders did not realize how strongly entrenched Buckingham was in the House of Lords; while Charles did not appreciate how stubborn the majority against him in the House of Commons could be if it did not get its way. Sir John Eliot, fighting for justice as he conceived it, had won up to this point. But idealist that he was, he did not understand that justice had long fled the halls of arrogant power.

Even now Eliot had not exhausted all his ammunition against his bitter enemy. There still was the *St. Peter*. Sir John had not forgotten it. As we have seen, he introduced the incident again on May 1[2] and succeeded in having the treatment of this ship by the Lord Admiral declared a grievance against him and turned into the tenth and final charge.

The prosecution had prepared its case and must organize itself to proceed into court with it. The first step in that direction was taken on May 2 when Digges reported from the committee of twelve to the House the two evils, the ten causes of those evils, and the Duke of Buckingham as the cause of those ten causes.[3] A long debate developed[4] in which one of the vital questions was whether to transmit the charges to the Lords or to the King. Though the leaders of the opposition may already have decided upon impeachment, it was not until this day that the House resolved that the Duke should be accused before the Lords. And the committee of twelve was ordered to prepare the accusations for transmission to the upper House.[5]

2. BUCKINGHAM ACCUSED BEFORE THE LORDS

On May 3 Sir Dudley Digges informed the House of Commons that the charges against the royal favourite would be entrusted to eight

---

[1] *C.J.*, I, 851. [2] See above, p. 111.

[3] *C.J.*, I, 853. To the 8 resolved upon on April 24 (see above, p. 128 and note 4) were added the plaster charge and the arrest of the *St. Peter*.

[4] Sir Dudley Carleton at great length declared himself opposed to making the arrest of the *St. Peter* a charge against the Duke. Eliot answered Carleton and defended the charge with many words and arguments. The House sustained Eliot. Grosvenor, and briefer in Whitelocke.

[5] Grosvenor and *C.J.*, I, 853.

managers and sixteen assistants. The eight, one of whom was Sir John Eliot, were of course drawn from the committee of twelve.[1] The Commons were ready to begin their impeachment proceedings. But Charles still had hopes of postponing, if not averting, the inevitable. On the previous day he had sent a message to the lower House in which he accepted a bit prematurely the extra subsidy and requested the Commons to hasten the supply bill. And now the House approved that subsidy and set the time for its payment. No bill for four subsidies and three-fifteenths, however, had as yet been introduced. At this time Sir Richard Weston explained the King's message of the previous day and informed the Commons that his Majesty 'desired and expected there should now be an end of the inquisition', and that he expected them not to entertain any new matters. Such language stirred the wrath of Sir John Eliot. He jumped to his feet and cried: 'If we desert our freedom we wrong ourselves. Have not we power to enquire of such things as are for the honour of the King for the safety of the commonwealth?'[2] Sir John was getting more touchy every day on the subject of freedom of the Commons, freedom to do and say what they pleased. He could brook not even the suggestion of interference with freedom of speech. Here was being displayed the development of that spirit which eventually was to lead to his martyrdom.

And yet again Charles urged haste with the subsidy bill. The result on May 5 was a long debate on supply which made little progress that would satify the King. During the discussion one of the 'courtiers' suggested that the Commons were bargaining with his Majesty for justice. As last to speak Eliot denounced such a thought. They were not trying to buy justice, he argued, but intended to give freely. He hoped that his Majesty would grant them the justice they desired in the same spirit. He closed with the motion that a a select committee, with its first meeting on May 9, be named to draft the preamble to the subsidy bill. The House passed the motion and named the committee.[3] For a second time Eliot was ignoring reality. In spite of what he might say, the Commons were buying justice from the King with money.

While Charles was prodding the Commons for money, he was running into trouble in the House of Lords. There the Earl of Bristol,

[1] *C.J.*, I, 854. Besides Eliot and Digges they were Wandesford, Erle, Herbert, Pym, Whitby, and Selden. As will be seen, Glanville took the place of Erle and Sherland that of Whitby.

[2] Grosvenor. Briefer in Whitelocke.

[3] Grosvenor. Also Whitelocke and *C.J.*, I, 856.

former ambassador to Spain, was accused of treason by the King. And
the Earl in turn made the same accusation against the Duke of Buckingham before his peers.[1] On May 2, the day after the charges were read,
Bristol sent a copy of them to the Commons in order to give his case as
much publicity as possible. Unfortunately, the two sets of accusations
against the Duke could not be combined because those of Bristol dealt
essentially with Buckingham's popish tendencies and his activities in
Spain. Influenced by the Earl's attack but without guidance from the
committee of twelve, the Commons on May 4 revived the old charge
against the Duke that he was responsible for the increase of popery in
England.[2] The discussion in the House had not progressed very far
when Eliot intervened. First he commented briefly on the subject under discussion and then turned the attention of the Commons to a new
angle of the charge made by the Earl. As Buckingham was charged
with treason he should most certainly be imprisoned. Sir John felt it
was dangerous to the King and Kingdom for a man with such power
and charged with such a crime to be at liberty. He suggested that the
Commons 'move' the Lords to imprison the Duke of Buckingham.[3]
This was a bold stroke proposed by Eliot. Could the accused be put
behind bars by the Lords, there would be much more hope of success
in the impeachment proceedings about to begin. But Sir John desired
the Duke's imprisonment not because of the accusations the Commons
were about to put before the Lords, but because of a charge made by a
peer in the upper House. He was suggesting that the Commons violate
the privileges of the House of Lords. That they would not do. Though
Eliot had the right end in view, he was a bit premature and was proposing the wrong approach. The Commons would not listen to him
and continued their inquiry about the Duke and popery without
reaching a decision.

By May 6 the House of Commons had completed its preparations
for the impeachment of the Duke of Buckingham before the House of
Lords. Sir Dudley Digges, as spokesman of the committee of twelve,
introduced the articles and assigned them to the managers. Digges was
to open proceedings by delivering the preamble, while Eliot was to
bring them to a close. The Commons approved the articles and the
assignments made by the committee. On Monday, the 8th, they requested a conference with the Lords 'by a committee of both Houses',

[1] Gardiner, VI, 93–97.
[2] It had been rejected on March 24. See above, p. 116.   [3] Grosvenor.

GEORGE VILLIERS, DUKE OF BUCKINGHAM, by Miereveldt
From the portrait at Lamport Hall
reproduced by permission of Sir Gyles Isham, Bt.

in which they would listen to an impeachment and accusation of a great peer. The Lords approved the meeting of the Houses and fixed it for that afternoon at two o'clock in the Painted Chamber.[1]

The stage was set on which to enact the drama which Eliot and his friends had been preparing for nearly three months. To change the figure of speech, the Commons were about to cast the net over their victim. Would the meshes hold which they, and particularly Sir John Eliot, had worked so hard to make secure? Impeachment is a trial in which the defendant is accused of having committed crimes. Surely most of the accusations against the Duke were hardly what a court of law would consider criminal. For example, had Buckingham committed a crime by holding many offices of state? Even if some of the charges by a stretch of imagination could be called criminal, was the proof, common fame, sound law? I do not think so. If the peers were to act as true judges in a court of law, the Commons had a flimsy case indeed. The only chance they had to succeed was to make use of politics, to appeal to the political sense of the peers, to show them that the career of the Duke of Buckingham had ruined the nation. That is what they did. That was the basis of the articles presented against the favourite. The leaders of the opposition in the Commons knew that a strong minority of the peers were as bitter against the Duke as the majority in the lower House. They hoped to convince enough of those who were only lukewarm supporters of the favourite that he was a menace to the country. It was a gamble. But Charles and Buckingham were certain that the gamble would fail, that a majority of the peers would make sure that no harm came to the Duke.

Before we can proceed to the Painted Chamber to watch the actors on that stage, we must follow an important little episode which took place in the Commons on that very morning and on the next day. A commentator reported that an extremely long debate took place over the question whether to ask the Lords to imprison the favourite. The motion to request the imprisonment of Buckingham was not made by Eliot and was not because of Bristol's charges, but was made because the Commons were about to impeach him. When the debate was resumed on the next morning it was again long and heated and lasted well into the afternoon. Sir John, it seems, felt that words from him were not needed to sway the House in the right direction. The flow of opinion for and against appeared to be endless. Finally, at four o'clock

[1] C.J., I, 856–57, and L.J., III, 589.

in the afternoon a division was taken which disclosed that 225 members favoured imprisonment and that 105 were against it.[1] The majority in the House of Commons against the Duke of Buckingham was growing apace. No wonder Eliot felt it unnecessary to speak on the question. He knew the vote would go heavily against the 'court'. That party was making a last stand fight in the lower House for its leader. Its failure, though only of a technical nature, meant that Buckingham would have to be saved by the House of Lords and the King. The power of the government in the Commons was completely broken for the rest of the life of this Parliament. Not until the day after the Commons had completed their accusations against the Duke before the Lords did Sir Nathaniel Rich, instead of the Speaker,[2] followed by most of the House, carry the request for the imprisonment of Buckingham to the House of Lords. The peers replied shortly that they would take the Commons' request into consideration and give them an answer in due time. That answer never came. The Duke exerted such power over his colleagues, that they were afraid to act against him.[3]

The only hope the Commons now had was that their accusations before the Lords would drive him out of power and lodge him in the Tower. As Sir Dudley Digges arose on the afternoon of Monday, May 8, in the Painted Chamber to deliver his preamble, Buckingham sat directly in front of him to confuse and disconcert him with a cold and intrepid stare.[4] But he was unaffected. Accusing this great peer of crimes and offences shortly to be presented, he launched into a figure of speech typical of much of seventeenth-century oratory. The Duke, a comet, was threatening the sun, stars, and universe itself. Having unburdened himself at length along these lines he summarized four of the charges against the favourite. In closing Sir Dudley divorced King Charles from all the actions of the Duke and from the blame the Commons were placing on his head.[5]

There followed the articles of impeachment. The first three were

[1] P.E. MSS., 'Eliot and Bucks', ff. 72–74. This diary by an anonymous member covers only the vital days of May 8 to 12 inclusive. It has been preserved among Eliot's papers, is not in his hand, and seems to be a copy of the original. Folios are written only on the recto. See also Grosvenor, Whitelocke, and C.J., I, 858.

[2] This was decided after a brief debate on May 9 in which the House followed the wishes of Eliot and others. Ibid. and Grosvenor.

[3] L.J., III, 628. See also letter of Mr Thomas of May 17 in Bodleian Library, MS. Rawl. C. 674, f. 16v.

[4] Anonymous diary, P.E. MSS., 'Eliot and Bucks', f. 72.

[5] L.J., III, 595–6, also Rushworth, I, 302–6.

read and 'enlarged upon' by Mr Herbert. John Selden came next with the fourth and fifth. And Glanville presented three more. Then 'growing late and Lords and all in a sweat with heat and thrusting, we could go no farther. But the Lords desired that the rest of the charge might be the next day. And so we went all weary home to our lodgings about six o'clock at night.'[1]

On the next morning the Commons were told that Mr Whitby, one of the managers who was to speak that day, was ill. So Sherland was substituted, and a request was sent the Lords to postpone the reading of the remaining charges to the afternoon to permit the new manager to prepare his speech. The Lords granted the request and even extended the time of the intermission to eight o'clock on the evening of May 10.[2]

That morning the two Houses assembled in the Painted Chamber to conclude the business against the favourite. Pym began and disposed of the next three articles. Sherland followed with the twelfth, and Wandesford closed with the thirteenth. With such meshes cast over Buckingham, who was not present on this day to unnerve his accusers, it was the turn of Sir John Eliot to draw the net firmly around the victim with a flashing, stinging epilogue.[3]

He began his speech with a summary, a summary of the deeds and conduct of the Duke of Buckingham which had brought only misery and misfortune to the land. From this black picture he turned to the 'patterns' of the favourite's mind where he found

'crimes in themselves so odious and uncertain, as the ancients knew not what name to term them; and therefore they expressed them in a metaphor, calling them *stellionatus*, from a discoloured beast so doubtful in appearance as they knew not what to make it.'

As an example of such crimes he cited the ships taken from English merchants, loaned to France, and used against Rochelle. Broadening his picture Eliot declared that Buckingham had brought under his

[1] For the charges given by Herbert, Selden, and Glanville see *L.J.*, III, 596–608, and Rushworth, I, 306–34. The last quotation in paragraph comes from the anonymous diary, P.E. MSS., 'Eliot and Bucks', f. 73.

[2] *C.J.*, I, 858; *L.J.*, III, 590; P.E. MSS., 'Eliot and Bucks', f. 73.

[3] For the charges given by Pym, Sherland, and Wandesford see *L.J.*, III, 610–17, and Rushworth, I, 334–53. The original of Eliot's speech is in P.E. MSS., 'Eliot and Bucks', ff. 80–85v. I have found a great many separates of this speech printed and in manuscript. The obvious printed sources for this speech are *L.J.*, III, 617–24, Rushworth, I, 353–6, and Cobbett, *State Trials*, II, 1367–70.

power and will 'the pleasure of his Majesty, his known directions, his public acts, his acts of council, his decrees of courts'. Nothing had escaped him. But the worst aspect of such crimes as loaning ships to France and arresting the *St. Peter* was that the Duke had declared the King responsible for them. If his Majesty had supported such proposals —and Eliot could not believe that he had—Buckingham should have used all the means in his power to dissuade him from them.

Commenting briefly on the favourite's exactions from the East India Company, which was one of the charges Glanville had explained, Sir John reminded their Lordships with what skill that gentleman had made his points. 'That skill was lately gotten in the late voyage, to which you know who sent him.' He was referring to the Lord Admiral's punishment of Glanville by making him secretary to the fleet sailing for Cadiz. But one of the peers was overheard to say that it was the King who had sent Glanville to the fleet. Here Eliot interrupted his speech to say:

'Because I hear a mention of the King,[1] his sacred name in this . . . [I must protest] that in nothing we intend to reflect the least ill odour on his Majesty or his most blessed father of happy memory, but with all honour of their names we do admire them, and only strive to vindicate their fames from such as would eclipse them.'

He returned to the attack by citing more charges against the favourite and expressing wonder that 'this man, so notorious in ill, so dangerous in the state' was able to 'subsist or keep a being'. His existence was made possible through 'art to help and underprop it'. That art was manifest in the creation of a party at court and in the country with which he worked in all fields of government to keep himself in power. Having made himself supreme throughout the nation Buckingham was able to tap the revenues of the crown and employ them for his own selfish interests, Sir John declared.

'His profuse expenses, his superfluous feasts, his magnificent buildings, his riots, his excesses, what are they but a chronicle of his immense exhausts out of the crown revenues? No wonder, then, the King, is now in want, this man abounding so. And while he abounds, the King must still be wanting.'

[1] Did Eliot actually hear this remark, or was he using his imagination while writing this speech in order to give himself the opportunity to uphold the King?

Pointing in the direction which this boundless power and ambition were headed but only hinting at their purpose, the speaker declared that the Duke's 'attempts go higher to the person of his Sovereign, making on that his practice in such a manner and with such effects as I fear to speak it, nay I doubt to think it'.

Having shown the peers the man, his power and his practices, his relations with the King and with the state, it was only necessary to compare him with men of the past and 'so considering what may now become [of] him'. 'Of all the precedents I can find,' Eliot said, 'none so near resembles him as does Sejanus.'[1] The evil ways of the two men were placed side by side and those of the Englishman appeared even blacker than those of the Roman. 'It is too, too manifest,' the speaker cried. 'I have done, your Lordships, know the man, what have been his actions, whom he is like; I leave him to your judgments.'

But Eliot had not finished. The pull of precedents was too strong on him. One more he must present. That was the case of the Bishop of Ely in the time of Richard I whose death was demanded by the people for his faults. Reading the formal conclusion of the charges against the Duke of Buckingham, Sir John Eliot closed his epilogue by requesting indulgence from the peers for his own imperfections and weaknesses and by desiring that in no way should his words reflect upon the Commons, his masters.

'This was a bold and as worthy a speech as ever I heard, only a little too tart', was the discerning comment of that 'countryman' whose notes are so entertaining and enlightening.[2] That was the trouble. The speech was too tart, too cutting in its denunciation. But for the Cornish knight, hating as only a man of his disposition knew how to hate, there was no *via media*. His enemy must be pictured as the foulest creature on earth with no hint of that bit of good to be found in every man. The thought of the truth of what he said, of his ability to prove all those vilifications, never entered his head. Sir John was carried away by his feelings. He became a free lance in the art of abuse. The result was oratory of a kind rarely heard in the halls of Parliament. To Eliot it did not matter that the formal charges against the Duke were by no means water-tight. He thought they were and therefore felt free to trim them with epithets, statements, and terms far from acceptable to a rational

[1] He was the unscrupulous praefect of the praetorian guard and minister to Tiberius, emperor from 14 to 37 AD. In the city of Rome Tiberius was a tyrant.
[2] Anonymous diary, P.E. MSS., 'Eliot and Bucks', f. 74.

and impartial legal mind. With closely reasoned arguments his predecessors in these proceedings had appealed to the intelligence of the
peers, he believed. Now it was his function to play upon their feelings.
But he over-played his part and raised sympathy rather than hatred in
many a noble's heart. Buckingham had many faults, some blacker than
even Eliot could evoke, but he also had his good points. These the
Commons forgot, while many a peer could remember them. Barring a
strong minority who looked at the favourite through the same glasses
as did the Commons, many Lords found much to praise as well as to
blame in the Duke. These men were not turned against him by the
stinging oratory of Sir John Eliot.

In his epilogue Eliot constructed a political ideal which shattered the
Tudor tradition of implicit loyalty to the sovereign. In its place he put
loyalty to the nation. The interest and well-being of the state, as expressed in seventeenth-century Parliaments, were paramount to those
of the Sovereign. Ideally stated, King, ministers, and Parliament should
work together towards the same ends. In practice that was rarely the
case under the Stuarts. But the radicals, who in the early seventeenth
century were prying into affairs of state which had hitherto been none
of their business, who were finding a multitude of faults where for the
last century few if any had been discovered, could not break completely
with the past. Tudor loyalty to the crown itself still gripped the hearts
of most members of Parliament. Therefore, a minister might make mistakes, might be base and evil, might do wrong, but never a King. This
thought was so imbued in the mind of Eliot that it has resulted in diminishing his popular historical stature.

The reaction of Charles I to this volcanic eruption of the Commons
against the favourite is of immediate interest. Early on the morning of
May 11 the King hurried to the House of Lords to explain to the peers
his position in relation to the Duke. 'To approve his innocency as
touching the matters against him,' he told them, 'I myself can be a witness to clear him in every one of them.' When he said: 'I have thought
fit to take order for the punishing some insolent speeches lately spoken',[1] he must have aroused the apprehension of the 'country' peers.
Such a statement was the logical consequence of the remark reported to
have been made by the King when on the previous day Eliot's epi-

[1] Rushworth, I, 357. *L.J.*, III, 592.

logue was related to him. 'If the Duke is Sejanus, I must be Tiberius',
Charles had said.[1]

3. THE ARREST OF ELIOT AND DIGGES

On the morning of May 11 the Commons had returned from the Lords
to their own House, where they had requested the imprisonment
of the Duke,[2] and were engaged in debate when Eliot and Digges
were summoned to the door. 'And when they came out there was an
officer with a warrant from his Majesty to carry both to the Tower.'
That was how Charles was punishing 'some insolent speeches'. As soon
as the Commons realized what had happened to the two members they
were shocked, so shocked that they stopped abruptly in the midst of
their business and adjourned for the day.[3]

When they returned on the next morning 'the House was very full
and sat very silent long'. The silence was finally broken by Mr Wild, a
lawyer, who said that 'the loss of our friends is grievous . . . and that it
was against privileges and the great Charter'.[4] After these words the
members found their tongues again. One of the first to speak was Sir
Dudley Carleton, the Vice-Chamberlain. After making some ill-timed
and unbecoming threats, such as that the Commons had better be careful about trenching on the royal prerogative, he told them that his
Majesty was displeased with Sir Dudley Digges when he spoke of the
plaster applied to King James. Sir Dudley had hurt the King's feelings
in implying that he had indulged in underhand dealings in applying the
plaster. In the case of Sir John Eliot his Majesty did not like his 'over-
bitterness in the aggravation upon the whole charge'. To speak of the
Duke as 'this man' or 'the man', as Eliot had, had given offence to the
King. Finally Charles had been offended also by the way Sir John had
referred to the 'composition' of the plaster. These were the reasons, the

---

[1] Gardiner, VI, 107–8. See also letter of Sir Simonds D'Ewes to Stuteville of May 11
where, using Sir Robert Cotton as his authority, he tells, among other matters, of the
ignorance of Charles about the charges against the Duke and his great loyalty to him.
C. and T., Chas. I, I, 101, and Halliwell, *Autobiography and Correspondence of Sir Simonds
D'Ewes. Bart.* (London, 1845), II, 187.

[2] See above, pp. 133–4.

[3] P.E. MSS., 'Eliot and Bucks', ff. 74–5, Grosvenor, and *C. and T., Chas. I*, I, 103.

[4] P.E. MSS., 'Eliot and Bucks', f. 75. This is part of the closing passage of the anonymous diary.

Vice-Chamberlain said, which 'drew his Majesty . . . to use his regal authority in committing them to the Tower'.[1]

Such absurdities did not strike the sense of humour of the House of Commons because, as all present must have realized, they concealed far more serious reasons, which the King had no intention of telling the Commons at the time. All the members could do was to continue their protests and shortly, in committee of the whole, resolve to present a remonstrance to King Charles touching the imprisonment of their two members.[2]

For the next two days[3] the Commons spent most of their time with the reason Carleton had given for the imprisonment of Sir Dudley Digges. The trouble with the accusation against Digges was that he had not used those words whose implication was distinctly treasonable. This aroused the Commons and caused them to drop Eliot out of the picture for the time being. In the end a protestation was made by every member of the House, even those who were absent due to illness, that they had not consented to any such words, had not heard any such words, did not believe such words were spoken, did not give Sir Dudley any such information, and did not know who gave the information.[4] The Commons even asked the Lords for a conference to learn from them, if possible, who had informed the King of the words attributed to their member. Finally on Tuesday, May 16, Digges was returned to the House with the excuse from Charles that he had been misinformed about the words Sir Dudley had spoken.[5]

The case of Sir John Eliot was another matter, Sir Richard Weston, the King's messenger, declared. 'His Majesty believes that he exceeded his commission of the House [and] charges him with some things that are extra-judicial to this House'. When Weston was asked to explain the word 'extra-judicial', he said that the word was his Majesty's and that he could not do it without permission from the King. After the Commons had cleared the six other managers in the impeachment pro-

---

[1] Rushworth, I, 358–60. C.J., I, 859–60.

[2] Grosvenor. Also E.P.N. 1626(1), f. 37. Between May 11 and 20 when Eliot was a prisoner these notes are blank except for three days, May 12, 13, 17, when they are quite full. As there is no change in the handwriting or in the shade of the ink, it shows that the notes as a whole were not originals taken by Sir John in the House. It is interesting to speculate who gave him his information for those days when he was a prisoner. Actually there are no notes between May 4 and 22 except on the three above-mentioned days.

[3] Saturday, May 13, and Monday, May 15.

[4] E.P.N. 1626(1), ff. 38–38v. Rushworth, I, 360.

[5] C.J., I, 860. Rushworth, I, 360.

ceedings of having exceeded their commission from the House, Mr
Kirton moved that Sir John Eliot might also be cleared by a vote. But
the House postponed this motion 'until they have had consideration of
the King's message this day sent'.[1]

That message was discussed on Wednesday, May 17, in committee of
the whole. First Weston arose to say 'that he hath leave to explain the
word extra-judicial, which is that his Majesty hath committed him for
high crimes against his Majesty done out of this House'. Carleton followed to clear Eliot 'in all things he spake by commandment and to
petition the King for him that he may be here to answer for himself'.
The debate continued at some length without making much progress.
Near the end the Vice-Chamberlain interposed again to make an interesting explanation of the attitude of King Charles towards Sir John
Eliot. He said:

'That no slip in words should be laid to his charge. That he hath here no
accuser. His accusation proceedeth from his Majesty and that is mixed
with that which happened at the conference and with something else
which might be discovered by the sight of his papers, or some other
means.'

'No slip in words' was being charged against Eliot but something
'which happened at the conference' where Sir John delivered his epilogue. To reconcile these two statements is difficult. At most it could be
quibbling on the part of Charles or even Carleton. But the investigation of Eliot's papers was a different matter. The Commons were not
prepared to interfere in such an examination. All they did was to instruct the sub-committee, which was composing a remonstrance to the
King on their liberties, 'to take therein what concerns Sir John Eliot
and to add it to the rest'. When the Speaker resumed his chair it was
decided to adjourn until Friday, May 19.[2]

In the meantime Charles was exerting every effort to discover evidence against Eliot which would assure his permanent imprisonment.
At his lodgings his papers were carefully searched for incriminating
data, but without success.[3] On May 18 he was brought before Sir

[1] Whitelocke, C.J., I, 860, and Grosvenor (misdated May 17).
[2] E.P.N. 1626(1), ff. 38v–39; Whitelocke; C.J., I, 861.
[3] S.P.D., Chas. I, XVIII, nos. 68, 69, 70, are abstracts of papers found in Eliot's chamber
at this time. See C.J., I, 865, for Eliot's motion to have certain members appointed to see
that his returned papers were all there.

Randall Crewe, Chief Justice of King's Bench, and Sir Robert Heath, the Attorney-General. Seven questions were asked the suspect with the intention of trapping him. Most of them centred around the precedent from the reign of Richard II which he had cited in his speech of March 27.[1] One asked whether he had had a conference with deputies from Rochelle, and another, whether he had ever had correspondence or a conference with a foreign ambassador or agent. To six of these questions the answers of Sir John were in the negative. He said he was not sure just where he had obtained the precedent from the reign of Richard II. As to having any message from a foreign ambassador or agent, he said that about three years ago, when he was a prisoner in the Marshalsea, Philip Barnardo came to him about prize goods in the west.[2]

Little did this examination avail Charles and Buckingham. Nothing 'extra-judicial' could be found against the prisoner. It is not surprising that on Friday, May 19, when the House had sat in silence for over an hour, Sir Dudley Carleton informed his mute colleagues that he had seen a royal warrant for Sir John Eliot's release. It had been despatched in a hurry by messenger to the Tower. He moved that the House get down to business, for he did not know whether Eliot would come directly to Westminster or first visit some friends in the city.[3] This was cheering news and set the wheels of parliamentary procedure in motion again.

The business of Sir John Eliot was the first item undertaken on Saturday morning. Coryton moved to take this subject into consideration, and if Eliot 'have done or spoken amiss to punish him, and if not to hear him'. Members had various ideas as to what steps should be taken. And when Sir Thomas Hoby desired that the Commons first be told how Eliot 'stands in the King's eyes', Sir Richard Weston replied that Sir John had been examined at the command of the King, given negative answers which his Majesty had accepted, and thereupon set at liberty as far as any extra-judicial charges were concerned.[4] At this point Eliot was sent for and entered the House of Commons nine days after his arrest to resume his seat among his colleagues.

One of the first to speak after Sir John Eliot's return was Carleton. He wished 'not to charge him but to give him occasion to discharge

---

[1] See above, p. 119.
[2] S.P.D., Chas. I, XXVII, nos. 17 and 18 contain the questions and Eliot's answers.
[3] Grosvenor. Also Whitelocke.   [4] *Ibid.*

himself of whatsoever might be objected against him for anything passed from him at the conference'. The Vice-Chamberlain enumerated five remarks in the epilogue which had given offence—presumably to the King—such as comparing the Duke to a *stellionatus* and to Sejanus, and calling the favourite 'that man'.[1] The government, having failed to find that Eliot had committed any high crimes against the state, was falling back on the ridiculously weak charges Carleton had presented to the House on May 12. To be sure, on May 17 Sir Dudley had guarded against such a situation when he said that the reasons for Eliot's imprisonment were mixed. But Carleton had confused his listeners by saying that 'no slip in words should be laid to his charge'. Now he said that Sir John was not being charged with these slips, but simply that they had been 'objected against him'. Charles certainly was forcing his officials to do a lot of fine splitting of hairs to get out of an unfortunate situation into which he had probably been enticed by the gambling spirit of Buckingham.

Eliot, of course, seized this opportunity to free himself of the stigma which was blackening his name.[2] He took it as a great favour to be given this occasion to explain himself. But because there were so many separate items, he could not cover them all adequately 'in a continuous discourse'. Therefore, he requested that the points be presented individually, and he would endeavour to give satisfaction in each instance. So the Speaker repeated the offending phrases one by one, and Sir John explained each as it was introduced. His expositions were simple and straightforward. At every opportunity he declared that the King was in no way implicated in his accusations and denunciations. He showed that the terms he had used did not exceed the task which had been set him by the Commons. But Carleton had also remarked 'that for the manner of his speech, it was conceived, it was too tart and harsh to the person of the Duke' and that 'in the matter' Eliot had gone beyond his charge.[3] In closing Sir John replied to these statements:

'What my nature is, and what I have received from [the] Commons in that particular I am not master of it. If a tone or sound might prejudice,

---

[1] *C.J.*, I, 861. Also Grosvenor and Whitelocke.

[2] Grosvenor. This speech is found also in Whitelocke, *C.J.*, I, 861, E.P.N. 1626(2). The speech in Eliot's notes differs considerably from that in *C.J.* Other printed versions of the speech are in Rushworth, I, 362–63 and Cobbett, *Parl. Hist.*, II, 123–24. MS. separates of the speech are to be found in Harl. MS. 160, ff. 79–88, and Add. MS. 22474, ff. 146–53.

[3] *C.J.*, I, 861.

it might do so now. Seldom here have I felt passion; and there I spoke not passion but so far to give life to that I was commanded. So this I hope pardonable, a fault of nature and not of me.'

As to the 'matter' Eliot felt he could say nothing until it had been shown specifically that he had gone beyond the charges against the Duke in his conclusion. 'If any please to charge me I shall give the best answer I can.'

With this weak explanation of his oratorical temperament Eliot left his case in the hands of his colleagues. Of his own free-will he withdrew from the chamber while the Commons unanimously resolved that Sir John Eliot had not exceeded his commission from the House of Commons at the conference with the Lords on the impeachment of the Duke of Buckingham. The same resolution was passed for Digges, who had not yet been officially cleared by the House of having exceeded his commission.[1]

In reading private and official accounts of the eight days of business devoted essentially to these two men, the impression is left that Digges was more popular than Eliot in the House of Commons. The Commons seem to have displayed greater dismay at the imprisonment of Sir Dudley than at that of Sir John. This impression remains even after discounting the anger aroused in the House by the charge against Digges and after remembering that the immediate interest in Eliot was dampened by the 'extra-judicial' charges against him. That sharp-tongued, loquacious idealist gifted with pre-eminent eloquence, who was still officially an officer under the Lord Admiral and was only recently an apostate from the hated ranks of the followers of the favourite, could never be loved and worshipped by the many. A few intimate friends he was sure to make,[2] but his enemies were bound to be numerous. In his own party he was admired for his ability and followed as a leader when his trumpet sounded true; but one cannot imagine the Commons cheering when he returned to their midst from the Tower. They would be happy to have the services again of so able a person, but that would be the extent of their feelings. Such is the picture of the

---

[1] *C.J.*, I, 862.

[2] Forster, *Eliot*, I, 565, quotes two letters of Bevil Grenville written on May 18 and 20, of which I could find no trace, in which he speaks with great enthusiasm of Eliot and his release from prison. This is the view of one of Eliot's closest friends and can in no way be said to illustrate the feeling of the House. Grenville sat for Launceston in this Parliament.

relation of Sir John Eliot to the House of Commons at this point, and it will not be greatly changed in the end.

Sir Dudley Digges, on the other hand, was intensely admired, if not actually loved, by the majority of the Commons. Nearly ten years the senior of Sir John, he had experienced more years of service in the House of Commons.[1] The knowledge and training he had obtained early in his manhood from association with trading companies and from connections with several minor diplomatic missions[2] all helped to give him a saner and more practical view of life than Eliot had hitherto acquired. In the House of Commons Sir Dudley had gained political insight which made him invaluable to any cause that was stirring. Imbued with common sense he had a greater opportunity of gaining success in life than Eliot blind to the growing conflict of his idols. But in this second Parliament of Charles I with its definite task to accomplish there was no better combination to produce success than this idealistic orator and that practical politician. In the arena of the House of Commons they were triumphant, but against a government controlled by Charles and Buckingham they were bound to fail.

One of the results of the arrest of the two members on May 11, as we have seen, was the preparation of a remonstrance by the Commons on this violation of their liberties.[3] That document was put in the hands of a sub-committee to which it had been referred by a committee of the whole. But on May 22 it was proposed in committee that the remonstrance be changed into a bill vindicating the liberties and privileges of Parliament. Nut until June 3 was it definitely decided to substitute a bill for the remonstrance. Many difficulties arose in making the transition from one form to another, especially as certain parts of the bill were to be referred to a conference with the Lords. Such was the confused situation on June 5 when Sir John Eliot entered the debate on this subject for the first time. Even though his interest in the remonstrance and bill would normally have been greater than that of most members, Eliot presumably had felt that silence was the best policy because he was directly involved. Now his interference in a discussion in committee of the whole was tactical. He wished to help remove the confusion the members were in over the form of their measure. His intrusion had nothing to do with the matter of the bill. His suggestion was accepted and helped to clear the atmosphere. On June 13 the bill on the

---

[1] He was a member of every Parliament from 1610 through 1628–9.
[2] D.N.B.   [3] See above, p. 140.

liberties and privileges of Parliament was read a second time and committed. But because of the imminent dissolution of Parliament it got no further.[1]

4. THE FINAL ATTACK ON BUCKINGHAM

On that June 5 when Eliot gave a helping hand, another subject of even greater interest to him was proposed. This was a declaration[2] against the Duke of Buckingham. 'That man' had been untouched by King or Lords. The request of the Commons for his imprisonment had been ignored by the upper House. No action had been taken by the peers on the accusations made against him. The Duke himself had not even replied to the charges of the Commons.[3] To make matters worse, late in May the University of Cambridge decided to choose a man under threat of impeachment as its Chancellor.[4] A storm raged in the House of Commons. Little wonder the members decided upon a public denunciation and request for removal of the man they hated so bitterly. In debating the declaration in committee of the whole on June 6 Walter Long berated the Duke and declared that he prevented good men from advising the King who received only 'the poisonous information of those vipers that do us so much harm'.[5] Such language Sir Richard Weston, the Chancellor of the Exchequer, took as a personal insult and lashed out against his too bitter colleague. Here Eliot intervened to soothe the angry official. He said that he did not believe that the gentleman meant 'to lay any aspersions upon the King's good officers'. Too many bad men had secured positions of influence around the King through the power of the Duke. Against those, Sir John believed, the attack was directed. But 'there are many, and that honourable gentleman for one, that have done good offices, but their good deeds excuse not others' faults', he declared.[6] With such language Weston was appeased and the debate on the declaration continued. After various heads of the document had been proposed, it was decided to entrust them to a sub-committee as the basis for a denunciation of the favourite and the policy of the government in the immediate past.

[1] *J.M.H.*, IV, 377; Grosvenor; Whitlocke; *C.J.*, I, 870.
[2] Also called a remonstrance.
[3] For the Lords' treatment of the charges against the Duke see *L.J.*, III, 630, 650, 652.
[4] Gardiner, VI, 115–6.
[5] Whitelocke.   [6] *Ibid.*

Words of this new attack quickly reached the ears of Buckingham and helped to induce him to take action. Exuding confidence he presented to the Lords on June 8 his defence against the charges of the Commons.[1] At the same time the King realized how serious this declaration against his favourite was. Having failed to prove him guilty before the Lords, the Commons were now trying with the help of public opinion to force King Charles to dismiss the Duke. What the King must do was to obtain his subsidies as quickly as possible and then dissolve Parliament before the declaration could be presented to him. With this as his policy Charles sent a letter to the Speaker of the House on Friday, June 9, in which he asked that the subsidy bill be passed immediately.[2] After a brief debate the Commons decided to take the King's letter into consideration on Monday, the 12th. Earlier on that Friday, Eliot, having heard of the Duke's reply to the charges of the Commons, desired that a copy of it be requested of the Lords so that it could be answered by the lower House. The proposal was accepted and Sir Humphrey May, Chancellor of the Duchy of Lancaster, despatched to the Lords.[3]

In the debate on the declaration against the Duke in committee of the whole on June 10 Eliot is recorded to have spoken only once.[4] He denounced the practice of disposing of royal lands in the form of bounties. Nothing was settled, however, and the discussion was interrupted by a message from the Lords in which they declared themselves ready to present to the Commons Buckingham's reply to the accusations against him. This document, containing the Duke's request that the Commons give a speedy answer, was then read in the House and referred to the committee of twelve.

As had been planned, there developed on Monday, June 12, a long debate in committee of the whole on the King's subsidy letter. Many of the speakers supported the request of Charles, but others wanted the Duke tried before supply was voted. What they really desired was his dismissal, either by means of a trial or as a result of the action of the King on their declaration. Towards the end of the debate Eliot expressed his opinion and displayed his naïve, unflagging faith in the King.[5] He said he believed there was not the slightest intention 'of any diversion from the course of justice which is already taken for the Duke's trial'. He agreed that there seemed to be some hesitation among

---

[1] L.J., III, 655–63. Gardiner, VI, 116. Rushworth, I, 376–90.
[2] C.J., I, 869.   [3] Whitelocke. Also Grosvenor.   [4] *Ibid.*   [5] Whitelocke.

the Lords. But he attributed this in part to the report he had heard that the attack on Buckingham was based on 'private spleen or malice'. That was quite untrue, for he reminded the Commons that the denunciation of the Duke had begun in the Oxford session of the previous Parliament by men who were absent now. All they wanted was justice. The King owed them that. And he was sure they would receive it in time. Sir John believed 'that the King in his honour cannot forbear the protection of one so near him. In this we but desire that he may come to his trial'. He continued by illustrating his argument with a precedent from the reign of Henry IV when that King dismissed his minister who had been impeached by Parliament. 'This much I am confident we shall have of our King', he asserted. 'This makes the difficulty with me, that if we give our money now we cannot hope it shall be converted to those ends which we intend', because Buckingham is still in power, he might have added in closing. A little later in the debate he said again: 'I am confident that upon our declaration the King will be pleased to respect the intent of these counsels, truly understanding both the Duke and us'.[1] When Sir Humphrey May warned the Commons that a persistence in the declaration might produce a conclusion of their counsels, Eliot replied immediately that 'where we are not guilty we need not fear. I am confident of the goodness of our Sovereign and desire no more such arguments may be made as conclusion of counsels'.[2] Little did he know of the man in whom he had such confidence! And genuine confidence it was. He was not bluffing. In spite of what we may think, he had not discovered the true feelings of Charles for Buckingham. Sir John Eliot was not alone in his faith in his Sovereign, but he voiced his belief more earnestly and insistently than anyone else. Such implicit trust was not based on the mantle of Divine Right with which James I habitually had clothed himself. Its roots lay deep in the traditions of English kingship and were immeasurably strengthened by the Tudors, particularly by their great Queen. Now, just before the crash this faith in the Sovereign was stronger than ever among many Englishmen, especially in a man like Eliot imbued with a loyalty based on custom and precedent.

Though Charles appeared to have many vocal supporters in this debate, he did not have a majority of the votes. It was decided in committee and then in the House that the declaration against Buckingham

---

[1] Whitelocke.   [2] *Ibid.*

should take precedence over the bill on supply.[1] In that declaration an answer to the King's letter requesting funds was to be inserted.

The debate on the heads of the declaration was continued on June 13. When Richard Spencer suggested that the sequestration of the Duke of Buckingham be requested, Eliot displayed moderation and absence of vindictiveness by insisting that they only wanted justice and desired merely that 'he may be removed from [the] administration of affairs of state'. And so it was decided. On Wednesday, the 14th, the declaration was completed, engrossed, and formally read to the House. After some discussion as to how it was to be presented to the King, it was resolved to request a presentation by the Speaker and the whole House.[2]

But Charles had no intention of letting the Commons cap this session with such a climax. He realized at last the futility of expecting subsidies from Parliament and at the same time keeping the Duke of Buckingham at his side. Either one or the other had to be sacrificed, and he chose to give up the money. But before the Commons were summoned to the upper chamber on June 15 to hear the commission of dissolution, Sir John Eliot closed proceedings in the lower House with a speech exuding love for his Sovereign.[3] He said he thought it was unnecessary to remind them 'with what affection, with what hearts' they had come to this Parliament. They had had many interruptions which had caused delays. It was to be regretted that they had to sit so long. In fact, their expenses amounted close to a subsidy, Sir John asserted. But their greatest grief was 'that we should fall into dislike with his Majesty, and he be misinformed of us'. And then he moved that the House by a vote support a general acclamation 'that we retain a dutiful and loving heart and opinion towards the King, and likewise express it so in our countries'. Such enthusiasm was a bit too much for the House. Whitelocke remarked in his diary: 'Hereat many say such acclamation need not, for our hearts are full of loyalty and love and good opinion of the King, and so every man will express in his country.'

Parliament was dissolved on that Thursday in the middle of June, 1626. But King Charles still had some unfinished business to conclude in which he needed the assistance of a few of his Commons. Buckingham was not yet acquitted of the charges brought against him by the lower House. To prove his innocence to the nation the King ordered

[1] For interesting comment on this debate see *C. and T., Chas. I*, I, 111.
[2] Whitelocke; Rushworth, I, 400–6; *C.J.*, I, 871.
[3] Whitelocke.

the Court of Star Chamber to try the Duke.[1] The idea, of course, was to enact a farce on this stage in which 'justice' and the royal favourite were to play leading roles. Even members of the late House of Commons were offered a part.

On Saturday, June 17, Heath wrote a letter to the members of the former committee of twelve. He said that his Majesty had ordered him to request them not to leave town before they had had a brief conference with him at his chamber in the Inner Temple on Monday morning. When the twelve arrived they were told that the King had decided to bring the Duke of Buckingham before the Star Chamber. For the trial these gentlemen were requested to supply proof of the accusations the Commons had made against the Duke before the Lords. The members decided not to reply to the Attorney-General until they had consulted privately among themselves. That afternoon Eliot, acting for the group, wrote to Heath that they had considered his request. He was reminded that whatever they had done in the business of the Duke of Buckingham 'was done by the command of the House of Commons and by their directions'. Certain proofs had been delivered to the Lords together with the charges. 'But what other proofs the House would have used . . . we neither know nor can undertake to inform.' In other words, the accusations against the Duke were the business of the House of Commons. Therefore, they could give no further information without instructions from that body.

Charles was not satisfied with this answer, so he requested Heath to question Sir John Eliot alone on the next day. Eliot was asked for proofs and the names of witnesses who would substantiate them. In fact, Sir Robert wanted him to tell anything known to him which might be useful in the coming trial. Sir John replied that he had forgotten all the details and had not preserved any books or papers dealing with the charges. But his chief reason for refusing to give Heath any information was that 'my first knowledge and intelligence happening in Parliament, after discharge of mine own particular duties to the House, I remitted to that again wholly the memory and consideration thereof'.[2]

The King could do no more with Eliot and his colleagues. As for Buckingham, he was charged before the Star Chamber. He put in his answer. Several witnesses were examined. 'But the cause came not to a

---

[1] Rushworth, I, 413.
[2] The letters on which the episode in the two above paragraphs is based are in *Letter Book*, pp. 6–11.

judicial hearing in that court.'[1] Two years later Charles wiped the slate clean for his beloved minister.[2] Thus 'justice' had played her part.

In this Parliament Sir John Eliot had played more than a part. With bitterness and unflagging zeal he had led the attack on the government. That attack quickly centred on the Duke of Buckingham. With eloquent, fearless words Eliot pushed it harder day by day. Hour after hour he worked behind the scenes to discover all the evil he could find against his man. By the time opinion from all sides of the House had come to his support Sir John permitted the final stages of the attack to be guided by more practised parliamentary hands. And then he reached his zenith on May 10 when in his epilogue he denounced his great enemy in the strongest language at his disposal. But Eliot's imprisonment seems to have taken some of the starch out of him. His defence of himself does not have the ring of his remarks and speeches of the past weeks and months. During the last days of this Parliament we find him far less bitter against the Duke of Buckingham. What is more important, he is repeatedly speaking of his loyalty and devotion to the King. The nine days in the Tower acted like a cold shower upon Sir John Eliot. He seems to have realized that possibly King Charles did not think so well of him. Though still hostile to the Lord Admiral, he must assure his Majesty of his loyalty. Of course, he could not understand that to Charles loyalty to him meant also loyalty to the Duke of Buckingham. This man, Lord Admiral of England, knew now without a doubt who his enemy was. The vice-admiral of Devon must be made to pay.

---

[1] Rushworth, I, 413. Gardiner, VI, 124, says 'the Star Chamber gave a sentence in favour of the Duke'. This is based on Forster, *Eliot*, I, 580 (2nd edit., I, 351, not 350 as Gardiner cites). But Forster, obviously paraphrasing Rushworth without citing it, does not say 'the Star Chamber gave a sentence'. All Forster says is that 'then the thing dropped out of sight'.

[2] Rushworth, I, 626-7, gives an order of the Star Chamber dated June 16, 1628, in which King Charles ordered all the proceedings of the trial 'taken off the file that no memory thereof remain of record against him [the Duke] which may tend to his disgrace'.

CHAPTER VIII

Punishment

July, 1626, to January, 1628

WITH the energy of a fanatic Sir John Eliot had taken the offensive against the Duke of Buckingham. He had persuaded a majority of the House of Commons to support his attack. Still he had made no dent in the armour of his enemy. From the other side a brief and futile counter-attack had been launched when Eliot and Digges had been sent to the Tower. But real danger lurked for Sir John in the tactics of Sir James Bagg, especially when they were combined with the vindictive spirit of the Lord Admiral. Eliot was soon to be in dire straits. Yet he seems to have been totally unconscious of the peril he was in until it was too late.

I. ATTACK AGAINST ELIOT IS LAUNCHED

Trouble began in the spring of 1626 when Eliot was pressing hard against the Duke of Buckingham in the House of Commons. It appears that the accounts of the vice-admiral of Devon for the year 1625 were unacceptable to the Admiralty. Already early in March Bagg wrote to Buckingham that Eliot could not pay his dues.[1] On the 16th of that month Edward Nicholas, secretary to the Lord Admiral, instructed Richard Wyan, proctor of the Duke in the Court of Admiralty, 'to except generally to the whole body of Sir John Eliot's accounts' and particularly to the three hundred pounds the vice-admiral claimed was due him from Hyatt's ship. On the same day Bagg wrote a memorandum in which he made the same proposals and suggested that a commission be appointed to examine the proceedings of the vice-admiral of Devon.[2]

[1] See above, p. 111, note 2.
[2] 'Eliot and Vice-Admir.', p. 16, and S.P.D., Chas. I, XXIII, no. 7, LIV, no. 32, DXXVI,

This ship, the *Joshua*, Captain Robert Hyatt had taken from a pirate and brought into Dartmouth. Buckingham then gave the entire ship to Sir Edward Seymour. According to articles introduced into the Court of Admiralty in May on behalf of Eliot, in reply to the exceptions taken to his accounts, we learn that he valued the ship at £1,000 and claimed his moiety. At the same time in his accounts for the past year he appraised the ship at £675 10s. 10d. and claimed £337 15s. 5d. as his share. Furthermore, according to the testimony of Sir Edward Seymour given over a year later, he asserted that Eliot had demanded £300 from him for the ship. These discrepancies in the vice-admiral's claims, even what appears to be a double claim, are hard to reconcile without more evidence from both sides. At least it is obvious that Sir John wanted to make sure that he was not deprived of his rights. But the incident looked extremely bad in the eyes of Eliot's enemies. There appears to be some basis for Bagg's suggestion that action be taken 'by commission and examination'.[1]

With the dissolution of Parliament on June 15, 1626, the offensive, as far as Eliot and Buckingham were concerned, had changed sides. Now Sir John was to be hounded. On July 1 the commissioners of the Duke of Buckingham's estate wrote to Edward Nicholas that a committee composed of the right men should be appointed by the Court of Admiralty in order to bring Sir John Eliot to account. They suggested such men as Bagg, Sir Bernard Grenville, Mr Drake and Mr Kifte, and thought it would be a good idea to consult with Sir Henry Marten and let him name one or two men. Finally they asked whether Sir John Eliot might not in the meantime be sequestered from his office.[2] Real trouble was brewing for Eliot. Bagg's suggestion was indeed fruitful.

Not until August 4 did the Court of Admiralty issue a commission of inquiry into the vice-admiralty of Devon. The commissioners who were named included Bagg, Kifte, Drake, John Mohun, Sir Edward Seymour, Sir William Strode, and Sir Bernard Grenville. Most of these men were enemies of Eliot, or at least friends of Bagg. Nothing

---

no. 34. In comparing the last item with *C.S.P.D.*, *Addenda, 1625–1649*, pp. 12–3, it can be seen that it should be dated 1626 and not 1627 as in the *Calendar*. No name is attached to the memorandum. But the tone and handwriting are so much like those of Bagg that I have not hesitated to call it his criticism of Eliot's account.

[1] S.P.D., Chas. I, XXVI, no. 15, and 'Eliot and Vice-Admir.', pp. 19, 20–1, 46. No record has been found of the action of the Court of Admiralty on Eliot's account for 1625. It was probably unacceptable.

[2] S.P.D., Chas. I, XXXI, no. 2.

was said in these instructions about the sequestration of Eliot from his office. By October 2 the commission had not begun to function. The reason, according to a letter Bagg wrote to Nicholas on that day, was that an admiralty solicitor had to be attached to it before the investigation could be held. Sir James begged Nicholas to send such an official as soon as possible. None was sent for many months.[1]

But on October 25 the Privy Council requested the Lord Admiral to suspend Sir John Eliot as vice-admiral of Devon.[2] It made this request because of 'divers foul abuses and misdemeanours committed by Sir John Eliot' which brought with them 'both scandal and dishonour to the state and damage and hindrance to sundry particular persons'. Buckingham was also asked to appoint some other person, or persons, in his place who would manage and execute the vice-admiralty of Devon. The Lord Admiral doubtless lost little time in discharging this order.[3] From the scanty records available it seems that before the end of 1626 Sir John Drake and Sir James Bagg shared the duties of the vice-admiral of Devon.

Not until late in August, 1627, however, did Edward Nicholas inform Bagg that William Davyle had been sent to Devon as the solicitor 'to see the execution of the commission for the examining the abuses of the officers of the vice-admiralty of Devon'. Nicholas indicated that the King was vitally interested in bringing Eliot to account. At last the commissioners under the direction of Bagg could proceed with their long-delayed plans.[4]

Returning to 1626 mention must be made of the trouble one of the commissioners was giving. This was William Kifte, judge of the admiralty court in Devon. It seems that Kifte had not sent Bagg all the information about Eliot that had been requested. In fact, the judge appeared unimpressed by the blustering, domineering outburst of the vice-admiral of south Cornwall against him. And then just before the close of the year Kifte interfered with the administration of the vice-admiralty of Devon and ran afoul of Sir John Drake, acting in the place of Eliot. Drake asked Nicholas to dismiss this unruly judge from office.

---

[1] P.E. MSS., 'Coll. by and con. Eliot', ff. 131–38v, and S.P.D., Chas. I, XXXVII, no. 6.
[2] A.P.C. June 1626–Dec. 1626 (London, 1938), pp. 328–9.
[3] Already on July 8, Eliot has been dismissed at the order of the Lord Keeper from the commission of the peace for Cornwall. This punitive action had nothing to do with Eliot as vice-admiral but was taken because of his opposition in Parliament. H.M.C. 3rd Rept.. App., p. 282b.
[4] S.P.D., Chas. I, LXXV, no. 24.

These activities of Kifte are difficult to understand. He seemed to be pulled between his loyalty to Eliot and his desire for advancement through Buckingham. Kifte's fundamental honesty was bound to fight against the unscrupulous methods of Bagg. He could not be dismissed as judge of the Admiralty or from the commission because his presence on that body was vital if Eliot was to be condemned. In September, 1626, Kifte had mentioned in a letter to Bagg that he had knowledge of 'things', for which no examination of witnesses would be necessary. Such 'things' were against Eliot, but, as far as is known, they were never disclosed. Of course a man with such information must be retained at all costs on the commission against Sir John. In the end the judge of the Admiralty for Devon remained loyal both to Eliot and to Bagg. He functioned as a commissioner without giving any more trouble, but he does not appear to have told what he knew against Eliot.[1]

A glance must also be taken at Sir John Eliot as vice-admiral before he was displaced. During the summer and autumn of 1626 his enemies took every opportunity at their disposal to harry him and interfere with his duties. There was the *Fortune* of Hamburg with her valuable cargo of pickled oranges and lemons from Brazil. Was she a prize of war for some Welshmen who had captured her as the Privy Council held, or should she and her cargo be restored to her owners as Eliot desired? Before the Court of Admiralty could settle the case Buckingham sent John Drake, senior, to Barnstaple to investigate and report. Though he found most everybody on the side of Eliot he sent the Duke a thoroughly unfavourable report on the actions taken by Sir John. In the end the Court of Admiralty gave a decision which technically supported the policy Eliot had followed. But by that time he was no longer functioning as vice-admiral.[2]

There was also the incident of the derelict French ship laden with fish which Capt. Jelly brought into Plymouth in September, 1626. Eliot bought the ship and her cargo from Jelly, while Bagg insisted to Buckingham, Nicholas, and Marten that the ship should have been seized. To the Duke he wrote: 'I hold it convenient your Grace should in all things express your dislike of that ungrateful villain Eliot'. He

[1] For this paragraph see S.P.D., Chas. I., XXXVII, no. 6, I, II; no. 92; XLVII, no. 50. C.S.P.D., *1627–1628*, p. 375.

[2] S.P.D., Chas. I, XXXVI, no. 118; XXXVII, nos. 78, 79; XXXVIII, no. 52; LXXXIII, no. 44; LXXXVI, no. 79; LXXXVII, no. 28; *A.P.C. 1625–1626*, pp. 478–9.

used similar language to Nicholas; and he asked Marten for a commission for himself and two others to seize the ship until further order. No record has survived as to whether Bagg obtained his commission for Jelly and his derelict. But the affair illustrates how Sir James was relentlessly hounding the vice-admiral of Devon.[1]

Sir James Bagg was doing everything in his power to put Eliot in as unfavourable a light as possible. He knew that a blackened, backward vice-admiral of Devon would help his commission of inquiry immeasurably in obtaining evidence against him. Bagg, it seems, made himself believe that Eliot was thoroughly dishonest. Therefore, he was justified in using any means at his disposal in uncovering and punishing his rival's baseness. From their earliest contact as admiralty officials the vice-admiral of south Cornwall must have disliked his brother officer in Devon. Sir James believed solely in his own advancement, which he hoped to obtain by following blindly the star of Buckingham. The good of the nation found no place in his scheme of life. With Eliot, on the other hand, his own fortunes were closely coupled to that ideal which Bagg studiously ignored. In consequence there was bound to be trouble between the two whenever their paths crossed. It was unfortunate for Eliot that his unscrupulous rival was always eager to defame him and cause his undoing, while Sir John, fighting a far greater enemy, merely looked with contempt upon Bagg until it was too late.

It is to be regretted that Sir John Eliot's side of the incidents of the summer and autumn of 1626 cannot be told. No letters or records of this period have survived, save his official vice-admiralty account for 1626 which is dated October 1 of that year.[2] Unfortunately this document throws no light on the controversies of the period. It contains no items which could be applied to the *Fortune*, to Jelly's derelict, or to any other incident that had caused trouble. It discloses no important seizures or expenditures. Eliot must, indeed, have been over careful in compiling this account. The testimony of Eliot's enemies, therefore, has to serve for both sides. Fortunately for him it is so full of holes at times and the evidence against him is so very weak that it is easy to see he was not nearly as culpable as he was pictured. Regardless of the justice of his case Sir John was bound to lose, for the Duke was as anxious as Bagg to procure his disgrace and punishment.

Between the time of Eliot's sequestration from his vice-admiralty

[1] S.P.D., Chas. I, XXXVI, nos. 37, 38.
[2] 'Eliot and Vice-Admir.', pp. 24–6.

and the investigation conducted against him by the commissioners, Sir James spied on him and reported to the Lord Admiral all the evil against him he could discover. On April 20, 1627, Bagg wrote to Buckingham that the Earl of Warwick with Sir Francis Stewart and Sir Michael Gayre, his vice-admiral and rear-admiral, had just arrived in Plymouth.[1] As soon as Warwick put foot on shore his invited familiars were 'that pattern of ingratitude Eliot', 'malicious' Coryton,[2] and a man no more true to the Duke, Sir Ferdinando Gorges. Six days later Bagg wrote again to the Duke that 'the Earl of Warwick and his friend Eliot are still together and still walk in the way they entered'.[3] Warwick was one of the greatest privateers of the age and by this time openly hostile to Buckingham.[4] Consequently, his friendship with Eliot and Coryton is not the least surprising. Gorges, that pioneer in New England colonization, was not on good terms with the Lord Admiral after refusing in 1625 to follow Pennington into the service of France and calmly sailing his ship, the seventh of the merchantmen, back to England.[5] Little wonder that Bagg had no love for these two men.

2. THE 'FORCED' LOAN

By the spring of 1627 Sir James had been presented with another reason, totally divorced from Admiralty business, for decrying Sir John Eliot and his friends. This was the refusal of many Englishmen to lend money to their King.

When by September, 1626, Charles discovered that the benevolence he had asked his rich subjects to pay was producing little money, he listened to a suggestion possibly made by Sir Allen Apsley, friend and co-worker of Bagg.[6] That was that the four subsidies and three fifteenths Parliament had failed to vote might be raised by means of a general loan. It was decided that all taxpayers would be induced to lend

---

[1] *C.S.P.D.*, *1627–1628*, p. 143.

[2] On Sept. 22, 1626, Bagg wrote to Buckingham and asked him to displace William Coryton from the vice-wardenship of the Cornish stannaries to make room for his friend John Mohun. This was a punishment for Coryton because of his misdirected energy in the last Parliament. It meant that the Duke would have to induce the Earl of Pembroke, Lord Warden of the stannaries and no intimate of the favourite, to make the change. S.P.D., Chas. I, XXXVI, no. 37.

[3] *C.S.P.D.*, *1627–1628*, p. 150.

[4] *The Hispanic American Review*, 1930, X, 'The Earl of Warwick, A Speculator in Piracy', by W. F. Craven, pp. 400, 466–7.

[5] Gardiner, V, 394.   [6] *Ibid.*, VI, 143.

at the rate of five subsidies. When the loan commissioners began to appear in the counties they found that their demands were far from popular. Men began to refuse to pay. They said that the King was actually taxing them without consent of Parliament. The refusers were greatly strengthened when the judges declined to declare the loan legal.[1] By the spring of 1627, though much money was flowing into the coffers of the King, many prominent gentry were among the refusers.

Of course, Sir James Bagg informed the Duke in April that in Cornwall all were lending except Eliot, Coryton, Arundel, and their associates.[2] He hoped that his Majesty would make an example of them for the future. We can only imagine Eliot's bitterness when confronted with an order to 'lend'. Undoubtedly he directed this feeling against Buckingham whom he must have blamed for this latest act of tyranny.

Bagg's hope that examples would be made of these contumacious Cornishmen was hardly uttered when it was fulfilled. On April 27, a week after he had expressed his wish to the Duke, the Privy Council issued a warrant to Simon Wilmott to bring Eliot and Coryton before their Lordships. On May 23 Sir James wrote the Duke that 'Eliot and Coryton are gone to London, now or never to receive their rewards'. Five days later the two gentlemen appeared before the Council and were ordered 'to give their attendance until they shall be dismissed by their Lordships'. And by June 5 Sir John Eliot, with no legal justification whatsoever, was lodged in the Gatehouse in London where he remained for the rest of the year in spite of an attempt to confine him outside the metropolis.[3]

The Duke of Buckingham, preparing to sail on his disastrous expedition to the Isle of Rhé, must have been pleased to have Eliot behind bars before his departure. The Lord Admiral sailed for the western coast of France from Portsmouth on June 27.[4] On the next day Sir James Bagg, having wished his noble benefactor God-speed and put the finishing touches on his job as one of the victuallers of the fleet, wrote to Nicholas from Southampton.[5] In this letter he gave the Lord Admiral's secretary his master's last wishes. One was that his Grace 'is very desirous to have the refusers of the loan sent for to the Council, which will "make the western people sensible that Eliot and Coryton

---

[1] Gardiner, VI, 149.   [2] C.S.P.D., 1627–1628, p. 143.
[3] A.P.C. Jan. 1627–Aug. 1627 (London, 1938), pp. 248, 249; C.S.P.D., 1627–1628, p. 187; H.M.C. 10th Rept., App., p. 125; C. and T. Chas. I, I, 236, 239.
[4] Gardiner, VI, 171.
[5] C.S.P.D., 1627–1628, pp. 232–3.

do not lie by the heels for my Lord's sake".' This request, peculiar in itself, showed how the feud between Eliot and Buckingham had become a local, if not a national, topic of discussion. It was peculiar because Eliot and Coryton, as we have seen, had already been called before the Council late in May. That audience may not have been given enough publicity. People may have thought that the two west countrymen had been arrested because of trouble between themselves and the favourite and not because of their refusal to lend. Now Buckingham wanted it made clear that their reaction to the loan was the real reason for the loss of their liberty. The only result of the Duke's wish seems to have been an order of the Council dated two days later to the sheriff of Sussex. He was commanded to take into his custody the persons of Sir John Eliot and William Coryton and to provide each with a suitable house in his county. In other words their prison was to be changed from London to some house in the country. But the order was never executed in the case of Eliot; and though it was twice repeated for Coryton, he too remained in London.[1]

3. MEETING OF THE COMMISSION OF INQUIRY

With Eliot a prisoner because of the 'forced' loan, the time was ideal for Bagg's commission of inquiry to begin its proceedings against the vice-admiral of Devon. Of course, it could not have been a worse time from the point of view of Sir John. We have seen how the commission was finally provided with a solicitor in the person of William Davyle late in August, 1627.[2] By September Davyle was getting the commission organized; and on October 10th and 11th it held its first formal meeting at Plymouth. There were present Sir John Chudley, Sir Bernard Grenville,[3] Sir William Strode, Sir James Bagg, John Mohun, John Drake, and William Kifte. On October 23 and 24 Chudley, Grenville, Drake, Kifte and Walter Younge sat at Totnes to listen to the evidence of more witnesses. Among these was Sir Edward Seymour 'who, being a commissioner and not taking upon him the burden of

[1] *A.P.C. Jan. 1627–Aug. 1627*, pp. 295, 430, 447.
[2] See above, p. 154.
[3] Bevil Grenville, Eliot's great friend, was not at this time on good terms with his father, Sir Bernard. Sir Bernard, on his death in 1636, left neither money nor personal goods to Bevil. Mary Coate, *Cornwall in the Great Civil War and Interregnum 1642–1660* (Oxford, 1933), pp. 87–8. Roger Granville, *The History of the Granville Family*, p. 161, *passim*.

the execution of the said commission, was produced, sworn, and examined as a witness'.[1]

There appeared before the commissioners at Plymouth and Totnes thirty-two deponents. Among them were Thomas Hardwen and Richard Randall, deputy vice-admirals of Plymouth and Dartmouth, who had helped Eliot capture the pirate Nutt. The evidence presented by the witnesses or deponents can be divided into fifty incidents. As there were a number of duplications the fifty boil down to thirty-two different denunciations of the vice-admiral of Devon. In comparing the two sets of Eliot's vice-admiralty accounts, neither of which any of these witnesses had seen, with the thirty-two points presented against him, it is clear that eleven of the incidents were perfectly honest and duly recorded transactions. On the other hand eight appear to be far from honest practices. In three suspicion against Eliot exists without enough evidence for proof. And in the ten remaining cases the evidence cannot be checked far enough to warrant its being held against him. Such is an impartial analysis of all the facts obtainable on the financial side of Sir John Eliot's vice-admiralty.[2]

The eight cases against Eliot leave an unpleasant impression of him. They do not fit at all into the picture of close co-operation between Sir John and the Lord Admiral during the first two years of his vice-admiralty when all eight occurred. Near the beginning of his third year as vice-admiral, Eliot wrote to Buckingham, as we have seen,[3] and declared that his practice was to show the appraised value of goods as a basis for the owners' claims. But he gave the Lord Admiral, he said, the benefit of the actual sale value of all goods.

But why should Eliot declare himself to be honest in one way only to be dishonest in another? If he was bound to earn a few extra pounds as vice-admiral, he should have followed the customary practice, which he denounced to his chief, of basing the Lord Admiral's moiety on the assessed value of confiscated goods rather than on their sale value. But in those earlier years Eliot was as anxious as Bagg to ingratiate himself with the Duke of Buckingham. The trouble was that he was not as clever as Sir James, and fortune played him some nasty tricks. Moreover, having declared his honesty he believed that his dishonesty would be extremely difficult to trace.

[1] 'Eliot and Vice-Admir.', p. 46.
[2] For this paragraph see *ibid.*, pp. 1-48.
[3] See above, p. 63.

This is what he did. The official sale value he recorded was always a bit higher than the assessed value. But in certain instances, where he thought it would be difficult to catch him, the money he received was a good deal more than the declared sale value. And then on occasion he would fail to record in his official accounts the sale of goods, particularly where the seizures were not too prominent. Probably Sir John was no worse than most vice-admirals of his day. Had he not been caught by Bagg's commissioners and had he destroyed his personal accounts Eliot's reputation as a public official would have remained impeccable to his contemporaries as well as to prying posterity.

Let us glance at a few examples of the vice-admiral's misrepresentations. Of the three most flagrant instances one shows that in confiscating sugar from pirates and selling it he kept over £300 instead of paying the sum into the Court of Admiralty for the use of the known owners of the sugar.[1] The second concerns itself with the recovery of silver bullion from freebooters and its sale in the legitimate market. Here Sir John pocketed about £85 instead of dividing it with the Lord Admiral. Finally Eliot made an undeclared profit of £38 2s. 7d. on ordnance he had seized.[2] Possibly he could have explained these and other discrepancies.

Mention must also be made of the three cases in which the impartial investigator might be suspicious of Sir John's honesty but would not be able to decide for or against him. The first of these, the case of the *Joshua*, has already been discussed. In the second it can be asked whether the sale of a ship called the *Flying Hart* produced £50, as Eliot declared, or £73, as uncertain evidence leads one to believe. And the third confronts us with the question whether the vice-admiral sold 259 quarters of rye, as he reported, or 529 quarters, as a customs house warrant supposedly stated. Confronted with these six as well as other instances, it could not have been too difficult for the commissioners to present a damning report against Sir John Eliot.

During the interval between the two meetings of the commissioners at Plymouth and Totnes the elder Drake wrote to Nicholas.[3] Addressing his letter at Ash on October 14 he told about examining the wit-

---

[1] 'Eliot and Vice-Admir.', pp. xii–iii. See also p. 1 *passim* for this and other examples cited below.

[2] According to a proclamation of July 10, 1621, 'The export of iron ordnance is prohibited'. Robert Steele, *Tudor and Stuart Proclamations, 1485–1714* (Oxford, 1910), I, no. 1314.

[3] S.P.D., Chas. I, LXXXI, no. 41.

F

nesses at Plymouth. The evidence they presented 'falls foul on the vice-admiral's part . . . so foul that if extremity be used it will go near to touch his life in my poor opinion', he wrote. Eliot had deceived the Lord Admiral, Drake declared, had taken the goods of honest men by force, had abused his authority, and had deceived men with bonds which were out of date. When Nicholas saw the particulars, Drake believed, he 'could think it impossible that any man that carries the face of an honest man should do such things. And yet', he continued, 'we have examined few or none of those things which were complained to me before'. Undoubtedly the picture he painted was much too black.

In this same letter John Drake mentioned 'a strange business' involving Eliot but in no way connected with the inquest. The Council had sent letters for billeting of troops in Devon and Cornwall. 'In the Cornish letter St. Germans, which is the town where Sir John Eliot lived,' Drake wrote, 'is exempted from taking soldiers, and no parish else, which as the Cornish gentlemen sayeth that it is one of the richest parishes in their shire, which they marvel at.' To exempt St. Germans from billeting troops, who were being levied to reinforce Buckingham's expedition to Rhé, was indeed 'a strange business'. Bagg writing to Sir John Coke at the same time confirmed this information.[1] He said it was a favour to Sir John Eliot which 'he hath gained out of some conceit to popularize himself among his western friends and faction'. Clearly Eliot, in spite of his intense hostility to the Duke of Buckingham, in spite of his refusal to pay the 'forced' loan—for which he was still lingering in the Gatehouse—still had friends on the Privy Council. In the absence of the Lord Admiral on his ill-starred expedition those friends exerted enough influence to obtain this slight favour for Sir John. Undoubtedly, his best friend on the Council was the new Lord Steward,[2] the Earl of Pembroke. He was the most likely person to have asked for the exemption of St. Germans from billeting, especially as he also was Lord Lieutenant of Cornwall. Possibly, too, Lord Conway had a soft spot in his heart for Eliot, in spite of his unswerving loyalty to his absent master, Buckingham. But to men like Bagg and his tribe, who were doing their best to compass the complete ruin of Sir John, the slightest partiality from above to their enemy produced only surprise and denunciation.

Four days after Drake wrote to Nicholas, the Duke's secretary re-

---

[1] *H.M.C. 12 Rept.*, App., Pt. I, p. 329.

[2] Raised from Lord Chamberlain to Lord Steward in August, 1626. Gardiner, VI, 133.

marked in a letter to Bagg[1] that he 'hopes now to see Mr Davyle shortly with a good despatch of that business. Mr Drake and Mr Kifte have fallen short of the expectation themselves raised'. Apparently these two gentlemen had information against Eliot which they failed to impart to the rest of the commissioners. As Drake had told Nicholas, they had examined 'few or none of those things which were complained to me before'. Such complaints against Sir John the secretary expected Drake to disclose to his fellow commissioners and was disappointed when he remained silent. In his next letter to Nicholas, John Drake revealed why there was also dissatisfaction with Kifte.[2] Writing on October 29 he said that Kifte and Staplehill, his registrar, were not examined. But they were the principal informers to him of Eliot's carriage, 'who say they will be examined above, but there is no great trust in their words'. Drake wanted them called 'by process, if they come not in voluntarily, for they can prove by their acts made in court many of those things which were proved by witnesses, which will be a good confirmation'. So Drake wanted Kifte and Staplehill to be forced to tell what they knew against Eliot, while he refused to volunteer any information they had given him. It looks as though a few of the commissioners were not completely devoid of loyalty to Sir John Eliot, or else they feared that somehow he would escape their trap and lay his heavy hand on them.[3]

Though Nicholas had hoped that Davyle would complete this business soon, it was still unfinished early in December. In a letter Sir Henry Mervyn wrote to the Admiralty secretary from Plymouth on December 13[4] he said that 'William Davyle desires you will be pleased to write to Sir James Bagg to despatch him, from whom he receives naught but delays in his business and gets nothing done'. So it was Bagg who was causing the delay. Undoubtedly his numerous duties in Devon and Cornwall prevented him from helping Davyle to conclude the work of the commission against Eliot. Sir James had been eager to bring his enemy to heel. But now that damaging evidence against Sir John had been obtained, Bagg's interest immediately flagged and centred once again on his own aggrandizement. The vital consummation of the whole affair was merely a troublesome detail which should not interfere with his own important duties. Presumably Sir James Bagg

[1] *C.S.P.D., 1627–1628*, p. 396.

[2] S.P.D., Chas. I, LXXXIII, no. 24.

[3] Sir John Drake in a letter to Nicholas of Oct. 29, 1627 (*ibid.*, no. 23) discloses such a fear.

[4] S.P.D., Chas. I, LXXXVI, no. 63.

did give the Admiralty solicitor the necessary co-operation to enable him to complete his business against Eliot. Writing to Buckingham on December 20[1] about a storm of a different kind which Eliot's pen had just aroused in his breast, Sir James said that Davyle had returned to London with his commission, and that he (Bagg) believed it advisable for the Duke to issue an order concerning it before it was presented to the Court of Admiralty. What that order was to be and whether Buckingham took Bagg's advice is impossible to say. The conclusions of the commissioners against Eliot were presented to the Court of Admiralty early in January, 1628. A brief of this document, dated the middle of that month, has survived.[2]

This brief is divided into two parts, the first of which is headed: 'It appears that Sir John Eliot hath not dealt truly in his accounts with my Lord Admiral, as in these particulars.' The first two declared Eliot had defrauded his chief in the sale of iron ordnance and chests of sugar, both of which incidents have been mentioned above as proven against Sir John. The three remaining particulars were those three cases, described above, in which there were suspicions against Eliot, but where, because of insufficient evidence, proof was impossible.

The second part of the brief begins: 'It appears that Sir John Eliot hath misdemeaned himself in the execution of the office of vice-admiral in those parts.' There follow four charges with evidence drawn from the testimony of the witnesses before the commissioners. Sir John offended first 'in suffering pirates for composition to come in safety into the King's harbours and to depart again'. Next he released 'pirates whom he had committed, after he had received money or goods from them, without further prosecution or trial'. Thirdly he extorted 'sums of money from the King's subjects by threatening to imprison them and bind them over to answer above in the Admiral Court'. Finally he was charged with 'seizing goods unduly'.

Unfortunately none of the accounts of Sir John Eliot give any assistance in estimating the truth of these accusations. All four of them, however, have the ring of being practices indulged in commonly by most vice-admirals of the coast, particularly if circumstances warranted such actions. It is obvious here, as in all the charges made against him, that Eliot should have been heard in his own defence. He surely would have been able to dispel much of the cloud the commissioners had hung over

---

[1] S.P.D., Chas. I, LXXXVII, no. 11.
[2] 'Eliot and Vice-Admir.', pp. 49–51.

his head. But as far as is known he was never given the opportunity to state his position. His release from the Gatehouse about the time the Admiralty received the report of the commissioners did not change the situation. If he did reply to the charges against him, any document containing his answers has escaped the eyes of searchers. The attack against the sequestered vice-admiral of Devon seems to have faded into the air. It was forgotten by the government. The burden of many troubles was so great that Charles and Buckingham finally decided to summon another Parliament.

Sir John Eliot was never officially deprived of his vice-admiralty. Late in 1628 he had his proctor make a motion in the Court of Admiralty to have his accounts for the years 1624-5 and 1625-6 allowed and secure his dismissal on that score.[1] On November 7, 1628, his old friend, Sir Henry Marten, wrote him that the late Lord Admiral's proctor had declared that, because of the death of the Duke, no action could be taken on Eliot's request until an executor had been appointed for the estate of the deceased. At the same time Eliot sent the patent of his office to his legal friend, John Selden, to obtain his opinion on its validity. Selden replied on November 7 that the patent 'be void by the death of him that made it'.[2] Furthermore Selden believed that the patent was voided also by the fact that Eliot had failed to give an exact account of his vice-admiralty each year on the day named in the document. In other words his sequestration had made it impossible for him to render his account on Michaelmas, 1627, for the preceding year. Consequently, technicalities and not the King, Buckingham and Bagg had forced Sir John out of his vice-admiralty of Devon.

4. THE PETITION FROM THE GATEHOUSE

We have been moving ahead too fast. Sir John Eliot was left a prisoner in the Gatehouse in consequence of his refusal to pay the 'forced' loan. The actions taken against Eliot in his absence have been detailed at great length. But nothing has been said of his own activities during the seven months of his imprisonment. All Sir John could do at first was to listen to the ominous rumblings of the country against the loan and enjoy the companionship of John Hampden, Sir Oliver Luke, Sir William Armyne, Sir John Corbet, and others who were all suffering the same

---

[1] As may be seen in the letter Marten wrote to Eliot on Nov. 7, 1628. *Letter Book*, p. 27.
[2] *Ibid.*, p. 28.

fate for the same cause. Even though the common law judges were unwilling to sanction such an arbitrary act of the royal prerogative, some
of the churchmen were eager to give it their hearty support. The sermons preached, and later published, by Drs Robert Sibthorpe and
Roger Manwaring in February and July, 1627, must have been
brought to the attention of Sir John Eliot while in the Gatehouse. These
two men advocated implicit obedience to the will of the King, even
to the paying of the loan. Eliot's innate loyalty to his Sovereign must
have been put to a severe test. But he could not support the principle
of obedience when it was applied to the loan for which he could only
have blamed Buckingham. The arguments employed by the two clerics
no doubt helped to induce Sir John, aided and abetted by his fellow
prisoners, to use his pen to justify his opposition to the loan.[1]

In the form of a 'Humble Petition' to King Charles, dated November 10, 1627,[2] Sir John Eliot expressed his views on the 'forced' loan.
His arguments, once they began to filter through the land, were eagerly
accepted by that growing class of people whose representatives were to
form such a powerful opposition to the government in the Parliaments
of the next twenty years.

Eliot begins as a suppliant filled with sorrow and unhappiness at the
long displeasure of his Majesty. He is eager to display his obedience and
loyalty to the King and to prove to him that obstinacy was not responsible for his refusal to lend. And then, throwing himself at his Majesty's
feet, he presents the reasons for that refusal which his duty to religion,
to justice, and to the King himself have forced upon him.

Considering that law constitutes justice, acts as the 'impartial arbiter
of government and obedience', and forms 'the support and strength of
majesty', Eliot decided to weigh the loan in the scales of justice against
the laws of the land.

He cites five precedents to prove that taxes, loans, or benevolences
were either prohibited or were not to be levied without the consent of
Parliament. The first two, taken from the reign of Edward I, are the
well-known words from the Confirmation of the Charters of 1297[3]

[1] Gardiner, VI, 206–8.

[2] P.E. MSS., 'Coll. by and con. Eliot', ff. 165–67v. Rushworth, I, 433–5; Cobbett, *Parl.
Hist.*, II, 209–11; a pamphlet printed, London, by M.E., 1649, pp. 91–95. I have found four
copies in the *H.M.C. Repts.*, six among the mss. in the Bodleian library, and ten among
the mss. of the British Museum.

[3] William Stubbs, *Select Charters* (Oxford, 1905), p. 497. *Statutes of the Realm* (London,
1810), I, 124, 125.

and the similar language from the apocryphal statute *de Tallagio non concedendo*[1] of the same year. Turning to the reign of Edward III he finds his third example in the second statute of the fourteenth year of that King's reign according to which all taxes must originate in Parliament.[2] Fourthly he quotes from the rolls of Parliament of the twenty-fifth year of the same King in which it was stated that loans made to the King should be repaid and that in future no such loans should be requested.[3] Finally, Sir John cites the statute of the first year of Richard III's reign which abolished benevolences.[4] Having stated that in his opinion these laws were binding on posterity, particularly those of the reign of Edward I which were to be enforced by a curse and the threat of excommunication, the petitioner gives further reasons for his opposition to the loan.

In the first place Sir John declares that the instructions for raising the loan 'imported a constraint' and contained 'tacit and implied commands'. Consequently, he maintains, such instructions prevented 'that readiness and love, which in a free way would have far exceeded those demands'.

Secondly he says he felt he could not lend to the King at this time without violating the liberties of the subject, which had been carefully preserved by former kings, because this loan was being enforced by imprisonment and restraint contrary to *Magna Carta* which had been so frequently confirmed in the past. But he was confident that there never was a King who had 'a more pious disposition to preserve the just liberties of his subjects, than your sacred self'.

And then Eliot declares his belief in the promise of the King not to make this loan a precedent for his reign. He fears, however, that posterity might employ it as a precedent 'contrary to the intention and piety of your Majesty'. Therefore he is opposed to it.

In conclusion Sir John Eliot briefly summarizes his arguments and most humbly prays that his Majesty will be pleased to take them into his princely consideration. 'He is hopeful . . . that, according to your innate clemency and goodness, you will be pleased to restore him [your

---

[1] Stubbs, *Constitutional History of England* (Oxford, 1877–8), II, 142; D. Pasquet, *An Essay on the Origins of the House of Commons* (Cambridge, 1925), p. 155; Holdsworth, *Hist. of Eng. Law*, II, 301, note 3.

[2] *Statutes of the Realm*, I, 289.

[3] *Rotuli Parliamentorum* (N.D.), II, 239, 240. Gardiner, VI, 213.

[4] *Statutes of the Realm*, II, 478.

petitioner] to your favour, and his liberty; and to afford him the benefit of those laws, which in all humility he craves.'

These precedents and arguments were considered irrefutable by those of Eliot's contemporaries who believed that their Sovereign should rule with limited powers. To them the King was bound by statutory precedents whose enforcement in the past neither they nor the supporters of the Crown took the trouble to check. Charles and his followers, however, believed in the existence of such a serious emergency that the King could justly appeal to a higher law, the preservation of the nation, as the reason for demanding payment of the loan. On the other hand the refusers of the loan denied the seriousness of the emergency and insisted it was necessary only to remove the incompetent advisers of the King, particularly Buckingham, to bring the English ship of state into the smooth waters of solvency and power. That is what was in their minds; that is what they had announced so boldly in the last Parliament; but that is what Sir John Eliot now refused to say.

If he hoped to secure his release from prison by means of this petition, he knew that to cast blame upon anybody would fasten the bars even more securely around him. If, on the other hand, this petition was a justification of his and his fellow prisoners' refusal to lend and was meant as much for the eyes of the nation as for those of the King, then it exhibits the weakness of condemning government action without placing the blame for such action on the head of anybody, not even the government collectively. Eliot's petition denounces the loan on count after count. But not a hint is dropped that the Duke of Buckingham or any minister was responsible for this measure. The loan and the method of its enforcement not only violated the people's 'just and decent liberties, which to this kingdom are derived from the clemency and wisdom of [his Majesty's] progenitors' but also conflicted with *Magna Carta*, 'by so many glorious and victorious kings so many times confirmed'. It is only necessary to read between these lines to realize that Eliot was blaming King Charles for having levied the 'forced' loan. In his next sentence he almost, but not quite, removes that blame when he says: 'Being therein most confident of your Majesty, that never [a] king that reigned over us had of his own benignity and goodness a more pious disposition to preserve the just liberties of his subjects, than your sacred self'. But that phrase, 'pious disposition to preserve', has the strong implication that in spite of best intentions, his Majesty was not preserving the liberties of the subject when forcing him to lend. Eliot could not bring himself to condemn openly the man he had placed on so high a pedestal. Loyalty and possibly fear were struggling against veracity.

Charles would not be fooled by this document, and it is difficult to see how Eliot could have thought that he would be fooled. But the majority of his contemporaries hostile to the government hurriedly reading this petition might still believe in Sir John's implicit loyalty to the King and might be puzzled that the Duke of Buckingham was not openly blamed for this last villainous act.

But here seems to have been the real purpose of that petition. Sir John Eliot was asking the careful reader to be even more careful. He was sending him a message. And this is what he appears to be conveying to him: 'The King is responsible for failing to preserve our liberties; but let us by no means publicly announce it; let us try, when the opportunity presents itself, to limit the power of the King and curb the activities of the government without referring to any minister such as the Duke of Buckingham; we can accomplish all we are after by making our attack as impersonal as possible, by never suggesting that we even have the King in mind'. Such may have been the thoughts of Sir John Eliot when he composed his petition in the Gatehouse. His fellow prisoners may have helped in his composition and may even have induced him to accept this point of view which was so contrary to his loyalty to King Charles and hatred of Buckingham.

This policy of impersonal attack was to prevail in the struggle for the Petition of Right during the next session of Parliament. If our deduction is correct, the petition from the Gatehouse set the tone of that struggle, made it unnecessary for the leaders of the opposition to hold a conference before the opening of the session to discuss the form their attack should take.[1] Even if a meeting was held, and our inference is correct, there was no need to persuade Eliot. The persuading had been done in the Gatehouse several months earlier.

There was one person at least who realized that Eliot in his petition intended to place the blame for the 'forced' loan on the shoulders of the King. That was Sir James Bagg. Writing a long letter to the Duke on December 20[2] he began:

[1] See below, Chap. X.
[2] S.P.D., Chas. I, LXXXVII, no. 11. It is printed in parallel columns with Eliot's petition in Forster, *Eliot*, II, 87–93.

'I met this petition wandering amongst the subjects, directed to, or rather against, my Sovereign, not repenting, but justifying an offence, not accusing the recusant subject of disloyalty but his Majesty of injustice in the business of the late loan.'

Bagg felt that it was dangerous for such a document to be circulating among the 'many-headed people' at a time when discontent was being aroused among them by Eliot and his accomplices. Therefore, he had made it his duty to bring this petition to the attention of his Grace who was guarding the safety of the people. Sir James was afraid that it might 'rekindle that fire of discontent and murmur in those unquiet spirits' which are of Eliot's opinion. Bagg was forgetting that the 'fire of discontent' had already been rekindled by the loan and was raging among the middle and upper classes of the land. Eliot's petition was both a manifestation of this feeling and, as Bagg feared, a call to gain support against the government in every nook and cranny of the country.

After this introduction in which Sir James showed the Duke that he was in no sense being fooled by Eliot's petition, he launched into a thorough denunciation of the hypocrisy of the document. But the greater part of his letter is devoted to throwing the light of history on the precedents presented by Sir John. This entailed a study of medieval sources, he said, which forced him to encroach on time he should have spent in his Majesty's service.

Bagg turned historian displays considerable insight into the past. His spectacles, coloured by the royal prerogative, enabled him to discover as much, if not more, truth than Eliot read into the documents. His opening comment on Sir John, that 'he forgets that law without circumstances observed is no law', shows Sir James to be imbued with the sense of history. But frequently he errs in his observation of the circumstances.

For every precedent presented by Eliot, Bagg had his own interpretation. Even *Magna Carta* he saw in a different light and tried to destroy its sanctity, which exudes from Sir John's petition.

Why was Sir James Bagg writing all this history to the Duke of Buckingham? Probably he hoped that some of it might be employed by the Duke and the King in printed propaganda against Eliot's appeal. That appeal, Bagg feared, might exert a real and widespread influence. Pens might be, as they were, busy copying it in many corners of the realm. An authoritative reply might do much to counteract it. Either the King and his favourite were not impressed by the historical research of Sir James Bagg or else they were too busy with other matters to be bothered with it. No public reply to the petition of Sir John Eliot was issued.

Possibly Charles and Buckingham hoped that the ruling of the judges in the Five Knights[1] case might act as an antidote to anything that had come from the pen of one of those imprisoned for refusing to lend. But the reaction was just the opposite. Many regarded the King, or more likely his favourite, as a tyrant when five of those imprisoned gentlemen suing out their writs of *habeas corpus* were refused bail by the judges because they were being held at the special command of the King.

By the end of 1627 one is bound to ask a question. Did Charles and Buckingham realize the extent of their unpopularity among the tax-paying classes of the nation as a result of their method of governing during the past twelve months? Apparently they did not.

Actually both Crown and people were in a sad plight. Even though the 'forced' loan produced close to a quarter of a million pounds, not far below what was expected of it, the Crown could not stem the flood of its debts which the war against France and Spain was raising month by month to higher levels. In December, 1627, the government was parti-cularly troubled by its inability to provide pay for the soldiers and sailors who were being held in the south of England with the hope that they would soon be employed in another attempt to relieve Rochelle. These men were so discontented that their continual pillag-ing was liable at any time to turn into open mutiny.[2] Worse than that they were quartered in the homes of peasants and small townsmen, who were both driven to distraction by the depredations of their lodgers and turned into bitter enemies of the government because of its inability to pay them for housing these unwanted guests. All classes, high and low, were feeling the nasty prodding of Charles and Bucking-ham. And these two gentlemen instead of trying to pacify their subjects and make peace with their enemies abroad were only looking for more money. Eventually, just before the turn of the year the Duke, heedless or blind to the feeling of the country, advised the summoning of a Parliament. Charles, still tasting the 'generosity' of his late Commons, was not easily persuaded to accept this last resort. Ultimately the plead-

---

[1] On Nov. 28, 1627. See Gardiner, VI, 213–17.
[2] With the result that martial law was declared in certain parts of England.

ing of the courtiers and the inability to raise money had their effect. At the end of January, 1628, the King ordered that writs be issued for an election.[1]

In the meantime the seventy-six gentlemen confined for their refusal to pay the loan were being turned into martyrs instead of glaring examples of royal justice. On January 2, 1628, Sir John Eliot and his fellow prisoners in the Gatehouse and other places of detention were released.[2] That these men should show gratitude to their King when, two and a half months later, most of them took their seats in the House of Commons could hardly be expected.

---

[1] Gardiner, VI, 218–21, 226.
[2] Ibid., 225, A.P.C. Sept. 1627–June 1628 (London, 1940), p. 218.

CHAPTER IX

Participation in the Cornish Elections

February to March 16, 1628

THE membership of the third Parliament of Charles I, the last in which Sir John Eliot was to sit, was about to be determined at the polls. Early in February, 1628, the writs for the elections were in the counties, and the two Houses were to assemble on March 17. That gave the country nearly six weeks in which to indulge in one of the most spirited campaigns of the century. Englishmen had become thoroughly aroused over the 'forced' loan, billeting of soldiers, martial law, and arbitrary arrests. Now they had a splendid opportunity to show their resentment at such despotic acts of the government. All the 'loan martyrs' who desired to stand had little trouble in finding seats. But the 'court' had to employ more electioneering energy than ever before and found its candidates rebuffed and rejected on every hand. Many of its leaders, such as Sir Humphrey May,[1] Sir John Coke,[2] and Sir Thomas Edmonds,[3] had to rely on pocket boroughs in the unquestioned control of the party. Others crept into the House after the fight of their lives or failed to obtain seats.[4] Only a few short scenes have been flashed on the screen of history. But they are so full of colour and activity that they whet the desire for more. One of the most exciting and hard-fought battles, of which enough facts have survived to reconstruct a fairly accurate picture, was waged over the seats of the two knights of the shire for Cornwall.

Sir John Eliot and William Coryton, the two worst enemies of the 'court' in the south-west of England, decided to stand for their home county. This was an insult, a direct challenge to those Cornish gentry

[1] Returned for the borough of Leicester, Feb. 29. *O.R.*, I, 476.
[2] Returned for Cambridge University, March 11. *Ibid.*, 474.
[3] Returned for Penryn, Cornwall, March 3. *Ibid.*
[4] Edward Porritt, *The Unreformed House of Commons*, I, 388–89.

whose gods were Charles and Buckingham and whose self-appointed prophet was Sir James Bagg. The candidates of the 'country' party must have known that they would not have an easy triumph, and that the tactics to be employed against them under the direction of Bagg, the political boss of Cornwall, would be far from clean. Their own campaign, therefore, must be cleverly conducted and free from all illegal practices.

It was decided that Sir John Eliot should make a silent appeal to the electors. He should rely on his reputation made in the last Parliament, his imprisonment in the Gatehouse, and his petition from those premises, to bring in enough votes to defeat any opponent. As Sir John later declared in Parliament: 'In this election I neither sent, spake, nor sued any man. I never intended opposition'.[1] On the other hand, Coryton, with not as black a reputation in opposition as that of Eliot, was to be the active and vocal partner in this campaign. The method he employed to bring his and his colleagues' candidacy before the freeholders of the county was most effective. He sent to the clergy of all the parish churches in Cornwall his 'ticket', which he asked them to read to their congregations on one or more Sundays previous to election day.[2] It was not an impassioned appeal but a notice to the 40 shilling freeholders of the county that an election was to be held for knights of the shire on March 10 at eight o'clock in the morning at Bodmin. It requested these men to attend so that there might be a due election. Unquestionably the ministers in most churches stated that Sir John Eliot and William Coryton were standing for election. And it would be most surprising if some of the clergymen, influenced by neighbouring squires, did not urge their parishioners to vote for these candidates. Regardless of any such unsolicited support Coryton's low-pressure electioneering was bound to bring results. But the 'country' party in Cornwall also employed high-pressure methods. Bevil Grenville, who had been returned for Launceston on February 24, wrote letters to influential electors in which he extolled the merits of Eliot and Coryton. And then on election day Grenville, John Arundel of Trerise, and Charles Trevanion of Carryhayes rode into Bodmin with fifteen hundred men at their heels to overawe the oppositing candidates and their supporters.[3]

[1] Borlase, March 20, 1628.
[2] S.P.D., Chas. I, XCVI, no. 48 and I, CVI, no. 14.
[3] Bagg to Buckingham, March 17, 1628, ibid., XCVI, no. 36.

These practices, indulged in by the 'country', were necessary to counteract the thoroughly reprehensible procedure of the 'courtiers' in Cornwall. It could only have been the hand of Sir James Bagg which guided their policy. He was too busy with his own affairs to take an active part in the campaign. A committee of nine was formed to conduct the opposition against Eliot and Coryton.[1] It was composed of some of Bagg's closest friends, all strong supporters of the government, and all deputy-lieutenants or justices of the peace in the county. There were that bitter enemy of Eliot, Sir Reginald Mohun, his son John, and his son-in-law John Trelawney of Trelawney. Another Trelawney, Edward of Plymouth, distantly related to John, was a fourth member of the committee. A fifth was old Sir Bernard Grenville who had caused Eliot much trouble and now was clearly on the other side of the political fence from his son Bevil. The other four were Sir William Wray, Sir Richard Edgcombe, Walter Langdon, and Richard Trevanion of St. Goran, cousin of Charles Trevanion of Carryhayes who was campaigning for Eliot. All these men were gentry of prominence in the county, their words carried weight with the 40 shilling freeholders, especially those who were still neutral in the growing conflict of the nation.[2]

The first step taken by the committee in charge of the 'court' party's campaign in Cornwall was to hold a meeting early in February. There they constituted themselves a nominating board and chose Sir Richard Edgcumbe and John Mohun as the party candidates for the two seats of Cornwall in the House of Commons. With this procedure there was nothing wrong. But then they wrote letters to the leading gentry and freeholders of the shire. They said that they had been entrusted with the care of the county and implied that this trust had been granted them by the King. In executing their commission they had chosen Edgcumbe and Mohun to stands as knights of the shire. These were the men for whom they wanted the electors to cast their votes. In their letters the committee spoke of the action they had taken as a laudable custom of the county and openly claimed that their procedure had the approval of the King. The letters went on to denounce Eliot and Coryton as 'unquiet spirits having perverse ends, . . . such as might breed mischief to the state, and were in his Majesty's ill opinion'. They told the voters

---

[1] *C.J.*, I, 874.

[2] Vivian and Drake, *The Visitation of the County of Cornwall*, pp. 229–30. Vivian, *The Visitation of Cornwall* (Exeter, 1887), pp. 142, 275, 501, 504, 564.

of Cornwall that if the candidates of the 'country' party were chosen, it would be impossible for Cornishmen to obtain their petitions from the King. These letters the committee sent throughout the county not by its own messengers but by 'those posts that are appointed for his Majesty's special service'. Not satisfied with such tactics, the nine also wrote letters to Eliot and Coryton, in which they threatened to use all their strength against them if they did not withdraw from the election. Finally, fearing trouble on election day and probably hoping to display their own strength, Bagg's satellites ordered the captains of the trained bands to be present at the election.[1]

These high pressure methods made the serious error of dragging the King into every phase of the campaign of the 'court' party in Cornwall. Though the county was to show its strong royalist bias in the civil wars of the none too distant future, at this time its freeholders were far too independent, far too incensed at the arbitrary acts of Charles and his ministers to be browbeaten by such tactics. This is conclusively proved by the return to Parliament of Sir John Eliot and William Coryton in the election on March 10.

If the majority of the voters disapproved of such proceedings and displayed their faith in Eliot and Coryton, so did the Commons. But before investigating the actions taken by the House, it is necessary to view the squirming of Sir James Bagg after such a stinging blow to his political pride. On March 17, the day the Houses assembled, he wrote a long letter from Plymouth to the Duke of Buckingham.[2] The methods employed by the victorious candidates and their supporters he denounced and declared to be unlawful. He thought something should be done and suggested that a commission be sent to investigate the activities of the 'country' party in Cornwall. After naming the nine who had conducted the election, he made another proposal whereby his chief enemy and two of his followers might be removed from the House. Because Eliot, Grenville, and Arundel were outlaws he believed the House would not accept them as members. So he wanted a motion made to expel them for that reason. He apologized for not being at Westminster and promised to be there 'as soon as I can see the fleet off the coast or fitted'.

---

[1] C.J., I, 895, 896, and P.E. MSS., 'Coll. by and con. Eliot', ff. 169–70, which are notes on the proceedings of Sir Robert Cotton's committee of investigation appointed by the Commons.

[2] See above, p. 174, note 3.

This last accusation was probably correct; at least it was in the case of Eliot. On May 28, 1627, Sir John had been outlawed in the city of Exeter at the suit of Geoffrey Weeles for a debt of £46 7s.[1] But outlawry for debt was no longer a serious disability. As a legal process it had become a matter of form and had lost its sting on the goods, person, and character of the individual concerned.[2] Moreover, Bagg was not aware of the parliamentary precedents in favour of outlaws. In 1624 the House resolved that 'outlawry [was] no hindrance for serving in Parliament'.[3] The suggestion made by Sir James was not put into effect, for the subject of outlawry was not mentioned in this session. Bagg was kept so busy in and around Plymouth that he did not proceed towards London until early in May[4] and only took his seat in the House shortly before the middle of that month.

But Bagg on March 17 had not said enough to Buckingham about the election in Cornwall. Two days later he addressed his Grace again.[5] He described the practices indulged in by Coryton, insisted that they were illegal, and suggested that he be examined by the House. Either the Duke did not agree with his henchman's proposal or was powerless to carry it out. Certainly the Commons did not criticize Coryton for circulating his 'ticket' among the parish churches of his county. Bagg had failed completely to instigate trouble for his two archenemies.

At the time the Cornish boss laid aside his pen, his opponents drew their swords in the House of Commons and struck most effectively against the followers of Sir James. On March 20 William Coryton presented to the House letters from various deputy-lieutenants and justices of the peace in Cornwall by means of which they had tried to prevent the election of Eliot and himself as knights of the shire. Sir Robert Phelips expressed regret that this Parliament should be confronted with such practices. Though some of the men involved were related to him, he wanted them summoned to the House. Then Eliot arose and said that he wished he could maintain silence as he was involved in this incident. But he was speaking 'out of zeal to the freedom of the commonwealth'. He had not suggested himself as a candidate for knight of the shire, he asserted, 'but wished some other more able might stand for it'. Thereupon he outlined in a few sentences the activities of the 'courtiers'

[1] S.P.D., Chas. I, CXXXIX, no. 53.
[2] Holdsworth, *History of English Law*, IX, 254-5.
[3] *C.J.*, I, 714, note. See also *ibid.*, 176, for precedent of 1604.
[4] Bagg to Nicholas, May 2, *C.S.P.D., 1628-1629*, p. 99.
[5] S.P.D., Chas. I, XCVI, no. 48.

in Cornwall and desired that a committee take this matter into consideration.[1]

Eliot and Coryton might be expected to remain silent in this phase of the struggle which was about to be enacted in the House. Yet they introduced it and were in the thick of it because freedom of election in Cornwall had been seriously endangered. They knew much more about it than anybody else and therefore were the obvious leaders in this discussion. Knowing Sir John's idealism and his zeal for the rights of Englishmen one is tempted to believe in the sincerity of his reason for introducing this subject. But remembering the humiliations he and Coryton had undergone during the last two years at the hands of these same local enemies, the inclination is just as strong to say that the two men were doing all in their power to take personal revenge and were liking it.

After Sir Edward Coke had seconded Eliot's motion, a committee was named to examine the letters of the Cornish gentlemen. Most of the prominent opposition leaders, such as Coke, Phelips, Wentworth, Pym, and Selden, were on this committee. It would have been too flagrant a breach of good taste had Eliot and Coryton been among them.[2]

On the next day Coke reported from the committee. The House, acting on his report, ordered the nine Cornishmen to be summoned to attend the House of Commons by the serjeant-at-arms. When it was suggested on March 22 that the serjeant might take bail of these men, it was resolved that under no condition should he fail to produce them in person. The Commons were too aroused to compromise with men who in their eyes had indulged in very shady and dangerous practices.[3]

A month later the House received its first word from the Cornish culprits in the form of a petition. They excused themselves for not appearing before the Commons because they had been busy on the King's business, executing martial law, pressing mariners, and the like. The members were enraged at this contempt. Sir Guy Palmes, Selden, and Phelips protested strongly. Palmes maintained that they did not want to answer the law in Parliament because they were breaking the law in their county. From the point of view of the nine men it was most unfortunate that in their petition they had spoken about executing martial law. The Commons had just been denouncing such proceedings in England when no state of war existed. But it was Sir John Eliot who

---

[1] *C.J.*, I, 873; Harl. 1601; Borlase; Mass. MS.
[2] Borlase and *C.J.*, I, 873.
[3] *Ibid.*, I, 874; Borlase; Mass. MS.

gave the House the real reason for the petition from Cornwall. Yesterday, he said, he had received letters from his county in which he was told that the gentlemen had sent their petition because 'they desired protraction in hope the Parliament might break up'. This charge, Eliot asserted, he could prove. The Commons were furious. The accused were just 'stalling' with the hope that time would save them. Now the serjeant was ordered to send messengers to the south-west to bring the delinquents to Westminster within a fortnight barring all excuses.[1]

The task of the serjeant-at-arms was far from easy. These gentlemen were veritable eels.[2] Quickly they began to squirm out of the clutches of the Commons. On the same day the House had become so aroused, April 22, Sir Bernard Grenville, on the plea of his son, was spared.[3] Two days later the Commons were informed that Mr John Mohun had been created a peer and therefore could not be forced to attend the House.[4] On the next day his father, Sir Reginald, because of his age and infirmity, was excused from presenting himself.[5] And of course, Sir Richard Edgcombe, sitting for Bossiney in Cornwall was a member of the House and could be called to account at any time. That left five of the delinquents whom the serjeant's messengers had to bring to Westminster.

It was not until May 8 that the serjeant-at-arms reported to the Commons that the gentlemen who had been summoned had arrived.[6] But only four of the five were awaiting the pleasure of the House. That officer informed the Commons that Richard Trevanion had been 'sixty miles further'. Therefore he had not been able to take him into his custody. The House did not appear greatly perturbed that Trevanion had escaped and ordered the serjeant to take security from the four to attend when called.

The fate of the four plus that of Sir Richard Edgcombe was put in

[1] Mass. MS. Grosvenor (2); Borlase; *C.J.*, I, 886.

[2] Eliot knew this and wanted all sheriffs, justices, and other officers to assist the serjeant in order that he might be sure of bringing them before the House. But the Speaker assured Sir John that in a case of contempt in any other court the serjeant was 'the last process'. Grosvenor (2) and Borlase.

[3] *C.J.*, I, 886; Grosvenor (2); Borlase. None of the sources say whether it was Bevil or Sir Richard or give any reason for this clemency. Probably it was Bevil because Sir Richard's indiscreet remarks in March had imposed silence on him.

[4] Bagg's urgent pleas to Buckingham had finally brought results when on April 15 Mohun was created Baron Okehampton in Devon. G.E.C., IX, 25. *C.J.*, I, 888 and Borlase.

[5] Grosvenor (2) and *C.J.*, I, 888.

[6] *Ibid.*, 893.

the hands of a select committee headed by Sir Robert Cotton.[1] This group performed a thorough investigation of the actions of the accused. In the process it excused Edgcombe who appeared before it with an 'ingenious declaration' that seemed to satisfy.[2] Thus five of the nine had escaped without the slightest punishment. There were left Walter Langdon, Sir William Wray, and John and Edward Trelawney.

Not until May 12 did Cotton report at length from his committee and the House debate the punishment of the four Cornishmen. On the second day of this discussion when the point before the House was which of the four should be spared the most severe punishment, Christopher Sherland declared that Sir James Bagg had had a hand in this business. But Bagg replied that he was willing to sign any charge against these men which the House might determine. Bagg was indeed successful in hiding his activities from the prying eyes of the Commons. A political boss must avoid all scandal![3]

The Commons on this day, May 13, finally decided upon the punishment of the four delinquents from Cornwall. Walter Langdon and John Trelawney were to be sent to the Tower to remain at the pleasure of the House and were not to be discharged until they had acknowledge their offence. Sir William Wray and Edward Trelawney were committed to the serjeant-at-arms under the same conditions. But that was not all. A debate developed as to whether these gentlemen should make a public recognition of their offence at the next Cornish assizes. In a division the affirmative was carried by a majority of thirty-five with over four hundred members voting. A committee was appointed to compose the statement to be made in public by the four gentlemen. And in conclusion they were called to the bar to receive judgment from the Speaker.[4]

Though punished by the Commons these gentlemen did not have long to wait for their reward. To be sure, on June 3 they sent a futile petition for their release to the King. But Charles was much too concerned over the Petition of Right to pay any attention to such a trifle.

---

[1] This committee was originally named on March 20. *C.J.*, I, 873. On May 9 seventeen members were added to the committee. *Ibid.*, 894.

[2] He said that he had refused to sign the letter of Feb. 26 when it was presented to him. But he had signed the postscript to the letter, as he understood that Eliot and Coryton did not intend to stand. If they had, he said, he would gladly have supported them. Coryton in part substantiated this statement. P.E. MSS. 'Coll. by and con. Eliot', ff. 169-70.

[3] *C.J.*, I, 895-6; Grosvenor (2); Nicholas (2); Mass. MS.; Borlase.

[4] *C.J.*, I, 896-7; Grosvenor (2); Borlase; Mass. MS.

When Parliament was prorogued on June 26, Wray and Edward Trelawney were automatically released from the custody of the serjeant-at-arms. On the same day Langdon and John Trelawney were liberated from the Tower at the King's command. And then the manna began to fall. In a few days both Sir William Wray and John Trelawney were created baronets. They did not have to pay a penny for this honour. Within six months Edward Trelawney was given a gift of £200 from his Majesty. Only Walter Langdon seems to have escaped the bounty of the King. Though he had lost in the gamble of politics Sir James Bagg was able to reward his faithful followers.[1]

Sir John Eliot, on the other hand, had been riding high in the winter and spring of 1628. He was the greatest power in the south-west of England. In his country thousands of men were willing to follow him blindly. Under those circumstances he was bound to exert influence on several Cornish boroughs in their search for men to represent them in Parliament. We know of at least two such constituencies where Sir John played a vital role.

He presented two seats for St. Germans to members of his party and deprived the Bishop of Exeter of all influence in that constituency. One of those seats went to Thomas Cotton, the son of his old friend Sir Robert. The other went to Benjamin Valentine, friend and soon-to-be fellow prisoner for a great and mutual cause.[2]

Newport was another Cornish borough with which Eliot had had close relations in the past. This constituency had returned him, presumably through the influence of the Duke of Buckingham, to the last Parliament of James and to the first of Charles. Now in 1628 the control over at least one of the two seats of this borough was passing from Buckingham to Sir John Eliot.

The sixty or more voters headed by two 'vianders'[3] were no longer submitting quietly to the dictates of the court. The election for Newport in 1628 was not as simple as in the past. Too many returns were made. Of this situation the House of Commons was informed on

---

[1] S.P.D., Chas. I, CVI, no. 14; *C.S.P.D., 1628–1629*, pp. 178, 179, 180, 182, 369; G.E.C., *Complete Baronetage*, II, 41, 43. Porritt, *The Unreformed House of Commons*, I, 386–8, gives a summary of Bagg's activities at this time.

[2] *O.R.*, I, 474.

[3] Browne Willis, *Notitia Parliamentaria*, II, 162. T. H. B. Oldfield, *The Representative History of Great Britain and Ireland* (London, 1816), III, 221–2. Browne Willis says: 'Two persons called vianders are here yearly chosen at the Lord's court, who are the returning officers.'

March 22 by Sir John Eliot himself.[1] The circumstances of the election
are very confused, but the main facts can with some difficulty be
picked from Eliot's speech.

He was present on March 5 when the voters, sixty to ninety strong[2]
headed by the 'vianders', gathered to choose their representatives. They
were all anxious to have Sir John represent them again. But having
cause to believe that he would be chosen knight of the shire five days
later, he refused the offer and suggested Nicholas Trefusis of Landew,
Cornwall, as a substitute. This gentleman, a neighbour of Eliot and
nephew of Coryton,[3] had come to grief during the previous summer
by refusing to contribute to the 'forced' loan.[4]

The trouble, however, was that one of the 'vianders', probably under
the influence of the 'court' party, would not follow the lead of the other
officer backed by a majority of the voters. He made a return of his own
which contained the names of Sir John Wolstenholm and John Herne.[5]
Though the majority headed by the other 'viander' could agree on
Trefusis, they could not settle on the second candidate. Some wanted
Sir William Killigrew and others Pierce Edgcombe. It seems that a return for both these men was made even though Killigrew did not want
to be elected for Newport, as he had already been chosen for Penryn.
The situation was further complicated by the clerk of the Crown who
refused to accept the certificate returning Edgcombe and possibly that
for Killigrew also, as well as the sheriff's return of Trefusis. The return
of Wolstenholm and Herne made by the single 'viander' the clerk approved. No wonder Eliot denounced him to the Commons for such
arbitrary action.

[1] Harl. MS. 6799, f. 336v. It is dated here March 22. But Forster, *Eliot*, II, 107, note,
using the same source, misdates it March 28. None of the diaries mention any part of this
speech. But *C.J.*, 874, March 22, says: 'A motion made concerning the election at Newport Medina in Cornwall. This referred to the committee of privileges to be heard according to former orders.'

[2] My copy of Willis, *op. cit.*, contains marginal additions and corrections in the author's
hand. As regards Newport, *op. cit.*, II, 162, he has the following additional information:
'all the inhabitants of St. Stephen and in Newport elect the members, there are in both
places about 90.'

[3] The mother of Trefusis, Mary, daughter of Peter Coryton, was a sister of William
Coryton. Vivian, *The Visitation of Cornwall*, p. 567.

[4] For refusing to pay the loan Trefusis had been dismissed as one of the royal justices in
Cornwall and from the commission of the peace. But he seems to have been intimidated
into lending by a threat of being called before the Council. See *C.S.P.D.*, *1627–1628*,
pp. 231, 232–33, 255, and *Addenda, 1625–1649*, p. 224.

[5] *O.R.*, I, 474, note.

The case was referred to the committee of privileges which reported on April 14 that Trefusis and Edgcombe had been duly elected.[1] When the Commons accepted the report,[2] it assured the 'country' party of two more seats in the House. Pierce Edgcombe was the nineteen-year-old son of Sir Richard.[3] Like Bevil Grenville, Pierce did not follow in his father's political footsteps. He is said to have opposed the loan[4] and with Nicholas Trefusis can be counted in the growing following of Sir John Eliot.

That Sir John played a part in any of the other numerous Cornish elections is impossible to say. If his close friends, like Bevil Grenville or John Arundel, needed help, he was undoubtedly glad to give it. Though Bagg slipped into the House, it must have given Eliot great pleasure to learn that Sir John Drake failed to obtain a seat.[5] The elections throughout the nation gave the 'country' party an outstanding victory. Not a single prominent leader, old or new, of the party failed to obtain a seat. Sir Edward Coke, Phelips, and Seymour were back again, as was that superior, haughty Yorkshire baronet, Sir Thomas Wentworth. They were all there with plenty of rank and file behind them to outvote the 'court' on every occasion. With such a plethora of leaders it is difficult to see who was to guide the 'country' party.

[1] *C.J.*, I, 883, and Mass. MS. The latter source says that only 12 freeholders voted. Either the majority of the 60 or more showed no interest in the election, or else there were not nearly as many freeholders in Newport in 1628 as at the end of the century when Browne Willis compiled his *Notitia*. Mass. MS. also gives another confused speech by Eliot.

[2] *C.J.*, I, 883.

[3] Vivian, *The Visitation of Cornwall*, p. 142.

[4] Mary Coate, *Cornwall in the Great Civil War and Interregnum*, p. 31.

[5] Forster, *Eliot*, II, 104. He gives no source for this statement. I am unable to find any supporting evidence. It may be just another example of Forster's fertile imagination. Drake may not have stood for election.

CHAPTER X

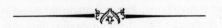

Defeat of a Bill of Rights

March 17 to May 5, 1628

I. PRELIMINARIES AND THE LEADERSHIP OF WENTWORTH

WE are told that four days before King Charles opened his third Parliament leaders of the 'country' party met at the house of Sir Robert Cotton. There they discussed the question of reviving the impeachment of the Duke of Buckingham. Sir John Eliot, in favour of renewing the attack, was overruled by the majority. It was decided to subordinate all grievances to safeguarding the liberties of the people which had been so flagrantly violated during the past twelve months. Such is the story related by Forster which he has based on a paper he allegedly found at Port Eliot.[1]

Unfortunately this paper is no longer in existence, or, what is as likely, never existed. The incident may be the brain child of that ingenious biographer of Eliot.[2] There are signs, of course, which would lead one to suppose that some sort of a meeting of the leaders of the opposition was held about this time. Why was not a word spoken against Buckingham in the Commons until the King on June 2 had given his first answer to the Petition of Right? Why, in explanation of his speech on June 3 in which he denounced the past policy of the government from every angle as a preliminary to a new attack on the Duke,

---

[1] *Eliot*, II, 114–5, and accepted by Gardiner, VI, 230–1.

[2] Forster does not quote a word from this paper. He is not certain as to how many were present at the meeting. Neither at Port Eliot nor among Forster's own mss. in the Dyce-Forster collection at South Kensington does a paper of this type exist. Forster prepared the Eliot papers for binding, as is seen in *Neg. Post.*, I, Supp., 129. I have found that a number of papers he says he saw at Port Eliot no longer are there. Either Forster's memory played him tricks, he appropriated the papers, or they were taken or lost by the binder. As Forster has, on several occasions, brought into existence marginal notes and other written statements on Eliot papers which never were there, is is possible that his brain, while writing his book away from Port Eliot, fabricated entire records which actually never existed.

did Eliot imply that he had an agreement with certain members to introduce this topic of widespread grievances only when the suitable opportunity appeared?[1] Such evidence would lead one to believe that Eliot, Wentworth, Coke, Phelips, and others had met prior to the opening of this Parliament and had decided on a general plan of campaign. But, as we have seen, the main points of such a plan had already been indicated in Sir John's petition from the Gatehouse less than six months earlier. This document showed that the glaring breaches of the law in the matter of the loan and its enforcement must be remedied. That opportunity was now at hand. If at any time Eliot had to be persuaded to sheathe temporarily his sword against his foe, that must have happened while he was composing his petition. Months before the Commons assembled, therefore, it was known to the leaders of the opposition what general plan would be followed after the Speaker had taken his chair. There probably were meetings before the opening day, possibly even one at Sir Robert Cotton's house. With broad principles defined in November, 1627, only the details must have been discussed at one or more gatherings in March, 1628. But it could hardly have been necessary to put any pressure on the author of the petition from the Gatehouse to induce him to follow the path he had so clearly indicated in his public appeal.

That the Duke's impeachment would not be renewed—at least for weeks, if not months—was known at court some time before the opening of the session. Pembroke and others, having read Eliot's petition and having conversed with some of the 'country' leaders, assured Charles, before he had decided to summon Parliament, that his favourite would not be touched when he brought the Lords and Commons back to Westminster.[2]

In opening the session on March 17 Charles addressed both Houses in firm but hardly diplomatic language. It was a speech of a severe yet kindly father to an erring son. Addressing his words more to the Commons than to the Lords he declared that he had called them together because a Parliament was the 'speediest and best way' in time of danger to obtain supply. Every man must act according to his conscience. But, he admonished them, if they should not do their duty 'in contributing what the state at this time needs', he would 'use those other means, which God hath put into my hands, to save that which

---

[1] Rushworth, I, 492; Grosvenor (2); Borlase; Mass. MS.
[2] Gardiner, VI, 226.

the follies of particular men may hazard to lose'. And in closing he cautioned: 'Take not this as a threatening, for I scorn to threaten any but my equals'. Rather it was a warning from him who has 'most care of your preservations and prosperities'.[1] Such words did not please the majority of the Commons. They now considered themselves fully the equal of the King and were in a mood to prove it to him. The desire of Charles to let bygones be bygones and the absence of vital information or concessions of any kind did not improve the feelings of the Commons. His words indeed disclosed a deep chasm, much too wide for the members of the lower House even to think of bridging, between the government and Parliament.

The next few days were devoted to the usual formalities of swearing in the members, choosing Sir John Finch as Speaker, and delivering official opening speeches. It was not until Wednesday, March 20, that the Commons got down to business. On that day the customary motion was made 'to petition his Majesty about a general fast throughout the kingdom'.[2] This proposal enabled Sir John Eliot again to display his deep religious nature. That he delivered the speech is not at all certain.[3] That he wrote it is without question.

Eliot declared that he was not opposed to a motion for a fast. But he wanted to warn the Commons, possibly even the nation, that the forms of religion were worthless unless they were imbued with a sincere religious spirit. Man might pray and fast, but unless he lived a godly life these formalities were entirely worthless. Sir John felt that the Commons, the leaders of the country, had not in the past lived up to their acts of devotion. He warned them in language worthy of Eliot at his best not to worship God by a fast and then renounce Him by irreligious acts filled with evil.

'Religion is the chief virtue of man', he declared. 'Devotion of religion, prayer and fasting, are the chief characters of devotion. Let these be corrupted in their use, the devotion is corrupt. If the devotion be once

---

[1] *Eph. Parl.*, pp. 1–2; Rushworth, I, 476–7; *L.J.*, III, 687.

[2] *C.J.*, I, 873.

[3] *Neg. Post.*, I, Supp., 171–3; P.E. MSS., 'Eliot speeches, etc.', ff. 34–5; Forster, *Eliot*, II, 117–20, where the wording is thoroughly confused. None of the parliamentary sources indicate that Eliot spoke a single word on this occasion. Sir John might easily have prepared the speech, with the full intention of using it, but actually never have had the opportunity. From the ms. of the speech, it appears to be a first, rough draft.

tainted, the religion is impure. It then becomes but an outward form of godliness denying the power'.

He was only cautioning his listeners, he said, so that if they were guilty of this type of religion they could repent. But he reminded them that repentance was not in words but in doing 'the will of our Father which is in heaven'. In closing Sir John declared that it was 'religion, not the name of religion, that must guide us'. They must not play with God 'as with the powers of men'. But in the sincerity of their souls they must do the work for which they had come.

These were noble sentiments. They may have moved his listeners, if they were actually spoken. They disclose a puritan tinge in Eliot's religious thoughts which indicates the direction his spiritual development was taking.[1] Of course his speech, delivered or not, had no effect on the petition for the fast which followed the usual course of procedure during the next few days.

The first indication that the Commons were on the warpath against the recent acts of the government came on Friday, March 21, when Sir Edward Coke in a lengthy speech introduced a bill against long and unjust imprisonment.[2] This being the first reading of the bill no debate resulted and no other controversial matters were mentioned that day. But on the next the storm broke. Robert Goodwin proposed that the House discuss the subject of supply,[3] and at the same time do something to preserve the rights and privileges of the people which had been broken. Sir Francis Seymour, who spoke next,[4] recognized the impossibility of driving such a team together. The fiery speaker denounced the recent breaches of the law and insisted that they be thoroughly aired before there was any thought of supply.

With the fighting spirit of the Commons aroused, the courtiers, Sir Thomas Edmonds and Sir Humphrey May, did their best to allay it.[5] But it was to no avail. Expressions of peace and harmony and any thought of co-operation were swept away by the stinging and overpowering language of Sir John Eliot.[6] Keeping his listeners in the dark

---

[1] Here Eliot, like the puritans of his day, was putting more stress on the spiritual side of religion and less on its forms and ceremonies.

[2] Mass. MS.; Borlase; Harl. 1601.   [3] Borlase and *Eph. Parl.*, p. 18.

[4] From here on I am following the order of speakers used by Borlase, Mass. MS., and Gardiner, VI, 233-7.

[5] Borlase; Mass. MS.; *Eph. Parl.*, p. 30.

[6] This speech has not survived at Port Eliot. Forster, *Eliot*, II, 123-7 (2nd edit. II, 8-11)

for some time as to the point of his speech, he dramatically progressed from one climax to another. Not for himself, was he speaking, not for his county, not for all the counties, but for the ancient laws and liberties of England. And then by means of a series of rhetorical questions he came to the point. They were confronted by one vital question. Did the law of the land have sufficient force to preserve the interests, the just possessions, the lands, and the goods of the people? The immediate situation showed that it did not have such power, Eliot implied. But in the past the law covered fully the points at issue. Employing a summary of the main argument in his petition from the Gatehouse he showed that according to the common law of the land, *Magna Carta*, and the many statutes confirming and explaining that great document 'no subject should be burdened with any benevolences, loans, tasks, prises or such like charges'.

Having made his point with all the oratorical ability at his command Sir John introduced the hypothetical claim that only certain laws at special times had been violated. To this he replied that if the government could at any time annul an act of Parliament under the plea of special circumstances, it could dispense with all laws whenever it pleased.

Turning readily from the evil to its causes Eliot found himself on dangerous ground. His words carried the members back into the previous session and must have aroused fear in the hearts of some of his colleagues, fear that he was about to break the agreement not to attack the Duke of Buckingham. He spoke of 'a great projector' 'who contrived the plot, and brought it to the state to be commended to the counties. I will not now name him. He is well known to you'. He was pointing so directly at the favourite that not even the deaf could have mistaken his meaning. By a hair Eliot avoided a breach of faith. Now those who were a party to the agreement could breathe more easily, provided this firebrand did not return to such a direct allusion. He led his auditors from high to low and accused the 'officers (I dare not call them justices) who in their several quarters did execute, did persuade it'. Again the object of his attack was manifest. Sir James Bagg and his kind scattered throughout the country were being given a lashing by

gives it as though it had been taken from a Port Eliot ms. Briefer versions of this speech are in Borlase; Mass. MS.; *Eph. Parl.*, p. 30; Cobbett, *Parl. Hist.*, II, 232; and half a dozen mss. in the Bodleian library, British Museum, and Public Record Office. Forster has combined this speech with another, the ms. of which exists at Port Eliot. See below, p. 189 and note 1 for second speech and reasons why it should not be combined with the first.

Eliot's tongue. Had Sir John been able to speak freely he would have said that Buckingham, Bagg and Co were the causes of the evil, were responsible for breaking the fundamental laws. He did say: 'In one we see the efficient and original cause that disposes of the work, . . . in the other the instrumental cause by which it is wrought'. In conclusion he desired that a committee be named to investigate the evil work of such men to prevent a recurrence of recent misfortunes and to preserve the liberties of the people.

That Sir John Eliot delivered a second speech on March 22, or during the next few days, with religion and the liberties of the people as its topic, is highly improbable. But that he wrote the speech, which he must have intended to deliver when the opportunity presented itself at the beginning of this Parliament, is substantiated by the surviving manuscript.[1] Whether his words were stillborn or made their appeal to the minds of his colleagues, they cannot be ignored, for they represent the opinion of Eliot at a critical time in his career.

In this speech Sir John coupled the preservation of religion with the maintenance of the liberties of the people and the prosperity of the King and state. His chief interest, to which he devoted most of his words, was the menace of Roman Catholics who were endangering religion in England. If the papists were permitted to break the law, then the laws defending the liberties of the people could be broken just as easily, and vice versa, he maintained. Not only Catholics were to be condemned but also Arminians who hindered the employment of the truly pious and religious. Working step by step he showed that the loyalty of a Catholic to the Pope would prevent him from being loyal to the King—an old Elizabethan doctrine. Thus Catholics, or even Arminians, undermined the liberties of the people and endangered the welfare of the state.

In his brief but stirring denunciation of the violation of the people's

---

[1] *Neg. Post.*, I, Sup., 164–71, and P.E. MSS., 'Eliot, speeches, etc.', ff. 36–39v. Forster, *Eliot*, II, 127–33 (2nd edit., II, 11–15), combines this speech with one Eliot actually delivered on this day. See above, p. 187, note 6. It is my contention that this speech (call it second speech) should not be combined with the first and that, though written, it was never delivered. No other parliamentary source gives any indication that Eliot ever delivered such a speech as this second one. Had the second speech been delivered as the second part of the first (as Forster contends), one of its two main themes, religion, could and would not have been ignored by Phelips (who introduced this subject) and other speakers who followed Eliot. Also the two speeches should not be considered part of one as they have different endings. Furthermore, the beginning of the second speech sounds much more like an opening than a transition from one part to another of the same speech.

liberties Sir John displayed a narrowness which, on becoming known to
his colleagues, was partially responsible for keeping him from becoming a truly national leader in 1628 and 1629. His ideal was not high
enough; it was confined within four walls; it placed the nation and the
people on a lower plane than Parliament. Having enumerated many
branches of the law he said:

'That which is more than lives, more than the lives and liberties of
thousands, than all our goods, all our interests and faculties, [is] the
life, the liberty of the Parliament, the privileges and immunities of this
House which are the bases and support of all the rest.'

Though raising Parliament to such heights Sir John could not forsake the King. In the midst of vindicating the laws and liberties of Parliament and the nation, he went out of his way to clear King Charles. In
speaking of breaches of the law he said: 'Such actions could not pass
without the knowledge of his Majesty in whose intention lives nothing
but truth and goodness'. He was confident that the virtue of the King
would not permit him willingly to sanction a violation of the law.

As Seymour had shown that the Commons could not drive the team
of finance and privileges without one getting ahead of the other, so Sir
John Eliot could not do the same with his two idols. Parliament was
already several strides ahead of the King. But he was trying hard to
keep the King abreast of Parliament. A conflict was in progress in the
mind of Eliot. As yet he refused to recognize it. In the end he must follow one or the other, King or Parliament. Which it will be can be seen
by us; but it is more than doubtful that in March, 1628, Sir John was
even conscious of the trouble in store for him. The presence of Buckingham blinded him completely to the inevitable decision he would
have to make.

Three speeches of Sir John Eliot have been discussed during three
days of this session of Parliament. We are sure that he delivered only
one of the three. What must have happened was that shortly before the
Commons assembled at Westminster or even during the first days of
the session Sir John wrote these speeches. He knew in general the subjects which would come before the House. He could even fit the opening of a speech into a discussion that was bound to take place in the
House. He felt strongly on the important issues of the day. He had
ideas. He must express them. But in the end he had the opportunity of

delivering only one of his three prepared speeches. All three show the man, where he stood in politics and religion, what he believed was the right and the wrong of the great issues of the day.

We must now return to the debate on March 22 in which Seymour and Eliot had aroused such opposition to the government that the conciliatory words of its spokesmen fell like drops of water on a roaring pyre. Even though Sir John had destroyed all hope of compromise, Sir Benjamin Rudyerd made another attempt and addressed the House with honeyed words of anguish.[1] Praising the excellence of the King he proposed, what was now impossible, to trust their Sovereign, vote him a large supply, and humbly present their grievances at his feet. Orator though Rudyerd might be, his words sounded flat after the brilliant denunciations of Eliot.

Then arose Sir Thomas Wentworth who ignored Rudyerd's plea and in the footsteps of Seymour and Eliot returned to the charge.[2] But Wentworth's pace was so firm, so straight that he stepped into leadership with the greatest of ease. Without any theorizing he went to the root of the trouble. Both King and people had been harmed by billeting of soldiers, the 'forced' loan, and illegal arrests. Who was responsible for these evils? 'Projectors', said Wentworth, 'who have extended the prerogative of the King beyond the just symmetry, which maketh a sweet harmony of the whole'. What should be the remedy? Not punishment of such men, not a discussion of their crimes by a committee, as Eliot had suggested. Sir Thomas proposed to prevent projectors or any of their kind from ever committing such evils again 'by reinforcing the ancient laws made by our ancestors; by setting such a character on them, as no licentious spirit shall dare to enter upon them'. He declared that his motion was to invigorate the old laws on four points, namely to prohibit for all time illegal imprisonment, compulsory employment abroad, forced loans, and billeting of soldiers without the assent of the householder. How this should be done, he declared, 'will be fit to determine . . . by a grand committee'. The practical Yorkshireman wasted little breath on theories of any kind. That had been done for him by the Cornish knight who took more than twice as many words as Wentworth used in his entire speech merely to disclose the evil and its causes. Sir Thomas quickly picked these up, stated then clearly, and in as few words as possible put them in their proper relationship to

[1] Rushworth, I, 501, also *Eph. Parl.*, p. 27; Borlase; Mass. MS.
[2] Rushworth, I, 500, also *Eph. Parl.*, pp. 20–21; Borlase; Mass. MS.

King, country, and people. But then he placed the emphasis on the remedy. What it should be, he clearly stated. How it should be carried out, he left to discussion in committee of the whole. On the other hand Eliot had thrown the evil and its causes into the lap of a select committee, much as Seymour had done, and expected this group to discover the remedy. On this day Sir Thomas Wentworth laid the foundation for a bill of rights which, blocked by the King, was to be turned into the Petition of Right by Sir Edward Coke.

Before that aged lawyer spoke on March 22, Sir Robert Phelips added his measured, weighty words to the rising tide of denunciation. He expostulated against the same evils as had his predecessors; 'yet one, and the main (as I conceive) hath not been touched, which is our religion'. He denounced papist and Arminian alike, but reserved his strongest language to attack an incident of arbitrary imprisonment which had barely been mentioned, the *habeas corpus* or Five Knights case. In the end Phelips ignored Wentworth's motion and proposed that a select committee be appointed to compose a petition to the King containing all their grievances. All that was necessary was to put the suggestion of Wentworth and and Phelips together and the Petition of Right could have been born weeks before Sir Edward Coke gave it corporate existence. But now he too spoke, like those who had preceded him, on the grievances of the moment. Yet on only one did he concentrate—the 'forced' loan. With wave upon wave of precedents he completely annihilated this practice and obliterated his more conciliatory opening words, that he was 'for giving, yet conditionally'.[1]

With such learning Secretary Coke (Sir John Coke) had no intention to compete. His desire was to induce the House to put supply ahead of grievances. Of course, such an attempt was futile after all the censures the Commons had been listening to that Saturday. As the morning wore on there was one more to be heard from the side of the opposition. That was Sir Dudley Digges.[2] He agreed with Secretary Coke on the need of giving supply but argued strongly for observing the laws. He placed most of his emphasis on examples of kings who had broken the law. But though he made no reference to Charles, he treated him rather roughly by insinuation. He closed with the same suggestion as had Seymour and Eliot, that a committee be appointed to take the outstanding grievances of the Commons into consideration.

[1] *Eph. Parl.*, p. 28; Rushworth, I, 501–5; Borlase; Mass. MS.
[2] *Ibid.* and Borlase.

That was the proposal of three of the 'country' leaders. Phelips, a fourth, had suggested that a committee prepare a petition to the King which would contain their grievances. And Wentworth, the fifth, had said that the Commons should discuss in committee of the whole the question of how to strengthen existing laws in order to prevent their being broken in future.

March 22, a Saturday, had indeed been a memorable day. It produced a great debate in which the government had been attacked by many, including most of the acknowledged leaders of the 'country' party. And it produced a plan to follow in carrying this attack to its goal. To be sure, there was no official announcement that Wentworth's plan had been accepted. But the debates on subsequent days showed that it had.

In this session on that Saturday Sir John Eliot had displayed ability, but not the effective kind that would produce results. Wentworth and Phelips, and later others including Sir Edward Coke, showed that they had clearer heads in understanding the problem confronting the Commons and how to solve it. Practical men, they exerted a greater influence over the Commons than did Eliot whose love of words and of ideas frequently put him out of touch with his colleagues. But because he had the gift of words and because he had ideas Sir John maintained a place of prominence, though not of outstanding leadership, in this session.

During the first three days of the new week the Commons spent much time organizing their attack. They seemed to be floundering around, not knowing what subject to tackle first. It was decided that the most important was liberty of the person. Two violations of this liberty, compulsory employment abroad and confinement to one's house, were mentioned and briefly discussed on two separate days. On Wednesday another topic was debated and a resolution passed 'That the subjects of England have such a propriety in their goods that they cannot be taken from them nor no laws to be made in any kind but by their consent in Parliament'.[1]

When it was proposed on Tuesday that the liberty of the person be discussed first, there developed a debate of considerable interest in committee of the whole. Both Digges and Pym spoke on the point and ex-

---

[1] *Eph. Parl.*, pp. 39–40; Borlase; Harl. 1601; Harl. 2313; Bodleian MS. Eng. hist. c. 203, ff. 48v–49, 55–56. The last-mentioned is a copy of the 'True Relation' and fills the gap in Mass. MS. for March 25, 26, and part of 27.

pressed the same desire, that the lawyers be heard with their records and precedents. Then Eliot arose. He apologized for introducing a new variant of the subject. Mentioning three methods of violating the liberty of the person, he laid particular stress on 'this *habeas corpus* which hath lately been so unlegal a detention, where, though great opposition was made, the judges nevertheless prevailed'. He closed with the desire 'that there be some intimation given to the King's counsel that if anything can be said either from reason or authority to come and make it known here'. This suggestion was supported by Phelips and forced a reply—rather an excuse—from the Solicitor-General, Sir Richard Shilton. He said he had been too ill to attend the case, but as it was so important he desired to consult with Heath, the Attorney-General, before making any statement. Immediately Sir Edward Coke gave the government another sample of erudition from a mind packed with legal lore by citing precedent after precedent against the use of imprisonment without showing cause. These precedents he wanted Mr Attorney to digest and declared that he was keeping other cases in reserve to use against him. It was then resolved that this subject should be 'solemnly argued on Thursday next, 9 o'clock'. That, as we shall see, was to be the beginning of a debate on this topic lasting several days before it was decided that imprisonment without showing cause was a breach of the law.[1]

During these first three days of the week the 'court' was also active in the House. On Monday, March 24, Secretary Coke again urged the Commons to consider supply before discussing grievances. On the next day he read a message from the King in which he told of the problems confronting the government but not of its actual financial needs. This time he suggested that supply and grievances go hand in hand. But his words had no effect on the Commons. Finally, on the third day Mr Secretary presented fourteen propositions[2] which were causing the

---

[1] Borlase; Harl. 1601; Bodleian MS. Eng. his. c. 203, ff. 44–48v; *Eph. Parl.*, pp. 39–40.

[2] They were: '1. To furnish with men and victuals 30 ships to guard the narrow seas and along the coasts. 2. To set out ten other ships for the relief of the town of Rochelle. 3. To set out ten other ships for the preservation of the Elbe, the Sound, and Baltic Sea. 4. To levy arms, cloth, victual, pay, and transport an army of 1,000 horse and 10,000 foot for foreign service. 5. To pay and supply £6,000 more for the service of Denmark. 6. To supply the forts [stores] of the office of ordnance. 7. To supply the stores of the navy. 8. To build 20 ships yearly for the increase of the navy. 9. To repair the forts within the land. 10. To pay the arrears of the office of ordnance. 11. To pay the arrears of the victualler's office. 12. To pay arrears of the treasurer of the navy. 13. To pay the arrears due for the freight of divers merchants' ships imployed in his Majesty's service. 14. To provide

government much financial worry. After some comment on a few of these proposals and the suggestion that the members receive copies of all of them, the debate was diverted to one of the grievances before the House. Charles was certainly making no headway against the stubborn and determined Commons.[1]

2. LIBERTIES OF THE SUBJECT AND SUPPLY

With these preliminaries concluded the House of Commons got down to business on Thursday, March 27. That business, conducted for five days in committee of the whole, was a thorough airing of the King's right to imprison without showing cause. The debate, a technical one, was in the hands of the lawyers. Men like Richard Cresswell (or Cresheld), John Selden, and Sir Edward Coke spoke at great length for the opposition, while Solicitor-General Shilton was the chief spokesman of the government.[2] With legal arguments and precedents filling the air it was not until April 1 that it was possible to pass three resolutions. The first was against commitment without cause; the second, against denial of the writ of *habeas corpus*; and the third, against refusal to bail a person thus unlawfully imprisoned.[3]

There was little opportunity for Sir John Eliot to speak in a debate dominated by the law and lawyers. But he found a way. In the midst of the second day's discussion when the rush of precedents was not too great Eliot arose to praise the slowness, temperance, and discretion which were being employed. He compared this deliberation with the emblem of Augustus, a snail creeping up a pyramid. Then he moved that the committee of the whole adjourn to the next day.[4] Why such a motion? Can his remarks be considered facetious? It is quite possible that Sir John was becoming bored and desired a change of subject so that he might have more to say. Of course his motion was completely ignored.

a magazine for victuals for land and sea-service.' Rushworth, I, 513–14. *Eph. Parl.*, p. 32, gives practically the same list.

[1] Borlase; Mass. MS.; Harl. 1601; Harl. 2313; Bodleian MS. Eng. hist. c. 203, f. 52; Rushworth, I, 505–6; Gardiner, VI, 239–40.

[2] By bringing to the House a copy of Chief Justice Anderson's book which he had in his possession Eliot was able to assist Coke in proving that Shilton was wrong in claiming that the Elizabethan Chief Justice had upheld prerogative arrest. Mass. MS. and Borlase.

[3] Rushworth, I, 513; *Eph. Parl.*, p. 32; Harl. 2313; Harl. 1601.

[4] Mass. MS. and Borlase.

A similar situation arose on the fourth day of debate. Silence fell upon the lawyers. Their reservoir of precedents was nearly empty. To refill it Eliot called upon the 'law of nature and nations' and quoted from his favourite classical authors, Cicero, Seneca, and Pliny, examples to show that rulers had no power to punish or injure. But Sir John was not really trying to add to the argument, he was not really serious. As he said: 'This I speak to entertain time now others are silent'.[1] One might call this a protest against his long silence enforced by the technical nature of the discussion. Eliot was bored. He must talk, for he was a poor listener.

Because of the prolixity of the Commons King Charles as well as Eliot was getting bored. On the morning of April 1 he sent a message through Sir John Coke urging the members to hasten supply. After Rudyerd had strengthened Coke's appeal Sir John Eliot came to their support.[2] He said they were all agreed on speedy and plentiful supply. They must remember the business in hand and complete it that morning. Then he moved that his Majesty's business be taken into consideration on the next day. The Commons, finding that the lawyers had about talked themselves out on the subject of the King's right to arrest without showing cause, immediately accepted Eliot's motion.

As a result of that motion supply became the subject of debate on Wednesday, April 2. The means to finance the fourteen propositions[3] of the government was the topic discussed in committee of the whole. The debate was long but futile with many members participating. Throughout there was an undercurrent, never clearly expressed, that little could be done for the King until he had changed his ministers. When it was obvious that no progress was being made Secretary Coke decided to change the tactics of the government. He hoped to arouse enthusiasm and financial backing for one of the propositions instead of trying to obtain supply for all of them. That one was the fourth, to raise an army of one thousand horse and ten thousand foot for foreign service. Coke spoke at length of an offensive war on the continent in which a large body of troops would be sent across the Channel; and he said as little as possible about strengthening the defences of England. Unfortunately for Mr Secretary this plan gave Sir John Eliot an opportunity made to order for him.[4]

---

[1] Borlase.   [2] *Ibid.*; Mass. MS.; Harl. 2313.
[3] See above, p. 197, note 2.
[4] Forster (*Eliot*, II, 136–40) finding among the Port Eliot mss. ('Eliot, speeches, etc.',

In a typical rhetorical reply Eliot dashed any hopes Sir John Coke may have had.[1] 'It is not ostentation or desire to be heard to speak that calls me up now', he began, 'but my necessary service to my country and this House'. What had brought him to his feet was the proposal to send an army abroad, he said. There might be some necessity for an offensive war, Sir John felt, but looking back on a recent disaster 'I tremble to think of sending more abroad'. Then he rehearsed not one but two disasters, those at Cadiz and Rhé. He told about the mistakes that had been made in those expeditions, how errors of judgment and tactics had brought nothing but disgrace and defeat. 'Consider what a case we now are in, if on the like occasion, or with the like instruments, we shall again adventure another expedition,' he declared. With the motion that we 'would decline the sending of an army and apply ourselves for defence of the coast', Eliot closed his speech.

Mr Secretary had put his eggs in the wrong basket. Sir John Eliot smashed them with the greatest of ease. The Commons now had no thought of financing an army for foreign service. Underlying the rhetoric of Sir John was the old theme of course—England's failures were caused by the Duke of Buckingham. As long as that man was at the helm, Eliot would oppose all offensive actions. In as subtle a fashion he was supported by Sir Edward Coke who prayed that God 'send his Majesty good counsel, good supply, and good employment'.[2]

In the broad picture of what the 'country' leaders were planning to do, the fourteen propositions and the one Eliot and Coke had just denounced were a diversion. Wentworth realized this and led the Commons back to the serious problem confronting them. The House had only begun to prevent the infringement of the liberties of the subject, Sir Thomas asserted, and therefore should return to that task.[3] He had no intention of diverting the subject of supply, but 'unless we be

ff. 40–41v) a speech labelled 'against supply in the beginning of a Parl' declares it was delivered on April 2, 1628, and even asserts without any warrant that it contained the 'endorsement that it had been spoken this day'. Forster proceeds to doctor the speech by omitting several passages which refer to the Parliament of 1628 (one or two escape him). Actually the speech was written by Eliot for the session of 1629 but, as frequently was the case, he found no opportunity to deliver it. Grosart in his *Neg. Post.*, II, 115–16, has printed the speech and included the passages omitted by Forster.

[1] Mass. MS. and Rushworth, I, 520. Also in Borlase; Nicholas (2); *Eph. Parl.*, p. 129; Cobbett, *Parl. Hist.*, II, 254. Eight separates of this speech have been found in the Bodleian library and British Museum.

[2] Borlase; Mass. MS.; Harl. 2313; Harl. 1601; Nicholas (2); *Eph. Parl.*, pp. 139–40; Rushworth, I, 520–21.

[3] *Ibid.*, 521; *Eph. Parl.*, p. 140; Mass. MS.; Borlase.

secured against our liberties, we cannot give', he said. He asked the committee of the whole to postpone any further debate on supply until Friday, April 4, and to return to the discussion of the people's liberties. The seventeenth-century isolationist, to whom domestic felicity was an ideal always to be sought, had spoken. To obtain that ideal a balance had to be maintained, a balance between the rights of the people and the prerogative of the King. Wentworth clearly saw that somebody, not King Charles, had weighted the scales heavily against English liberties. To rectify and prevent for the future this disparity was his predominating aim. No wonder he now insisted on turning the committee of the whole from what to him would be a fruitless discussion.

After Phelips had given a strong second to Wentworth's motion, it was resolved by the committee to postpone all further discussion of supply until April 4. As noon was at hand it was decided by the House that the afternoon should be relinquished by all committees to the committee of the whole 'for the liberty of the persons of the subjects and propriety of their goods'.[1]

That afternoon the members in committee listened to many learned invectives by the leaders of the 'country' against confinement of men to their houses, compulsory employment abroad, and billeting of soldiers. On the first point a denunciatory resolution was passed; debate on the second was to be continued the next morning; while the third was referred to a sub-committee.[2]

Eliot had nothing to say against confinement, but he used strong words in attacking employment abroad.[3] He claimed, in fact, that 'neither imprisonment of the person nor loss of goods [was] so great'. At the same time he made it clear that he did not want the Commons to rush to a conclusion on this subject. Rather, 'for the liberties already concluded (which are chief)', he said, 'let us determine how shall we right ourselves in them'. Presumably his words helped the committee to decide to continue the discussion of this subject at a later time.

By far the longest debate took place over billeting of soldiers. Virtually all the opposition leaders, including Wentworth, Phelips, Selden, and Digges, had much to say. Of course, Sir John Eliot was far from silent. Characterizing this practice as the 'greatest of grievances' he re-

---

[1] Mass. MS.; Borlase; Harl. 2313; Harl. 1601; *Eph. Parl.*, p. 140; *C.J.*, I, 878.

[2] Borlase; Mass. MS.; Harl. 2313; Harl. 1601; Rushworth, I, 522–3.

[3] Borlase; Mass. MS.; Rushworth, I, 523. The speech given in the last of these three sources differs considerably from that in the first two. Probably the words given by Rushworth were actually spoken on the next afternoon in a debate on confinement.

lated in great detail an incident[1] that had taken place near Plymouth in which soldiers began to 'make spoil' of a house belonging to a gentleman and drove him to the city. There he found no relief except to be landed in jail. In conclusion Eliot asked: 'Can this people give supply that are not masters of themselves?' Similar incidents were narrated. Crown officials, particularly deputy-lieutenants, were blamed and defended for instances of billeting. In the end it was decided to refer this vital and involved subject to a sub-committee for the purpose of adjusting the facts and theories presented.

The day closed with much said and little accomplished. Progress had been made in enabling a large number of the members to air their views on a variety of subjects. This was a sport beloved by the seventeenth-century gentlemen who sat in the House of Commons. They knew enough to denounce, and denounce most effectively, a great many policies of a government growing more autocratic every day. Of this vocal group Sir John Eliot stood head and shoulders above the rest. There was a smaller number who likewise could condemn but with their denunciation coupled remedies and correctives. These men with Sir Thomas Wentworth at their head, ably supported by Phelips and others, chafed at the time expended by destructive criticism and were eager to make cords with which to bind the hands of their government. To be sure, Eliot had a remedy—oust the Duke and all his kind. That would lead to greater and greater denunciation. And that corrective was taboo in this session. No wonder leadership fell to Wentworth. By a constructive attack on impersonal government he hoped to tie the hands of ministers and even kings. Eliot, on the other hand, had difficulty in working from the particular to the general. His mentality forced him to make his appeal more personal, though he frequently showed subtlety in his approach to an individual. At the same time he lacked the legal and practical background which gave the combination of Wentworth, Phelips and Sir Edward Coke such power in this session.

Thursday, April 3, was noteworthy for a conciliatory message from King Charles on supply and the liberties of the subject which was well liked by Eliot, Wentworth, Phelips, and others. And then as soon as several resolutions had been passed by the House on the liberty of the person, most of the afternoon was devoted to a discussion in committee of the whole on compulsory employment abroad and pressing men into the army. After the leaders, including Eliot, had had their say

[1] Mass. MS. See also Borlase; Harl. 2313; Harl. 1601.

Wentworth's motion to refer these subjects to a select committee to be framed into 'a moderate law' was passed by both the committee of the whole and the House of Commons. Here we see being fashioned one of those cords with which Sir Thomas hoped to bind the government. His plan at the moment was to have a number of laws passed each of which would make it impossible in future to violate a certain liberty of the subject.[1]

And now the Commons did not know which liberty to discuss. So at the suggestion of Sir Robert Phelips another select committee was appointed to decide what to do next under the heading of the liberty of the subject and the propriety in his goods. The following morning Sir Edward Coke reported from this last select committee that it had been unanimously decided to have a conference with the Lords on Monday about the liberty of the subject. After the report was accepted Sir John Coke presented another message from the King. Again his Majesty gently urged the granting of plentiful supply and encouraged the Commons to proceed to vindicate their liberties by bill or any other means, provided they took care 'of his honour and the public good'. This tactful persistence was hardly necessary, for the Commons had already resolved to discuss supply on that day, April 4.[2]

Soon after the debate on this subject began in committee of the whole, it became more and more confused. Some members wanted the fourteen propositions discussed before any decision was reached on supply. Others stated definite sums to be voted the King. After many had spoken and confusion was growing worse confounded Sir Thomas Wentworth cleared the air.[3] He opposed a reconsideration of the propositions of the government. He felt the Commons were not ready for them yet. He did not like these 'pressings and importunacies'. But, he said, 'let this business go by degrees, go one step for the King another for the subject'. In the end he urged the members to settle by a motion whether they should proceed with the propositions. In other words, he wanted them to decide that it was time to determine the amount of money to be voted the King. Then they could return to the liberty of the subject. In the process, he hoped, they would forget about the fourteen propositions and the foreign policy of the government.[4]

---

[1] Rushworth, I, 523–4; C.J., I, 878, 879; Mass. MS.; Borlase.

[2] Borlase; Mass. MS.; C.J., I, 879; Rushworth, I, 524; Eph. Parl., p. 44, misdated Apr. 7.

[3] Mass. MS.; Borlase; Harl. 2313; Nicholas (2).

[4] Wentworth is clearly in favour of granting supply, but not necessarily a large amount as Gardiner, VI, 250, says. By not connecting the grant of money with the propositions no

When Wentworth had spoken Eliot arose to say that now that they had taken some steps towards their liberties and some towards supply, he had had 'an affection and an opinion to retain some debate still upon the propositions. But it was not out of art and cunning to gain time, but with our fathers to hold a parliamentary way'.[1] But now, he implied, he had changed his mind and was in favour of proceeding with supply. Without saying it Sir John admitted that Wentworth's speech had influenced him.

The committee of the whole accepted Wentworth's suggestion and relegated the propositions to the distant limbo.[2] But as soon as the motion with its decision to discuss supply was passed Eliot spoke again.[3] It suddenly seemed to dawn on him what the Commons were about to do. Clearly and emphatically he advised against a hasty settlement of so vital a question as supply. He wanted to delay a decision if it was in any way possible. Monday, after a day of fasting on Saturday[4] had put them in a more thoughtful frame of mind, would be a much better day on which to discuss this all-important topic, he asserted. Sir John was obviously afraid that if the amount of the grant was settled so early in the session, the subsidy bill might be pushed through the House before the Commons had made any progress in protecting the liberties of the people.

But when Seymour, Phelips, and Sir Edward Coke all opposed further delay, the words of Eliot fell on deaf ears. Member after member arose to declare himself in favour of either five or four subsidies. Most of the leaders of the 'country', including Digges, Wentworth, and old Coke, favoured the higher figure.[5] Sir John Eliot was swept with the tide and had to state his preference. One authority[6] reports him as say-

strings would be attached to the money voted by Parliament, Wentworth felt. Obviously he did not want Parliament to support a large-scale foreign campaign by granting supply under each of the fourteen heads proposed by the government.

[1] Mass. MS. Nicholas (2) reports Eliot as saying: 'Would have us put off the further consideration of the supply till Monday, and now to enter on the propositions'. This sounds much like his second speech. See text below and note 3.

[2] Mass. MS.; Nicholas (2); Harl. 2313.

[3] Mass. MS. Practically the same meaning is to be found in the words which Nicholas (2) gives as Eliot's second speech which he makes as fifth speaker after the resolution against the propositions was passed. In other words both Mass. MS. and Nicholas (2) have Eliot make two speeches. Both Borlase and Harl. 2313 give only one speech by Eliot in which he asks that the consideration of supply be delayed until Monday.

[4] This was the day set for the general fast. C.J., I, 875, 879.

[5] Borlase; Mass. MS.; Harl. 2313; Nicholas (2).

[6] Borlase.

ing 'I would go in the highest company and give 5', while another[1] has
him say 'that he knoweth not how 4 subsidies will be levied without
soldiers; would give 4 subsidies'. Eventually it was determined that five
subsidies should be paid the King. But before the committee adjourned
for the day Wentworth directed his colleagues into a clever move.
He said that there should be no report to the House of this resolution,
'for this gift is upon assurance that the King will settle the fundamental
liberties of the subject'. He wanted a sub-committee appointed which
would compose a law that 'may assure us of our liberty of our persons
and propriety of our goods, before we report the resolution of our gift'.[2]
No record has survived to show that the committee of the whole accepted the proposal of Sir Thomas. But that is unnecessary, for the
resolution to vote five subsidies was not reported to the House until the
liberties of the subject had been vindicated.[3] Eliot must have been
greatly relieved to find the delay he so much desired made far more
effective than by any scheme his cloudy brain might have concocted.

In this proposition Sir Thomas Wentworth disclosed that he had
changed his tactics. Instead of having a separate law for each of their
liberties, as he had suggested on the previous day, he now proposed
that all their liberties be guaranteed in one statute. Possibly that morning's message from King Charles, where he had given the Commons
permission to vindicate their liberties by a bill, was responsible for this
change. But what is of greatest importance is that here we have for the
first time the appearance of Wentworth's bill of rights. That bill will
become the direct antecedent of the Petition of Right.

Having passed a more religious week-end than usual, the Commons
assembled on Monday, April 7, to be presented with two messages
from his Majesty by that dull but faithful clerk, Sir John Coke.[4] In one
message the King gave a most favourable reply to the petition against
recusants, while in the other the Commons were told how pleased his
Majesty was at their decision to vote five subsidies. Had he only known
how long these subsidies would lie secluded in committee of the whole,

[1] Nicholas (2). It must be remembered that Edward Nicholas, secretary to the Lord
Admiral, was no friend of Eliot.

[2] Nicholas (2) Harl. 2313 and Borlase give a somewhat different version of Wentworth's speech. Mass. MS. gives no speech by Wentworth, only the motion passed in
committee.

[3] Littleton did not report the resolution of the committee of the whole to vote five
subsidies until May 8. C.J., I, 894.

[4] Rushworth, I, 525–6; Mass. MS.; Borlase.

his joy at such a noble gift would have been greatly diminished. But now the Secretary was all aglow with the pleasure the King had expressed over the performance of his faithful Commons. His Majesty was so delighted with the promise of five subsidies that he had had to call his Privy Council and tell the Lords about it. Unfortunately Coke lacked discretion. In telling the House about these pleasant scenes he coupled the Duke's praise of the Commons with that of the King. Immediately the good effect of all he had said was spoiled. With his blood set to boiling on hearing the tribute of a devil coupled with that of a deity Sir John Eliot arose and caught the Speaker's eye.[1] He spoke of the pleasure and satisfaction his Majesty's gracious answer had given the Commons, of the King's goodness and of their loyalty and obedience to him. But then he declared: 'I do not like these commixtures of other names with that of his Majesty. Can any man add grace to that royal goodness of his?' After further praise of the goodness of the King, Eliot requested that 'his name only may hereafter bear and bring to us whatsoever happiness we shall receive.'

'Well spoken, Sir John Eliot!' cried the House as he took his seat.[2]

Well spoken it was from more than one point of view. It voiced exactly what the great majority of the Commons at that moment felt. And it voiced those sentiments extemporaneously in vigorous and distinguished language. As we have seen, and will continue to see, Sir John spoke a great many times; but his words did not always move his audience. It was when his thoughts were born in his heart and his words were carried on the wings of his feelings that he could bind the House with his spell. Unfortunately it had been, and would continue to be, chiefly the affections of hatred, anger, and displeasure and not those of love, pleasure, and delight which carried Sir John Eliot to oratorical heights. No doubt the circumstances of his parliamentary career and not his nature or personality built his reputation as an orator on such foundations. To be sure, Sir John enjoyed praising his Sovereign as much as attacking the favourite. But usually either his heart and soul were not in his words of praise, or else the light of understanding between himself and his listeners refused to shine when he acclaimed the King. On this day, however, commendation and condemnation were

---

[1] *Ibid.* It is not so well expressed in Mass. MS. and Harl. 2313. It is much longer but not as effective in *Eph. Parl.*, pp. 43–4, misdated April 5. This last source is the basis of the speech as found in a number of ms. separates and in Rushworth, I, 526–7.

[2] *C. and T. Chas. I*, I, 338, 339–40.

joined together in such perfect harmony of phrase that the House of Commons rose to applaud the unquestioned orator of his day.

After so stirring a beginning the rest of the day was, indeed, a tame affair. The Commons spent most of the time preparing for the conference with the Lords on the liberty of the subject to be held that afternoon.[1] Even though Wentworth tried to arouse an interest in the subject of billeting of soldiers, it was quickly reserved for debate in committee of the whole on the morrow.[2]

For the next two days, Tuesday and Wednesday, April 8 and 9, the liberties of the subject kept the Commons busy. They were particularly interested in billeting of troops. At the same time it was decided to discuss commissions for martial law.[3] Sitting in committee of the whole on the first of the two days the Commons, after a long debate, passed a resolution on billeting. It provided for a sub-committee to prepare a petition to the King on this subject.[4] Here we have more evidence that there was no agreement on how to present their grievances to the King. Resolutions, separate bills, and now petitions were all being employed. Wentworth's suggestion of a bill of rights had not been accepted as yet.

As soon as the resolution concerning a petition on billeting was passed Sir John Eliot reminded the committee that martial law needed airing badly. He declared that in the west country the commission for martial law had displaced the commissioners of oyer and terminer as well as the justices of the peace. Therefore, it was against the law.[5] But there was time only for Robert Mason to support Eliot's denunciation before proceedings were adjourned for the day.

Besides being thoroughly aroused because one of the members of the House had billeted troops without proper authorization, the Commons on this Wednesday, April 9, also became interested in adjournment over Easter. This holiday fell on the following Sunday, April 13, so it was high time that something was done about it. It was Sir Francis Seymour who moved for the Easter recess. He was immediately supported by Sir John Eliot who proposed that the recess extend from this Thursday noon until the following Thursday morning with a fine of £10 for those who were absent when the House reconvened. This proposal the House accepted by resolution.[6]

---

[1] *C.J.*, I, 880.   [2] Mass. MS.; Borlase; Harl. 2313; Harl. 1601.   [3] *C.J.*, I, 880.
[4] Borlase; Mass. MS.; Harl. 2313; Nicholas (2).   [5] *Ibid.*, also Mass. MS.
[6] Borlase and *C.J.*, I, 881.

That Thursday morning the Commons received a blow. In a message from the King transmitted by the Speaker they were requested not to adjourn over Easter but to continue their proceedings as the Lords were doing. Immediately Seymour expressed dismay at this demand and declared that it would cause great inconvenience, as many members had already left on their week's holiday. Sir Francis moved that the Privy Councillors in the House should go to his Majesty and acquaint him with the embarrassment his request was causing. There followed a discussion in which the courtiers defended the message and their opponents expressed their distress at the royal command.[1] Sir John Eliot asserted that his sorrow was so great that he could not hide it. 'The King is all goodness and all comfort to us,' Eliot asserted. But he wondered why they had been administered this lash. He thought there might be some plot behind it. The message should have been delivered on Tuesday, Eliot like others insisted. Why had the Privy Councillors said nothing about it on the previous day when they had been discussing the recess, he wondered. That time was getting short Sir John was willing to admit. And then accepting the royal command, he agreed with Rich and Coke that 'not a man of us may stir'. But he also moved that, as so many members were absent, 'there may not any motion be made of supply until Thursday next'.[2] It is not difficult to see what Sir John Eliot had in mind. He was recalling the first Parliament of the reign when, in a House thinned by fear of the plague, the Duke of Buckingham, through the mouth of Sir John Coke, had tried to push through a motion for additional supply. Now when at least a hundred members were absent[3] Eliot felt that a similar trick or plot might be tried again. He may have been right. Both May and Secretary Coke immediately took all the blame upon themselves for the failure to deliver the request sooner and asked forgiveness of the House.[4] This apology looked a bit too white. By hasty confession they were trying to conceal the black. Though no other member appeared to suspect the good faith of the government, still Eliot had put the House on its guard.[5]

With an order passed that no member was to depart without permission, the Commons found themselves on Good Friday pursuing

---

[1] Borlase; Mass. MS.; Harl. 2313; Harl. 1601; Nicholas (2); *C.J.*, I, 881.

[2] Borlase. Also Mass. MS.; Nicholas (2); Harl. 2313.

[3] *C. and T. Chas. I*, I, 343.

[4] Borlase; Mass. MS.; Nicholas (2); Harl. 2313.

[5] As Gardiner, VI, 254, says. See also Willson, *Privy Councillors in the House of Commons*, pp. 274–75, for an account of this debate.

their business as usual instead of participating in the solemnities of the pre-Easter festival. After a round of bills, remarks, and reports, the House adjourned into committee of the whole to discuss martial law. The debate was opened by Sir Edward Coke who was followed by Sir William Beecher. The latter asserted that commissions of martial law were sent at the request of gentlemen in various counties who feared the unruliness of the soldiers. Martial law was never executed where common law was in force, Beecher asserted. To this Eliot replied that such was not the case in Cornwall and Devon. 'I am sure martial law hath taken place where common law was debarred,' he said. 'If a justice of the peace offered to meddle he was menaced and threatened, as if he had passed beyond his limits.' He concluded: 'I humbly desire the latitude of these commissions may be examined. But first I would willingly know his Majesty's answer concerning these soldiers.' The debate continued at some length with half a dozen members participating until Selden moved to postpone the discussion to the coming Monday. The committee, however, decided that it should not be resumed until Tuesday morning.[1]

And then like a bolt out of the blue Sir Edward Coke, of all people, desired that the time for paying the five subsidies should be settled.[2] Sir John Strangways was giving his support to Sir Edward when Eliot interrupted him with the remark that this was not the time to discuss that subject. 'This committee sits only for martial law, therefore the motion is untimely,' he said. After being so rudely interrupted Strangways was 'bid go on'. He insisted that, as martial law had been postponed till Tuesday and the House had decided that supply and grievances should go hand in hand in committee of the whole, he be allowed to speak on the time for paying the subsidies. Again he was interrupted. This time it was Sir Walter Erle who said that had they not lost so many members because of their resolution for a recess, he would gladly support a discussion of this subject. 'But to debate it in a thin House, I can not assent.' The urge to express himself struck Eliot anew. He supported Erle's remarks by saying: 'I will not call to mind any late jealousies.' This was a pointed statement, for by jealousies he meant fears. He continued: 'I fear, should we proceed, the gift will come less freely, and it will worst of all suit with the considerations of his

---

[1] Borlase and Mass. MS.

[2] Borlase and Mass. MS. Rushworth, I, 537, attributes this speech incorrectly to Secretary Coke.

Majesty.' Nothing daunted, Strangways stuck to his guns and said: 'I see no thinness nor no empty places in the House. I desire we may go on and add advantage to all sides. Sir Edward Coke said we have many petitions, and I doubt not but this may help them on.' Coke and Strangways got their way.[1]

The preliminaries having been completed the debate continued with nearly a dozen members participating. Among them was Digges who showed that he also desired a time should be fixed for payment of the subsidies. After Secretary Coke in a long speech had urged the committee to hurry the vote of the time for payment, Sir Thomas Wentworth again displayed his common sense and presence of mind in an emergency. Grievances and supply should go hand in hand, he said. Therefore he proposed that the grant of the five subsidies and the time they were to be paid be reported from the committee of the whole to the House of Commons at the same time. A simple solution of the worries of many of the 'country' party! Upon the motion of Rich that the subsidies be paid within one year of the time they were voted, Sir John Eliot declared that he was pleased the motion to set a time for payment had originated with the Commons and not with the King, that is, with the 'country' party and not with the 'court'. But he still appeared a bit afraid that the subject of supply was being rushed. He showed no belief in the adage, 'the better the day, the better the deed', when he said: 'It is a step nearer to conclusion. Consider what day this is and how this question came.' He remembered that it was Good Friday but seems to have forgotten that Sir Edward Coke had introduced this 'question'. If only the 'country' leaders could occasionally have gathered together, exchanged views, and made plans.[2]

This whole incident is another example of Sir John Eliot's becoming greatly aroused over a minor point, gradually submitting to the will of the majority, and in the end simply cautioning against anything which might harm the main objective of the session, vindication of the liberties of the people. His exuberant temperament induced him to express his thoughts before weighting them with the balance of common sense, so often produced by Sir Thomas Wentworth. Consequently, Eliot frequently leapt before he thought and in the end found himself leaping half way back again.

[1] Borlase. Occasionally Mass. MS. supports this source.
[2] Borlase; Mass. MS.; Rushworth, I, 538. The last named source attributes the speech of Secretary Coke incorrectly to Digges.

With the passage of the motions of Wentworth and Rich and a few more remarks of no great consequence, this rather heated day was brought to a close.

Rarely a day passed now on which Charles did not send a message to his faithful Commons. Saturday, April 12, Mr Secretary Coke again announced his master's wishes and commands.[1] Their gist was that the King had become impatient while waiting for the lower House to supply him with the many thousands of pounds he so badly needed. Consequently he requested 'that without any further or unnecessary delay . . . [they were] . . . to proceed in this business'. Though he had agreed that supply and grievances should go hand in hand, yet he did not mean 'that the one should give interruption to the other', the Commons were told. Coke closed the message itself with 'he bids us therefore take heed that we force not him to make an unpleasing end of that which was so well begun'. Such words had an evil ring, so evil that Sir John Coke immediately explained that his Majesty in no way was threatening to dissolve Parliament. Possibly many members of the 'country' party accepted this explanation. But their fears were not allayed when they were told by Coke 'that notice is taken, as if this House pressed not upon the abuses of power only but upon power itself'. In other words Charles was becoming conscious of the end towards which Wentworth's campaign was leading. No wonder he instructed his Secretary to tell the Commons to keep their hands off the royal prerogative.

After such a message with such an explanation it is not surprising that the House of Commons was intensely disturbed. Some of the members were not even sure they had heard aright. Rich wanted the message written out and presented to the House again. Phelips asked that it be repeated. And so it was. Whilst its true meaning was soaking into the minds of the Commons, that amusing henchman to Elizabeth of the Palatinate, Sir Francis Nethersole, decided to break the growing tension by relating to the House the dream he had had on the previous night. He had just begun to tell about two pastures, some sheep and a ram when the Speaker interrupted him to say that the House was no place in which to tell one's dreams. But at the request of many members Nethersole continued with his dream. He might easily have intended it as an analogy to the state of the nation rather than a mere incident to divert the attention of his colleagues. Whatever its purpose,

[1] Rushworth, I, 538–39, also *Eph. Parl.*, p. 46; Borlase; Mass. MS.; Nicholas (2); Harl. 1601.

the mind of Sir John Eliot was much too preoccupied with a national crisis growing more serious day by day to be either amused or interested in Nethersole's palaver. When Sir Francis took his seat Eliot 'thanked the Speaker for interrupting the gentleman, saying it became not the gravity of that House to hear dreams told'. That was the trouble, and Nethersole knew it. Many of the Commons, of whom Sir John Eliot was a glaring example, were taking themselves much too seriously. Such a state of mind must be broken or dissipated. Otherwise grave trouble was bound to arise.[1]

After this brief interlude the House got down to business with Wentworth, as usual, taking the lead. He desired the appointment of a select committee to compose an answer to the King in which his Majesty would be told that the Commons were not wasting time and in a few days would have all their grievances completed. This proposal received general approval with Seymour, Digges, and Sir Edward Coke supporting it as well as Eliot. Sir John declared that a select committee was 'very pertinent'. He was glad that a distinction was made between the King's business and theirs. As to supply, he requested the King be informed that it would be rushed through the House as fast as their consciences would permit. He begged his Majesty not to try to push them, for such a course might tie their hands. Then by means of the analogy of the two Kentish towns which mariners must keep in view in order to avoid shipwreck, he asked that King Charles keep in mind both supply and liberties of the subject, so that he could be 'a King of freemen to his own honour and safety'. A few more suggestions having been made, it was agreed by the House to accept Wentworth's motion. A committee of ten, including its originator, Eliot, Phelips, and the two Cokes, was named and ordered to get down to work. By that afternoon a reply to his Majesty under nine heads was completed and approved by the House. The Speaker was ordered to embody it in his address to the King.[2]

During the past week the Lords and Commons had been conducting conferences dealing with the resolutions of the Commons on the liberties of the subject. Digges, Littleton, Selden, and Sir Edward Coke had been acting as the spokesmen of the lower House. By the end of the week rumours were drifting about London and Westminster that the peers were not at all impressed by the arguments of the Commons. In

[1] Borlase; Mass. MS.; Harl. 2313; *C. and T. Chas. I*, I, 344-45.
[2] Borlase; Mass. MS.; *C.J.*, I, 882.

fact, it was said that 'the Lords . . . are all settled in a contrary opinion to the lower House'.[1]

These reports were being mentioned in the House of Commons on the afternoon of April 12. Fearing that harm might come to the principles for which the majority of his colleagues were fighting, Sir John Eliot in a moment of impulse presented a plan. He wanted the Lords to reply to the resolutions of the Commons before they could be influenced any further against them by the legal advisers of the Crown. Then in a conference 'a final resolution and determination of the cause' could be made, he said. But the saner heads of Selden and Phelips saw the danger of the proposal. They spoke against such a step and assured the House that the Lords would not come to any decision before giving the Commons another hearing. After Eliot's motion was rejected, Sir Edward Coke and Littleton justified themselves and denounced the rumours. Upon this note proceedings for the week were terminated.[2]

The day after Easter Eliot was still worried that the Lords might nullify the labours of the Commons to strengthen those liberties which were so dear to him. Having failed in one attempt he now had another scheme in mind which would salvage some of the work of the Commons, if worst came to the worst. This would at least give permanence to the points made before the Lords by the four spokesmen of the lower House. He moved[3] that copies of their arguments be brought to the House and 'that they remain here to posterity and to every particular [person] that desires to look upon them for the present . . . and here to be kept in safety'. This motion was immediately accepted. Digges and his colleagues were asked to bring to the House by the coming Thursday copies of their speeches and the records they had employed.[4]

As so often happened in the House, a storm suddenly broke from a most unexpected quarter. Edward Kirton informed the Commons that the Earl of Suffolk had said that Selden ought to be hanged for 'razing' a record. That was a startling accusation, and 'after a great pause Sir John Eliot spake'. He said that if the accusation was true, it greatly concerned the House. It implied dishonour both to the gentleman accused

---

[1] For this paragraph see *C.J.*, I, 879, 880, and Borlase.

[2] Borlase and Mass. MS.

[3] The speech and motion are attributed in Borlase to Phelips. In Mass. MS. they are accredited to Eliot. I am following Mass. MS. but am quoting words from Borlase. The speech, when taken in conjunction with Eliot's activity on Saturday, fits him much better than it does Phelips who on that day expressed faith in the peers.

[4] *C.J.*, I, 883; Borlase; Mass. MS.

and to the House itself, and thereby involved them all, Sir John declared. Two things he proposed. First that Selden was to be heard and,
if possible, was to give the reason and occasion for such a charge.
Secondly, Eliot said, witnesses 'of this imputation' should be produced.[1]

And then a great deal of time and energy were expended to no purpose. Strangways said that he had heard the Earl make the charge.
Selden defended himself and denied the accusation. And Suffolk denied
he had ever used those words. At the suggestion of Eliot a committee
of investigation was named. More evidence and witnesses were discovered. With Sir John acting as the driving force of the committee charges were presented four days later against Suffolk to the
Lords. Here this little storm vanishes from sight. What the Earl of
Suffolk had said John Selden had done was forgotten as both Houses
became more and more interested in the great controversy over the
liberties of the subject. But the episode must have given Sir John Eliot
considerable pleasure. He must have been reminded of his battle with
the Duke of Buckingham which might break out again with renewed
vigour in the near future.[2]

In the meantime on Monday afternoon, April 14, the Speaker and
all the Commons attended King Charles in the Banqueting House.
First the Speaker addressed his Majesty in answer to the strong royal
message on supply of the previous Saturday; and then he presented the
petition of the Commons against billeting of soldiers. Responding immediately Charles urged haste in the vote of the subsidies and begged
the Commons not to spend so much time in preserving their liberties.
With the remark that he would answer the petition later, he left the
Commons to disperse to their lodgings.[3]

During the next two days the members of the lower House were enlightened by more arguments against martial law in committee of the
whole, by still another plea for harmony and supply from Sir John Coke
supported by several 'courtiers', and by a conference with the Lords
over the liberties of the subject.

Such a conference was held on Wednesday and Thursday, and again
in the next week on Wednesday and Friday, April 23 and 25. Interspersed between these conferences and reports on them, the Com-

---

[1] Mass. MS.; Borlase; Nicholas (2); Harl. 2313; *C.J.*, I, 883.
[2] Borlase; Mass. MS.; Nicholas (2); Harl. 2313; Harl. 1601; *C.J.*, I, 883, 884–5; Rushworth, I, 539; *Eph. Parl.*, pp. 136–7.
[3] Borlase; Mass. MS.; Rushworth, I, 540–5; *Eph. Parl.*, pp. 47–54.

mons held a number of sessions in committee of the whole where they discussed martial law without reaching any conclusion.

Monday, April 21, was the day on which the two conferences of the previous week were reported. First Digges, then Littleton, Selden, and finally Sir Edward Coke spoke. The general impression these men created was that the Commons had fared rather well in matching their brains against those of the peers and the legal advisers of the government. Of the four Coke gave the longest report in which he spent most of his time denouncing Serjeant Ashley. The ex-chief justice declared that Ashley had insulted the Commons on five occasions in his speech, particularly when he said in reference to the 'King's supreme power in matters of state' that he conceived 'it to be a question too high to be determined by any legal direction'. In closing Sir Edward moved for a conference with the Lords on Serjeant Ashley.[1]

When the reports were completed Sir John Eliot was so elated that he felt the urge to sing the praise of his learned colleagues.[2] He greatly admired the 'strength' of their 'wisdom' and the skill with which they presented their points. He asked those sitting near the chair to bring to the attention of his Majesty that his power rested on the fact that he was 'a King of freemen not of slaves'. And then he talked about Sir John Ashley. He praised the Lords for the action they had taken against him. They had stopped him and told him that he was speaking without their authority. He informed the Commons that he had heard that since then the peers had debated Ashley's words and as a result had imprisoned him.[3] 'This is a great satisfaction,' Sir John concluded. 'And if we find the punishment too easy for the offence, we may hereafter petition to have it increased.'[4] Eliot was right about Ashley, for the Lords on the

[1] *C.J.*. I, 886; Borlase; Grosvenor (2); Mass. MS.; Nicholas (2); *Eph. Parl.*, p. 144.

[2] Borlase; Mass. MS.; Grosvenor (2); Nicholas (2).

[3] From the wording of Mass. MS. and Grosvenor (2) it seems that Eliot was the first to give this information to the House. Sir Edward Coke knew nothing of the action taken by the Lords.

[4] It is to be hoped that Eliot delivered this brief and appropriate speech (as is indicated in the diaries) and not the long-winded oration filled with inapt examples of his learning, of which a copy is to be found among the P.E. MSS., 'Eliot, speeches, etc.', ff. 42–45v. A good version is printed in *Neg. Post.*, II, Sup., 119–23. It is also given in Forster, *Eliot*, II, 161–6 (2nd edit., II, 33–7), but is misdated April 19. Probably this speech, which says nothing about Ashley, was prepared in advance. When Eliot spoke in the House he used only a small part of it and added the remarks about the Serjeant. Of course he may have written the speech some time after its delivery, omitted all he had said about Ashley, and embellished it with classical allusions.

previous Saturday had punished him for his strong statements and had committed him to the gentleman usher.[1]

The first conference of the second week, that of April 23, disclosed from the report given by Sir Edward Coke that the Lords were becoming worried about 'pinching' the royal prerogative.[2] The picture becomes clearer at the second conference held two days later. Here a committee of thirty-six including Sir John Eliot attended the upper House with instructions only to listen and have nothing to say. That same day Sir Dudley Digges reported what the peers had said. They had decided to attempt a compromise with the Commons. In lieu of the resolutions of the lower House on the liberty of the subject they offered five propositions.[3] They were so important that Digges felt they should be studied before they were considered by the Commons. On his motion it was agreed that the propositions should be debated the next morning in committee of the whole.

Candles must have burned low on Friday night, as members of the lower House studied at their leisure the proposals of the Lords. On Saturday morning the Commons quickly adjourned into committee of the whole to discuss what was on the mind of almost every member of the House. Over a dozen spoke, mostly opponents of the government. The consensus was that the fourth and fifth propositions, particularly the fifth with its royal prerogative 'intrinsical to his sovereignty' and its permission to the King to express cause of imprisonment 'within a convenient time', were impossible to accept. The first three were felt to be harmless and might be used by the Commons in conjunction with their own resolutions. Both Sir Edward Coke and John Selden denounced all five and would have nothing to do with any of them. But Sir Dudley Digges thought that some of the propositions might be combined with the Commons' resolutions and presented to the King in the form

[1] Francis H. Relf, *Notes of the Debates in the House of Lords* (London, 1929), p. 118.

[2] *C.J.*, I, 887; Borlase; Mass. MS.; Grosvenor (2); Harl., 2313.

[3] Rushworth, I, 546–7 and *Eph. Parl.*, pp. 153–4. See Gardiner, VI, 259, for explanation of how the five propositions were the product of a defeat of Buckingham and the 'court' party in the House of Lords. The gist of the propositions is: 1. That the King declare *Magna Carta* and the six supporting statutes to be in force. 2. That the King declare that according to the ancient laws every subject had propriety in his goods and liberty of his person. 3. That the King would confirm in the most ample fashion the liberties, privileges, and rights of his subjects. 4. That the King would promise to proceed in all matters which fell under the common law according to that law and the law of the land. 5. That the King would not use his 'royal prerogative intrinsical to his sovereignty' to deprive his subjects of propriety in their goods or liberty of their persons. And that the King on imprisoning a subject would within 'a convenient time' state the cause of such imprisonment.

of a petition of right.[1] He suggested that a smaller committee be appointed to confer with the Lords on how to combine the two sets of proposals. Others recommended either a select committee or a subcommittee to examine the propositions and prepare a reply to the upper House. As the discussion neared its close Wentworth arose to speak. Though he agreed that the propositions must be entrusted to another committee, he felt they were not ready for that yet. Like Digges and others Sir Thomas thought the first three might be used and was opposed to the last two. But unlike Digges he did not favour a petition of right which would be buried in the parliament rolls. Instead he advocated a bill which would be printed and be seen by all.

Again, as three weeks earlier, Wentworth put before the House his plan for a bill of rights. A petition of right, as proposed by Digges, would not have the legal strength or the publicity value of a bill. The greater utility of a bill was manifest, provided the Commons could frame one which the King would sign. Furthermore, there was a good chance that the House would now be interested in a bill. The Commons had thrashed out the details of their grievances and knew what they wanted. At the beginning of April it would have been extremely difficult to state those grievances clearly enough to be able to shape them into a bill. Now the task was fairly simple.

In all this discussion, which ended without a decision and an adjournment to Monday, Sir John Eliot, as far as the records available show, did not say a word. It hardly seems possible that he could have been in the House that Saturday morning and kept his thoughts to himself. Thoughts he must have had on the propositions of the Lords, as well as a desire to express himself. What held him in his seat? The presumption is that his views were the same as those of the majority of his colleagues who spoke that morning.

3. A BILL OF RIGHTS

Soon after the Commons had assembled on Monday the King sent them a message asking them to come immediately into his presence in the House of Lords.[2] Obediently the members appeared before their

---

[1] Borlase and Harl. 2313 give Digges as advocating a petition of right. The other diaries do not use this phrase. But none of the diaries say that Sir Edward Coke advocated a petition of right to the King as does Gardiner, VI, 262.

[2] C.J., I, 889; Mass. MS.; Grosvenor (2); Borlase; Nicholas (2); Harl. 2313.

Sovereign to listen to the words of Charles from the mouth of Lord Keeper Coventry. After reminding his audience of the needs of the nation and of all the time spent on the liberties of the people without furthering those needs, Coventry said that the King had decided to hasten matters by declaring his own intentions. His Majesty held *Magna Carta* and the six other statutes, which were being insisted on as guarantees of the subject's liberty, 'to be all in force'. He assured the Commons that he would maintain 'all his subjects in the just freedom of their persons and safety of their estates'. He would govern 'according to the laws and statutes of the realm'. And finally he assured them that they would find 'as much security in his Majesty's royal word and promise as in the strength of any law you can make'. In consequence they would hereafter 'never have cause to complain'.[1] With such concessions Charles hoped to end the wrangling of the Commons and obtain in the shortest possible time the promised subsidies. As usual his estimation of the minds and wills of men like Wentworth, Coke, Phelips, Eliot, Digges, Selden, and a host of others was wrong. He did not understand what they were after. They trusted the King to adhere to the law, but not his ministers. They wanted to be sure that in future no minister of any king would break the law. Had he understood this, it is more than doubtful that Charles would have been willing to differentiate between the act of the King and the act of his minister. Therefore, it can be argued that the Commons were more ignorant, if anything, of the point of view of King Charles than he was of theirs. This misunderstanding was an important aspect of the rift which was eventually to lead to revolution.

As soon as the Commons had returned to their own House Sir John Coke dotted the 'i's and crossed the 't's of the Lord Keeper's speech. He closed with the motion that 'we would show ourselves the best of subjects, as he hath showed himself the best of kings, and without further interruption proceed in the King's business'. In order to make sure that the members were being put in the right frame of mind to do his Majesty's bidding, Sir Benjamin Rudyerd showered his listeners with honeyed words. But even Rudyerd took pleasure 'to see that good old decrepit law of *Magna Carta*, which hath so long kept in and lain as it were bedrid, . . . walk abroad again with new vigour and lustre attended by the other six statutes'. He went so far as to say: 'I hope we

---

[1] Rushworth, I, 549, also *L.J.*, III, 772 and *Eph. Parl.*, pp. 157–58.

may have a bill, to agree in the point, against imprisonment for loans or privy seals.' The King and 'court' had spoken.[1]

Now there stood before the House its greatest orator to destroy whatever good King Charles, Coke, and Rudyerd had done in the interest of speeding the royal cause. Sir John Eliot could not have picked a more opportune time to expiate his silence of the previous day. He began by saying that he had no intention of commenting on the two preceding speeches. He would simply present a prayer that God might grant both the King's and their wishes. Eliot was not going to insist too much on particulars nor on a confirmation of the laws, now that his Majesty had promised to enforce them. Nobody doubted that he would do this, Sir John declared. What he was interested in was the preservation of the liberties of the subject and a method to accomplish this quickly. Briefly he reviewed what had been done.

Now, Eliot declared, it was the intention of the Commons to send to the Lords a law which would be approved by the King. He saw no reason why they should not carry out this plan, as there appeared to be no opposition to it. The King had told them that he would uphold the laws and their 'just' liberties, Eliot asserted. 'But the difficulty still rests upon the word "just", what interpretation it shall bear, who shall expound it.' He moved that the Commons frame a bill in which their own resolutions and the propositions of the Lords 'may be so interwoven that we may give them satisfaction and proceed to the great work desired by his Majesty'.

They were expecting a conference with the members of the upper House, he continued. There his colleagues should observe carefully what the Lords did not like about their own propositions and what they approved in the resolutions of the Commons. Let us return this answer to the Lords, he concluded, that as the message of the King did not contradict any of their conclusions and did not oppose a law which explained those good old laws, 'that we will without further trouble apply ourselves and make use of their propositions in a bill as will give them satisfaction'.[2]

The implication of this speech was that Sir John Eliot did not trust the King's 'just' interpretation of the laws, rather the interpretation his

---

[1] Rushworth, I, 549–52; *Eph. Parl.*, pp. 155–57; Grosvenor (2); Borlase; Mass. MS.; Nicholas (2).

[2] Chiefly Grosvenor (2), but also Borlase; Mass. MS.; Harl. 2313; Nicholas (2).

ministers would give them. Therefore it was necessary for Parliament to interpret them by means of a bill. Eliot grasped the reins which Wentworth had dropped on Saturday. Sir Thomas had not moved that they proceed by a bill. He had merely suggested it and hoped that it would soon be put in a motion. That Eliot did and got more credit than he really deserved. There had been no time for such a motion on Saturday. Now on Monday after the King had made some sacrifices, it was time to show exactly what the Commons wanted and demonstrate to Charles the limitations of his concessions. Sir John took full advantage of this opening and made use of the medium Wentworth had proposed. After Glanville had seconded Eliot's motion, the House 'ordered that a select committee should be named to draw a bill concerning the liberty of the subject in his person and goods and to make use of the resolutions of this House'.

The committee in charge of the bill worked fast, for already on Tuesday morning, April 29, it reported as a sub-committee to the committee of the whole.[1] Sir Edward Coke made the report and introduced the bill. The first part of this document contained a re-statement of *Magna Carta* and the confirming statutes on the liberty of the subject. The second part consisted of the resolutions of the Commons on imprisonment, taxation, and billeting of soldiers, that is, what amounted to an explanation of the first part.[2] A long debate took place in which, according to Sir Edward Coke, 'there are two questions before the committee: whether or not the resolutions of the House should be included in the act'.[3] Most of the discussion was over stating the cause of imprisonment. A few did not want it expressed at all. More wanted it declared on return of the writ of *habeas corpus*. While the majority favoured expressing the cause at the same time a man was imprisoned.

To this last group Eliot belonged. He gave some excellent reasons for his contention out of his own experience. But first he said it was supported by *Magna Carta* in its famous article 39. Then he cited his imprisonment in May, 1626, when no cause was given except that he was being imprisoned for things extra-judicial. Finally he reminded the

---

[1] This is an interesting mixture of parliamentary procedure. A committee obviously named as a select committee (*C.J.*, I, 890) now reports as a sub-committee. Borlase and Mass. MS. call it a sub-committee when it reports, while Nicholas (2) calls it a select committee. Grosvenor (2) and Harl. 1601 speak of it just as a committee.

[2] For the bill see Gardiner, VI, 264.

[3] Nicholas (2).

Commons of his imprisonment and that of many others for refusing the loan.[1]

Of the opposition leaders Sir Dudley Digges and William Hakewill would not side with the majority in supporting the vital point of the debate. As might be expected Sir Edward Coke favoured stating the cause of commitment at the time a man was imprisoned. And near the close of the debate Sir Thomas Wentworth declared that Privy Councillors 'who would deprive us of liberty and goods' should be punished. In spite of all this talk, no decision could be reached on the bill of rights and the committee of the whole adjourned to the next morning.[2]

On that last morning in April the discussion of the bill continued in committee with Rudyerd trying his best to clip its claws. Sir Benjamin was answered by Phelips who argued ably and forcibly for the bill as it stood. He reminded the committee that they had been invited to proceed with a bill, for 'his Majesty assured us he would confirm our liberties by bill or any way'.[3]

Eliot was not satisfied with this reply to Rudyerd. In addressing the committee after Phelips, he admitted that whatever the Commons did must have the approval of the Lords. But even though the peers did not agree with the Commons on all matters, they had not as yet opposed the resolutions of the lower House, he said. Then he described the attitude of the Lords towards the resolutions and their own propositions.

Another matter they must consider, Sir John continued, was the request of his Majesty not to make anything new. He was sure that nothing they wanted was new. Their desire was only an explanation of the old. Furthermore, it was objected, Eliot said, that the bill the Commons were preparing might dishonour the state and the government. On the contrary, they were trying to increase the honour and power of the King. 'The greatness of the King is like the glory of the sun, not capable in itself of any obscurity, but by intervenient and dark clouds it may seem to be eclipsed and diminished to us.' Through 'the interposition of officers the goodness of the King may be darkened to us. The King's goodness hath no prejudice', he said. In conclusion Sir John declared that he had no doubt but that the Lords would confirm them,

---

[1] Grosvenor (2), also Mass. MS.; Nicholas (2); Harl. 2313; Harl. 1601.

[2] For this paragraph see all six diaries so far cited, particularly Grosvenor (2).

[3] Mass. MS.; Grosvenor (2); Nicholas (2); Borlase; Harl. 5324 which is the continuation of Harl. 2313 beginning with April 30.

and therefore they should proceed with the details of the bill. After this glorification of the King, typical of Sir John Eliot, the debate was soon brought to a close without any decision being reached.[1]

Another day[2] brought forth another debate on the bill of rights. The time of stating the cause for imprisonment was still up for discussion. Among others Wentworth argued strongly for the bill. But unlike the more radical members of the 'country' party, such as Sir Edward Coke, Sir John Eliot, and Robert Mason, he believed it unnecessary to show cause before the return of the writ of *habeas corpus*.[3]

On Wentworth's resuming his seat Sir John Coke announced he had a message from the King, so the Speaker took his chair. The communication from Charles was brief. If the Commons would adhere to his 'royal word' as declared to them by the Lord Keeper two days previously, he assured them 'it shall be royally performed'.[4] After the Commons had shown by a prolonged silence their lack of enthusiasm for the royal word thus expressed, Secretary Coke broke in with an explanation which exasperated the House even more. He made it quite clear that the King would not accept a new law or an addition to the old. A restatement of the old laws was all that was necessary. And then Mr Secretary enraged many of the members when he said that if he had to commit a man to prison he would 'neither express the cause to the jailer, nor to the judges, nor to any counsellor in England, but to the King himself'.[5]

Such foolhardy words merely produced the motion from Sir Edward Coke, seconded by Phelips, that the royal message be discussed on the morrow. But Sir John Eliot could not let this opportunity pass without telling Secretary Coke what he thought of him. He praised the moderation of the House. He wondered why 'this message should stay so long within these walls'. The delay in delivering it was 'a prejudice to his Majesty [and] a dishonour to this House'. Eliot did not like Mr Secretary's 'speech of suspicion'. He disclaimed that the Commons were trying to add to the existing laws and thereby would diminish the power of the Crown. And in closing he denounced in no uncertain terms Coke's assertion that he would commit without showing cause. Such language made Sir John Coke furious. He replied that 'what concerns myself I submit to your judgment. But as for that, that this

---

[1] Mass. MS.; Borlase; Grosvenor (2); Nicholas (2).   [2] Thursday, May 1.
[3] All six diaries.   [4] Rushworth, I, 552; *Eph. Parl.*, p. 161; all six diaries.
[5] *Eph. Parl.*, p. 162, also Rushworth, I, 553; Nicholas (2); Grosvenor (2); Borlase.

message came no sooner, he that gave me the command commanded me the time when to speak'. With tempers rising the Commons decided it was time to put an end to this business for that day and passed the motion of Sir Edward Coke to consider the message on the morrow.[1]

Before the House could adjourn into committee on May 2 Sir Walter Erle suggested that a remonstrance be sent to his Majesty in which he would be told exactly what the Commons were intending to do.[2] This proposal added confusion to the long debate that developed in committee of the whole. Some wanted a remonstrance, others opposed it. Some wanted a bill, others asked the House to trust the King. As usual it was Sir Thomas Wentworth who had a plan which received the most support.[3] He desired that Sir John Coke report to his Majesty the thanks of the Commons for his gracious message. But they wanted to be sure, he continued, that 'his Majesty's goodness may remain to posterity'. Therefore, as the law had been publicly violated by the ministers of the King, it was necessary to make public reparation. That should be done by means of a bill which would vindicate the subject's rights, Sir Thomas declared. Such a bill would contain no more than was 'laid down in former laws with some modest provision for instruction, performance, and execution'. All this Wentworth implied should be included in the reply of the Commons to the message of the King. The bill itself Sir Thomas wanted presented to the King by the Speaker and the entire House. This suggestion was received by the committee with increasing favour. The gist of Wentworth's proposal, which he was asked to read to the members, was that in their answer to the royal message his Majesty should be told that in the near future a bill concerning the liberties of the people would be presented to him. After a discussion over the wording of the reply,[4] it was entrusted to a subcommittee.

This committee was to complete its work by four o'clock that afternoon and report back to the committee of the whole.[5] After the House

[1] See all six diaries, particularly Mass. MS., and *C.J.*, I, 891.

[2] Nicholas (2); Mass. MS.; Borlase; Grosvenor (2); Harl. 1601. According to Forster, *Eliot*, II, 183, Eliot made a speech at this point which sounds much like that of Erle. None of the diaries mention Eliot as speaking at this time. Forster in a footnote to the above says: 'I find the remark in the text in his own hand among the Port Eliot MSS'. I could not find it.

[3] Rushworth, I, 554, also all six diaries.

[4] Eliot as well as Digges, Secretary Coke, Wentworth, Seymour, and Glanville spoke among others.

[5] Borlase. *C.J.*, I, 891.

had waited until seven in the evening, the answer of the Commons was finally ready to be reported. But Charles, informed of the intention of the Commons, decided to forestall them. Before the Speaker could leave his chair Sir John Coke announced that he had another message from his Majesty.[1] This time the King sent word that he would govern his people according to the laws and customs of the realm and would maintain them in the liberties of their persons and the proprieties of their goods. The Secretary went on to say that as his Majesty, refusing to encroach upon their lawful liberties, 'will rank himself amongst the best of our kings', so the Commons, shrinking from violating the royal sovereignty 'which God hath put into his hands' for their good, will match themselves with the best subjects. In conclusion Coke said that his Majesty wanted them to keep themselves 'within the bounds and laws of our forefathers without restraining them or enlarging them by new explanations, interpretations, expositions, or additions in any sort, which he telleth us he will not give way unto'. The Commons were told that as time was pressing, his Majesty could not endure 'long debate or delay'. He intended to prorogue this session a week from the coming Tuesday, that is, May 13, 'in which time his Majesty for his part will be ready to perform what he promised. And if the House be not as ready to do that is fit for themselves, it shall be their own faults'. Charles promised another session at Michaelmas to complete what was left undone.

The day was far gone. The hearts of many members were full of anguish. The communication from the King was so important that it must be considered with the greatest care. So the Commons accepted the motion of Sir Thomas Hoby that the royal message be delivered to the House in writing on the next morning.[2]

Soon after proceedings had begun on Saturday, May 3, Sir John Coke carried out the last request of the Commons of the previous day. Immediately Eliot moved that the House adjourn into committee of the whole to discuss the bearing of this last message on the proposed answer of the Commons to the former royal communications. The debate was long and futile. Many of the 'country' felt that the King had been misinformed about the intentions of the Commons to introduce anything new in their bill. They wanted him to know this and proposed an addi-

---

[1] Rushworth, I, 554, also *Eph. Parl.*, p. 167; Grosvenor (2); Borlase; Nicholas (2); Mass. MS.
[2] Grosvenor (2) and Nicholas (2).

tion to the answer prepared by the sub-committee on Friday and reported to the 'grand' committee this morning. Others were opposed to
sending any answer to his Majesty. They were anxious that the bill be
completed to see whether it could be made acceptable to both King
and Commons. Such procedure would take much less time than first
amending the answer, presenting it to the King, and then enacting the
bill. Naturally, 'courtiers' like Sir Humphrey May and Secretary Coke
were in favour of the greatest possible speed and therefore advocated
that action first be taken on the bill.[1]

In the midst of the debate after May had spoken in support of the
bill, Sir John Eliot declared himself in favour of an addition to the
answer of the Commons and requested that the consideration of the
bill be postponed temporarily.[2] He believed that 'to the best of kings'
they should make it apparent that they were 'the best of subjects' and
had no intention of encroaching on his prerogative. But he was sure
that it would be impossible to complete their business by May 13. There
had been so many messages, letters, and misreports which had caused
them to delay the King's business. His words had little immediate
effect, as the controversy over the answer to the royal messages and the
bill continued to wax with member after member expressing his
opinion and party lines becoming more and more blurred. Finally, it
was resolved that the sub-committee which had penned the answer
yesterday should add to that answer some reassuring remarks, that the
intention of the Commons had been misrepresented to his Majesty and
that they had no thought of encroaching on his prerogative, as Eliot
and others had suggested.[3] That afternoon the sub-committee reported
to the committee of the whole its completed answer which in turn was
reported to the House. There it was resolved that Mr Speaker accompanied by the whole House should present it to King Charles.

On Monday morning Sir John Coke brought word that his Majesty
would give the Speaker and the House of Commons immediate audience in the Banqueting house. There the King heard from the mouth of
the Speaker that the Commons still insisted on their bill. He was told
of their intention not to encroach upon his prerogative and of their desire to enact a law with some necessary explanations 'for execution and
performance, as in times past upon like occasions have been used'.

[1] All the diaries except Harl. 1601, with Borlase as the most important.
[2] *Ibid.*; Mass. MS.; Grosvenor (2); Rushworth, I, 555.
[3] Harl. 5324; Harl. 1601; Mass. MS.; Nicholas (2); Borlase.

When the Speaker had concluded the Lord Keeper addressed the Commons in the name of the King. They had declared their trust and confidence in his Majesty. But had they shown it in accepting his word and promise? What need was there of explanations unless the Commons doubted that the laws would be executed according to their true meaning, they were asked. 'Explanations will hazard an encroachment upon his prerogative,' the Lord Keeper continued. But to show that his Majesty was sincere in what he had said, he would accept a bill confirming *Magna Carta* and the other six statutes. But, Coventry warned in closing, 'so as it may be without additions, paraphrases, or explanations'.[1]

The Commons were deeply disappointed by these words of the Lord Keeper. On returning to their chamber they displayed their feelings by refusing to take any action that morning on the all-important subject before them. Expressions of opinion and the making of a decision were left to that memorable Tuesday, May 6.

There was no doubt about the issue now. Charles had had his say four times since Wentworth's proposal of a bill of rights on April 26. The King would not accept a new law, nor would he sanction an affirmation of old law to which any explanation was attached. But the old laws had been broken; even the King's ministers admitted that, though Charles ignored both breach and admission. The King had begged the Commons to trust him, trust him to adhere to the existing law of the land. If they would not do that, he was willing they should enact a measure in which the old laws which preserved the liberties of the people were restated. But this measure must under no circumstances contain any explanation of the law it contained.

To Wentworth and the leaders of the 'country' party such a simple bill was not nearly enough. If old law, far too vaguely stated to meet existing conditions, could be broken, an affirmation of that law could just as easily be violated in the near or distant future. But the minds of these parliamentarians, imbued with the early seventeenth-century sanctity of law, could not take the next logical step.[2] That was, if old law could be broken, any law was at any time at the mercy of constitutional vandals.[3] A bill of rights in the hands of a Stuart king might

---

[1] *Eph. Parl.*, pp. 171–3 and Rushworth, I, 555–7.

[2] Margaret A. Judson, *The Crisis of the Constitution* (New Brunswick, N.J., 1949), pp. 240–57, for an excellent exposition of the part played by the sanctity of the law in the discussions over a bill of rights.

[3] Eliot stated this clearly in his speech of March 22. But his application was general. See

be of no greater value than the Petition of Right was to be. But it was to take a dozen to a score of years to make these gentry see the error of the reasoning they exhibited in 1628.

The fundamental error of men like Wentworth, Eliot, and their kind went much deeper. The King can do no wrong, long live the King! There was the real fallacy. Only the King's minister can do wrong, or a king misled by evil ministers. The King alone is pure goodness. These men believed that law could tie the hands of the most autocratic minister. In that way the influence of such officials could be eliminated. The King by himself, or aided only by good ministers who believed as he did in the law, would rule perfectly. Wentworth and others thought that a bill of rights would securely bind the hands of the Duke of Buckingham and his worthless tribe. As we shall see, Wentworth and a few believed that the Petition of Right would accomplish the same end. So they left the ship of state to Charles I and his advisers. But Eliot and a growing number felt that the great Petition was not strong enough to prevent an evil minister from breaking its bonds. What was more important, these men began to doubt that their King was all goodness, all perfection and right. The Petition of Right was followed by the first rocking of the pedestal on which the English King had stood for years. Within two short decades he was to be standing on the ground, standing in dire peril of his life. There could be no compromise for rebels against their King, between the Stuart prerogative and the law of the land.

Now on May 5, 1628, the situation, as yet many paces away from rebellion, appeared impossible to compromise. The Commons must have their bill with explanations; the King would have the bill but no explanations. In all the preliminaries leading to this crisis the House of Commons had followed the unquestioned leadership of Sir Thomas Wentworth. Hard thinking along one straight line, which resulted in the best possible advice stated simply and clearly, had put him and kept him in that position ever since the beginning of the session. Sir John Eliot, on the other hand, was just one of the many who had supported the policies of Wentworth. The past ten days had been no time for oratory, no time to attack, no time when Eliot could put his best foot forward. Of course he expressed himself, but his words were not particularly arresting, his ideas by no means original. To be sure, he seems to have had

above, p. 188. Now that matters had become far more specific, he seems to have been afraid to state the issue as clearly as he did in March.

the knack of taking the ideas of other men and sometimes making much of them. He could talk sense, good sense, on occasion. But one gets the impression that his ears rather than his mind were responsible for such sense. Sir John Eliot up to this time in the Parliament of 1628 was simply one of the dozen or more leading members of the 'country' party. On occasion when the opportunity presented itself, he rose far above the rest and stirred the House to its depths. But those occasions were none too numerous. In brains and common sense, great necessities for leadership in this Parliament, Wentworth, Phelips, and even Digges were his superiors, not to mention a number of prominent lawyers in the party who were at least his peers. But as will shortly be seen, the ability of neither Wentworth nor Eliot, Phelips nor Digges, was able to solve the dilemma confronting the House of Commons on May 6. It took a keen old legal mind to find a satisfactory compromise.

H

CHAPTER XI

Victory of the Petition of Right

May 6 to June 26, 1628

I. BIRTH OF THE PETITION OF RIGHT

ASSEMBLING on Tuesday morning, May 6, 1628, the Commons were in a state of Stygian gloom.[1] The reply of the Lord Keeper on the previous day to the Speaker's address had not been conducive to peaceful slumber during the night or happy thoughts on arising that morning. One of the first motions made in the House was to adjourn into committee of the whole where the knotty problem confronting them could be threshed out more easily than in formal session. Before the motion could be put into effect it was decided to read the two addresses of Monday, the 5th.[2] Their reading produced such dejection that a half-hour of silence had finally to be broken by Sir John Coke. He reminded his saddened audience that the King had given them a choice, either to proceed by a bill of confirmation without explanations or to rely on his royal word to govern according to the laws in force. Sir John first showed the advantages of such a bill and then turned to the much greater benefits which would result from trusting the King. After painting a glowing picture of the latter proposal, he strongly advised the House to proceed in formal debate rather than in informal discussion of the committee of the whole.[3] With the ice broken Edward Alford advocated a complicated plan of action which aroused no interest in the House. Eliot, the next speaker, ignored his suggestion and replied to Secretary Coke with a strong plea for adjournment into committee. So it was ordered. Now debate was opened wide to the whims and mental acrobatics of all who had plans, proposals, or propositions to propound.

[1] The events of this day are to a large extent covered by my note on 'Opinion in the House of Commons on the Proposal for a Petition of Right, 6 May, 1628', *E.H.R.*, L, 302–6.

[2] Borlase and *C. and T. Chas. I*, I, 353.   [3] Rushworth, I, 557, and all six diaries.

In a long discussion the 'courtiers', on the one hand, presented the simple solution of trusting his Majesty. Their pre-eminent advocate was, of course, Sir John Coke, followed with less heart by Sir Roger North, Sir William Beecher, and Sir Humphrey May. Closely associated with this group were John Hoskins and Richard Dyott, who suggested that a bill confirming *Magna Carta* and the six statutes without any explanations be passed. Thus they showed that trusting the King was likewise implicit in their political philosophy. On the other hand, we have the extreme element of the 'country' party represented by Littleton and Coryton who advocated what Charles had prohibited, a confirmatory bill with explanations. To avoid this dilemma Alford and Peter Ball desired that the grievances of the Commons, royal messages, and old laws be tacked on to the subsidy bill. Finally, a novel idea, differing only in the means and not in the end from that of Littleton, was presented by Sir Nathaniel Rich and was supported by Pym and Robert Goodwin. This was a double plan in which Rich suggested that first it be determined by a vote whether the satisfaction already promised by the King was sufficient. If the decision was in the affirmative then Charles should be asked to explain the law himself, even to declare certain practices illegal, so that the Commons would know what he meant when he asked them to trust him to rule according to the law of the land. Sir John Eliot had no plan and did not as yet give his support to any of these propositions.

With progress barred by all these related but conflicting proposals it seemed impossible to reach a solution. Then arose Sir Edward Coke. The first words of the former chief justice dealt with trusting. They must trust his Majesty, he felt, because under God he was the only one they had to trust. Next he turned to their grievances. They were particular, he said, and therefore could not be answered by the general words of the King. Likewise royal messages delivered by the Lord Keeper and Privy Councillors were not a parliamentary method of procedure in the opinion of Sir Edward. After making this point he turned from the negative to the positive and reminded his listeners that in the past Parliaments had always petitioned their sovereign. Let them, therefore, join with the Lords in a petition of right. That would be proper parliamentary procedure, a matter of record, and yet not a bill which had been prohibited.[1]

This proposal was clearly a compromise at a time when no solution

---

[1] All six diaries; Rushworth, I, 558; *C. and T. Chas. I*, I, 354.

seemed possible. It was not novel, for Sir Dudley Digges had suggested a petition of right on April 26.[1] But at that time no barrier had been raised to a statutory settlement of the troubles confronting the Commons—no compromise was necessary then. Now on May 6 it was in such demand that Sir Edward Coke easily reverted to the only possible method of solving their dilemma, the passing of a petition of right.

Where Digges had failed Sir Edward now succeeded, but the proposal was not immediately accepted. It had to sink into the minds of the members. What is more to the point, it was practically ignored by the next speaker, Sir John Eliot. Returning to the plan of Sir Nathaniel Rich he reminded the Commons that it was not the question of refusing to trust his Majesty, but on what point they were going to trust him—a fine distinction indeed. Sir John admitted that it was useless to work for a law with explanations, as that had been forbidden by the King. To the first suggestion of Rich he turned and proposed that the committee of the whole decide whether the general word of the King 'can satisfy our duty and conscience'. When that had been settled Eliot was willing to state his opinion whether they should proceed by a bill or a petition. 'But for the present,' he said, 'put it to the question whether this general word of the King's will serve our turns or no.'[2] What heresy was Eliot speaking! His royal idol was beginning to totter. Would he regain confidence in the King?

But Sir John's motion fell on deaf ears. Seymour combined the proposals of Eliot and Coke by suggesting that the way to learn in what to trust his Majesty was to join with the Lords in a petition of right. Then came Glanville, Littleton, Hoby, and Pym, all of whom approved such a petition and suggested heads to be included in it. The next speaker was Sir Thomas Wentworth, who presented his ideas for the first time on that day. He was opposed to putting a motion on trusting the King to a vote and also abandoned his own measure when he said that a bill with or without explanations should not be put to the question. He too supported a petition of right. After such a petition had received the royal assent they should be free to proceed with other debates and resolutions. He closed with the remark that he believed the present was not the proper time in which to decide what the heads of a petition of right should be.[3] At this point Eliot realized that he was on the wrong

[1] See above, pp. 213-7.
[2] All six diaries, particularly Borlase.
[3] All six diaries.

side of the fence. As so often was the case, the words of his rival swayed him. First, however, he must explain himself. 'The question,' he said, 'was not intended for the King's trust but for the manner of the trust. But upon better judgments I recede from that. As for the petition of right I agree too, but withall let the liberty of our persons be inserted.'[1] Again Sir John was splitting hairs about trusting the King in trying to extricate himself from a situation which belied his ideals. But he was far from enthusiastic about the petition of right, as is seen by the reservations other diarists report him requesting.[2]

At this point more of the leaders of the Commons came to the support of Coke's timely suggestion. Though Coryton and Hakewill threatened for a moment the movement of the tide in favour of the petition, Rich set it in motion again. As a result a resolution was passed by the committee of the whole in favour of proceeding by a petition of right. Any remaining doubts were dispelled by further arguments from Wentworth and Rich; and heads to be included were proposed by Alford, Phelips, and Pym. Finally a resolution was passed which contained three of the four well-known articles of the Petition of Right. They protested against 'forced' loans, arbitrary imprisonment, and compulsory billeting. Tuesday, May 6, 1628, was a day not to be forgotten. Englishmen could cry: 'Well done, you members of the House of Commons.'[3]

On the next day the illegality of martial law was the subject of a long technical discussion. But it was not until the following morning, May 8, that this abuse of the law was put in such form that it was accepted for incorporation in the Petition. Now that the points to be included had been approved both in committee and in the House, it was decided to compose the document and ask the Lords for a conference at which it could be presented to them.[4] A conference of select committees was granted for that afternoon.

2. THE PETITION OF RIGHT IN THE HOUSE OF LORDS

For several days the Commons marked time by discussing such subjects

[1] Mass. MS., also the other diaries except Nicholas (2).
[2] Borlase; Grosvenor (2); Harl. 1601; Harl. 5324.
[3] See all six diaries.
[4] All six diaries. According to Borlase, Eliot suggested that the Lords be told that the Petition was closely related to their former conferences.

as the dates on which the subsidies were to be paid,[1] the scandalous actions of Richard Burgesse,[2] vicar of Witney in Oxfordshire, and minor incidents, on all of which Sir John Eliot had some remarks to make. There were few subjects that came before the Commons that did not bring him to his feet. But only occasionally were Eliot's words of importance or did his suggestions find favour with his colleagues.

In the meantime Sir Edward Coke reported on May 9 that the Lords had agreed to take the Petition of Right into consideration. And on Monday, May 12, the subsidy bill was given its first reading. Not until the latter day did the two Houses, sitting as committees of the whole have their first conference on the Petition. Sir Edward Coke reported from this conference that the Lords and Commons were generally in agreement on the Petition of Right. The peers proposed seven slight alterations in the wording of that document. On only one article had they failed to reach a decision. They were about to discuss the clause which deprived the King of his right to imprison without showing cause, Sir Edward reported, when they received a letter from his Majesty which was 'so full and so gracious that their Lordships conceive it may without further dispute give satisfaction to both Houses'.[3] In this letter, a copy of which was sent to the lower House and read to the Commons, the King promised that neither he nor any of his Privy Council would ever again imprison a man for refusing to lend money, 'or for any cause which in our conscience doth not concern the state, the public good and safety of us and our people'. Should a man be imprisoned his Majesty promised to state the cause of his restraint 'so soon as with conveniency and safety the same is fit to be disclosed and expressed'.[4]

The first to speak after the reading of the letter was Sir John Eliot. He divided Coke's report into its natural parts and moved that the proposed alterations of the Lords and the King's letter be debated on the next day.[5] Though Sir Edward Coke desired this debate be postponed for two days, Eliot's motion received the support of Sir John Coke and

[1] At the conclusion of the discussion over the dates Eliot denounced the rumour that the Commons were granting supply out of fear rather than love. Borlase, also Grosvenor (2); Mass. MS.; Nicholas (2).
[2] He had made and used a scandalous catechism.
[3] Borlase, also Grosvenor (2).
[4] *Eph. Parl.*, pp. 180–81; *L.J.*, III, 789–90; Rushworth, I, 560–61.
[5] Borlase, also Grosvenor (2) and Mass. MS.

the majority of the House.[1] Thus began the dispute of the two Houses over the Petition of Right.

For the next ten days that dispute raged over two points: what to do with the King's letter and the alterations to the wording of the Petition desired by the Lords. It can be followed in numerous conferences between the two Houses and in the debates in the lower House, chiefly in committee of the whole.

The royal letter was an interposition for which the Commons were not prepared. When carefully analysed it was far from 'full' and 'gracious' in their eyes. Charles was willing to surrender little of his power to imprison without showing cause. Something had to be done with the letter to clear the decks for the Petition of Right. Again it was Eliot who set the ball in motion by proposing that the letter either be sent back to the Lords or set aside.[2] A brief debate resulted in no decision. Not until the next day, Wednesday, May 14, was the subject discussed and settled. Wentworth this time took the lead to show why his Majesty's letter should be ignored. His main point was that by discussing it delay would be caused in preparing the Petition of Right for presentation to the King. The arguments of Sir Thomas were immediately supported by Eliot. In addition he wanted the reasons why the Commons wished to disregard the royal letter sent to the Lords in a special message. In other words Sir John was anxious to separate the letter from the Petition and place them in air-tight compartments. The Commons were not willing to go that far.[3] But the Lords could not persuade the members of the lower House to combine the royal letter with the Petition of Right in their deliberations. Finally the will of Wentworth, Eliot, and the majority of the Commons, that the Petition be considered without reference to the letter of the King, was accepted by the peers. Of course their Lordships now understood the attitude of his Majesty towards the Petition. Consequently the 'courtiers' in the upper House were bound to seek a solution which would come closer to the royal wishes expressed in the letter than was to be found in the Petition of Right as it stood at that time.

As to the alterations in the wording of the Petition proposed by the Lords, there was no serious difficulty confronting the Commons. But it

---

[1] Borlase; Grosvenor (2); C.J., I, 896.

[2] Grosvenor (2) makes Sir Edward Coke introduce this subject. But Borlase, Mass. MS., and Harl. 5324 say nothing about Coke and give Eliot as the first speaker.

[3] In a division Eliot's motion to send a special message to the Lords was defeated by 38 votes. C.J., I, 897.

took a good deal longer to reach an agreement with the peers than it did in the case of the royal letter. Between May 13 and 20 the Lords and Commons haggled over minor changes in the wording of the Petition, with the Commons spending many hours debating whether they would accept the phrase 'by means' in place of 'by pretext' and similar picayune variations. In the end the Commons accepted three of the seven alterations proposed to them by the Lords. During the numerous discussions most of the leaders of the 'country' party, including Sir John Eliot, expressed themselves several times. But the member for Cornwall had no outstanding ideas to present and was usually in agreement with his colleagues.[1]

A new issue in the fight over the Petition of Right had been introduced by the Lords during a conference on Saturday, May 17.[2] Now that the letter of King Charles had been rejected by the Commons something had to be done to protect the power of the Crown. It was proposed that a clause be added at the end of the Petition by which it was to be declared that his Majesty's sovereign power was left intact.[3] When the report was made to the House of Commons Sir Robert Phelips thought that this clause was so important that debate on it should be postponed till Monday. The House agreed.

Not until the afternoon of Tuesday, May 20, were the Commons able to discuss the additional clause of the Lords. As might be expected opinion in the House sitting informally was strongly opposed to bolstering the royal prerogative in so obvious a fashion. Eliot spoke twice on matters of procedure. But his words indicated that he was behind the will of the majority. The peers were told in conference that their clause was unacceptable to the Commons. And the Lords in turn gave many arguments in favour of the clause.[4]

Sitting in committee on Thursday, the 22nd, the Commons debated at length the arguments which the peers had presented on the previous day. Late in the discussion as usual, Sir Thomas Wentworth spoke and briefly gave his objections to the controversial addition of the Lords. He moved that a sub-committee be named to collect the reasons which had been presented against it. As was becoming his habit, Sir John Eliot spoke shortly after Wentworth, expressed his opposition to the clause

---

[1] The five diaries (Harl. 1601 ends with May 8) and *C.J.*, I, 897, 900, 901.

[2] *C.J.*, I, 899; Borlase; Mass. MS.; Grosvenor (2); Harl. 5324.

[3] For clause see Rushworth, I, 561, and *L.J.*, III, 801.

[4] Grosvenor (2); Borlase; Harl. 5324; *C.J.*, I, 901; Rushworth, I, 562; Frances H. Relf, *Notes of the Debates in the House of Lords* (Royal Historical Society, 1929), pp. 185–7.

in a few words, and seconded the motion for a sub-committee. The motion was passed by the committee of the whole. But the sub-committee, though ordered to report that afternoon, was not ready until the next morning.[1]

The committee of the whole on Friday morning listened to the report of Sir Nathaniel Rich from his sub-committee. With much detail he reported the reasons why the Commons could not consent to the 'saving' or additional clause. When Rich had concluded Wentworth rose to make a plea for co-operation with the upper House. He said now that they had decided on a petition of right the Lords must support it or else 'the stamp is cut off that gives value to the action'. If the peers joined with the Commons, Wentworth declared, it would be a record for posterity. But if the Lords did not, 'it is like the grass on the house top that is of not long continuance'. So he urged the Commons to induce the Lords to approve the Petition of Right. He continued by declaring that it was essential to refuse to accept any change whatsoever in the Petition. The peers should be told, he said, that the Commons were proposing nothing new, nor were they attempting to limit the prerogative of his Majesty. But his last remarks were that 'if their Lordships can find out any way to keep untouched this petition, we will consider of it and join with them'.[2]

In his speech Wentworth showed complete understanding of the constitution. Both Houses must approve a petition of right to give it permanence and the force of law. Should the upper House fail to approve it, the King would be given encouragement to refuse his assent. But should his Majesty be persuaded to endorse a petition emanating from only one of the two Houses, it would unquestionably fail to have the strength, the legal standing, of a petition of right approved by both Houses. Where Wentworth's logic weakened was when he insisted that the Petition of Right be left as it stood without any changes, and then suggested that 'if their Lordships can find out any thing which way to cause an agreement, let them express it and we shall condescend'. By making such a suggestion he implied an addition or alteration in word or phrase. But he had just refused the additional clause of the Lords and had asserted that the Petition must go to his Majesty as it stood, that is, without changing in the slightest degree any of its vital

---

[1] Borlase; Grosvenor (2); Mass. MS.; Harl. 5324.

[2] Mass. MS.; Grosvenor (2); Borlase. The speech is also found in Earl of Birkenhead, *Strafford* (London, 1938), pp. 100–1.

principles. If the Lords were going to help Charles at all, they must do that very thing. It is hardly conceivable that this plain-spoken York-shireman meant his last suggestion to be a subtle way of telling the peers that the only thing for them to do was to accept the Petition of Right as it stood. That was not his way of speaking, for he always meant what he said. No wonder the last part of Wentworth's speech confused his fellow members and found no favour with them. On the other hand his opening plea was acceptable to the majority of the lower House.

Only Sir John Eliot took offence at it.[1] But first he declared that he was in agreement with Sir Thomas Wentworth. He agreed that the Lords should concur with the Commons in order to give strength to the Petition. He agreed that the support of the Lords would have influence on the King. He agreed that when both Houses had given their approval the result would produce 'more authority and force'. But he did not like the arguments Wentworth used to induce agreement. He did not like the figures he had employed. 'As though the virtue and perfection of this House depended upon, and were included in, their Lordships,' Sir John declared. He did not consider the Commons 'mere cyphers to nobility'. He felt sure that if they were deserted by the peers, they 'should yet continue flourishing and green'. 'Therefore,' he said, 'I disagree and must vary from that gentleman.' Sir John continued with a denunciation of Wentworth's proposal that the Lords be asked to find some form of accommodation to which both Houses could agree. He asserted that the suggestion was 'at least in interruption, if not in contradiction' to the decision of the House to refuse the additional clause. He showed that the Commons had never suggested any addition or alteration to the Petition and that much time had been consumed before they were willing to accept even a few unimportant words. He insisted that Wentworth's proposal, if carried out, would result in endless discussion and debate. Previously Sir Thomas had been determined to keep the liberty of the subject intact, but now this proposition seriously endangered such a principle, Sir John said. Any 'saving' clause, he declared, however subtly worded, was bound to weaken, if not destroy, the value of the Petition of Right. In fact, he

[1] Forster, *Eliot*, II, 223–7 (2nd edit., II, 69–71). The ms. of the speech Forster says he found at Port Eliot. I have been unable to find a trace of it anywhere. That the speech was delivered is attested by briefer versions in Mass. MS.; Grosvenor (2); Borlase. Undoubtedly Forster doctored the speech so that it would run smoothly.

had heard from 'an honourable gentleman near the chair', by whom he meant Sir Humphrey May, that the King was not in love with the Lords' additional clause, 'taking it rather as tending to his prejudice than his advantage'. With Buckingham in mind no doubt, Eliot said the clause was being insisted on as 'a colour and an art to give satisfaction to some ministers whose worths will hardly merit it'. In conclusion he moved that they urge the Lords to hasten with this business so that no more time be wasted.

Though we may admit that the figure of speech employed by Wentworth in describing the nature and worth of the Commons when acting by themselves was a little too strong, a little too colourful, we must agree that he was right in his constitutional interpretation. It was Wentworth's language rather than the thought behind it that aroused Eliot. His idol had received a resounding slap in the face. Little wonder he sprang to its defence, though in so doing he contradicted himself. At the beginning of his speech he had approved the co-operation of the two Houses in the Petition of Right, and on April 30 he had said that the business of the Commons must have the approbation of the Lords.[1] But when Wentworth compared the Commons acting without the Lords to dry grass, Sir John's anger blinded him to the constitutional truth put forward by his Yorkshire rival. Actually Eliot's condemnation of Wentworth's figure of speech had no effect on his colleagues in the committee of the whole, while the rest of his speech received the approval of the members of his party.

Wentworth, however, could not be attacked so openly without replying. As soon as Sir John had taken his seat Sir Thomas arose to clear himself. The member for Cornwall, he said, was mistaken, for he did not intend 'to trench upon the liberty of this House' by means of his figures of speech. He placed 'the happiness of this House' above his own life. But again he said that if the Lords did not join the Commons in the Petition of Right, it was 'of no use'. He had not spoken 'unseasonably', Wentworth said. The House could do whatever it pleased with his suggestions.[2] Clearly Sir Thomas had been annoyed by Eliot's attack on him; but now there was no mistaking his meaning. Not even Sir John could rebut such straightforward language.

But Eliot had also brought the King's opinion, through the mouth of May, into his speech. That needed an explanation, and Sir Humphrey

[1] See above p. 218.
[2] Borlase, also Mass. MS. and Grosvenor (2) as well as Birkenhead, *Strafford*, p. 101.

gave it as soon as Wentworth had finished. He believed that the Petition of Right 'do stretch very far'. If it was going to be strictly enforced, it would 'give a blow to the government'. In that case the King believed the additional clause 'would do him no good'.[1]

After a few more speeches on Wentworth's proposal it was ordered to report to the House the arguments against the addition of the Lords to the Petition of Right. When this had been done a conference with the peers was requested, granted, and held at which Glanville and Marten delivered long speeches.[2] As the Lords desired to discuss the Commons' arguments immediately and had hopes of reaching some decision that day, they requested the Commons to sit in the afternoon. To this they agreed.

But the peers were too sanguine. No decision was reached. They did arouse the wrath of the Commons when the proposal was made that a conference of select committees be held to try to reach an accommodation. Eliot was outraged at such procedure. And when the point was debated on the next day, he was supported by Phelips, Rich, and Digges. Sir John declared it was unparliamentary and without precedent, unnecessary, and inconvenient. Such important business should not 'be committed to the judgment of a few'. For a second time Wentworth disagreed with Eliot. He declared the practice was parliamentary and should be employed in this instance. What a tempest in a teapot! The House refused a conference of select committees. In the meantime the Lords had begun a long debate on the Petition of Right and had lost all interest in any conference.[3]

Now that it appeared that the Petition was making some progress, Sir Henry Marten proposed that the subsidy bill be given its second reading. To this Eliot objected that it would hinder the King's business and might actually delay the final settlement of this bill. But when Pym moved that the subsidy bill be given its second reading on Monday morning, the House approved.[4]

That Monday, May 26, was a momentous day. The Lords accepted the Petition of Right as sent to them by the Commons.[5] After a conference of committees of the whole of both Houses Sir Edward Coke reported to the lower House that the peers had unanimously agreed to

---

[1] Grosvenor (2), also Borlase and Mass. MS.
[2] Rushworth, I, 568–84 and *Eph. Parl.*, pp. 186–94.
[3] All five diaries and *C.J.*, I, 904.   [4] Borlase.
[5] Relf, *Notes of the Debates in the House of Lords*, p. 205 and Rushworth, I, 584–85.

the Petition as it stood. Then some of the leaders of the 'country' party urged their colleagues to rush the Petition through the House,[1] while others wanted the subsidy bill passed as quickly as possible.[2] But there were two who did not appear to share the enthusiasm of their fellow members. Sir John Eliot was silent, possibly because the struggle of the past weeks had dampened his spirits, or else because his mind was filled with a new topic. It was not of national importance, but for the moment it was vital to him. He would shortly disclose it to the House of Commons. The other was Sir Thomas Wentworth who tried to curb the headlong rush of his colleagues to pass the Petition of Right through the House.[3] It was an important document to him, so important that it should be read carefully before its final passage. To Wentworth the Petition freed the King from the baneful effects of evil councillors and gave full sway to a sane and sound prerogative. He could not imagine that the prerogative as exercised by a Stuart had been and would become as evil as had been the sway of the Duke of Buckingham. As has been said before, both Eliot and Wentworth desired above all else good government. They both had believed that the King of England, if left to his own devices, would give his country such a government. Had not the idealized Elizabeth done that for a generation and a half? Wentworth still believed, believed implicitly, in his ideal of benevolent royal government. But for Eliot that ideal had received rude shocks and, imperceptible to him, was gradually being displaced by a government in which the House of Commons dominated the partnership of King and Parliament. The clear thinking Yorkshire baronet marched relentlessly ahead. He looked neither to the right nor to the left of him, while the confused Cornish knight began to flounder midst conflicting loyalties.

But on this Monday morning the Commons could not easily be checked. The Petition was read twice and ordered engrossed. In the afternoon, after a session of the committee of the whole for religion, the Speaker took his chair at five o'clock. The subsidy bill was given its second reading and Wednesday appointed for a discussion of its preamble. At last Charles was in sight of obtaining what he had been demanding for months. Was it worth the price he would be asked to pay?

[1] Erle, Phelips, Rich, and Seymour. As will be noted above, p. 229, the Petition of Right had not been formally passed by the Commons on May 8.
[2] Digges, Sir Thomas German, and Littleton.
[3] Borlase, Mass. MS., Grosvenor (2).

For the next two days the Commons were intensely interested in completing their labours on the Petition of Right. What caused discussion when this document was given its third reading on Tuesday was the question as to where and in what form it should be presented to his Majesty.[1] To Eliot it did not matter where the presentation was made. All he cared about was that the King give a 'speedy answer'. But others showed themselves to be sticklers on procedure. Eventually the Petition of Right passed the Commons and was ordered sent to the Lords with the request that Charles give his assent in Parliament. Finally on May 28 his Majesty agreed to meet both Houses that afternoon at three o'clock in the Banqueting house at Whitehall. There the Lord Keeper presented the Petition of Right. King Charles replied that he would consider it. But he would not spend as much time in answering it as the two Houses had spent in framing it. The Petition of Right balanced by the promise of five subsidies rested precariously on the knees of the King. Would he accept or reject them both? He could not receive one without giving the other. The month of June was to provide an answer to this question.[2]

While Charles was considering his answer to the Petition of Right, let us glance for a moment at Sir John Eliot's denunciation of Lord Mohun. It may be remembered that late in the summer of 1626 after the dismissal of William Coryton from the vice-wardenship of the Cornish stannaries, John Mohun was appointed to fill the vacancy.[3] At the request of Sir James Bagg the Duke of Buckingham had induced the Earl of Pembroke, Lord Warden of the stannaries, to name Mohun to the position. But the stannaries in Cornwall had not run smoothly under the guidance of the new vice-warden. On April 10, 1628, Hannibal Vivian, MP for St. Mawes and comptroller of the Duchy of Cornwall, read a petition against the vice-warden in the House of Commons.[4] It was resolved 'to let it rest a while'. Thus were brought to light the unwarranted activities of Mohun in the Cornish stannaries at the very time he was seriously implicated in the unsavoury Cornish election for this Parliament. No wonder Bagg, who had for some time been seeing that trouble would sooner or later engulf his henchman, worked hard to procure him a peerage as a reward for his pains and as a cushion to ease any fall he might sustain. On April 16, the day after the date of

[1] Without any support Eliot tried and failed to obtain an adjournment of the House over Whit Monday. Borlase; Mass. MS.; *C.J.*, I, 905; Grosvenor (2).

[2] For this paragraph see *ibid.*, also Borlase; Mass. MS.; *C.J.*, I, 905–6.

[3] See above, p. 157, note 2.   [4] *C.J.*, I, 881.

Mohun's peerage, Mr Vivian again brought the attention of the House to the activities of the vice-warden by moving that a select committee be named to consider his petition against him.[1] The motion was passed. A committee of twenty-two was named plus the knights and burgesses of Cornwall and Devon with power to send for witnesses. As MP for Cornwall and chief opponent of the Bagg-Mohun faction Sir John Eliot played a leading role in the sessions of this committee. For weeks he and his colleagues worked like tireless ants gathering evidence against Mohun from every possible source.[2] By May 24 their task was completed. And on May 27 and 28 Eliot delivered a long detailed report to the House of Commons.[3]

The member for Cornwall made numerous charges against the vice-warden of the stannaries. Mohun had admitted men to the body of tinners who were not really tinners. He had ignored the jurisdiction of the primary stannary courts and had drawn all cases directly to himself. He had increased and demanded unwarranted fees. And worst of all he had misused the stannary parliament, or convocation as it was called in Cornwall. Not only had he personally nominated stannators, as the members were styled, but also had asked for a totally unwarranted grant of £500. After Mohun had tried to bribe and intimidate the members, convocation finally voted the sum. But then the whole body of tinners protested against it. Collections were stopped only when the tinners proposed to lay their case before Parliament. Such were the outstanding offences Sir John Eliot disclosed and denounced with his usual oratory.[4]

Many of his colleagues were astounded at such abuse of power. The opinion of the House was that Lord Mohun should be warned of the charges which had been brought against him and should prepare to answer them. The upshot was that the vice-warden finally decided to defend himself in the House of Lords and requested that the charges be sent there. Of course the Commons decided that Sir John Eliot should

---

[1] *C.J.*, I, 884.

[2] As may be seen from Eliot's notes preserved in the muniment room at Port Eliot.

[3] Forster, *Eliot*, II, 284–301 (2nd edit., II, 129–44). See also Grosvenor (2); *C.J.*, I, 905–6; Mass. MS.; Borlase. The report of Eliot against Mohun has been lost from the Port Eliot MSS, though Forster says he found it among them. In the muniment room at Port Eliot there are several sheafs of papers headed 'Stannary Business' which Forster never saw. None of these papers contains the report of Eliot, but taken together they are obviously the material from which it was constructed.

[4] For an explanation of various technical points in Eliot's report see G. R. Lewis, *The Stannaries, A Study of the English Tin Miner* (Cambridge, 1924), pp. 96–103, 109, 126, 245–7.

deliver the accusations against Mohun in the upper House. Actually the formal charge against this peer was not presented to the House of Commons until June 3.[1]

At this point Lord Mohun and his activities among the Cornish tinners grow dimmer and dimmer in the proceedings of Parliament. Not until June 14 was 'the charge against Lord Mohun read, allowed, and ordered to be ingrossed' in the lower House. Of course it was Eliot who read it.[2] But there is no evidence that this worthy knight appeared before the peers to accuse the vice-warden of all those villainies which he had presented to the Commons on May 27 and 28. That he prepared the speech he was to deliver against Mohun, at least a first draft of it, is attested by fragments at Port Eliot in which Sir John is far from being at his best.[3] In spite of Forster's statement that he delivered this speech in the upper House on June 17[4] there is not the slightest evidence to corroborate the biographer's words. The last days of Eliot's attendance in Parliament were too full of important problems to give him an opportunity to appear before the Lords on so irrelevant a matter.

But Sir John had no intention of letting Mohun escape scot-free and was planning to revive the charge against his enemy in the second session. When the noble peer wrote to Bagg on October 8, 1628, that 'Eliot and Coryton have incessantly roamed up and down all Cornwall in inquisition of my carriage in the vice-warden's place'[5] he could only have been referring to the summer of 1628 after the close of the first session. Apparently these two were not satisfied with the facts obtained by the committee of the Commons during the spring of 1628. They were searching for more evidence to make the charge against the vice-warden irrefutable when it was revived in Parliament again. But it never was revived except for an intensive but futile attempt made by Eliot late in January, 1629.[6]

On returning to the business of the Commons sitting on Thursday, May 29, we find Sir Humphrey May delivering a message from his Majesty.[7] Charles assured the Commons of a speedy answer to the Petition of Right and requested them not to adjourn over the Whitsun holidays as he desired 'to expedite the finishing of this session'. The first to speak on this message was Sir John Eliot. After a friendly comment

[1] C.J., I, 906–7; Borlase; Grosvenor (2); Mass. MS.
[2] C.J., I, 913; Grosvenor (2); Borlase; Mass. MS.
[3] P.E. MSS., 'Eliot, speeches, etc.', ff. 47–49. Neg. Post., II, Sup., pp. 125–30.
[4] Eliot, II, 304.   [5] C.S.P.D., 1628–1629, p. 347.
[6] C.J., I, 923, 925. See below p. 302.   [7] Ibid., 906; Grosvenor (2); Borlase.

on the King's remarks about the Petition, Sir John declared that he was dismayed that there was to be no Whitsun recess. He reminded the Commons of his request on May 27 for such a recess. He reminded them that discussion had been postponed until more of the members had returned to their seats. Now, as many had believed his Majesty would request an adjournment, the House was even thinner, Eliot declared. Consequently he felt that the only thing to do was to prevent more from departing. But in the end his motion was directly opposed to the King's request. It was to 'sit till Saturday and meet again on Wednesday'.[1]

Sir John seems to have been worried that the subsidy bill would slip through the House before the King had answered the Petition of Right. He feared that Buckingham was up to tricks and might now succeed where he had failed in July, 1625. The rest of the members were not as apprehensive as the Cornish knight. Many supported the request of the King. And the subject was deferred until the next morning when more would be present.[2] There is no record, however, that Eliot's motion for a recess was discussed again.

When the Commons met on Saturday, the last day of May, a nervous turbulence ran through the House. After Mr Solicitor Shilton had taken the chair of the committee of the whole to discuss the subsidy bill 'the great noise in the House and the going out of many made Mr Sherville [Henry Sherfield] make this motion. . . . I desire silence. We that sit here at the lower end know not what you above do. We hear nothing. You may give ten subsidies for ought I know'.[3] When silence had been obtained Sir John Strangways spoke. In the course of his remarks he introduced the question of whether Oxford or Cambridge should be named first in the money bill.[4] Immediately the dam which had pent up an age-old university rivalry was broken. The bill under discussion was lost sight of for that day in a rushing roar of words. The Commons forgot the problems of the nation, cast off the burdens of their years, and participated in a clash of youthful rivalry. In the end such a mix-up in procedure took place that the question whether to name Oxford or Cambridge first in the bill was never put. The Speaker took his chair again. And discussion in committee of the subsidy was postponed until Monday, June 2.[5]

---

[1] Borlase; Grosvenor (2).   [2] *Ibid.*; Borlase; *C.J.*, I, 906.   [3] Borlase.   [4] Grosvenor (2).
[5] This scene is based almost entirely on Borlase. Grosvenor (2) supplements Borlase but is not as complete.

On Whit Monday the House at the instigation of Sir John Eliot decided to call the roll on Wednesday and fine all absentees twenty
shillings. Shortly thereafter Mr Maxwell, the usher of the black rod, appeared at the door of the chamber and announced that his Majesty desired the immediate presence of the Speaker and all the Commons in the
House of Lords.[1]

3. THE KING'S FIRST ANSWER TO THE PETITION OF RIGHT

As the Commons trooped to the upper chamber they realized that
Charles was ready to give his answer to their Petition. They must have
hoped fervently that that answer would give them pleasure. They did
not have to wait long in the presence of their Sovereign to learn the
fate of their precious document. The King told them that he had come
to do his duty and that he had not taken as many days to answer the
Petition as they had spent weeks in framing it. After a short speech by
the Lord Keeper the Petition of Right was read and it was declared that
the King wished that right be done according to the laws and customs
of the realm. His Majesty would see to it that his subjects had no cause
to complain against the violation of their just rights and liberties.[2]

A visitor to Parliament watching Eliot and the leaders of the 'country' party straggling back into their chamber would have noted the
deep disappointment he saw pictured on their faces. The answer
Charles had given was worthless in the eyes of the vast majority of the
Commons. No mention had been made of the Petition of Right. No
correct and formal answer had been given. The labour of weeks was
destroyed. King and Commons were back to April 28 when Charles had
made virtually the same promise.[3]

As usual with the Commons, silence and contemplation were the first
resort when faced with bitter disappointment. Immediately upon their
return, on the motion of Sir Walter Erle they rose to think over the
royal answer to the Petition of Right.[4] Not a committee was to meet
that afternoon.

The Commons took their seats on the morning of Tuesday, June 3.
Mr Browne moved that the King's answer to the Petition be read again.
It was. Silence reigned. It was broken by Sir John Eliot. He confessed

---

[1] Grosvenor (2); Borlase; Mass. MS.; *C.J.*, I, 907, 908.
[2] *Eph. Parl.*, pp. 194–5, also Rushworth, I, 588–90.   [3] See above, p. 215.   [4] Borlase.

he did not know what to say. But somebody must begin. The royal answer was to their solution of the great business before them, their liberties. That business had consumed so much of the time of all the members in the House that it was a shame so few were present now to consider this reply. Therefore he moved that debate on the answer of King Charles be postponed until Friday. And so it was ordered.[1]

Once more not a whisper was heard in the House. Eliot had only cracked the icy silence. He arose again. As the business of the Petition and the answer were 'at rest', 'you are now at leisure and I cannot forbear to discharge my duty', Sir John began.[2] After these introductory words this man inspired by hatred and love, hatred of a fellow man and his policies and love of this country, launched into an oratorical denunciation of the English Government such as never before had been heard in the House of Commons. Of course Sir John Eliot had prepared this speech.[3] Possibly he even read it to the House. And later he made sure that anybody who wished to could make a copy of it.

The opening words of his formal address have appeared in print innumerable times. 'We sit here as the great Council of the King', he began; 'and in that capacity it is our duty to take into consideration the state and affairs of the kingdom.' Weakness abroad and weakness at home were most serious threats to that kingdom. To Eliot weakness at home was arousing the greatest fear.

'Our want of true devotion to heaven, our insincerity and doubling in religion, our want of councils, our precipitate actions, the insufficiency or unfaithfulness of our generals, the ignorance or corruption of our ministers at home, the impoverishing of the Sovereign, the oppression and depression of the subject, the exhausting of our treasures, the waste of our provisions, consumption of our ships, destruction of our men'—

---

[1] Borlase; Mass. MS.; *C.J.*, I, 908.   [2] Borlase.

[3] It is most unfortunate that Eliot's own version of this speech has disappeared. It is in Forster, *Eliot*, II, 237–47 (2nd edit., II, 79–88). He says it is the same as the copy in Eliot's hand he found at Port Eliot. But in the case of every speech of Eliot's where a comparison could be made between the original and Forster's version, that biographer has freely edited the speeches and at times changed them to suit his own purposes. No doubt, this speech is no exception to the rule.

I have found numerous separates of this speech in all the ms. collections I have examined. It has appeared in print a great many times, such as *Eph. Parl.*, pp. 195–201; Cobbett, *Parl. Hist.*, II, 380–5; the old *Parl. Hist.*, VIII, 155–63; Rushworth, I, 591–2; and in various reports of the *H.M.C.* The essential points of the speech are also in Borlase; Grosvenor (2); and Mass. MS.

such was the list of evils he presented to the Commons. By implication, but implication understood by every member of the House, Eliot absolved the King of all blame. And then he proceeded to elaborate on each of the charges he had made.

The papists had been tolerated and left unpunished. 'Want of council' was responsible for the loss of the Palatinate and the disaster at Rhé. Elizabeth, Sir John declared, would never have made such errors. She had allied England with France, kept that country unified, and had induced those two countries to join the Low Countries in their fight against Spain. Now it was just the opposite. Now there was war between England and France. And England was so weak that she could not help her neighbours, hardly defend herself. Indeed, policy had been changed to such an extent that it 'might be thought a conception of Spain than begotten here with us'.

At this imputation Sir Humphrey May arose from his seat. He declared this to be strange language. But the House commanded Eliot to proceed. Thereupon May interposed that if Sir John continued he desired to leave the House. He was greeted with cries of Be gone! Be gone! 'Yet he stayed and heard him out.'[1] The orator was in command.

After a few words of apology Eliot resumed his denunciation of the breach of the Anglo-French alliance, particularly at a time when Denmark was so badly beaten[2] and was in great need of assistance. Turning to the Privy Councillors he asked them whether they had advised such a policy. He could not believe it. What a subtle attack on the Duke of Buckingham!

Next Sir John went into detail on 'the insufficiency and unfaithfulness of our generals'. Again he brought the errors of the Cadiz, Rhé, and other expeditions before the Commons. Again he implied that somebody else, the Duke of Buckingham, was to blame for these errors.

Seizing upon 'the ignorance and corruption of our ministers', Eliot pointed to every aspect of government and to every corner of the land where instances of such ignorance and corruption could be found. Apologizing to the Speaker for the length of his discourse Sir John promised to curtail it. 'The impoverishing of the King' and the rest of his points he summarized with flashing, stinging oratory. Nearing his conclusion he declared that if a 'speedy reformation' be made of all

---

[1] Alured to Chamberlain, June 6, 1628, Rushworth, I, 609, also Borlase.
[2] He had in mind the defeat of King Christian of Denmark at Lutter on Aug. 17, 1626, and his expulsion from northern Germany by Wallenstein in Aug., 1627.

these disorders 'our ancient English virtue . . . will secure us'. The first step that must be taken to attain such a reformation Eliot declared was the preparation of a remonstrance. In order to inquire into all the facets of the proposed remonstrance he desired that the House ask his Majesty to give them more time.

This speech presents Sir John Eliot the orator at his best. If only we could hear his voice, know more about his manner of presentation. That he was eloquent, that he could carry the House of Commons with him, there is no doubt. Francis Bacon may have been an excellent speaker.[1] But did he have a cause such as inspired Eliot? Moreover, Sir John had the gift of choosing the right words and phrasing them in such a way that he stirred his audience as none before him and few after him were able to do.

In this speech Eliot was clearly, for all to see, aiming at the Duke of Buckingham. He had broken the spirit, though not the letter, of the agreement made before the session began.[2] The reason for the breach was obvious. The impersonal attack waged by the Commons through first a bill and then the Petition of Right was a failure now that Charles had given an entirely unacceptable answer. That answer had removed all bars, all restrictions, all promises which any of the Commons may have made. Furthermore, Eliot must have learned, or possibly only suspected, that Buckingham was largely responsible for that worthless reply the King had given to the Petition.[3] It was high time for Sir John to place blame for disasters and failures where it was due, to summarize in one great indictment the misfortunes of the nation, and to bring the culprit before the bar of the Commons without deigning to give him a name. Thus might the orator exchange charges to be proven for dramatic accusations. Somehow the favourite must be beaten. Ridding the nation of the Duke of Buckingham had become a sacred duty to Sir John Eliot, a duty which must be performed in order to save his ideals of perfection in government, in Parliament, and in the King. He still had faith in Charles—though it had been shaken—and believed that if he could remove the dark glasses from his Majesty's eyes, he (Eliot) would be revealed in the light of a saviour instead of a satan.

In the House of Commons where the members were catching their breath Sir Thomas Jermyn was the first to reply to Eliot. He cautioned

---

[1] In 1626 Sir Dudley Carleton spoke of Bacon as 'the best orator that ever sat within these walls'. Willson, *The Privy Councillors in the House of Commons*, p. 114.
[2] See above, pp. 184–5.   [3] Gardiner, VI, 298.

against starting a quarrel with the King now that they were so close to an agreement. But then he said: 'It is folly to conceal what every one thinks. This speech comes from the scantness of the King's answer to our Petition. Let us all apply ourselves to that and petition his Majesty for a fuller.'[1] At these words Sir John jumped up and replied: 'Where it is said that some distrust of the King's answer caused this, I protest the contrary. And I and others too have had this resolution to satisfy his Majesty thereon, only we stayed for an opportunity.'[2] That was just the point. 'Scantness of the King's answer', 'distrust of the King's answer', or what you will furnished the opportunity Eliot and others had been looking for. Jermyn was right and Sir John was just wriggling.

After Coryton had supported Eliot's attack, Sir William Beecher returned to the reason why Sir John had made it at this time. He felt that public causes were not so much to blame for the delivery of the speech that morning as 'private counsels and conference . . . of which I shall be able to say something when time is'. Cleverly avoiding the direct charge of Beecher, Eliot retorted: 'I am sorry I lie so obnoxious to mistakes. You may well judge I found a ripeness in myself for this notion, and that I as earnestly sought an occasion to utter it. For it may be it lay not in my breast only, but all men had the same thoughts.' And the House cried 'Yes! Yes! Yes!' Then spoke up Wentworth in defence of his rival and accepted the implications of Beecher's half-concealed charge. He said: 'God forbid but we may speak one with another out of that House concerning those things which concern this House, and yet no confederacy. And this tends much to the disservice of this House not to confer wtih one another. A man may light his candle at another man's fire.'[3]

The significance of this discussion is plain. The leaders of the 'country' party had held one meeting, if not more, at which it was decided that the oratory of Sir John Eliot or of anybody else should not be unleashed against the favourite until the occasion presented itself. It is doubtful that the circumstances under which such a speech should be delivered were defined or that a meeting was held after Charles gave his answer on the previous day. Later in the debate Phelips, supporting the remonstrance, declared that he did not expect this subject to be introduced at this time.[4] Possibly the answer to the puzzle is that Eliot,

---

[1] Mass. MS., also Borlase and Grosvenor (2).
[2] Mass. MS., also Borlase and Grosvenor (2).
[3] Borlase; Grosvenor (2); Mass. MS.   [4] Borlase; Grosvenor (2); Mass. MS.

knowing the general plan of his friends and intimates, found no opportunity on June 2 to consult with them and decided that they would all
support him if he chose this as the time to begin an astute attack on
Buckingham.

After the speech of Wentworth, support for a remonstrance began
to be expressed on all sides. The 'courtiers', to be sure, desired a moderate remonstrance and requested that it go hand in hand with the subsidy
bill. When the leaders of both sides had shown their approval, whole-
hearted or merely general, of Eliot's proposal, Richard Spencer reverted to particular words in the speech of the day. He desired Sir John
to explain what he meant by saying that English policy appeared to be
a conception of Spain. Eliot, thanking the gentleman, replied that all he
meant was English affairs had been so disastrous in the past that it
looked as though they had been undertaken on the advice of their
enemy, Spain, than at the behest of sane counsel at home.[1] The explanation satisfied Spencer and the 'courtiers'.

Having concluded the formal business of the day, it was decided to
discuss on the morrow in committee of the whole Eliot's remonstrance
and to adjourn immediately into committee to complete the reading
of the subsidy bill.[2]

But on the morning of June 4 the Commons did not return to Sir
John's remonstrance. Instead they listened to a message from his
Majesty[3] in which they were told he was satisfied with his answer to
the Petition of Right and had no intention of altering it. He planned to
end the session on June 11; hence there was no time for a discussion of
new grievances. They should be saved for the next session. The message
naturally irked the members of the 'country' party, but only by their
silence on the royal injunction did they show their feelings.

No discussion of the remonstrance took place. At the close of the day
the chairman of the committee of the whole on the remonstrance took
the chair and adjourned it immediately to meet the next morning at
eight. It had already been agreed that the House itself should meet at
seven. Could the King during that hour prevent a debate on the remonstrance? Could he force the Commons into a strait-jacket?[4]

[1] Borlase; Grosvenor (2); Mass. MS.
[2] C.J., I, 908; Borlase; Grosvenor (2); Mass. MS.
[3] Delivered by the Speaker. Rushworth, I, 593; Borlase; Grosvenor (2).
[4] For this paragraph and for the long report from the committee of the whole for trade
delivered by Digges with Eliot's remarks see Borlase; Grosvenor (2); Mass. MS.; C.J., I,
909; Harl. 5324; Eph. Parl., pp. 201–3; and Lowther who began taking notes on this day.

When the clock struck seven on the morning of June 5 Speaker Finch took his chair. One of the most moving and unforgettable scenes ever witnessed in the House of Commons was about to be enacted. The members prayed. The House was well attended. The threat of a heavy fine had filled the benches. Before the usual routine business was brought before the members, long before it was time to adjourn into committee of the whole, Mr Speaker delivered a message from his Majesty. Charles reminded his faithful Commons that a day for prorogation had been set. He had no intention of changing it. There was so little time at their disposal that he requested 'they enter not into or proceed with any new business which may spend greater time, or which may lay any scandal or aspersion upon the state, government, or ministers thereof'.[1]

Those last words were a bomb which shook the House to its foundations. That sacred privilege of freedom of speech had received a staggering blow at the hands of the King. But were the words put in the mouth of the Speaker by Charles any worse than the scolding given the Commons by the Lord Keeper on March 29, 1626? He told them in the name of the King to 'cease this unparliamentary inquisition' of the Duke of Buckingham.[2] Or was the imprisonment of Eliot and Digges in that same Parliament any less a violation of freedom of speech than this last command of his Majesty? No. Charles had hit as hard on previous occasions and had infringed that liberty as clearly and obviously as he was doing on this June morning of 1628. But why should the Commons be moved more deeply than ever before by this last prohibition? They must have remembered that the command and the imprisonment of 1626 had not benefited the King and had in no way harmed the practice of their privilege. The answer to this question can be found only in the changed mentality of the majority of the House of Commons. In 1626 the members, denying honestly that they had any quarrel with his Majesty, were fresh in their fight with the favourite. They were willing to exchange blow for blow. Thrusts from the King dismayed the Commons, but ignoring the source of the attack they quickly rallied and struck back at the Duke of Buckingham. The struggle of 1626 had been wearing indeed. But by June, 1628, the opponents of the Crown had participated in a long series of nerve-racking experiences. The 'forced' loan with its imprisonments, the struggle with Charles over a bill of rights, the protracted dispute with the Lords

[1] Rushworth, I, 605; *Lowther*; Borlase; Grosvenor (2).   [2] See above, p. 121.

over the Petition of Right, and finally the worthless answer of the King to the Petition had brought the majority of the House of Commons to a state of mind that was well-nigh unendurable. This last violation of their privilege was too much. Their nerves gave way under the strain. Undoubtedly, too, many of the Commons began to realize now, in spite of their continual protests and sincere belief in the past to the contrary, that the King was not blameless, that he was stepping down from his pedestal, that he was fallible like themselves. The old and firmly founded theory, the King can do no wrong, was disintegrating before the eyes of many in the House, though not all. No wonder tears of anguish and dismay welled up in place of anger and the desire to strike harder than ever at the great enemy of the state, the Duke. That policy seemed so hopeless now. A correspondent wrote: 'I have been told by a parliament man that there were above an hundred weeping eyes, many who offered to speak being interrupted and silenced by their own passions.'[1]

The first to attempt to express his feelings in words was Sir Robert Phelips. Even though he managed to say something, in spite of a commentator's remarks that he 'could not speak for weeping',[2] his observations were little more than an expression of his overflowing feelings. His last words illustrate this when he said that they should beg his Majesty 'to give us leave to retire to our houses to pray for him'.[3]

If Sir John Eliot, who spoke next, was dry-eyed it is remarkable. After some preliminary remarks about their great sins and the danger of God removing 'Himself further from us', Eliot declared that he believed that 'misrepresentation to his Majesty hath drawn this mark of his displeasure upon us'. Instead of trying to lay aspersions on the government, their only desire was to avenge the dishonours that had been placed upon King and country, he said. They were also reported to have cast aspersions on the ministers of the King. But Sir John believed that no servant could be as important to his Majesty as his kingdom and people. At this moment 'the Speaker started up from the seat of the chair, apprehending Sir John Eliot intended to fall upon the Duke and some of the ministers of state, said: "There is a command laid upon me that I must command you not to proceed".'[4] Eliot sat

[1] C. and T. Chas. I, I, 360.   [2] S.P.D., Chas. I, CVI, no. 55, and Rushworth, I, 609.
[3] Mass. MS.; Rushworth, I, 605–6; Borlase; Lowther; Grosvenor (2).
[4] Rushworth, I, 606; Mass. MS.; Grosvenor (2); Borlase. Rushworth has the Speaker intervene in the middle of a sentence. Both Grosvenor (2) and Borlase have Eliot complete his sentence as given in the text.

down. Insult had been added to injury. The King had not only prohibited freedom of speech, but now, through the Speaker, had also enforced the prohibition. The flood of tears and desolation in the House became even greater. Only Sir Dudley Digges was able to express himself. 'I have been heretofore glad to be of Parliaments,' he said. 'I am now sorry that I was ever of any because we are commanded from our liberties. I beseech you gentlemen that we may be silent.'[1] When Seymour had seconded the proposal to sit in silence, the Speaker, with tears streaming down his cheeks, protested that 'before God I mean all well. If you know what I have done, you would not blame me. For I am sure I have used my best faculties to do you service'.[2] Silence reigned in the House.

How long this stillness was punctuated only by sobs and blowing of noses it is impossible to say. At length it was broken by Sir Nathaniel Rich. He deprecated a long silence. 'Either we must now speak or forever hold our peace,' he said. He proposed that the Commons go as a body to the House of Lords and tell the peers how English liberties had been violated and the King endangered. The members of both Houses then could present themselves to his Majesty and 'fall prostrate before the King and desire him to save himself and the kingdom'. Rich was supported by Pym, who moved that a committee be appointed to compile the heads of a resolution dealing with the violations of their liberties and the danger to the kingdom. But then several members suggested that it had been Eliot's speech of June 3 which had given offence to his Majesty and in consequence caused them such anguish. Fearing the truth of these remarks Sir Robert Phelips with eyes far from dry arose again and declared that as this might be the last time he was to speak in the House he moved that the question be put 'for freeing every member of undutiful speech since the beginning of this Parliament'. The motion was passed. Shortly thereafter it was moved and approved that the House adjourn into committee of the whole to consider the royal message. At his own request the Speaker was granted leave from the House for half-an-hour. Whitby took the chair of the committee, whose members were instructed not to leave on pain of being sent to the Tower.[3]

After some discussion as to whether to proceed with their remonstrance or first go to the Lords, there arose Sir Edward Coke. Weighted

[1] Borlase; also Grosvenor (2); Mass. MS.; Rushworth, I, 606.   [2] Borlase.
[3] Grosvenor (2); Borlase; Mass. MS.; Lowther; Rushworth, I, 606, 609.

down by close to fourscore years[1] he was still buoyant, still keen, still ready to lead in the thick of battle. With his mind steeped in the past he first gave precedents of royal ministers attacked and punished by the Commons. Coming to the present he asked why should they now be afraid to do the same. 'I will not stick to name the Duke of Buckingham,' he asserted. 'This man is a grievance of grievances. I am the first to tell you so this day and I shall never repent it, for you will find that all that is amiss will reflect upon him.'[2] After such fearless leadership it was easy to follow. No wonder Thomas Alured wrote: 'As when one good hound recovers the scent the rest come in with a full cry, so they pursued it, and every one came on home and laid the blame where they thought the fault was.'[3] Coryton, Kirton, Sherland, Valentine, Fleetwood, Knightley, and many others raised their voices against the favourite.[4] But Sir John Eliot remained silent. He had had his say. He was not needed. But the Duke was not without defenders. Ashburnham, Sir John Scudamore, Beecher, Edward Nicholas, and others gave him their support.

As denunciation and defence grew hotter with every speaker, John Selden put a temporary stop to the controversy. He desired that the remonstrance or declaration, as it now was being called, be brought before the committee of the whole. But the Duke's supporters continued to talk. Their object seemed to be to kill time. At length Eliot growing impatient broke his silence and moved that a sub-committee to compose the declaration be named. No action was taken on this motion. After several points to be included in the document had been named Sir John spoke again. This time he introduced a grievance of his own, the quartering of Irish troops in Essex and Kent. But nobody paid any attention to his complaint. The members were too aroused, too concerned with their own feelings to follow the lead of anybody. Just as the motion 'that the Duke of Buckingham shall be instanced to be the chief and principal cause of all these evils and an enemy to the state' was about to be put to the question the Speaker appeared in the House. He had been absent and in conference with the King far beyond the half-hour allowed him by the House.[5] After a considerable dispute

[1] He was 76.   [2] Borlase, also Grosvenor (2); Mass. MS.; *Lowther*; Rushworth, I, 607.
[3] *Ibid.*, 610.

[4] Most of them are to be found in Borlase and Grosvenor (2), a few in Mass. MS. and *Lowther*.

[5] Alured in his letter says he stayed away three hours. Rushworth, I, 610. That seems to be an exaggeration.

Finch took the chair. The motion before the committee of the whole had not been passed. The Speaker announced that he had a message from his Majesty. Charles requested the Commons to adjourn immediately; no committees were to meet that afternoon; and the House was to reassemble the next morning. The Commons complied. Exhausted by their emotional strain they departed to their lodgings. Many must have wondered whether this was not the end, whether they would see each other at Westminster again that year.[1]

The Lords were also apprehensive that Charles might end this Parliament.[2] They had cause for their fears. From two until eight that afternoon the King was in consultation with his Council on the subject of the dissolution of Parliament.[3] The final decision was to leave June 11 as the date of prorogation.

The Commons met on Friday morning, June 6, to hear Speaker Finch explain his actions of the previous day and present another message from his Majesty. They were told that the King had no intention 'of barring you from what hath been your right'. In other words, they were not to be deprived of freedom of speech. The Speaker continued by saying that his Majesty's intention was 'only to avoid all scandals on his Council and actions past that his ministers might not be, nor himself under their names, taxed for their counsel unto his Majesty'.[4] The message had a touch of Tudor finesse and consequently put the Commons into a better frame of mind.

After Rudyerd, supported by Alford, had proposed that the King be asked to give a more satisfactory answer to the Petition of Right and Phelips in a tactful and friendly speech had insisted that they proceed with their remonstrance,[5] Sir John Eliot arose. Today he was full of joy, while yesterday he had been bowed down with sorrow. Now they must consider the royal message and the royal answer to the Petition. Sir John believed that the King would explain his answer without any request from them. Going to the Lords with such a request might cause disputes and delay. Eliot wanted the Commons to rest upon the goodness of the King which he was sure would drive all the clouds

---

[1] Grosvenor (2); Borlase; Mass. MS.; *Lowther*; Rushworth, I, 607; Gardiner, VI, 219; C.J., I, 909.

[2] Gardiner, VI, 306–07, and Relf, *Notes of the Debates in the House of Lords*, pp. 214–15.

[3] S.P.D., Chas. I, CVI, no. 55.

[4] Rushworth, I, 610, also *Eph. Parl.*, p. 203; Grosvenor (2); Borlase; *Lowther*; Nicholas (2).

[5] Grosvenor (2); Borlase; Mass. MS.; *Lowther*; Rushworth, I, 611–2.

away. The message, in which their liberties were preserved, had given comfort and joy to Sir John. He desired that the Commons make 'a short and humble representation' as to what they intended to do. His Majesty was to be told 'that we do not cast any aspersion on him or his Council, but where there is a want of duty in any to inform him thereof'.[1]

A kind, tactful word from the King had engendered in Eliot all the old loyalty and love of his Sovereign. Though these sentiments in Sir John had slowly been weakening for the last two years, the latest message from King Charles had restored, for the moment at least, his faith and confidence in royalty. But Eliot realized that the influence of the Duke of Buckingham over the House of Lords was so great that he might cause the Commons endless trouble and delay should they approach the King through or with the help of the upper House. Sir John was being turned against the Lords because the power of the Duke and 'courtiers' was infinitely greater there than in the House of Commons. He believed that the favourite was largely responsible for the three weeks of haggling between the two Houses over the Petition of Right. Now Eliot advised the Commons to trust the King and let the good within his Majesty express itself in the best interests of the nation.

After this lone display of enthusiastic loyalty a debate developed in which the question was whether first to ask the King for another answer to the Petition of Right or proceed with the remonstrance. It was Pym who finally convinced the House that a request for another answer must be made jointly with the Lords and would take all the remaining time of the session. Therefore, they had better proceed with the remonstrance and forget for the time the royal answer to the Petition. The House decided to discuss the remonstrance, or declaration as it was also called, in committee of the whole.[2]

In the debate in committee that morning various heads of the remonstrance were proposed and discussed.[3] At the afternoon session of the committee Strangways was the first to propose a new head. He called it innovation of government under which he put billeting of soldiers, martial law, and bringing German cavalry to England. Upon Strangways taking his seat Eliot arose and denounced along familiar lines billeting and martial law. 'As for the drawing on of foreign horses,' he

[1] Mass. MS., also Grosvenor (2); Borlase; *Lowther*; Nicholas (2).
[2] Mass. MS.; Grosvenor (2); *Lowther*; Nicholas (2).
[3] For Eliot's defence of Sir Allen Apsley as a victualler see Grosvenor (2); Mass. MS.; *C.J.*, I, 909; *Lowther*.

said, 'our English are not of so poor heart and courage but that we are able to make our King great at home and abroad.' To give strength to his point he cited the precedent of the Duke of Somerset who was charged with treason for bringing in 'straingers'.[1] In the debate which followed nobody actually knew whether foreign horse were in England or not. It was later ordered that Philip Burlemachi should be called before the committee on the next day to inform it on the whereabouts of this troop of foreign cavalry. The billeting of Irish soldiers in England was also thoroughly denounced, but no decision had been reached on it when the next head, the cause of disaster in all English actions abroad, was presented. Again Eliot had something to say. He declared that the lack of trained officers and generals was the cause of these failures and desired that this mistake be not made in future. As usual member after member denounced the officers of particular expeditions without mentioning any names. Sir John spoke a second time on this point and mingled his barbed shafts with unexpected moderation. 'I conceive the fault was in making such commanders as wanted courage and fidelity,' he said. 'As for that to Rochelle, we know who was employed; one that wanted experience, and so for that to St. Martins. But we do not complain of what is past but desire his Majesty to take this into consideration for the future.' In conclusion Digges and a few others discussed the decay of trade and shipping, whereupon the committee of the whole, on the motion of Eliot, was adjourned for the day. Much had been said but no decision on any of the heads had been reached. As usual the Commons displayed their ability to talk without getting anywhere. What a boon the committee of the whole was to these loquacious Englishmen.[2]

After the Commons on Saturday, June 7, had denounced the export of ordnance and military supplies with Sir John Eliot making a typical speech in opposition, the House adjourned into committee of the whole. There Burlemachi declared that he had received funds to bring a thousand German horse to England. But they never crossed the Channel, he said, because the order had been countermanded. In spite of this statement the project was denounced by several speakers including Eliot.[3]

---

[1] Eliot is mistaken. It was the Duke of Northumberland and not the Duke of Somerset who proposed to bring foreign troops to England in his attempt to put Lady Jane Grey on the throne instead of Mary Tudor. J. A. Froude, *History of England from the Fall of Wolsey to the Death of Elizabeth* (New York, 1872), VI, 40.

[2] Grosvenor (2) and Mass. MS., but also on *C. J.*, I, 909; Rushworth, I, 612; Nicholas (2).

[3] Mass. MS.; Grosvenor (2); Borlase; *C. J.*, I, 909; Rushworth, I, 612-13.

While the members were attacking a proposed excise tax a message came down from the Lords and the Speaker returned to the chair. The peers desired a conference between the two Houses concerning the answer of the King to the Petition of Right. It was granted. At the conference the Commons were asked to join with the Lords in request-ing his Majesty to give a clear and satisfactory answer to the Petition. On returning to their chamber and receiving the report of the confer-ence Coryton requested that their reply to the Lords be delayed until Monday. But Eliot responded: 'Let us embrace this present opportunity and join with the Lords.' He felt that the proposal in no way contra-dicted 'that way we were in'. Sir John appears to be inconsistent in his attitude towards the peers. But he was not. He only objected to co-operation with the upper House when it meant delay in furthering the interests of the Commons or the nation, when it gave Buckingham and the 'courtier' peers an opportunity to frustrate the plans of the lower House. There was no threat of that nature on this occasion. Immediate concurrence should produce what the Commons desired above all, a correct answer to the Petition of Right. The House needed no further urging to join with the Lords. Sir Edward Coke was sent with the message that the Commons would gladly co-operate with the peers in making this request of the King. The two Houses agreed to sit that afternoon, and Pym, with a premonition of good news from his Majesty, proposed the naming of a committee to compose the pre-amble to the subsidy bill.[1]

4. THE SECOND ANSWER TO THE PETITION OF RIGHT

While the Commons were discussing the remonstrance in committee that afternoon a message from the Lords brought the Speaker back to his post. The members were informed that the peers had sent the re-quest of the two Houses to his Majesty, and that they might expect to be called into the royal presence at any moment. The Commons had not long to wait. When the Lords and Commons had assembled Charles addressed them briefly, had the Petition of Right read, and declared 'Soit droit fait come il est désiré'. That was the answer they had been hoping for. That was the answer which made the Petition a matter of record and gave it the force of a common law decision.[2] Joy

[1] Grosvenor (2); Mass. MS.; Borlase; C.J., I, 910.
[2] For the standard account of the struggle for the Petition of Right, which covers much

reigned supreme when the Commons returned to the House. Sir Edward Coke was especially pleased and explained the legal soundness of the King's answer. Others like Wandesford and Littleton wanted the Commons to express their gratitude by taking quick action on the subsidy bill. Eliot must have basked in this sunshine, but surprisingly there is no record of his giving voice to his feelings.[1]

With the hearts of the Commons more loyal and grateful to their Sovereign than they had been since the beginning of the first Parliament of the reign, the opening week in June, 1628, came to a close. Like children these impressionable members of the House of Commons could turn from tears to laughter, from anger to love, and back again on the slightest provocation. They were easily aroused and expressed their feelings freely. They would plunge themselves at a moment's notice, as we shall see, back into the gloom and fighting spirit of the past weeks. Sir John Eliot was no exception to the rule. He was rather an extreme example of the typical member of his day. No wonder his powerful and emotional language could influence his colleagues so easily.

When the Commons assembled on Monday, June 9, the order of the day appeared to be speed in all matters. The decks were to be cleared of everything except the subsidy bill and the remonstrance. Sir John Strangways, still imbued with the joyous spirit of co-operation, urged haste first with the subsidy bill and then with the remonstrance. He desired the Commons to confer with the Lords on the remonstrance and present it to his Majesty as the joint work of the two Houses. To Eliot this proposal was not conducive to speed. He wanted no more disputes with the Lords. By all means proceed with supply, he said, and have the preamble to the bill drawn that afternoon. But when they considered their remonstrance he was opposed to conferring with the Lords, for that would cause delay and delay was dangerous. Already the bell had tolled twice for the end of the session. There were many subjects awaiting their consideration which Sir John wanted referred to committees. Now he desired that 'you Mr Speaker to leave the chair that Mr Whitby may take it and we may go on with our remonstrance'. Remembering the three weeks' delay caused by the upper House on the Petition of Right, it was only natural when time was at a premium that Eliot should advise against working with the peers on

of the ground given here, see Frances H. Relf, *The Petition of Right* (Minneapolis, 1917).

[1] Grosvenor (2); Borlase; Mass. MS.; Rushworth, I, 613; *Eph. Parl.*, p. 204.

the remonstrance. Having disposed of a few pressing matters, his pro-posal to adjourn into committee of the whole was accepted by the House and Whitby took the chair.[1]

The head of the remonstrance that held the attention of the com-mittee all morning was the failure to defend English shipping and coasts. Twice Eliot intervened, once with the help of Phelips, to hasten a settlement and end the debate. Finally it was decided to turn the decay of shipping and trade and the failure to guard the seas and the coasts into three heads of the remonstrance. In the afternoon Sir Edward Coke reported the preamble of the subsidy bill which was to be referred to the House the next morning. Progress was being made in spite of the effusion of the members. But it would be nip and tuck between the remonstrance and prorogation if Charles adhered to the date he had set, June 11.[2]

Fortunately for the Commons and their remonstrance they were informed on the 10th that at the request of the Lords the King had postponed the prorogation for a few days so the subsidy bill could be passed. Another message from his Majesty informed the members of the lower House that the Petition of Right with the royal answer would be enrolled and printed. That pleased the Commons and in-duced Digges to move thanks to the King. But their attention was cen-tred on the subsidy bill which passed through its report stage by the end of the day. The only part played by Eliot in the proceedings of the day was to move that the remonstrance be reported to the House the next morning at nine o'clock. So it was ordered.[3]

On June 11 the remonstrance was the centre of all attention, and that in committee of the whole. On four occasions Eliot participated in the debate. Except in one instance his words had little significance. When May under the head of innovation in religion told the committee that the King would advance neither papist nor Arminian, Phelips was pleased. But Coryton denounced the Duke in connection with religion and requested that he be named under this head. After Sir Richard Onslow had defended the favourite, Sir John Eliot said: 'As for the intimation from his Majesty, we all conceive our head sound and per-fect and his Majesty's intentions are clear. Let us truly present to him what he doth not know already about his ministers and officers.' In the

[1] Mass. MS.; Grosvenor (2).
[2] Mass. MS.; Borlase; *C.J.*, I, 910; Grosvenor (2).
[3] For this paragraph see *ibid.*; Borlase; Mass. MS.; *C.J.*, I, 910–11.

I

end eight heads of the remonstrance were passed by the committee of the whole.[1]

And then the storm, which had been brewing throughout the debate, broke loose. Long and Coryton each addressed the committee with thorough denunciations of the Duke of Buckingham under all eight heads of the remonstrance. Many more followed this lead. But the favourite was strongly defended. And some like Rudyerd and Marten counselled moderation. The point at issue in the storm of words was the cry of 1626, the Duke of Buckingham must be named as the chief cause of the evils encompassing the nation. Speaker after speaker blamed Buckingham for this or that evil, for one or another cause, or for all put together. But defence met attack in a far from one-sided debate. Near its close Littleton exhibited a leaning towards compromise when he said: 'I will not say to the King he [the Duke] is the cause of all these causes. But if we say that the Duke in his person or in his power in general opinion, as we conceive, is the cause of all this.'[2] That was too much for Eliot who had been silent ever since the direct attack on his arch-enemy began. Now he arose to speak his mind as freely as he ever had in the past.[3] He differed with the gentleman who had spoken last, he declared. There was neither time, need, nor purpose in making the proposed distinction. As to naming others who were just as much at fault as the Duke, 'it is his power and greatness that turns the wheels to all the rest', Eliot insisted. On the subject of religion it had been argued that his mother's religion was not his fault. But, the speaker suggested, they should observe how papists were tolerated and employed. Places of trust, Sir John continued, were 'given through his interest'. 'It was said he is not the cause of particulars. But let us say he is a cause. And though immediately he is not the cause, yet he is the immediate cause by his power.' Eliot went on to remind the committee how the Duke as a general in time of peace had appointed men to places of danger. As an admiral had he guarded the seas? Did nations

[1] Mass. MS.; Grosvenor (2); Borlase, also Nicholas (2) and *Lowther*. For heads of remonstrance see *Eph. Parl.*, p. 206 and *C.J.*, I, 911.

[2] For this paragraph up to this point see Borlase; Mass. MS.; Grosvenor (2).

[3] Mass. MS. and P.E. MSS., 'Eliot and Bucks', ff. 86–87v. Forster, *Eliot*, II, 311–3 (2nd edit., II, 108–10), following Rushworth, I, 617, misdates the entire debate in which this speech was delivered, June 13 for June 11. There is a striking similarity in the P.E. version and that in Mass. MS., even though they differ in many details.

The rest of the debate in committee of the whole on this day, which includes two more speeches by Eliot, is to be found only in Mass. MS. The other diaries do not cover the debate from the first of Eliot's three speeches on.

respect the English fleet as they had done in the past? 'We are not in a way of a charge but of a remonstrance,' Sir John concluded.

To these words Nicholas replied. Alford showed he had lost some enthusiasm for the chase. But Rich again blew the hunting horn which Phelips echoed in a request to make Buckingham 'the chief cause of all these evils'. Again Eliot pushed his case against that hated man. To assure the glory and safety of the King was their only intention, he said. If they present a remonstrance to his Majesty without showing what the cause of their troubles was, how could he reform them, Sir John declared. He begged the members to consider the goodness and sweetness of the King in whose hands they were putting everything. What a contrast to the favourite with his excessive power who was the immediate cause of all the evils. But Seymour felt that there were others 'that deserve as ill of the commonwealth as he'. Again May pleaded with the members and told them that his Majesty would consider it a favour if the Commons did not name the Duke, if they did not make a personal charge against him. After Speaker Finch had strengthened this appeal Sir John Eliot put in a final word against the arguments of the last two men. It was necessary to name the Duke, he asserted. Their honour and their action in the last Parliament made it so. Since that time the reasons for naming him had multiplied. In fact, they had already named him. By declaring that the Duke of Buckingham was the cause of the evils, Eliot alleged, and doubtless believed 'we shall be free from his Majesty's displeasure'. They had gone so far in their labours, he insisted in closing, that the only thing left to do was to present the evils and their cause to the King. Thereupon 'it was ordered upon question that the excessive power of the Duke of Buckingham and the abuse of that power is the cause of these evils and dangers to the King and kingdom and that this be added to the remonstrance'.

With the Speaker back in the chair the division of the two parties in the House of Commons was clearly shown when, on a technicality dealing with the report from the committee of the whole, the House divided. The 'country' party mustered 235 votes to 145 for the 'court'. Whitby then made his report and the House approved everything that had been passed in committee, including the naming of the Duke of Buckingham. The last step was to frame the remonstrance for which a select committee of nine, including Eliot, was chosen.[1]

Now it was time to turn to the subsidy bill. That bill, granting five

[1] *C.J.*, I, 911.

subsidies to Charles I, was given its third reading and passed the House
on the morning of Thursday, June 12th. The first to speak after the passage of the bill was Eliot. He said that, as they had demonstrated their
loyalty and duty to his Majesty, they should decide when to send the
bill to the House of Lords. He implied that it should not be done
immediately. A clerical subsidy had not as yet been granted. And the
Commons had not been informed of the heads of the general pardon.
Sir John's motion that the subsidy bill be sent to the Lords on the
coming Monday was approved by the House.[1]

On the last day of the week the remonstrance was finally put in
shape by the Commons. Upon the motion of Eliot it was decided to
deal with it clause by clause. The debate was brief until the last clause
was reached. Selden declared that as they had decided to name the
Duke as the cause of all the evils, they should be more explicit in this
clause. The Duke of Buckingham, he said, had both too much power
and had abused that power, therefore his Majesty should be requested
to remove him. The abuse of power by the Duke was the phrase he
proposed to add to the remonstrance. May replied that if the King
was to be requested to dismiss a bad servant, he should be told in what
way that servant was bad. Eliot, addressing both Selden and May,
agreed with the lawyer that they should request 'redress as well of
the abuse of his power as of his power'. To the 'courtier' he retorted
with the suggestion that the declaration against Buckingham in the last
Parliament be examined. And to the House he moved that the clause
under discussion be recommitted. As he received no support his motion
had to be dropped. Shortly after these remarks of Sir John the remonstrance was referred to the committee of the whole meeting that afternoon. With Whitby in the chair after the mid-day recess Selden argued
for his addition about the abuse of power. At the suggestion of Eliot a
sub-committee was named to rewrite the clause. As soon as the new
draft containing Selden's proposal was reported, the committee of the
whole accepted it and presented it to the House. There it was immediately approved, whereupon the Commons passed the entire remonstrance and ordered it engrossed.[2]

When on Monday, June 16, it was moved that the subsidy bill be
sent to the House of Lords, Sir John Eliot protested that 'the ancient
manner of Parliaments was to begin with the affairs of the common-

---

[1] Grosvenor (2); Mass. MS.; Borlase; *C.J.*, I, 912.
[2] Grosvenor (2); Mass. MS.; Borlase; *C.J.*, I, 913.

wealth and to conclude with subsidies. But now it is clearly contrary.'
He feared that this step might serve as a precedent to break the rights
and privileges of the Commons. By implication he displayed his apprehension that the King with money in his pocket might never hear their
remonstrance. And he was afraid that if the subsidy bill got out of control of the Commons, the King might issue a general pardon which
would include Buckingham and other enemies of the Commons. He
asked that it be shown that 'this pardon take not off these offences that
concern the commonwealth'. To this request Shilton replied that any
member could see the heads of the pardon if they came to him. But the
heads could not be presented to the House without the pardon. When
that was to be done was up to his Majesty, the Solicitor-General
asserted. The subject of the pardon versus the subsidy bill caused considerable debate in which Wentworth, May, Coryton, Phelips, and
others participated. After Phelips had declared that he did not want to
couple the pardon with the subsidy bill, it was finally decided to send
the bill to the Lords.

The Commons having approved the remonstrance with its schedule
of shipping losses, the Speaker, over his own protest, was ordered to
deliver it with a short introduction to his Majesty. In the introduction
Eliot proposed to 'let his Majesty see how readily we have given him
the subsidies, and in this remonstrance we have no ends but only his
Majesty's honour and safety, and that we do not, or will not, lay any
aspersion on his Majesty's government'. Sensing the insincerity of these
sentiments Sir Edward Coke would have nothing to do with them. He
believed the remonstrance too important for such generalities. Coke
had his way. On Sir John Eliot's motion May, Mildmay, and Lord
Carey were sent to the King to request access of the House to present
the declaration or remonstrance. That afternoon the Chancellor of the
Duchy reported that his Majesty signified his intention to meet the
Commons headed by their Speaker the next afternoon at two o'clock
to listen to their grievances.[1]

The next morning the Commons were informed that the peers were
highly displeased with the preamble to the subsidy bill. They were
hurt because the Lords had not been mentioned when it spoke of the
grant as being made by the Commons. In a lengthy debate one group
in the House showed that it was afraid of endangering the privileges of

[1] For the last two paragraphs see Mass. MS.; Grosvenor (2); Borlase; Rushworth, I,
619–26; *Eph. Parl.*, pp. 206–16; *C.J.*, I, 914.

the Commons by changing a money bill at the request of the Lords. The other thought the point made by the peers not important enough to warrant a dispute between the two Houses. They said the Lords should send the preamble back and the Commons would do 'what is fit'. With this group Eliot sided. Troubled neither by fear for the Commons' privileges nor by the lack of desire to work with the peers he said: 'Let us show to the Lords how willing we are to retain all good correspondency. . . . We conceive we have done them no injury at all, but if it come down from them we will do what is fit.' Sir John was not antagonistic to the Lords. He only opposed co-operation when it meant delay. But the problem could not be settled in debate that morning, so it was 'deferred to to-morrow morning'.[1]

The Commons assembled in the presence of the King at two o'clock in the afternoon to hear Mr Speaker present the remonstrance. The reply of Charles was far from satisfactory. He said he had not expected such a declaration from the Commons after the answer he had given to their Petition of Right. He had thought that they had some understanding of the affairs of church and state, but now 'I perceive you understand these things less than I imagined'. Even so he would consider the points of their remonstrance 'as they deserve'.[2] It is easy for us to comprehend why Charles made this contemptuous and scathing reply. We are tempted to wonder why, under the circumstances, the Commmons would have expected anything else from the King. But that would not be fair to Eliot, Wentworth, Phelips, Rich, Selden, Pym, and many others. Though in some it had been jarred, in most the faith in their Sovereign was hard to shake. They knew so little of the working of the mind of Charles, of the place Buckingham held in the heart of the King, and of the contempt King and court felt for the opinions of the country gentlemen, lawyers, and merchants who composed the opposition in the House of Commons. They believed that Buckingham had forced himself on the King and was exerting an influence over him against his Majesty's better and sounder nature. They were certain that if Charles could be shown that the Duke was threatening the true interests of the nation, the King, imbued with the same love of country as was theirs, would immediately dismiss him. It is strange indeed that these men of the House of Commons had not learned a bitter lesson from the Parliament of 1626 and subsequent

[1] See particularly Mass. MS., but also Borlase and Grosvenor (2).
[2] *Eph. Parl.*, p. 217, also *C. and T. Chas. I*, I, 366.

events. In many cases, to be sure, faith in themselves had been shaken. But the Petition of Right had restored it. Buckingham had almost caused defeat or emasculation of the document in the Lords. But the persistence of the Commons had beaten him. So they argued. They believed him responsible for the worthless answer given by Charles on June 2. But their attack on the favourite had opened the eyes of the King, they thought, and was responsible for the answer of June 7. The advantage they had gained must not be lost. The remonstrance with its naming of the Duke must be completed and presented. Now the King would see eye to eye with them. But he did not. The Commons had not been informed that the day before they presented the remonstrance Charles had ordered the sham prosecution of Buckingham, begun in the Star Chamber after the impeachment proceedings of the last Parliament, completely quashed.[1] Continual display of ignorance of events, facts, and of the mind of their King was costing the Commons dear. When would they awaken? Some individuals, possibly including Eliot, may have begun to see the true light. But many like Wentworth were anxious to follow the royal prerogative as long as it was not being mistreated and abused by such men as Buckingham. They believed they had tied the hands of the Duke and his kind by the Petition of Right and were now presenting in their remonstrance a cold, untouched picture of the favourite to his Majesty. The love of Charles for Buckingham,[2] his complete faith in him, was understood by few in the 'country' party and not even all of the 'courtiers'. That their King could put a man before his country was inconceivable to them.

With the remonstrance shelved by Charles in so unsatisfactory a fashion, the Commons got down to business on Wednesday, the 18th. After participating in a debate over some minor point[3] Sir John Eliot reminded the House of the importance of having the Petition of Right properly enrolled and printed. He recalled that the peers had promised to send it to the courts and desired 'a message may be despatched to the Lords to put them in mind of it. And that if any doubt arise their Lordships would be pleased to yield to a present free conference'.[4] As soon as

---

[1] Rushworth, I, 626–27.

[2] C. and T. Chas. I, I, 366, letter of Mead to Stuteville, June 21.

[3] It concerned a private petition which was referred to a select committee on which Eliot sat. Grosvenor (2); Mass. MS.; C.J., I, 914. According to my count in C.J. Eliot was named to 29 committees during this session, Wentworth to 24, Phelips to 34, Digges to 48, and Sir Edward Coke to 60.

[4] Borlase; Grosvenor (2); Mass. MS.

Selden and Hakewill had explained what steps had already been taken to give the Petition publicity, Rich reintroduced the request of the Lords to change the wording of the preamble to the subsidy bill. After a brief debate in which Eliot displayed a conciliatory spirit towards the upper House, this trouble between the two chambers was resolved. And then a conference on enrolling the Petition of Right was requested, granted, and held, the result of which was complete agreement between the two Houses.[1]

On Thursday, June 19, Sir John Eliot spoke for the last time during this session.[2] In the three months of this Parliament he had addressed his fellow members on countless occasions. As we have seen, Sir John had to talk. He was a poor listener. But as we have also seen, during the greater part of the session he was overshadowed by men of the calibre of Wentworth, Phelips, and Sir Edward Coke. That Eliot was outstanding is without question. That he was the leader of this Parliament is untrue. But on June 3rd and 5th he once again jumped to the fore. He was attacking and denouncing. Under these conditions he was without a peer and could bring the Commons under his sway with the greatest of ease. For the two following weeks Sir John was frequently on his feet and on occasion was able to direct the House. Generally, however, he left to others the formulation of policy. There was the weakness of the man. Rarely was he able to present a positive programme that met with approval. Occasionally he helped, but more than likely his proposal was rejected. If it was accepted, the chances were that it had originated with some other member. To repeat, Sir John Eliot was at his best, was the leader without question, when he was attacking denouncing, or hounding some opponent.

Why did Sir John not speak after June 19th? The answer is found on the next day when Sir Robert Phelips moved 'the House to give leave to a worthy member upon a sad occasion to repair home. It is Sir John Eliot whose wife is dead. The House assents.'[3]

According to the parish register of St. Germans Lady Eliot was buried on June 13, 1628, and her son Nicholas was baptized two days later. Lady Eliot gave birth on June 11 or 12 to her fifth son and ninth child. Childbirth regularly every two years was too much for her physical

[1] This incident is based chiefly on Mass. MS., but see also Borlase; Grosvenor (2), and C.J., I, 915.
[2] On a private bill. Mass. MS. and *Lowther*.
[3] Borlase, also C.J., I, 916.

stamina. Sir John may have known that his wife was far from strong and therefore tried to obtain a Whitsun recess which would enable him to rush to Cornwall and back. It is more likely that the death of Lady Eliot was sudden and unexpected. Her husband could not be notified in time, even to attend the funeral. But it is strange that word of his loss should have taken a week to reach him at Westminster. Eliot returned to St. Germans to mourn the loss of a fertile and faithful wife and to provide for nine motherless children, the eldest of whom had not turned sixteen.

In the meantime Parliament was hurrying to its close without the assistance of the alert mind and gifted tongue of Sir John Eliot. He could not participate in the debate in committee of the whole on tonnage and poundage[1] nor help to formulate a remonstrance on this subject whereby, as the King said, you 'do intend to debar me of tonnage and poundage which is a flower of my crown'. He was not among the dismayed leaders of the 'country' party who listened to the sudden prorogation to Parliament on June 26 before the new remonstrance could be presented to Charles. But the voice of Eliot was not yet silenced forever in the hall of the Commons. A new session within seven months was to give ample scope to the abilities and powers of a great orator.[2]

---

[1] The only references to tonnage and poundage in this session are as follows: the bill was introduced on April 2; it was read a second time on April 4; it was reported from committee of the whole and recommitted on April 9; and on May 26 Phelips proposed that the bill for tonnage and poundage be prepared.

[2] Borlase; Rushworth, I, 628–30, 631; *Eph. Parl.*, pp. 218–20.

CHAPTER XII

The Widower

July, 1628, to January, 1629

DURING the summer of 1628 Sir John Eliot devoted his time to his family and property. The death of his wife was a severe blow. How deeply it affected him is impossible to say. The more or less conventional comments on his loss which appear in his correspondence of this period denote little more than that Sir John and Lady Eliot had been happily married. She had been a good wife in bearing him nine children. As the mother of his children and mistress of his house she had left nothing to be desired, as far as the meagre records disclose. But because of the tender ages of his children on the death of their mother a heavy burden was placed on the shoulders of Sir John.

The two eldest sons, John and Richard, were by this time at school in Tiverton.[1] But the seven younger children[2] were still at Cuddenbeak. It was probably during the summer or early autumn of 1628 that the younger Eliots were sent to live with their maternal grandfather, Richard Gedy, at Trebursey in Cornwall.[3]

During these same months, possibly earlier, Sir John disposed of his property in the interest of the future of his family. Having suffered three imprisonments, been suspended as vice-admiral of Devon, and had his activities in that office thoroughly investigated, he realized that it would be an easy step for his enemies to induce the government to seize all his property and turn him and his heirs into paupers. So he transferred his lands and goods to faithful friends to be held in trust for himself and his children.[4] When, within less than a year, he was again a

---

[1] *Letter Book*, p. 64.

[2] For the ages of the Eliot children see above, p. 24, note 6.

[3] *Letter Book*, pp. 34, 50.

[4] They were: Nicholas Gilberte, John Norleigh, Hugh Boscawen, John Trefuses, Leonard Treise, Peter Mayowe, and Maurice Hill. See Eliot's will in Forster, *Eliot*, 2nd edit., II, 370.

close prisoner of the King, he is reported to have said that 'a commission was directed to the high sheriff of Cornwall and five other commissioners, his capital enemies, to inquire into his lands and goods, and to seize upon them for the King; but they returned a *nihil*'.[1]

Eliot's forethought was thus not without its reward. Having carried out these plans in the summer of 1628 he was legally landless. Technically others should have been administering his estates. Actually there probably was little change. His trusted servant, Maurice Hill, and faithful officials continued to do the routine work. As true, though not titular, head of several manors Sir John, nevertheless, must have found much to keep him busy during the months following the death of Lady Eliot.

Of his friends one of the first to express sympathy over his loss and possibly inform him of the prorogation of Parliament was the famous old antiquary and fellow member, Sir Robert Cotton. On July 1 Eliot replied, thanked him for his words of condolence, and remarked on the isolation of Cornwall from the happenings in London. He was glad that the session of Parliament had been brought to an end 'because to our understandings it implies a concurrence in the general, and intimates a continuance of the Parliament'.[2] Sir John then elaborated on the provincialism of Cornwall whose mists threw a curtain over domestic and foreign affairs making names and places merely words without meanings.[3]

This description of Cornish ignorance of and remoteness from the events of the world throws an interesting light on provincial England of that day. But Eliot either ignored the proximity of Plymouth, a wide open door for continental news, or else knew that such intelligence was spread with difficulty over the moors to the south-west and took a natural course to the north-east and to London.

During this summer Eliot must have received news at St. Germans which made him more bitter than ever against the favourite and could hardly have increased his love for his Sovereign. William Laud, denounced by the Commons in their first remonstrance of the previous month, was advanced on July 4 to the see of London. Others of the Arminian persuasion received similar rewards. Richard Montague,

---

[1] *C. and T. Chas. I*, II, 62.

[2] By these words he must have meant that most people were satisfied with a prorogation of Parliament which would probably be followed by another session in the near future.

[3] Brit. Mus. Cotton MS. Jul. C. III, ff. 168–68v.

bitterly hated by the puritans, was made bishop of Chichester. And, worst of all, Roger Manwaring was pardoned from the sentence passed against him by Parliament and received the rectory of Stanford Rivers, just vacated by Montague.[1] Arminianism was in the saddle, and all the bucking of the enraged puritans and moderate Anglicans with puritan leanings, such as Eliot, would not be able to unseat it. A violent outburst was inevitable in the next session of Parliament—if Charles were actually to call one.

Thoughts about the future in Parliament could not have dominated the mind of Sir John Eliot during the summer of 1628. There was much for the lonely widower to contemplate. A new subject came to his attention early in August in a letter from Capt Henry Waller, a member of the House of Commons and an admirer.[2] Writing from London, Waller began by expressing his condolences on 'the loss of so worthy and virtuous a lady'. Leading gradually to his point he spoke of how tedious and solitary it must now be for Sir John. Under those conditions it was the duty of a true friend to help to replace Eliot's loss. Waller wondered whether Sir John would be interested, should a widow be found in London who for person, parts, and estate 'may be thought to be a fit wife for a gentleman of worth and quality'. The captain admitted that he knew of such a widow who had lost her husband at about the time of Lady Eliot's death. Already the widow was being 'solicited by men of great birth and worth'. But she had made no decision and was still free. Waller said that he had mentioned Eliot's name to a friend who knew the widow. The friend, who did not know Sir John personally but honoured his name, wanted particulars about his worldly status and his children which Waller could not give him. So much the captain had done. Expressing his love and friendship, he closed with the hope that he had not offended Eliot.

That the fluttering wings of Cupid should follow hard on the silent wings of death in no way jolted the widower. He replied on August 11 with expressions of the obligation he owed to the worth and goodness of his friend for his most recent act of kindness. Misery and unhappiness were his constant companions, he wrote. As to the proposal the captain had made, Sir John left that in his hands. Giving him no help at all, he declared 'the overture you make is an argument of such favour and

---

[1] Gardiner, VI, 330.
[2] Clothworker and MP for London. O.R., I, 476. He was probably a captain in the London trained-bands.

respect as I cannot repose myself more confidently than in you, from whom as I have had the intimation I shall likewise crave the direction and advise'.[1]

Eliot was bewildered and forlorn. He could not think of the future with the sad past so near at hand. Had he been able to look ahead he must have realized that his young family needed above all else a woman's hand to guide it. Re-marriage, therefore, must be considered and not put off too long. On the other hand he was fully aware that he had been publicly marked. The government might fall upon him at any moment. It was not fair to a woman to ask her to marry a man who might be thrown into prison without warning or direct action on his part. Some of his flowery language to Waller might be interpreted to mean that this was what he had been thinking about. Whatever his thoughts, he could not decide for himself. The captain must do that, must weigh his needs, his misery, his loss in the balance with what the future had in store for him.

Any doubts or questions in Eliot's mind were ignored by Henry Waller in his answer of August 27. After a humble and flattering introduction he turned to his widow and told her story. Her husband had been a merchant, the son of a London alderman. She was about thirty years old and had one son who was her ward. Her husband had left an estate of around £30,000, half of which at least would go to her. She had been courted so strenuously that she had left for the country to visit her kinsman, Matthew Craddocke of Staffordshire, a member of Parliament.[2] Among her suitors was Sir Heneage Finch, the recorder of London,[3] Sir John was told. The widow had asked Waller two questions about Eliot. One was as to his means and the other was as to the number of his children, the captain wrote. When he could not enlighten her on these points, she said that she wanted to marry a man without children. Waller's comment to Eliot was that a woman's 'resolutions are not always constant'. At any rate, he was writing to Craddocke to further Sir John's suit and fervently prayed that success would be granted him. He hoped that he would meet Sir John when Parliament reassembled, if not sooner, 'the only obstacle [to the assembly of Parliament] being now removed, of which I doubt not but you have

[1] *Letter Book*, pp. 16–18.
[2] He sat for Stafford, *O.R.*, I, 477.
[3] He had represented London in the three previous Parliaments (*ibid.*, 458, 464, 470) but had no seat in this one. He had been chosen Speaker of the Parliament of 1626. *C.J.*, I, 816.

heard together with the manner thereof which will produce some alteration'. In these words Waller referred to the murder of Buckingham and disclosed that he had no love for the favourite.[1]

The nameless widow with her money, pretty face, and numerous well-born suitors seemed a good catch. Would Eliot think so and enter into competition in spite of his handicaps?

It took Sir John over six weeks to answer Waller's August letter. He was at Tiverton on his way to London for the opening of Parliament which had been set for October 20.[2] While visiting his sons there at school he received word that Parliament was not to meet until January 20th.[3] As there was no need to go on to London he wrote his 'matrimonial agent', Henry Waller, from Tiverton on October 15. He admitted that he entertained the marriage proposal at first only because it came from his friend. He was still considering it but left it entirely in the hands of Waller. The bearer of the letter would give him any particulars he might want.[4] Enthusiasm was lacking. Eliot can hardly be called an active aspirant for the hand of the widow. The instructions he gave to his servant may have been a little more explicit, but they could not take the place of Sir John in person.

That is what Henry Waller thought when he wrote to Eliot on November 1. He was deeply disappointed that Sir John's trip to London had been postponed. But his hopes of successfully concluding the match still appeared to be high. The gentlewoman had returned to London, he wrote, and 'hath been often moved concerning yourself'. Her answer was that she intended to remain single for the present; but when she did marry it would be with a man without children. Displaying again the point of view of the conceited male Waller's comment was: 'I persuade myself that few women have that power over themselves but that when a man comes against whom no other exception can be made those resolutions are soon turned.' But he confessed that he was severely handicapped by the absence of Eliot from London where 'others are present and daily soliciting'. He admitted that he had not received enough encouragement from the widow to urge that Sir John come to London just for the purpose of wooing her. Still 'if she did but see your person and hear your discourse, she could not have so

---

[1] *Letter Book*, pp. 18–20.

[2] Rushworth, I, 632.

[3] The agitation over the enforced collection of tonnage and poundage during the autumn of 1628 led Charles to prorogue Parliament to January 20. Gardiner, VII, 4.

[4] *Letter Book*, pp. 20–21.

hard a heart as to deny'.[1] Captain Waller had as much faith in Eliot as Sir John had in King Charles. But both were slipping.

As far as Sir John Eliot, Henry Waller, and the desirable widow are concerned, this letter closed the incident. Eliot did not marry pretty Mrs Bennett—that was her name. Perhaps his grief over the loss of his wife turned him against marriage for the time being. Perhaps he feared that his own precarious position was too much of a burden for a second wife to bear. The nine children may have been a higher hurdle than the widow wished to take, or there may have been a combination of all these factors. Elizabeth, daughter of William Cradock (or Craddocke) of Staffordshire and widow of Richard Bennett of London, became the talk of the town in November, 1628. Not only was Sir Heneage Finch a suitor but also Sir Sackville Crow, treasurer of the navy, and Dr Raven, a prominent London physician. Of the three birds the more colourful Finch carried off the prize to the dismay of the drab Crow and dreary Raven.[2]

But the summer of 1628 was a time when political changes of interest to Sir John Eliot in his Cornish seclusion were taking place in London. Endeavouring to create better feeling between the 'court' and 'country' parties for the forthcoming session of Parliament, Buckingham and Charles restored the Earls of Bristol and Arundel to favour and made Sir Richard Weston Lord Treasurer. These men were all interested in economy and peace and therefore might serve as a bridge between the Government and the House of Commons. Of the honours granted by the King the most startling to Eliot and his friends must have been the barony conferred on Sir Thomas Wentworth. More than that, he was received into favour by Charles. Now that the Petition of Right had tied the hands, as Wentworth believed, of Buckingham and other evil ministers, he, true to his loyalty to the Crown, was only too glad to serve his King more closely than ever. That can be seen today. But it was not manifest to his contemporaries, many of whom branded the new baron as an apostate. History leaves Sir John Eliot silent on what to him must have appeared to be a new path chosen by his great rival. He may have been prepared for the break, but it is more likely that he too joined with the leaders of the 'country' party in denouncing Wentworth as a traitor to their cause.

But the man regarded as the real traitor to the nation was about to

[1] *Letter Book*, pp. 22–3.
[2] *D.N.B.*, Sir Heneage Finch, and *C. and T. Chas. I*, I, 436, 437.

meet his fate. Preparing another expedition to relieve Rochelle, be-
sieged more closely than ever by the forces of the French government,
the Duke of Buckingham and King Charles made every effort to bring
the English fleet into shape for an early sailing date. Ever since the first
of August the King had been near Portsmouth to help the supervision,
while Buckingham travelled between London and Portsmouth to hasten supplies. But since August 17 the favourite had been at Portsmouth, so that on the morning of the 23rd John Felton, a discontented
army officer, had no difficulty in finding his victim. With the thrust
of a tenpenny knife Felton snuffed out the life of the best hated man in
England and brought upon himself what was, in the eyes of many
Englishmen, the death of a martyr.[1]

When Eliot received this news it is impossible to say, but it must
have reached him in a very few days. Henry Waller's casual and veiled
remarks of August 27 could hardly have been the first harbinger of this
momentous event. What Sir John's thoughts and feelings were on the
murder of Buckingham is too obvious to need elucidation. But it
would be of interest had some comment of his, however slight, survived in his correspondence. At least his plans for the coming session of
Parliament—if he had any—must have been affected by the elimination
of his greatest enemy in the government. But where would Eliot and
others be able to place the blame for unpopular acts of the government
now that the broad shoulders of the Duke of Buckingham had been removed? Would other shoulders take the place of his and still keep the
King inviolate? The next session of Parliament was to answer these
questions.

In spite of the death of the Lord Admiral, the fleet for the relief of
Rochelle weighed anchor on September 7 under the command of the
Earl of Lindsey. But Rochelle was too heavily invested and the English
fleet too ineffectively commanded to give any hope of succour to the
starving Rochellese. News of English failures before the Huguenot
stronghold was reaching Plymouth by the middle of October. Its
actual fall on the 18th of that month, however, could not have been
reported to England for several days, if not weeks. Consequently, Sir
John Eliot knew about the lack of English success before Rochelle,
though not of its fall, when on October 15 he wrote from Tiverton to
Sir Robert Cotton. He apologized for not being able to see Sir Robert
in London. At Tiverton he had learned of the 'adjournments of our

[1] For the last two paragraphs see Gardiner, VI, 335, 345, 349-50.

good success abroad and the Parliament at home'. He confessed that he
had been afraid that the English would not be able to relieve Rochelle.
As to the prorogation of Parliament to a later date, he said it was 'so
doubtful to that little reason I conceive, as I cannot judge whether it
import either good or ill.' Sir John then philosophized on the value of
leaving decisions to time. When he asked for news at court and 'how
greatness is affected', he implied that the murder of the Duke was
bound to cause changes in the government.[1]

That Eliot should be worried about who was to succeed the late
favourite is only natural. Though he could not have known that no
man was ever to fill the void in the heart of the King created by the
death of the Duke, yet Sir John had cause to believe that some important shifts would take place at court. Would Pembroke be advanced? Would Bristol, Arundel, and other peers friendly to Eliot and
his party be given some of the trappings of the late Duke of Buckingham? Above all, who was to be the new Lord Admiral? The answers
to these questions might easily have a serious effect on the public, if not
private, life of Sir John Eliot. When he learned that the office of Lord
Admiral had been put in commission and the Mastership of the Horse,
formerly held by the Duke, had been given to the Earl of Holland,[2]
he could not have been elated.

Surely, in the lost correspondence between Sir John Eliot and his
friends during the autumn and early winter of 1628 much must have
been written about the affairs of the nation. These men could hardly
have failed to express some opinion about the controversy between the
government and the merchants over the payment of impositions and
particularly tonnage and poundage. Those merchants who refused to
pay duties had their goods seized. Both sides agreed to submit the question of the government's right to collect tonnage and poundage to the
next session of Parliament. But they could not agree on who should
have custody of the goods until the larger question was settled.[3] By
levying tonnage and poundage and by seizing the goods of merchants
Charles was considered by many of his influential subjects to be breaking at least the spirit of the Petition of Right. Furthermore, the publication of that document also gave dissatisfaction. It appeared in print
with the unsatisfactory answer of June 2 as well as the final one of the
7th. Moreover, there was added to the printed Petition the King's
explanatory speech in which he gave his own interpretation of that

[1] B. M. Cotton MS. Jul. C. III, f. 167. [2] Gardiner, VI, 360. [3] *Ibid.*, VII, 3–4.

much discussed document.[1] All these subjects, or at least a hint of them, might appear in the letters of Eliot and his friends had they survived the tidying hands of the seventeenth century and the ravages of modern progress. Coupled with religion, these subjects furnished ample material in the coming session of Parliament for as pretty a quarrel between King and Commons as had taken place up to that time.

For the moment there was to be no session. Sir John Eliot, having visited his sons at Tiverton and having learned that his immediate presence in London was not required, returned to Cornwall. There a letter from Benjamin Valentine written in London on November 4 reached him. That gentleman expressed his disappointment at Eliot's return to St. Germans. He told of friends, Sir William Armyne,[2] Thomas Godfrey,[3] and Sir Walter Erle,[4] who were most eager to see Sir John either in London or at their country homes. He also was a purveyor of foreign and domestic news, most of which has little to do with the story of Eliot. He did say that Arundel had been admitted to the Privy Council, while Essex, Saye, Lincoln, and Warwick had been received at court.[5] The letter shows the popularity of Sir John and also gives a glimpse of the attempt Charles was making to win over those peers who were closely allied to the 'country' party in the House of Commons.

Having heard from Sir Robert Cotton or some other friend soon after his return to St. Germans that the Admiralty had been put in commission, Eliot took steps to clarify his own position in that department of the government. He wrote to Sir Henry Marten and John Selden. As we have seen,[6] both replied on November 7[7] and explained the legal position of Sir John Eliot as the sequestered vice-admiral of Devon now that the Lord Admiral was dead. This was the first time in nearly two years that the correspondence between Eliot and Marten was resumed. Their friendship had not been harmed because the two men were on different sides of the political fence. The man at the head of the Admiralty rather than principles had separated them. In his

---

[1] Gardiner, VII, 30.

[2] A Lincolnshire baronet, M.P. for Boston, 1621, and for Grantham, 1625 (O.R.., I, 452, 464), who did not have a seat in this Parliament.

[3] Thomas Godfrey of Lincolnshire, close friend of Eliot, did not sit in this Parliament and must not be confused with Thomas Godfrey who sat for Romney in this Parliament.

[4] Knight of the shire for Dorset in 1628. O.R., I, 475.

[5] *Letter Book*, pp. 23–5.

[6] See above, p. 165.   [7] *Letter Book*, pp. 26–27, 28–29.

letter Marten thanked Eliot for writing and renewing 'that league of mutual love and friendship between us'. He excused himself for not having written for so long and reminded Eliot that until September last 'we forbore by convention and agreement' to correspond.

The relationship between John Selden and Eliot was somewhat different. They were friends, but their friendship does not appear to have been as close as that between Sir John and Sir Henry Marten. Selden, besides writing on the business of Eliot's vice-admiralty, gave a bit of news of the court, but otherwise excused his inability to write of 'the occurrences of the present time' because 'they are either so uncertain or so unsafe to relate to you'. That was the reason why so little news of importance is to be found in the surviving correspondence, and why there might be little more if all the letters written to Eliot were available. He was in such ill-repute with the government that it was dangerous to pass on to him news of a controversial nature. The letter might be intercepted with dire results to both writer and recipient.

One more letter has survived from this period. Undated, it was written to Eliot by his good friend Sir Oliver Luke of Bedfordshire. It falls obviously into the last six months of 1628. Its tone and tenor clearly put it after the death of Buckingham. But it could have been written in any of the autumn or early winter months of that year. Speaking, like all Eliot's friends, of the love he bore him and of the hope he had of seeing him soon in London, Luke told about a declaration Charles had made to his Council in which he said that he intended 'to go that way in his government that might suit best with his own honour and the safety and prosperity of his kingdom' and that 'he did not think to humour or prepare a Parliament'. Luke also said that it was expected that something would be done soon 'in [the] matter of religion for discountenancing both the popish and Arminian party'. His final bit of gossip was of particular interest to Eliot. 'Here is also a general restoration of all the refractory, as they termed them, to their ancient employments in commission; only I hear yourself and some such are not graced with these spangles.'[1] In other words, Sir John Eliot was not to be vice-admiral of Devon.

From such bits gleaned here and there it can be seen that Eliot was a marked man. If he did not watch his step he would get into serious trouble. Sir John must have been fully conscious of his status. There-

[1] *Letter Book*, pp. 11–4.

fore, any act with unfortunate results to him cannot be blamed on luck or chance.

The dangerous time was still a few weeks hence. Christmas was at hand. But Eliot did not, as might be expected, go to Trebursey to spend the holiday with his children and father-in-law. Instead he went to Essex to visit the Earl of Warwick. The presumption is that more than friendship brought him to the festive board of the Earl at this season. Undoubtedly plans for the impending session of Parliament were discussed with some of the leaders of the party participating in these holiday festivities in Essex. At a later date Eliot wrote his father-in-law that he did not reach London 'but newly before the Parliament'.[1] That sounds as though he remained in Essex well into January. The evidence which substantiates this visit to the Earl of Warwick is a letter, a most exasperating letter, which Sir John wrote on December 30 from Lees in Essex[2] to Sir Robert Cotton. There seems to be so little of importance in this letter; its style is so involved; it is so full of obscure words and hidden meanings. Indeed, it is hardly intelligible to any reader, least of all the modern.[3] And yet there may be method in this madness. Should the letter fall into the wrong hands its misleading terminology would hide its true meaning.

In it Eliot spoke of a power which had commanded him to come this distance. By that he meant the Earl had asked him to come to Essex. Sir John believed that Warwick was as sympathetic towards Cotton as he was towards Eliot. Still writing in the impersonal, he felt that in serving the Earl he was also serving Cotton. The news the gathering at Lees had from court was uncertain, but apparently the 'courtiers' were most anxious to postpone the meeting of Parliament, he wrote. To face the situation squarely, he continued, they knew little of the plans at court and were influenced rather by ignorance and fear. There was little news of value at Lees, he said; possibly Cotton in London had learned something of importance and would send it to Eliot before he and his friends returned to that city.

When Sir John arrived in London around the middle of January he wrote a charming note to his friend Thomas Godfrey in Grantham.[4]

---

[1] Jan. 29, 1629. *Ibid.*, p. 32.

[2] Lees Priory in Essex was granted by Henry VIII to Sir Richard Rich and was still in the possession of the family in the time of the 2nd Earl of Warwick. Philip Morant, *The History and Antiquities of the County of Essex* (London, 1768), II, 101–2.

[3] *Letter Book*, pp. 29–30.

[4] Jan. 19, 1629. *Ibid.*, pp. 30–1.

His ostensible reason for writing was to express thanks for the great debt and obligation Godfrey had laid upon him. What lies behind these words has to be left to the modern reader's imagination. Becoming a bit more specific Eliot wrote that there was no news. Their fears exceeded their hopes. The danger was so great that only heaven guarded them from despair.

What could Godfrey read into these lines? Was it the fear that the Commons had little chance of accomplishing anything, the fear that the King would block whatever path they took, even the fear of Sir John that his idol was being shattered, his ideal disintegrating? We cannot tell. Eliot and others may have been losing faith in the King and were afraid to say it, even admit it to themselves. So much had happened during the last few months in religion and finance that only the most impartial 'were of opinion that Charles was really anxious to avert all chance of a quarrel with the House of Commons'.[1] Buckingham was dead, but Eliot and his friends were sure that somebody equally obnoxious would take his place. The Earl of Carlisle and Lord Treasurer Weston were the first choice to fill the vacancy, and both were disliked by the men of Parliament. Though Weston was probably not a Catholic yet,[2] he was deeply suspected of being one. To have such a man in charge of the burning subjects of impositions and tonnage and poundage, however honest and well-intentioned he was, however anxious for peace and retrenchment he may have been, was bound to court disaster when the Commons could again raise their voices in protest and condemnation.

[1] Gardiner, VII, 29. [2] As Earl of Portland he died a Roman Catholic in 1635. *Ibid.*, 378.

CHAPTER XIII

Seditious Conduct

January 20 to March 3, 1629

WHEN Parliament assembled on Tuesday, January 20, 1629, King Charles did not deign to address it. He left the Commons in the dark about past events and future plans. Possibly he was afraid that anything he might say would do more harm than good. Better let the Commons take the initiative to see in what direction and with what strength the wind was blowing. On the first day the King learned nothing, 'nothing was done, but only the settling of the committees'.[1] Sir John Eliot had prepared a speech in which he denounced in typical language, with figures of speech and illustrations drawn from the classics, the foreign and religious policy of the government.[2] He had hoped to deliver the philippic as the first fruits of the session. But he never was given the opportunity or decided that the speech was either not good enough or not timely enough for delivery.

What were the issues of this brief session which lasted little more than a month? They were initially the Petition of Right, but chiefly religion and tonnage and poundage. These last two topics became so involved that they are extremely hard to follow as the Commons switched from one to the other without the slightest hesitation. In order to trace with some degree of clarity the part Sir John Eliot played in this session, it will be necessary to consider each of the three subjects separately. When the Commons were adjourned for the last week in February, it will be possible to examine the brief correspondence of Eliot during this session. And then religion and tonnage and poundage

---

[1] *C.D. 1629*, p. 4.

[2] *Neg. Post.*, II, Sup., 134–7, taken from P.E. MSS., 'Eliot, speeches, etc.', ff. 50–51v. No indication that this speech was delivered on this day or might have been delivered on any other day is to be found in any of the parliamentary sources. Gardiner, VII, 30, note, opposes Forster, *Eliot*, II, 395, in believing that the speech was ever delivered.

will be drawn together in that dramatic, tumultuous, and final day, March 2, 1629.

I. THE PETITION OF RIGHT

On Wednesday, January 21, the House became aroused.[1] Under the direction of John Selden a small select committee[2] investigated the publication of the Petition of Right. It discovered that the King's speech of explanation had been added to the Petition upon a royal order. In his report Selden denounced the government, declared that the Petition had been violated, and asserted that the liberties of the people had been infringed in various ways. In the debate on the procedure to be followed Sir John Coke was opposed to leaving the investigation in the hands of the select committee. He thought that the subject were best discussed in the committee of the whole for grievances. Pym asserted that the matter was too important to be debated when so few were present. He felt it should be deferred. Eliot agreed with Pym but believed it was good 'to prepare things'. Therefore he supported the select committee in its further investigation. Turning to the printed Petition of Right he objected to the inclusion of the answer of June 2 and asked that the committee discover why that had been done. His motion was that the printer be summoned and that he be asked to disclose by whose warrant he had done the printing. The Commons approved the motion and sent for Mr Norton, the King's printer. Before he appeared the House passed a motion that the violations of the privileges of the subject contrary to the Petition of Right should be considered on Tuesday next in committee of the whole. When Mr Norton presented himself at the bar of the House before the close of the day's session he was so uncertain as to the origin of the warrant for printing the Petition that the House ordered five members to go with him to learn the truth.

On the next day Selden reported that the King's printer had received the order from the Lord Privy Seal and Attorney-General Heath to withdraw the first printing of the Petition of Right and issue the second unsatisfactory edition. Heath had a royal warrant as his authority. Secretary Coke amplified this statement by declaring that his Majesty

[1] Unless otherwise indicated the proceedings for this day are taken from *C.D. 1629*, pp. 4–6.

[2] It was composed of five members to whom four were later added, one of whom was Eliot. *C.J.*, I, 920.

insisted that it was his warrant, and his warrant alone, which had directed the printer. But the House was not satisfied and ordered Norton to appear before it on the morrow with all his papers of instruction and his royal warrant.[1] As far as we know Norton never appeared. Possibly discretion was the better part of valour when confronted with a royal warrant. The House did not adjourn into committee of the whole on Tuesday to discuss the infringement of the privileges of the subject. The entire matter was dead by the end of January. The select committee named to 'search for the entry of the Petition of Right in the courts of record' had killed it.

2. RELIGION

In the meantime the Commons had become thoroughly aroused over religion and tonnage and poundage. On January 26 Francis Rouse introduced the subject of religion into the debates of the session.[2] After several speakers had denounced popery and Arminianism, it was decided to refer the subject to the committee of religion which was meeting that afternoon. No detailed account of this gathering has survived. We are left in the dark on the first big religious debate.[3]

On the next day Pym reported the gist of the discussion in which, for various reasons, not much progress had been made. After a brief debate, in which the King through his Secretary attempted to make way for the tonnage and poundage bill, it was 'resolved that the committee of religion shall have precedency before all other committees' and that this committee 'shall meet tomorrow morning at 8 o'clock'.[4]

But the House did not adjourn into committee of the whole for religion until the morning of January 29. Pym was in the chair. After introductory remarks by Rudyerd and Harley, Sir John Eliot delivered the speech of the day.[5] He began by thanking 'that noble gentleman, my countryman',[6] in a rather sarcastic fashion for the delay of this dis-

---

[1] *C.J.*, I, p. 921.   [2] *C.D. 1629*, pp. 12 and 109.

[3] Except for a brief summary in a letter of Nethersole to the Queen of Bohemia. *Ibid.*, pp. 246–47.

[4] *C.D. 1629*, pp. 16–21 and 110–2.

[5] Forster in his *Eliot*, II, 412–7 (2nd edit., II, 210–4), says he has taken this speech from a ms. at Port Eliot. There is only a part of the speech, a little more than the last half of it, at Port Eliot now. P.E. MSS., 'Eliot, speeches, etc.', ff.52–3. This is printed in *Neg. Post.*, II, Sup., 138–42. In *C.D. 1629*, pp. 24–8, there is an excellent version of this speech.

[6] See *ibid.*, p. 24, note *a*, for the opinion that the 'noble gentleman' was Lord Treasurer

cussion which prevented a confusing and dangerous situation from arising. But now the delay had given him an opportunity to contemplate 'this great business of religion, and what may be expedient'.

The fears of all were centred on the increase of popery and 'Arminianism creeping up', Sir John declared. Their objective must be to put a stop to this. On that policy he wished to express his thoughts. But 'to enter into the disquisition of writings and opinions, as it has been propounded', he wisely said, 'I doubt would be too intricate and involved. There is such diversity amongst men, such differences of learning, . . . that the reconciliation would be hard; and instead of light and direction to the way, we might by that search and scrutiny darken and obscure it.'

The Commons had no intention, Eliot presumed, to get into a dispute about their religion. That had been settled for a long time by the fundamental truth of the gospel. This truth, he asserted, 'not with words but with actions, we will maintain'. This truth was to be found in the 39 Articles which had been confirmed by Parliament in the 13th year of the reign of Elizabeth.

First, Sir John desired to express his fears and apprehensions, so that they could make plans on how to oppose and resist the work of their enemies with better hope of success. What had caused him the greatest worry, he confessed, was 'the late Declaration that was published under the name and title of his Majesty'. Eliot was referring to the Declaration on religion published early in December, 1628.[1] In it Charles asserted that the 39 Articles contained the true word of God and ordered his subjects 'to continue in the uniform profession thereof'. What aroused a storm of disapproval was when he said that, he being supreme governor of the Church, any differences about 'external policies', 'injunctions', 'canons', and 'other constitutions' were to be settled by the clergy in convocation at the order of the King. From this and further emphasis on the power of the clergy in convocation, it can be seen that Charles was simply saying that he and his clergy had the sole right to interpret the doctrine, ceremonies, and practices of the Church of England. He was enunciating a principle fundamental in the Erastian church established and maintained by Queen Elizabeth—a principle, to

Weston, whom Eliot was referring to in this satirical fashion, rather than Rouse or Coryton, whom these words would be honestly praising.

[1] Gardiner, VII, 21–23, and Gardiner, *The Constitutional Documents of the Puritan Revolution, 1652-1660* (Oxford, 1906), pp. 75–76.

be sure, which was far from acceptable to the puritans of her reign or those of her successors.

To return to Eliot's attack, he spent much time in clearing the King of all responsibility for the Declaration. He put the blame on ministers and friends of Charles, cited classical examples of similar situations, and concluded that if this document was given the protection of the royal name, it was done 'either without his knowledge or through the misinformation and importunity of some that are about him'. Sir John then proceeded to explain the danger in the Declaration. Proclaiming the papists and Arminians to be the enemies of the nation, he showed how this document was threatening it. The truth was, of course, to be found in the 39 Articles, he declared. But a difference might arise over the double meaning of some of the Articles. Then those clergy who were at the moment dominating the Church would give their own interpretation with the result that popery or Arminianism would be introduced. Should such men be permitted to decide upon the principles of religion of the country? he asked. The truth, which was in question, 'is not man's but God's and God forbid that man should now be made to judge it'. After lashing out against Laud, Neile, Montague, and their kind Eliot said in conclusion, 'I could grant to the humour of our adversaries even the admission of some ceremonies, those great idols which they worship'. Describing a ceremony of the Eastern churches of which he heartily approved, he told of men standing with drawn swords at the repetition of the creed. Here we catch a glimpse of the low church Anglican developing into the puritan.

Finally Eliot hoped that the danger from their enemies might be prevented now that it had been disclosed. By accepting the 'known truth' without question, all that should be necessary was to discover who had 'offended against it, whose actions, whose doctrines, whose discourses have been in prejudice thereof'. Such should be their procedure. Let them punish those who were guilty as examples to others. Actions not words, Eliot asserted, must be their defence against the evils of these times.

Thus our Cornish knight, believing that among the Commons there was an accepted interpretation of the 39 Articles, proposed to turn the House of Commons into a religious tribunal which would rival that established by the King in convocation and its allied enforcing bodies of High Commission and Star Chamber. At the beginning of his speech he had opposed a discussion of religious writings and opinions. In the middle he had declared that the truth of religion should not be judged by King and convocation but by God alone. At the end he had forgotten his previous words of wisdom. To determine in the House of Commons who had violated the accepted interpretation of the Articles was bound to result in heated discussions of religious writings and opinions. Such disputes, if carried to a decision, would deny the will of God and prevent both King and convocation from defining the truth.

The fundamental difficulty at this time confronting the leaders of the 'country' party in the matter of religion and other problems before them was the necessity of accepting the old relationship of a superior, if not supreme, Sovereign and an inferior Parliament. But only by rebellion could they hope to solve that difficulty, could they make their views dominant. As yet the vast majority of the opposition had no thought of so drastic a change, least of all Sir John Eliot. For him the King was still upon a pedestal. But he was trying to push the pedestal with its statue into a corner and make the supreme governor of the Church of England a mere spectator of religious strife in the nation. In Eliot's view, as implied in his speech, the King had no more power over religion in England than the Pope. God and the House of Commons, or even the House of Commons alone, he was unwittingly turning into the supreme religious authority in the nation. But had he been confronted with such a radical interpretation of his plans, he would have repudiated it. In looking back we can see that Sir John by the implication of his speech had hurdled a dozen years in the religious history of England. The speech shows Eliot to be as anti-clerical as most puritans of his day. His Church was to be Erastian. His state in matters of religion was to be composed not of the King and clergy but of the King and the House of Commons, possibly even the House of Commons alone.[1]

On the morning of January 29, 1629, the committee of religion was not willing to follow Sir John Eliot into the dangerous channel he advocated. After a few members had emphasized the importance of the 39 Articles, a resolution was passed, later to be approved by the House, upholding the truth of these Articles.[2] Any interpretations by Jesuits or Arminians were rejected. Such was the moderate result of Eliot's striking proposal for parliamentary control of the Anglican Church.

[1] Compare this point of view with Henry Parker's Erastianism of a dozen years later. J. W. Allen, *English Political Thought 1603–60* (London, 1938), I, 339–45.
[2] *C.D. 1629*, p, 118, *C. J.*, I, 924.

Not until February 3 did Sir John speak again in the committee of religion. Strengthened possibly by some propositions he had received from Sir Robert Cotton,[1] Eliot was the first to speak in committee.[2] He declared that the Commons had laid a strong foundation for proceeding in matters of religion. He felt that as a result of the 'late dispute' over the Lambeth Articles[3] the only differences that had manifested themselves concerned their use. Everybody had agreed as to their truth and value. Such unity Sir John was sure would produce joy in their hearts. Relying on this foundation he wanted the Commons to examine the cases of all who had denied the truth. Arminians should be watched, their books and sermons examined. 'Let us strike at them and make our charge at them and vindicate our truth that yet seems obscure.' If any Arminians defended their new opinions, then the Commons, Eliot asserted, should present proof of the truth of their religion. By such proposals Sir John Eliot was turning the House of Commons into a debating society on religious beliefs, doctrines, and ceremonies.

Francis Rouse approved in general the policy advocated by Sir John. But Coryton, though not denying the truth of the Lambeth Articles, did not want to make them public and binding acts of the Church. Then there was read to the House the Commons' remonstrance on religion of the last session, the King's Declaration on religion of December, 1628, and the proclamation against Richard Montague. As a result the debate turned into an attack on individual prelates, first Laud and Neile, then Montague. The general policy advocated by Eliot was being followed. Along these same lines the debate ranged in committee of the whole for the next two days. Montague's confirmation as Bishop of Chichester was questioned. The pardons of Montague, John Cosin, Robert Sibthorpe, and Roger Manwaring were ordered examined and investigated.[4]

Easily diverted, the Commons on February 6 became intensely interested in an incident only indirectly related to the main current of the debate. Sir Robert Phelips reported to the committee of the whole some remarks made by John Cosin. His informant had been Sir Robert Heath, who had obtained the statement from a third party. Cosin was

---

[1] See below, p. 301.   [2] *C.D. 1629*, pp. 33–4, 121.

[3] I have been unable to find any previous debate on the Lambeth Articles. For the Articles see Charles Hardwick, *A History of the Articles of Religion* (London, 1904), pp. 159–77, 363–7. The Articles, submitted to Whitgift in 1595, Hardwick does not consider binding on the Church of England.

[4] *C.D. 1629*, pp. 121–2. Gardiner, VI, 316, VII, 23, 46.

alleged to have said that 'the King was not supreme head of the Church; that in excommunications the King had no more authority than his man that rubbed his horse's heels'.[1] King Charles had been told of Cosin's words. Though his Majesty did not believe the story, he instructed the Attorney-General to continue his investigation. Having uncovered several conflicting statements as to the truth of Cosin's remarks Heath decided to drop the whole matter without saying anything more to the King about it. That was the story Phelips told the Commons.

What anguish it raised in the breast of Sir John Eliot. Not only did he denounce John Cosin but he bitterly attacked Sir Robert Heath for neglecting his duty. Cosin had slandered his Majesty and Heath had not brought the slanderer to justice. Disregarding the uncertainty of the evidence Sir John rushed to the defence of his Sovereign. No conflict with his beloved Commons was involved. He could lash out against a cleric tainted with hated Arminianism as well as against a royal official for whom he had little love.[2]

The debate, which raged for some time and in which Eliot was most active, concerned itself with the questions as to who should be summoned to give evidence and against whom the Commons should proceed. It was finally decided that Heath should attend the House on Monday, February 9. Instead of appearing in person he sent a letter which was read by the Speaker. It added nothing to the information the House had already been given. It produced no debate. The anger of Sir John Eliot had subsided. He, like the rest of the members, was no longer interested in the slanderous remarks attributed to John Cosin.[3]

In the meantime the pardon of the four Arminian clerics continued to interest the House. In particular, Neile, Bishop of Winchester, was under attack for his ardent Arminianism. The evidence presented against him on February 13 was most damaging.[4]

But again the interest of the Commons was diverted. Between February 14 and 17 in committee of the whole for religion the Clerkenwell Jesuits were the centre of several of the most bitter debates of the session. Ten of them had been arrested; three were tried and the rest released on bail. Of the three, two were acquitted and the third was con-

[1] *C.D. 1629*, p. 174.
[2] *Ibid.*, pp. 45–6, 131, 175–6.
[3] For this paragraph see *ibid.*, pp. 176–7.
[4] *Ibid.*, pp. 64–72, 144–6, 203–6.

demned to death, but his execution was stayed. When the Commons were told of such leniency a violent storm of words began to rage. The judges, the Attorney-General, the Recorder of London and the Earl of Dorset, who had acted as a royal messenger, were the chief culprits. On one occasion Secretary Coke informed the committee 'that we shall find that the King, being merciful in case of blood, gave direction for reprieving of the condemned priest'. Eliot immediately replied 'I doubt not but when we shall declare the depth of this to his Majesty, he will, instead of mercy, render them to judgment that gave him advice therein'. It seems impossible that intelligent men like Eliot and many of his colleagues could conceive such ignorance, such lack of information, in their King. The investigation proved to be entirely fruitless. The judges squirmed out of any blame placed upon them. In the case of the others the Commons found that the trail they were following eventually ended with a royal command given by word of mouth. There could be no comment, beyond the remarks made by Eliot, upon such a disclosure. By February 17 the subject was dropped and the debate centred on the futile question as to why so many priests were wandering about the streets of London. This was the last time before the closing day of the session that the members participated in a debate on religion.[1]

What did this prolonged attack on Arminianism and Roman Catholicism amount to? Exactly nothing. In his speeches of January 29 and February 3 Sir John Eliot led the way by denouncing Arminianism. To him, as to most of his colleagues, it was as bad as popery. The Arminian with his belief in episcopal authority and ceremonies was an apostate. He was an Anglican who was rapidly returning to Rome. So thought Eliot and a great many members of the Church of England, not to mention the puritans. Therefore he wanted to destroy this sect within the church and root it out of the land. But Sir John was not clear on how he intended to attain his objective. He had indicated the first step to be taken and the Commons had followed him when they proposed to examine the pardons of Montague, Cosin, Sibthorpe and Manwaring. Somebody must be responsible for them. If that person could have been found, the Commons would naïvely have said—and Eliot would have been the first to say it—that the King would surely punish that person and revoke the pardons. In that case the Arminians would eventually be deprived of authority and forced out of the Church of England. But the Commons could not even discover who was respon-

[1] C.D. 1629, pp. 74–5, 78–81, 83, 148, 151–5, 213–21.

sible for the pardons; they were repeatedly diverted from this primary objective with Eliot as erratic as the worst of them. Now it was the slanderous words of Cosin. Then it was the activities of the papists. Wicked men were continually being discovered who should be punished for their sins. These wicked men formed a black barrier in front of the King which must be removed. Had the Commons remained constant in working towards their objective, they would have found that Charles was responsible for the four pardons, that Charles was as strong an Arminian as any in the land, and that King Charles was not too unfriendly to Roman Catholics. Let us see if the discussion of tonnage and poundage was to prove as futile as that of religion.

3. TONNAGE AND POUNDAGE

On Thursday, January 22, John Rolle[1], an MP and a merchant, informed the House of Commons that his goods worth five hundred pounds had been seized because of his refusal to pay tonnage and poundage to the value of two hundred pounds.[2] His offer of security to pay what would be due by law or adjudged by Parliament had been refused. He had been unable to obtain his goods by means of a replevin because royal officials had stopped him in two attempts. This statement raised a storm of protest in the House. The liberty of the subject, the privilege of a member of the House of Commons must be protected. Thus cried Phelips, Littleton, Selden, Eliot, and others. To Sir John three points were involved: the right of John Rolle, the right of the subject, and 'the right and privilege of this House'. To him and to others the last was the most important. As had been moved, a committee[3] was named to investigate these proceedings, and the officers of the customs[4] were summoned to appear in the House. Such was the beginning of the most hotly disputed issue of the session.

In turning the floodlights of the House on the question of the privilege of a member and in dimming them on the subject of unparliamentary taxation, the Commons displayed a weakness in their quarrel with

[1] In spite of the fact that *C.D. 1629* and *C.J.* spell the name Rolles, I am following Gardiner, Pollard, Porritt, and other modern authorities in leaving off the *s*.

[2] *C.D. 1629*, pp. 7–9, is the basis for the proceedings of this day unless otherwise indicated.

[3] Of 20 members including Eliot, *C.J.*, I, 921.

[4] They were Sir John Wolstenholm, Abraham Dawes, Richard Carmarthen, Michael Measy, John Beaupell (or Baupage), and Bryan Rogers. *Ibid.*

the Stuarts which appeared time and again during the first three decades of the seventeenth century. The only exception to this statement, and it is an important one, is the Petition of Right. They were members of the House of Commons first, and Englishmen secondly. Their interest in that corporation at Westminster was so vital, so new, that it frequently dampened their age-old interest in the affairs of the nation. And of all the members, Sir John Eliot was one of the most easily diverted from the large to the small, from the national to the parliamentary.

When they accepted the case of John Rolle the Commons were on ground that was legally far from secure. Though they had asserted the right of members to their goods ever since the accession of James, there was still some doubt as to whether the goods necessary to the member during his stay at Westminster were not the only type covered by the privilege. More than that, Rolle's goods were seized on October 30. It was necessary, therefore, to introduce the fact that Parliament should have met on October 20, though it had been prorogued, in order to give him even a technical leg to stand on. But when the subject was first broached on January 22, all this was of little interest to the fire-eaters in comparison with the fact that the supposed privilege of a member of the House of Commons had been violated.[1]

Early on the morning of the 23rd Sir John Coke delivered a message from King Charles in which the Commons were asked to avoid all debate on the Rolle case until his Majesty had addressed the assembled Houses at Whitehall at two o'clock the next afternoon. The request was complied with, and the House adjourned until Saturday.

When the Lords and Commons had assembled in the Banqueting House the King pleased the Commons by saying that he had no intention to claim that the levying of tonnage and poundage was his by right. His action stemmed from necessity. That had been the meaning of his speech at the close of the last session, he said. Now he was most anxious that they pass the bill for tonnage and poundage, so that 'my by-past actions will be included, and my future proceedings authorized'. Not since the Commons had listened to the second answer to the Petition of Right was there such general satisfaction with the words of the King.[2]

---

[1] Gardiner, VII, 32-33, John Hatsell, *Precedents of Proceedings in the House of Commons* (London, 796), I, 184-6.

[2] For the last two paragraphs see *C.D.1629*, pp. 10, 11.

The tonnage and poundage bill was introduced in the House of Commons on Monday, January 26, by Sir John Coke.[1] He recommended it to the Commons in the name of the King and asked them to speed its passage. The first to speak to the bill was Sir John Eliot. After flattering the King and declaring the loyalty of the Commons, he attacked the bill indirectly and advocated delay in its passage. With a display of tact Sir John was trying to avoid a clash with the King over tonnage and poundage. But it was obvious that he was opposed to the bill under existing conditions. He was supported by Selden, who argued that a subsidy bill, that is, for tonnage and poundage, should not originate with the King but with the Commons and should not be introduced so early in the session. Digges, on the other hand, could not see why a subsidy bill should not have a royal origin. He did feel that a committee should be named to present it to the House. Finally, Phelips, supported by Henry Pelham, believed that the liberties of the House should be safeguarded first before they proceeded with the bill for tonnage and poundage. This suggestion terminated for the time being discussion on all phases of that subject.

It was reintroduced as a result of the presentation on January 28 of a petition from Mr Chambers to the House.[2] Like Rolle, he was a merchant whose goods had been seized for refusal to pay tonnage and poundage. Unlike Rolle, he was not an MP and had been imprisoned by the Council for his refusal.[3] As soon as the petition had been read Sir John Eliot remarked that 'he findeth the judges, the Council, sheriffs, customers, the Attorney, and all conspire to trample on the spoils of the liberty of the subject'. He wanted the party whose goods had been kept from him 'to take a legal course for release of his goods that we may see what ministers will refuse to do their duty therein'. Secretary Coke did not like Eliot's language. He desired 'that such words that all officers of state do trample on the liberty of the subject may be forborne'. As neither Sir John nor anybody else replied to Coke's reprimand, he proceeded to deliver a message from the King in which his Majesty again asked that the bill for tonnage and poundage be given precedence. After some words from Sir Thomas Edmondes, Eliot, and Coryton had failed to improve the situation, the

[1] *C.D.1629*, pp. 107-10, 12-6, are the basis for the proceedings of this day unless otherwise indicated.

[2] The proceedings of this day are based on *C.D. 1629*, pp. 22-23, 112-15.

[3] Gardiner, VII, 4-5.

K

House decided to put a reply to the last communication from his Majesty into the hands of a select committee.[1]

That reply was completed on Monday, February 2. It was called a declaration[2] and objected first to the manner of presenting the bill for tonnage and poundage—in the name of his Majesty by one of his ministers. The rest of it concerned itself with religion. On the next day Sir John Coke arose to explain some words he had previously used. In urging the bill for tonnage and poundage he had not said that his Majesty had commanded its passage, nor had he called these duties ordinary revenue. What he had meant was that the payment of tonnage and poundage would enable his Majesty to send the fleet to sea. He then read the King's reply to the Commons' declaration of the previous day. With some remarks on religion interspersed in his answer Charles upheld his Secretary in stating that the bill for tonnage and poundage 'was not to have been offered unto you in my name'. One reason he desired the passage of the bill was 'to put an end to those questions that daily arise between me and some of my subjects'. Therefore, the King urged the Commons to make haste with this vital financial measure.[3]

The only one to reply to Coke's explanation and to the royal message was Sir John Eliot. The words of his Sovereign had given him 'great satisfaction', he said. He was pleased to learn that his Majesty would listen to the opinion of the Commons. What troubled him was 'a difference between his Majesty's expression and the expression of his ministers'. Sir John reminded the House that the tonnage and poundage bill had been presented in his Majesty's name. 'Now we find that his Majesty disavows it, and that he did it not.' Declaring that a wrong had been done his Majesty and the House in presenting this bill in the name of the King, he felt that Sir John Coke was 'not worthy to sit in this House'.[4]

These words did not add to Eliot's prestige. His 'great satisfaction' with the King is beginning to have a hollow ring. Here he was balancing his expression of loyalty with an unnecessary and fruitless attack on the royal Secretary. Coke's words on introducing the bill for tonnage and poundage on January 26 could undoubtedly bear varying interpretations. But what of it? He had explained himself and might

---

[1] Composed of Sir John Coke, Rich, Erle, Digges, Eliot and Selden. *C.J.*, I, 923.
[2] For the declaration see *C.D. 1629*, pp. 29-30.
[3] *Ibid.*, pp. 31 and 121.   [4] *Ibid.*, pp. 32-33 and 121.

even be said to have apologized. To expel him from the House for so slight an offence would be an unwarranted act and unthinkable. After the Speaker and Sir Humphrey May had briefly intervened on behalf of Sir John Coke, and he had said a few words in his own defence, the matter was dropped.[1]

The attention of the House was focused on the case of John Rolle when Eliot made the first report from his select committee on Monday, February 9. He denounced Acton, sheriff of London, for giving totally worthless information to the committee because of his 'prevarications and contradictions'. As a result of the report, brief explanations by Sir John, and a short debate the Commons ordered the sheriff of London to present himself as a delinquent in the House at 9 o'clock the next morning.[2]

Before Acton had made his appearance on the next morning Rolle informed the House that on the previous day he had been served with a subpoena to appear in the Star Chamber. Even though Attorney-General Heath, according to Rolle, had by letter declared it a mistake and had apologized that very evening, many members were incensed. Men like Phelips and Eliot declared that it was a violation of the privilege of a member of the House. Sir John, as usual, committed the error of identifying the liberties of the kingdom with those of the Commons. Believing in their identity he centred his attention on the narrow field of the House of Commons and neglected liberties on a national scale which would be much more difficult to handle. After Selden had also raised his voice in protest, the House granted Rolle his privilege in this particular instance, and named a committee to investigate who was responsible. Though the Commons had refused to believe Heath's assertion that he was to blame for the subpoena, the committee in the end had to accept him as the culprit.

In the meantime Sheriff Acton had made his excuses, been sent to the Tower, brought back to the bar of the House, and assigned to the select committee on tonnage and poundage. It was becoming obvious that whatever actions the sheriff of London had taken against John Rolle and his goods had been on orders from a higher authority.[3]

On Thursday, February 13, Sir John Eliot presented a lengthy report

---

[1] C.D.1629, p. 121.

[2] Ibid., pp. 52, 133, 181, C.J., I, 928.

[3] For the last two paragraphs see C.D. 1629, pp. 55, 57, 136, 137, 186, 187–9, 190, 195, C.J., I, 928, 929.

from his committee to the House.[1] First he recited the royal commission of July 26, 1626, in which it was declared 'that subsidies, customs, and imposts should be levied in such manner as they were in the time of King James until it might receive a settling by Parliament'.[2] He then described the several recent grants of the farm of the customs to Sir Paul Pinder and others. Having painted this background he depicted the actions taken by the customers against those merchants who had refused to pay tonnage and poundage. From the general he turned to the particularlar and gave the steps taken by Mr Rolle and others to recover their goods. These measures had ended in the Court of Exchequer. That court had issued an order which stayed all suits which concerned themselves with the King's revenue in other courts and at the same time it prohibited the suing of a collector of royal revenue. The order of the Exchequer finally stated that the whole business could only be settled in the forthcoming Parliament. Eliot went on to tell how the Exchequer instructed the sheriff of London not to surrender any of the goods of the merchants. After the merchants had been heard by counsel it issued another order on November 27(13),[3] 1628, which prohibited them from obtaining their goods or suing elsewhere. As the merchants could obtain no justice in any court, they now came to Parliament for it.

The House ordered the report to be considered in committee of the whole for tonnage and poundage into which it immediately adjourned. There Selden felt that it was high time to find some method of having the goods restored to the merchants.[4] Eliot, supporting Selden's suggestion, expounded a novel idea.[5] Putting it into a nutshell, it was that once the farmers of the customs had paid the King the value of the farm they were no longer acting as royal officials. The money they collected from the merchants, after having paid the value of the farm, was not the King's but the customer's. Their activities were no longer royal but private. Eliot believed that if the Barons of the Exchequer were informed of this truth they would order the goods restored to the merchants. He moved that a message containing such an explanation be sent to the Court of Exchequer.

But Sir John's conception of the activities of the farmers of the customs was wrong. It did not matter when the customers paid the King

<hr />

[1] C.D. 1629, pp. 195–6, 140–1,   [2] Rushworth, I, 641.
[3] Grosvenor (C.D. 1629, p. 196) gives the 13th, while Nicholas (ibid., p. 141) gives the 27th.   [4] Ibid., p. 192.   [5] Ibid., pp. 60, 141–42, 196–97.

the money they had contracted to pay him. In collecting customs duties at any time they were acting as royal officials. And the money paid them was also paid, one way or another, to the King. They were never acting as private individuals, nor could the money paid them be considered as their private property.

On one point Eliot was right. If the customers maintained in their affidavit that the goods were being held only for the old, or common law, customs, then they were not telling the whole truth. Goods were being held for payment of both the old customs and tonnage and poundage. Sir John was justified in pointing out this minor discrepancy and in insisting that the Exchequer be informed of it.

The debate in committee was long and learned.[1] Eliot had had his say and did not enter the discussion again. To the 'country' party the real grievance was the detention of the goods of the merchants at the order of the Exchequer. Now it appeared that the customers admitted that under the head of duties in their affidavit they included tonnage and poundage. But under no circumstances did they consider themselves to be private individuals instead of royal officials. During the debate Noy attempted a compromise whereby the Commons would pass a bill for tonnage and poundage. In the bill it would be declared that the acts of the Court of Exchequer were void and of no effect. The result would be that the goods of the merchants would be restored immediately and the dispute settled. But the majority refused to accept this most sensible solution. Instead it was decided to inform the Exchequer of the admission of the customers that the goods of the merchants were being held for both tonnage and poundage and the old customs. The 'country' members believed that should the Exchequer know that such was the interpretation of 'duties', the Barons would order the goods restored, as a bill for tonnage and poundage had not been passed by Parliament. A message to the Barons of the Exchequer containing this explanation was drafted by Selden, Littleton, Noy, and Glanville.[2] It was presented to the House and accepted.

One point in Sir John Eliot's argument had thus been endorsed by the House of Commons. But nobody would follow him in his statement that the customers were collecting the money for themselves as private individuals and not for the King as royal officials. To be sure, the members were intensely naïve in believing that the Barons of the

[1] C.D.1629, pp. 142–44 and 197–201.
[2] Ibid., p. 200.

Exchequer had been ignorant of the true situation, and, now being informed of it, would act in the interests of the Commons against those of the King by releasing the goods of the merchants. Had the leaders of the 'country' party been better politicians, and had they not believed so intensely in the justice of their cause, they might have agreed that Noy's compromise had merits over Eliot's proposal.

On the last day of the week, February 14, the answer of the Barons of the Exchequer to the message of the Commons was read by Sir Humphrey May. The judges said that their orders in no way determined the right of levying tonnage and poundage. They were simply defending the financial interests of the Crown and had not prohibited the merchants from suing to recover their goods in the Court of Exchequer. That is what they should have done. After the reading of the answer a select committee of twenty-seven, including Eliot, was named to take it into consideration and to search for precedents in the course of the Exchequer. Upon the motion of Selden the customers were ordered to appear in the House on Monday 'to answer their contempt against the privilege and members of this House'.[1]

The first of these gentlemen, however, did not appear before the House until Thursday, February 19. He was Abraham Dawes who was followed by Richard Carmarthen. The chief point made by both men was that they believed the privilege of Parliament did not cover the goods of a member of the House of Commons, especially when it came to paying duties to the King on these goods.[2]

As soon as the two customers had testified Sir John Eliot arose to say that two questions confronted them: 'whether we conceive these parties to be delinquents or no and to have violated our privileges, whether one or both. And if they be delinquents, what punishment they shall merit'.[3] In other words Eliot wanted the actions of these two men to be regarded in the light of a breach of the privilege of the House of Commons and not from the broader view of the violation of the rights of Englishmen by royal officials. As we have seen, near-sightedness was one of Sir John's greatest weaknesses as a national leader. Here he clearly displayed it in requesting that Dawes and Carmarthen be judged as delinquents against the privileges of the Commons. He felt that the Commons would cease to exist without their privileges. He felt that his countrymen could be adequately protected against the encroachments

---

[1] For this paragraph see *ibid.*, pp. 73, 148, 206, *C.J.*, I, 930.
[2] *C.D. 1629*, pp. 155–56.   [3] *Ibid.*, pp. 85, also 222 and 156.

of the government only by a strong House of Commons. He apparently did not see that fundamental law as well as common law were protective forces which would function all the more effectively in conjunction with the House of Commons if the liberties of the people were put above the privileges of the Commons. Eliot could not think clearly or deeply on the affairs of state. He believed the people were suffering from the struggle of two forces, one good and the other evil. The good King and Commons were allied against the evil ministers in the government. Could he have realized that the King was actually in alliance with his wicked advisers against the Commons and the people, he would have recognized that victory in the broader field of battle would have far better results than success in the narrow field in which he was taking his stand. Such a view, however, was premature in 1629. It was revolutionary. In that year Sir John Eliot could not conceive of revolution as could Pym, Hampden, and their colleagues in 1642.

But in this debate others had a better perspective. First Wandesford saw that they 'should forbear and decline at this time to consider of the delinquency of these men'. He 'would have us first to take a course to establish the merchants in possession of their goods'. Then Pym declared it was not a fit time to debate the delinquency of the customers. 'The liberties of this House are inferior to the liberties of the kingdom,' he declared. 'To determine the privilege of this House is but a mean matter,' he felt. Pym believed that their main business was to establish the subject in possession of his goods. To do this revolution was by no means necessary in his eyes. Like many others he was unable to see King Charles as yet in the light of a dozen years hence. But at least he was putting first things first and not the reverse as Eliot had proposed.

Suggestions and proposals followed each other from member after member until Eliot spoke again, though the Commons were sitting in the formal house and not in committee. He struck back at Wandesford and Pym. 'I shall never undervalue the privileges of this House to think them inferior to any liberty of the kingdom, nay the ground of all,' he asserted. 'Let the examples of these times show us that if we dispute them not we may lose them.' That was Eliot's argument.[1]

Even Digges and Seymour refused to support Eliot's point. They were upheld by May who declared God forbid that the King's command should result in his ministers being brought before the Commons on a charge of delinquency, of having violated the privilege of the

[1] *C.D.1629*, pp. 156-57, and 222-23.

Commons. These words brought Sir John Eliot to his feet for a third time. He said they were not 'making a question of bringing the King's command to delinquency. But the question is whether an act done on pretence of the King's command to the breach of the privileges be a delinquency or no.' That was quite a different matter to Sir John. He went even further and said that 'he hath heard that the King cannot command a thing which tends to the breach of parliamentary privilege'. Repeating May's words 'that if we did go about to bring the King's commands for delinquency, *actum est de Imperio*', Eliot asserted it would be 'an act of the highest treason'. He moved that May explain himself. Again Eliot was blind to and at the same time true to his Sovereign. He forgot the past in his zeal for the present. He forgot his own arrest in 1626 and the Protestation torn from the Journals by King James in 1621. Had he been confronted with these precedents, he would have said immediately that his Sovereign had been misadvised, that the ministers of the King were responsible for these mistakes. So he denied that questioning the delinquency of the customers would put the Crown at stake, for that would be high treason.[1]

Of course May had to explain himself, which he did without retracting a single word. It was far from his meaning to wrong the gentleman, he said. 'I told you that if you questioned those who justified their act by the King's command, the King would think his command were questioned.' The two points of view were far apart. May saw clearly what Eliot peered at through coloured glasses.

In spite of the arguments of Wandesford, Pym, Digges, Seymour and others the House of Commons followed Sir John Eliot. It was resolved 'that this House shall now take into their consideration the violation of the privilege of this House by Mr Dawes and Carmarthen'. As it was conceived 'to be a business of great consequence', it was 'ordered that the House shall be resolved into a committee for more freedom of debate'. But as it was getting late the committee of the whole was adjourned until nine o'clock the next morning.[2]

Before Mr Herbert took the chair that morning the third customer, Sir John Wolstenholm, appeared before the House. The questions asked and the answers he gave were substantially the same as those of the other two. The debate in committee involved all three customers even though Eliot's motion that they should be considered separately

[1] C.D.1629, pp. 157–58 and 224.
[2] For the last two paragraphs see *ibid.*, pp. 85, 158, 224. See also Gardiner, VII, 61–3.

was accepted. Two questions were salient. The first was whether the three men had collected money for themselves or as accountants to the King. The other was whether Mr Rolle had claimed his privilege when his goods were at the water side or when they were in the King's storehouse. The debate at times grew heated. But only once did Eliot intervene to assert, as he had already done, that the customers in collecting duties had made money for themselves and had not sent it to the coffers of the King. The debate was concluded when the three men were given until the next day to produce evidence to prove that their task was merely to account to the King for the customs and not to make any profit for themselves. This decision was made on February 20. But as we have seen,[1] on the 13th nobody in the House would accept the very same point made by Sir John Eliot. So often in the past it had been necessary for the views and arguments of that man to penetrate the minds of the members before they gave them their assent. With the Speaker back in the chair Mr Rolle was given permission to present witnesses for the time and place of his claiming privilege. They were to appear before the committee of the whole, which was to continue the business the next morning.[2]

With Herbert in the chair on February 21st Rolle presented two witnesses. Both asserted that he had claimed his privilege on October 30 when his goods were seized 'at Porters Kay near the custom-house'. Here Eliot intervened to express his displeasure at the practice of introducing witnesses. He saw no reason why the statement of a member of the House of Commons was not enough without any other proof. He was afraid that 'by such examples we introduce a kind of necessity to have witnesses to prove the affirmation of a member of this House'. Not only was the House of Commons a superior institution to Sir John but also a member of that House was a superior person to him.[3]

Shortly after Eliot had made these remarks there took place the greatest debate of the session on privilege of a member. It was conducted essentially by the lawyers of the 'country' party who called upon their armoury of precedents, while the 'courtiers' opposed them with a clever defence. Never before had the question of privilege posed such tantalizing difficulties for the leaders of the opposition. The King must not be involved, and yet he could not be avoided. The goods had been seized under royal warrants, therefore privilege could be claimed only

[1] See above, p. 293. [2] *C.D. 1629*, pp. 87, 158–61, 226–7.
[3] *Ibid.*, pp. 162 and 228.

against the King, was the gist of the argument of the 'courtiers'. The 'country' leaders did their best, but with little success, to divest the customers of their status as royal officials. Eventually the debate centred on the exact wording of the warrants, whether they permitted the seizure of all the goods of the merchants or allowed the officials to levy only a small proportion. Here Sir John Eliot was drawn into the argument. As reporter of the select committee on the case of Mr Rolle he should know. Sir John declared that he did not think that the warrants permitted seizing goods. Displaying impatience he asserted that whatever the wording of the warrants might be the Commons should grant John Rolle his privilege. Eliot was asked to present the warrants he had in his possession to the committee of the whole. He did so. They were read and no mention of seizing was to be found in them. During the debate it was resolved that every member of the House should have privilege for his goods, estate, and person. In the end a resolution was passed that Mr Rolle should have privilege of Parliament for his goods seized on October 30, January 5, and any time since then. But against whom he should claim his privilege was not stated. There was the rub. As Digges pointed out during the debate, it was almost impossible to avoid involving the interests of the King in this claim. The line between the farmers of the customs as private individuals and as royal officials was so fine that it would disintegrate at the slightest touch. If they granted Rolle his privilege, Sir Dudley asked, to whom should the warrant be directed? Here was a dilemma.[1]

When the committee of the whole had convened on Monday, the 23rd, Sir Robert Phelips summarized the work before it. But he ignored the insoluble issue of the previous debate. The delinquency of the customers must be discussed. If it was decided that they were delinquents, their punishment must be determined. Some method must be found of restoring his goods to a member of the House. But first the delinquency of the customers must be dealt with. Such were Sir Robert's proposals. With the 'courtiers', under the leadership of May, advocating that some means whereby Mr Rolle could secure the return of his goods be discovered, the debate grew intense. In the midst of it Sir James Perrott, a 'courtier', suggested that the enemies of their religion were trying to break this Parliament by introducing the issue of privilege. Thereupon Sir Humphrey May tried to erase any distinction between 'courtiers' and 'countrymen', between reasonable men and orators, as he put it.[2]

[1] *C.D.1629*, pp. 88–93, 162–66, 228–34. [2] *Ibid.*, pp. 93, 167, 234, 236.

These attempts at diversions brought Sir John Eliot to his feet. Making his colleagues conscious of the seriousness of the situation before them and of their duty to King and country, he declared he had thought the issue was whether to find a means to restore the goods of a member or 'to proceed to the delinquency'. But now it seemed, he said, that it was neither of these two points. If they persisted in attacking the customers, the King would dissolve Parliament. That was Sir John's interpretation of Perrott's remarks. Eliot continued by displaying his faith in the justice and goodness of the King. 'His goodness is so far clear that he will not break us,' Sir John asserted. 'Those that bring upon us these terrors let a curse light on them and their posterity,' he continued. In closing he supported a discussion of the delinquency of the customers.[1]

Eliot's great faith in the justice and goodness of the King was to receive one jolt after another. Shortly after he had spoken Sir John Coke delivered a message from his Majesty. The Commons were informed that whatever the customers had done closely concerned the King; 'what they did was either by his own direct order and command, or by order of the council-board, himself being present and assisting, and therefore he will not have it divided from his act'.[2] As Coke took his seat the cry of adjourn was heard on all sides. A blow had been administered to the opponents of the government. But first Digges wanted his Majesty informed that they were dealing with the privilege of a member of the House of Commons for his goods. He thought such exact information might put a different aspect on the whole affair in the eyes of the King. Eliot did not think so. He was opposed to the Commons picking out a particular instance. The privilege of the House of Commons was the issue. That 'the King hath ever used to give us', he assured his colleagues. Turning to another aspect of the problem before them, he believed the customers had not insisted so much on the King's command as that they had acted by virtue of the warrants which they had presented to the House of Commons. Sir John wanted the royal message reported to the House. He did not doubt but that his Majesty 'will come to a right understanding of this business by means of the grand council of this House'. Therefore, he wanted the Commons in formal session to consider what was best to be done.[3] Eliot was drawing much too fine a distinction between a royal warrant and a royal com-

---

[1] C.D.1629, p. 236, also pp. 93–94 and 167.   [2] Ibid., p. 94, also pp. 167–68, 236–37.
[3] Ibid., p. 168, very brief on p. 237.

mand. And as usual his boundless faith in the King and in the prowess of the House of Commons was far beyond their combined capabilities. Were his words and his thoughts identical?

On the motion of Sir Robert Pye to read the message in the House the Speaker took the chair. As soon as the resolutions regarding the privilege of Rolle, which had been approved by the committee of the whole on Saturday, were passed by the House of Commons, Sir John Coke repeated the message from King Charles. Phelips then disclosed how seriously the message affected him. 'The essential and fundamental liberty of this House is now before you,' he said. He wanted the Commons to adjourn and to spend the next day 'invoking God to consider what way to take in obedience to his Majesty'. To Phelips there was no easy way out, no means of informing the King of the truth, or casting the blame elsewhere. Eliot, who spoke next, now also realized the seriousness of the situation. He said there was 'a double obligation upon us, to our King, to our country, to posterity to preserve that right our fathers have left us'. But he refused to face the predicament they were in. He thought the message was caused by some 'great persons near the King' who feared that the punishment the House might inflict on the customers would lead to a disclosure of the sins and faults of the great. He continued to refuse to place the King under the slightest shadow. The few speeches which concluded the work of that Monday showed feeling to be in support of adjournment over Tuesday. One of the last to speak was Selden, who, like Phelips and Eliot, understood the importance of the royal message. Unlike Eliot he could not suggest an easy way of escape. But he insisted that some action must be undertaken and that adjournment until Wednesday to think out their difficulties was the only thing to do at the moment. As a result a resolution to adjourn until Wednesday, February 25, was passed by the House of Commons.[1]

When the Commons had assembled on Wednesday morning they were informed by the Speaker that it was his Majesty's pleasure and express command that they adjourn until Monday, March 2.[2] The Commons could only obey. In their mood of subservience to the royal will they dared not protest or speak a single word. Unquestionably Charles was afraid, or even had been told, that in their communion with God on Tuesday some members at least had received strength,

[1] For this paragraph see C.D.1629, pp. 168–69, 237–39, and C.J., I, 932.
[2] Ibid., and C.D. 1629, pp. 169–70.

such strength that they might dare to launch their shafts at him. Five more days of contemplation might raise fears among even the boldest at taking such an unheard-of step. Five more days would give greater opportunity than one for hot blood to cool off.[1] But five more days might also galvanize weakness into strength, contemplation into action. Charles was gambling with time. Possibly he hoped to break this Parliament, saw his opportunity, and decided to give the Commons enough rope to hang themselves. But the main reason for summoning this session, the passage of the tonnage and poundage bill, had been lost sight of by the Commons. In the present temper of the House there was little chance of that bill being revived. Possibly Charles had also given it up and was concentrating on leading some of the members into a trap. Or, what was more likely, he felt that when the Commons saw that in their attack on the customers they were confronted with the will of the King they would submit and return to the bill for tonnage and poundage. Privilege of a member, the rights of the subject, and hatred of Arminianism had stirred the Commons to their depths. Confronted with the will of the King could they forget the goods of John Rolle, the actions of the customers, and the opinions of Manwaring and Montague? Could they again turn to impersonal attack as they had in the Petition of Right?

4. CORRESPONDENCE

There could be no better time to consider the correspondence of Sir John Eliot than when the House of Commons was adjourned for a few days. Though one gets the impression that Eliot was always busy, at least when away from home, he was not too busy to write and receive letters. Part of his preoccupation was to carry on a voluminous correspondence with friends and relatives, most of which, one gets the feeling, has been lost. But we are fortunate in having preserved for us a few of the letters Sir John wrote and an occasional one he received during the first two months of 1629.

Richard Gedy, his father-in-law, was one of the first to hear from Eliot after the opening of Parliament. Three letters to Gedy have sur-

---

[1] Or as Gardiner, VII, 66–67, says: 'His agents were busy with the leaders to induce them to desist from their pretensions, in order that, as he afterwards said "a better and more right understanding might be begotten between him and them".'

vived, written on January 29, February 2 and 19.[1] In the first Sir John graciously excused himself for not having written sooner, mentioned that he had spent Christmas with the Earl of Warwick, and told of his arrival in London shortly before the opening of Parliament. He also spoke of the 'treaty with the Bishop' which will be discussed shortly.

Writing on February 2 Eliot told his father-in-law of sending messengers to Cornwall to bring witnesses in the case of Lord Mohun to London. He asked Gedy to encourage any of them who lived nearby to obey the order of the Commons and explained how their refusal would gain them nothing but 'danger to themselves'. The case against the vice-warden of the stannaries had been reopened on January 27[2] and three days later a resolution was passed to send for witnesses.[3] But when Eliot wrote to Gedy on February 19 he could report no progress against Mohun. Not a hint has survived that any witnesses appeared at Westminster or that any steps were taken against Lord Mohun by the House. It appears that he remained untouched.

In his letter of the 19th Sir John wrote of many private matters of little importance. He concluded it with the statement that the interest of the Commons was wholly fixed on religion, and that if they did not do something about it quickly they might become involved in serious danger. There was no hint in the letter that tonnage and poundage was also becoming an issue.

Let us turn to the 'treaty with the Bishop' Eliot mentioned in his first letter to Gedy where Sir John said that Gedy's servant, having received general instructions on this matter from his master, had accomplished nothing. Eliot said he would take over the business himself. The bishop was Joseph Hall of Exeter who was now in London for the Parliament. From him the Eliots leased Cuddenbeak in St. Germans. Undoubtedly the 'treaty' with Hall had to do with an alteration in the lease for this manor. In 1608 it had been leased for the lives of Bridget, Sir John's mother, Sir John Eliot, and his intended wife, Radigund. On January 27, 1620, after the death of Bridget in 1618, the name of John Eliot, eldest son of Sir John and Radigund, was substituted in the lease for that of his grandmother. And now unquestionably it was the intention of Eliot to put the name of one of his younger sons in place of his deceased wife in order to preserve the time element of three lives which is characteristic of every lease made in the early seventeenth century

---

[1] *Letter Book*, pp. 32, 33–34, 51.
[2] See above, p. 240. [3] *C.J.*, I, 923, 925.

between the Bishop of Exeter and the Eliots for the manor of Cudden-beak.[1]

In his letter of February 2 to Gedy Sir John told him that he was going to see the Bishop that afternoon. If the opportunity presented itself he would 'give some overture to the treaty for my lease'. It is impossible to be sure that he obtained the desired alteration in his lease of Cuddenbeak when he talked to Bishop Hall at his Drury Lane house. There is no mention of the lease in his letter to Gedy of February 19. Probably Eliot was successful, for in a most friendly exchange of letters on February 6[2] on a different subject the bishop requested a favour of his prominent Cornish tenant. Such a request Joseph Hall could never have made of Sir John Eliot had he refused to alter the Cuddenbeak lease.

According to the bishop's letter he was having trouble with the rabid puritan, Henry Burton. Burton in one of his writings had accused Hall of helping 'popery over the style'. The bishop had replied with a pamphlet in which he refuted such a charge. To Hall's support came his chaplain, Hugh Cholmley and Robert Butterfield, Cholmley's friend. Answering these pamphlets with a book dedicated to Parliament[3] Burton suggested that the Bishop of Exeter and Cholmley 'have sure some plot in hand of restoring popery to England, or England to popery'. Hall now wrote a strong defence of Cholmley and himself in his letter to Eliot because some mention of this business had been made in the House of Commons.[4] He had even heard that steps were to be taken in the case of Cholmley. The bishop asked Sir John to notify him as soon as anything more was done in the House about his and Cholmley's troubles and also to put in a good word with Mr Speaker, who was an old friend of theirs.

In his reply of the same day to the worthy bishop Eliot mentioned his visit to him on February 2 and showed that he had complete faith in the Bishop of Exeter. He associated him in no way with popery. There had been no further mention of him and Cholmley in the House, Sir John wrote. If there should be, he assured the bishop he would do

---

[1] P.E. MSS., Muniment Room, Manor of Cuddenbeak, Title Deeds, Bundle LXVIII. Between 1620 and 1632 no lease or record of the alteration of a lease has survived.

[2] *Letter Book*, pp. 40–4.

[3] For the writings of these clerics see *D.N.B.* under their names.

[4] On Feb. 4, Sir James Perrott complained to the House of Commons that Dr Thomas Turner, chaplain to the Bishop of London, refused to license the printing of certain books while he granted licences to Cholmley and Butterfield for their pamphlets. *C.D. 1629*, pp. 39, 125, *Eph. Parl.*, p. 245.

all in his power to help him. The troubles of the Bishop of Exeter do not appear again in the records of the Commons. But these letters display the prestige and repute Sir John Eliot had acquired in the eyes of a man as prominent as Joseph Hall. Friendship existed between the two men, favours could be asked and granted on both sides. If there was any expression of servility, it came rather from the bishop than from his Cornish tenant.

On returning to his lodgings on February 2 after his above-mentioned visit to Bishop Hall, Eliot found a communication from Sir Robert Cotton.[1] That worthy, unaccountably absent from the House at this time, proposed that Sir John present to the Commons four points on religion which he hoped would break the plot of those bishops who proposed to introduce an innovation in the government of the Church by enhancing the power of convocation. Cotton believed that a resolution containing his four points voted by the Commons and recorded in their register would be 'a happy conclusion of your dispute of religion'. The gist of the four proposals was that the catholic body of the Church of England was not composed solely of the spirituality and temporality under the headship of the King, that convocation could not determine the doctrine and discipline of the Church without full assent by Parliament, that the doctrine of the Church was to be found in the 39 Articles approved by Parliament in the 13th year of Queen Elizabeth, and that anybody advocating any other doctrine than that to be found in the Articles was to be punished as a breaker of the law. Sir John did not follow Cotton's suggestion and introduce these assertions in the House of Commons. But, as we have seen, he made a strong speech on February 3 in which he denounced Arminianism.[2] Undoubtedly these proposals helped him in composing that speech. They strengthened his anti-clerical stand for saving Anglicanism from Arminianism by parliamentary action.

In spite of his expressed attitude towards Arminian bishops, Sir John was on good terms with other members of the Church. We have seen his friendly relations with the Bishop of Exeter. At this same time Eliot's good friend Thomas Godfrey of Grantham in Lincolnshire hoped that he had influence with John Williams, Bishop of Lincoln. Writing on February 4 to Sir John,[3] Godfrey told how Grantham was 'miserably served with two base vicars'. He implied that Eliot might be able to induce Williams to remove Tytler, an Arminian clergyman of

[1] *Letter Book*, pp. 36–8.   [2] See above, p. 284.   [3] *Letter Book*, pp. 38–9.

some repute.[1] as well as his colleague who seems to have been of the same persuasion. Unfortunately, the absence of any further correspondence on this subject makes it impossible to tell whether Sir John Eliot was able to help Thomas Godfrey and his poor town of Grantham.

Yet another friend had a request to make of Eliot. This time no bishop was involved. Bevil Grenville of Stow in Cornwall writing on February 14[2] regretted that he was unable to attend this session of Parliament but gave no reasons save that 'my occasions have not been ordinary'. His purpose in writing Sir John was to beg him to procure for him a letter from the Speaker of the House 'to the judges of our circuit' to stop a trial which concerned some land of his. For an unstated reason Grenville could not attend the assizes. Therefore, he wanted to avail himself of his privilege as a member of Parliament.

Sir John replied on February 29 with some gracious remarks about expecting to see him soon and needing his help.[3] But he was puzzled about Grenville's request. He had given him so little information about the trial, the name of the parties involved, the county in which 'the scene is laid', etc., that he found it difficult to give him the assistance he desired. But he had moved it 'in general', and the House had ordered that a mandate should be granted.[4] He felt sure that a letter from Grenville to the judge stating his position and requesting his privilege would be all that was necessary. To have at our disposal Bevil Grenville's reply filled with apologies and explanations would be most entertaining and instructive.

Our knight of the shire of Cornwall was indeed a man of influence in this session. So thought Michael Oldsworth, secretary to the Earl of Pembroke, who wrote Eliot from Whitehall on February 19.[5] Making his apologies for having invited him yesterday 'to some trouble', he now asked Eliot to prevent the second reading of a private bill, called 'Brookers' bill, which concerned itself with a settlement of land in Kent.[6] We know neither what help Sir John had given Pembroke on the previous day nor whether he was able to use his influence against

---

[1] See Gardiner, VII, 16–8. [2] *Letter Book*, pp. 46–7.
[3] *Ibid.*, pp. 47–9. [4] *C.J.*, I, 932.
[5] Forster, *Eliot*, II, 427. Grosart has printed only the most important letters of Eliot's corespondence in his *Letter Book*. Many letters of no great significance are to be found only in the ms. Letter Book at Port Eliot. This is one of them. Forster has printed in one form or another all these minor letters. I have compared them all with the originals. As these letters appear in print only in Forster's *Eliot*, reference will be made to this work for these letters. [6] *C.J.*, I, 929, *C.D. 1629*, p. 202.

this private bill. At least there is no record that it came to a second reading.

One more letter of Eliot's correspondence for this period has survived. It was written to him by his old friend, Sir Dudley Digges, and dated 'this Wednesday evening'.[1] But as the first part of the letter deals with a quarrel between Sir John Eliot and Sir William Herbert which had taken place in the House on Wednesday morning, January 21, it is most likely that the letter was written on that day. The quarrel came as a result of some words used by Herbert which greatly displeased Eliot.[2] Nothing was done about it in the House. But Digges, according to his letter, had had a talk with Herbert and wanted to see Sir John as a result. Sir Dudley appears to have been acting as a mediator. Apparently Kirton also intended to talk with Herbert to see what he could do. Digges felt, however, that a conference between himself and Eliot should precede the mediation of Kirton. So he asked Sir John to prevent Kirton from seeing Herbert before such a conference. That is all we know of this little dispute.

In the second part of his letter Sir Dudley changed the subject to the policy he and Eliot intended to follow in this session. That their 'ways would seem to differ', as Digges expressed it, is carried out in practically every speech by that gentleman in the controversial issues of the session. In all, his moderation and leanings towards the court are apparent. Either the government had made overtures to Digges during the interval between the sessions and had induced him to leave the 'country' party, or, what is more likely, he felt, like Wentworth, that he could support the prerogative now that the Petition of Right was law. That the 'ends' towards which Eliot and Digges were working were the same is undoubtedly true, for they, like Wentworth and others at this time, were striving to attain the idea of good government by King and Parliament.

What is indeed perplexing are the words Sir Dudley Digges wrote in closing his letter. 'If this day any cast stones or dirt at my friend,' he said, 'let me pray you to preserve yourself clear, a looker-on, which credit me, if my weakness be worth your crediting, will both advantage you and much content him that is truly and faithfully your servant.' Whom did Digges mean by 'my friend'? It does not seem possible that

---

[1] *Letter Book*, pp. 49–50.

[2] Herbert had referred to a certain select committee supported by Eliot as coming 'near the Spanish Inquisition'. *C.D. 1629*, p. 6, note c.

he could mean King Charles. Could he have meant Sir Thomas Wentworth, now Baron Wentworth of Wentworth Woodhouse?

This letter must have hurt Eliot, for it showed him that his former
companion in arms, with whom he had fought and suffered in the
struggles of the House of Commons, could no longer be considered a
political ally. But a vaguely perceptible undercurrent runs throughout
the session and grows stronger week by week. It is that thoughtless
idealism expressed in more and more forceful language was bringing
Sir John Eliot out of touch with an increasing number of the level-
headed leaders of his party, call them moderates. Unconsciously he was
becoming the leader of the radicals and was relinquishing his place
among the parliamentary moderates in their struggle against the con-
servatives of the 'court' party—if such modern terminology can be applied to this stage of the great conflict of the seventeenth century. The
impression one gets is that Eliot, radical leader during this session, was
usually a potent influence in the House even if he did not always carry
it with him.

5. MARCH 2ND

During the recess from February 25 to March 2 these lines between the
radical and moderate opponents of the government were becoming
more clearly drawn. By March 2 there was little difficulty in distin-
guishing the groups. While the House was adjourned a meeting was
held at a tavern called the Three Cranes. There nine of the leading
radicals[1] made plans for the day on which the Commons were to reassemble. We can surmise that the government heard of the meeting
and decided upon an immediate adjournment as soon as prayers had
been read on the morning of March 2. Somehow the group of radicals
must have learned of the government's plan. They appear to have held
a second meeting at which they made sure that an immediate adjournment would be prevented. Much of what happened on March 2 could
not possibly have taken place spontaneously. Unquestionably Sir John
Eliot dominated the meetings at the Three Cranes. One cannot picture
him just sitting and listening. He had to do most of the talking. At
one of the two meetings, most likely the first, Sir John with the help of

---

[1] Sir John Eliot, Denzil Holles, Benjamin Valentine, Walter Long, William Coryton,
William Strode, John Selden, Sir Miles Hobart, and Sir Peter Hayman.

his colleagues prepared the speech he was to deliver as well as three resolutions to be presented to the House. Eliot had no rival as radical leader of the Commons. Except for John Selden, and possibly William Coryton, he was the only leader of the 'country' party who was willing to go to extremes against the government. As will be seen, there were a number of prominent members who sided with the radicals or can be labelled as such. But the majority of the old leaders against the 'court' either were silent on March 2, counselled moderation, or were as conservative as any royalist could possibly be.[1]

The Commons assembled in the House on the morning of March 2, 1629.[2] Prayers were read. Immediately Sir John Finch, the Speaker, delivered a message from the King. His Majesty requested the Commons to adjourn themselves at once until March 10. When Finch asked them whether it was their pleasure to abide by the wish of the King, he was met by the cry of 'No' from all sides of the House. At the same time, midst cries of approval, Sir John Eliot arose to speak. But the Speaker, still standing, informed the members that his Majesty 'had laid an absolute command upon him, that the House should be presently adjourned without any speech or other proceedings, and that if any in the House did offer to speak after the message delivered he should instantly leave the chair'. The royal instructions were greeted with cries that Sir John Eliot should be heard. As Eliot remained standing the Speaker moved away from the chair. Thereupon Denzil Holles and Benjamin Valentine jumped to his side, pushed him down, and held him in the chair. They remained at his side throughout the session. The attempts of May, Edmonds and other Privy Councillors to free Finch were futile and only caused Holles to swear by 'God's wounds he should sit still until they pleased to rise'.[3]

When a degree of order and quiet had been restored Eliot was able to address the House. Except for the adjournment of February 25 there never had been a similar incident, he asserted. One of the fundamental liberties of the House was to adjourn itself, Sir John said. He believed that the King had been misinformed about their intended proceedings. His Majesty apparently thought that they were about to trench 'too far

[1] S.P.D., Chas. I, CXXXIX, no. 8, and 'An Information' presented in Star Chamber on May 7, 1629, by Sir Robert Heath found in Rushworth, I, 666, and *C.D. 1629*, p. 239, note *b*.

[2] Unless otherwise indicated my description of the events and speeches of March 2 is based on *C.D. 1629*, pp. 252–67 (March 2nd Account).

[3] *Ibid.*, p. 104.

upon the power of sovereignty'. But Eliot insisted that they had always acted in accordance with his Majesty's justice. After glorifying royal justice he declared that they had prepared a 'short declaration' of their intentions which he hoped would agree with the honour of the House and the justice of the King. Sir John then threw a paper from his seat high up in the House down to the floor where it was picked up by Sir William Fleetwood and handed to the clerk.[1] Confusion and tumult resulted. Coryton struck one of the members.[2] The House resounded with the cry of 'Read', 'Read'. As soon as he could make himself heard the Speaker, standing between his guards, told the Commons that in the past they had always adjourned immediately upon a request from the King. When Finch again tried to obey the royal command he was restrained by Valentine and Holles and greeted with insistent demands to have the paper read. He begged the members not to press him to do this, asked them to think what they would do if they were in his place, and expressed the hope that his desire to serve them faithfully might not bring on his ruin.

When the tumult had subsided Edward Kirton, following the lead of Eliot about false reports carried to the King and elaborating the point about the Commons' having the right to adjourn themselves, desired to know by what warrant the Speaker had delivered the royal message to the House. He was supported by Sir Walter Erle with the statement that the Speaker usually brought a royal letter as a warrant for such a message. But Finch, citing numerous precedents, was able to refute the argument that a warrant was necessary and showed that an oral request for adjournment from his Majesty was all that was required. Sir John Finch was right, while Eliot and the rest were wrong. The Commons could make no headway in that direction.

Coryton, who spoke next, tacitly admitted the strength of Finch's precedents but cleverly ignored them. He ignored the royal message, turned a strong light of approval on the Commons' activities in relation to the King, and directed one of disapproval on the Speaker's actions in relation to the Commons. Thus the attention of the House was focused directly on the failure of the Speaker to act in accordance with the wishes of the members.

Henry Bellasis arguing along these lines moved that Finch should be replaced by another Speaker if he refused to put the question for the reading of the paper. Eliot showed the extent of his demands on Finch

[1] *C.D.1629*, p. 240.   [2] Gardiner, VII, 69, Rushworth, I, 667.

when he declared that he was ready to obey the royal command to adjourn as soon as the declaration written on the paper in the hands of the
clerk was read. Again the hard-pressed Speaker asked in desperation
what would they do if they were in his place. He begged to be allowed
to leave the chair.[1] But his plea fell on deaf ears. First William Strode,
then Valentine, Holles, Sir William Constable,[2] Sir Francis Seymour,
Clement Coke, and Sir Peter Hayman desired either the reading of the
paper or a vote as to whether it should be read, knowing full well that
a majority of the House in its present temper would support the proposal to have the paper read.

After this expression of the prevailing opinion Sir John Eliot again
entered the fray to see if he could not influence Finch by either persuasion or threats. He declared it was obvious that the opinion of the
House was to have the paper read. Therefore, the refusal of the Speaker
was in contempt of and an affront to the House. Eliot then threatened
Finch with calling him to the bar and having him judged a delinquent.
'To avoid that put it to the question,' he said, 'and if you do it by the
command of the House no doubt but it will satisfy his Majesty.' These
startling words stirred the temper of the House. Again confusion reigned
supreme. Midst the hubbub a demand that the door be locked and the
key 'brought up' could be heard. The serjeant-at-arms refused to carry
out the request. So Sir Miles Hobart said that if the House would trust
him he would lock the door and keep the key. As soon as his proposal
had been accepted he performed the task and pocketed the key.

When some order had been restored the unfortunate Speaker, more
afraid of how the King might punish him than of what the House was
threatening to do to him, replied to Eliot. 'Though I should hold it one
of the greatest miseries that can befall me to be called to that bar, yet I
will readily undergo any shame or censure you can lay upon me if that
will satisfy you.' The entreaties of Sir Walter Erle and Sir Edward
Giles that he permit the paper to be read had no effect on him. He
begged the House to let him go to the King and said that if he did not
return speedily, after having done them good service with his Majesty,
they might tear him to pieces. These words were greeted by cries of
'Aye' and 'No'. The sentiment of the House was beginning to change.

After Thomas Godfrey had suggested that if Mr Speaker had the
paper read he could go better instructed to the King,[3] Sir John Eliot

[1] *C.D. 1629*, p. 240.   [2] *Ibid.*
[3] *Ibid.*, p. 241.

took the floor again to make one more attempt to beat down his obstinacy. The paper Finch had refused to have read, Eliot assured him, contained matter which could emanate only from loyal subjects. Therefore, if he persisted in his refusal there was nothing left for them to do but fall upon his person. As he had refused to put the reading of the paper to the question, Sir John intended to have it restored to him. He then would give its substance, so that everybody might know of the loyalty and affection to his Majesty of the members of this House. To make the situation even more difficult for Finch, William Strode gave him the choice of being the servant of either the King or the Commons. To which the unfortunate Speaker replied that he was no less the King's servant than the Commons'. But he made his position clear when he declared, 'I will not say I will not put it to the question, but I must say I dare not.'

When threats and cajolery proved to be of no avail, Sir John Eliot, requesting his paper, stepped down from his high seat and retrieved it midst the cry of 'No', 'No'. To men keyed to a high pitch of excitement he spoke out with fire and vigour. 'I shall now express that by my tongue which this paper should have done. And I do it with as faithful a heart to the King as ever any man spake in this House.' Turning to his prepared speech Sir John declared[1] that the sad state of the country in religion and 'policy' made him fear for both the King and his subjects. He reminded his listeners of Arminianism stealthily creeping into the country and popery openly defying the law. The discovery of the Jesuit college in Clerkenwell, he said, demonstrated such an advance of popery and showed its power and insolence. It would be foolhardy, he continued, not to see the danger they were in, not to avoid it.

The danger, however, did not lie wholly in these Jesuits, Eliot asserted. It was increased by their patrons through whose influence they were brought into the country. Such men had power over the law, even could check magistrates in the execution of justice, he declared. What was worse, these men were responsible for another danger. Because of a feeling of guilt and out of fear of punishment, they had disrupted Parliament and had tried to divert attention from themselves by causing trouble and disturbances among the Commons. After letting his imagination get the better of him Sir John came down to facts and informed the House that some of the enemies of the commonwealth

[1] P.E.MSS., 'Eliot, speeches, etc.', ff. 54–55v. *Neg. Post.*, II, Sup., 142–7. *C.D. 1629*, pp. 258–61, also pp. 104, 170, 241–2.

were to be found among the churchmen. Of these he feared most the Bishop of Winchester and his 'fellows'. But there were others who helped to turn his Majesty against Parliament. 'Amongst them I shall not stick to name that great Lord Treasurer and to say that I fear in his person is contracted the very root and principle of these evils. I find him building upon the old grounds and foundations which were laid by the Duke of Buckingham, his great master.' After blaming Buckingham for the misfortunes of the last session and sounding a note of warning about ministers who tried to break Parliament and were in turn broken by Parliament, Eliot continued to denounce Weston as the head of all the papists in England. He was confident that a little investigation would prove that the Lord Treasurer was behind all Catholic plots and machinations. It was obvious therefore, he asserted, who was the real danger to their religion.

Here Sir John turned to what he called 'policy'. Under this heading he introduced the subject of tonnage and poundage where 'the interest which is pretended for the King is but the interest of that person', by whom he meant the Lord Treasurer. Eliot was sure that Weston was trying to drive trade away in order to 'subvert the government and kingdom'. He cited the advice given to Charles IX of France by his chancellor, which was that the best way to weaken a country was not to attack it from without but to hinder and divert trade from within. This, Sir John said, was what was happening in England at the present time. He thought that in a few days it would be made manifest that such was the purpose of Weston and his followers. It was the Lord Treasurer's guilt of attempting such a policy which made 'him mis-interpret our proceedings, misrepresent them to his Majesty'. Clearly the duty of the Commons was to uphold the rights of Englishmen, their religion, and the honour and safety of the King.

Upon completing this unjust denunciation of the Lord Treasurer, Eliot held up his paper and declared[1] that it contained a protestation against the 'new counsels' which were ruining the government, against those men, 'whether they be great or subordinate' who 'will persuade his Majesty to take tonnage and poundage without grant of Parliament', and against any merchant who was willing to pay these duties without consent of Parliament. The men who were harming the government and advising the collection of tonnage and poundage should be declared 'capital enemies to the King and kingdom', and the mer-

---

[1] From here to end of speech I have used *ibid.*, p. 261 instead of the P.E. MS.

chants who paid the duties should be 'declared as accessories to the rest'.
Without formally presenting them to the House Sir John told the Commons what his resolutions contained. He closed his speech by saying:
'Whensoever we shall sit here again, if I be here (as I think I shall), I
shall declare my resolutions fully to fall upon the person of that great
man', by whom he meant, of course, Lord Treasurer Weston.

Having had his say and done all in his power to put his plans into
effect against the will of a stubborn Speaker, Sir John Eliot believed
that he had finished his work for the day. Without anybody seeing
what he was doing, he threw the paper on which the resolutions were
written into a nearby open fire.

Eliot was followed by Coryton who told Speaker Finch that he was
not opposed to his going to the King, but he did not want him to go
until the resolutions had been read. He said that his Majesty needed
assistance from the Commons but was prevented from receiving it by
those who had been named by the last speaker. When he declared that
they had all come to this Parliament to grant the King tonnage and
poundage as well as further supply, he was greeted by cries of 'ALL',
'ALL', from every side of the House. Coryton then denounced the
practice of pleading the King's command in justification of the breach of
the law and closed with a motion to entreat his Majesty to advise 'with
his grave and good Council' and to dismiss those councillors who had
been named in the House.

Several members denounced and defended the Lord Treasurer.
When one of them described the circumstances under which he would
vote against Weston, Sir John Eliot realized that the purpose of his attack had been misunderstood. He arose to say that he did not want a
vote taken now on Weston's policies. He merely wished to name him
as the man he believed responsible for the troubles which confronted
the Commons. Sir John said that his plan, not to be initiated on this
day, was first to prove Weston guilty and then have a vote taken on
him. He hoped that an honourable person near the chair 'may faithfully represent our desires to his Majesty' sometime during the adjournment of the next week.

After a few more had expressed their opinions on the immediate
issue John Selden spoke for the first time and brought the debate back
to the point from which it had been diverted by Eliot's long address.
Passing over the previous speeches with the remark that he was 'not
ready for voting anything now', he launched into an attack on the

Speaker for refusing to put the question on the reading of the resolutions. With one cogent argument or pointed example after another he showed how Finch had failed to function as the Speaker of the Commons. 'We should make choice of a new Speaker,' he declared. 'But for the present all I shall move shall be that since you have refused to put the reading of this paper to the question, the clerk may be commanded to read it. Here Sir John Eliot said the paper could not now be read, for he had burned it.' Tension in the House was rising again. Mr Maxwell, gentleman usher of the black rod, sent word through the locked door that the serjeant-at-arms had been summoned to attend the King.[1] No step was taken to permit him to leave. Instead Digges moved that the House adjourn itself and end all dispute for the present. In spite of what had been said in the House he considered the Lord Treasurer innocent until proof had been presented against him. 'Whereupon some hissed.' Yes, Digges had gone over to the 'court'. Even Phelips wanted Weston tried and cleared in Parliament 'which I doubt not but may turn to his greater honor'. In naming and blaming the Lord Treasurer, Eliot had raised a greater storm than had been his intention.

At this point Denzil Holles asserted that Sir John Eliot 'hath done very ill to burn that paper'. He desired that the House declare by a vote that anybody who counselled the taking of tonnage and poundage or any merchant who paid it without consent of Parliament be proclaimed capital enemies of the state. 'To this Sir John Eliot answered that he gave that gentleman great thanks for reproving of him for the burning of that paper, and that all the obligations that had passed betwixt them he held this for the greatest.' Before more could be said on the subject Sir Thomas Jermyn reminded the House that Mr Maxwell was still waiting at the door and was wondering why the serjeant had not been sent to him. But the 'courtier's' words fell on deaf ears and Hobart made no attempt to unlock the door. Instead Christopher Wandesford, former ally of Eliot but intimate friend of Wentworth, came to the support of Weston and Finch by moving adjournment. The motion produced another violent attack on the Speaker by Sir Peter Hayman who desired that the House punish him in some way. Seeing that no progress was being made and that the moderates and 'courtiers' were gaining strength Holles said, 'since that paper is burned I conceive I cannot do my King and country better service than to deliver to this

---

[1] Immediately after Eliot's long speech Nicholas in *C.D. 1629*, p. 171, says: 'The serjeant of the House is sent for by the King'.

House what was contained in it'. Midst the expression of some opposition he read the three famous and well-known resolutions from a paper he had written himself.[1] They 'were jointly, as they were read, allowed with a loud Yea by the House.'[2]

Immediately several members called out for adjournment.[3] After Rich and Seymour had argued over a technicality of this procedure, the House of Commons, through the mouth of its Speaker, adjourned itself until March 10. Sir Miles Hobart unlocked the door. The members trooped out.[4] None returned for eleven years. Some never passed through those portals again.

On March 3 Sir John Eliot and eight of his colleagues were summoned to appear before the Privy Council. On the next day Sir Allen Apsley, Lieutenant of the Tower, received a letter from the Council ordering him to take Sir John Eliot into custody and keep him a close prisoner. On the same day the Council directed its messenger, Lawrence Whytacres to 'repair to the lodging of Sir John Eliot, knight, and carefully to seal up his study, trunks, cabinets, and any other thing wherein you may find or understand that he hath any papers'. Because of his fight for what he believed to be freedom and liberty, Sir John Eliot was deprived of both during the few remaining years of his life.[5]

---

[1] *C.D. 1629*, pp. 101–2. Rushworth, I, 660. *Eph. Parl.*, p. 267.
[2] *Ibid.*, p. 105.   [3] *Ibid.*, p. 172.
[4] For an interesting description of this last scene see *C. and T. Chas. I*, 11, 12.
[5] P.R.O., Privy Council Register, V, 119–20.

CHAPTER XIV

The Judges Take Action

March 10, 1629, to February 12, 1630

SIR John Eliot was not the only member of the House of Commons put into the custody of Sir Allen Apsley. Selden, Coryton, Holles, and Valentine were also sent to the Tower. Sir Miles Hobart and Sir Peter Hayman found themselves in other prisons. Strode and Long could not be found and were at liberty for a month, after which they too resided behind bars.[1] These nine men had met at the Three Cranes and supposedly had 'seditiously conspired' against the government. So thought Charles I and his Attorney-General, Sir Robert Heath. In the heated discussion of March 2 other members of the House had denounced the Speaker in stronger language than had been employed by some of the nine members.[2] But they were not touched by the government, for they had not been at the Three Cranes. However, it was not alone because of what the nine had planned at that tavern that they were arrested, but because they had also talked and acted contemptuously and seditiously in the House of Commons on March 2.

By March 10, to which the Commons had adjourned themselves, King Charles was ready to deal with Parliament. On that day he dissolved it. Addressing the Lords alone he declared 'that it was merely the undutiful and seditious carriage in the lower House that hath made the dissolution of this Parliament'. Exonerating the majority of that House, Charles declared that it had been 'but some few vipers among them that did cast this mist of undutifulness over most of their eyes'. Soothing the peers with his closing words he hurled another stone at Eliot and his friends when he declared that 'those vipers must look for their reward

---

[1] *H.M.C. Rept. MSS. of the Duke of Buccleuch and Queensberry* III, 341. *C.S.P.D., 1628–1629*, p. 506. According to a warrant dated April 2, 1629, William Strode was committed to the marshal of the King's Bench prison. Rushworth, I, 664.

[2] Clement Coke, Henry Bellasis, and several others made remarks which were far more offensive than anything said by Hayman and Long.

of punishment'.[1] And then in a proclamation to justify the dissolution, drafted on March 2 but not published till after the 10th, the trouble was said to have been caused 'by the malevolent dispositions of some ill-affected persons of the House of Commons' and 'by the disobedient and seditious carriage of those said ill-affected persons'.[2] Such language shows what Sir John Eliot and his compatriots might now expect at the hands of the King.

A week after the dissolution the imprisoned members were already being questioned. On March 18 it was Eliot's turn. To the numerous questions dealing with his activities on or before March 2 put to him in the presence of a group of Privy Councillors,[3] he had the same reply. It was that whatever he had done or said was as a member of the House of Commons. He would always be ready to answer any questions when brought before that House. But now as a private man 'he would not trouble himself to remember what he had either spoken or done in that place as a public man'.[4]

Of the others who were questioned, Coryton and Hayman were not as firm in refusing to answer as Eliot had been. Within a little over three months they had made their peace with the King and were released.[5] From the point of view of his colleagues as well as posterity, John Selden made the worst impression of the lot. Not a single question, as far as has been recorded, did he refuse to answer. When he was asked about Eliot's three resolutions, he said 'he did not nor well could observe [them] at that time'. When the resolutions were read to him he declared 'that if he had then understood those to have been the positions Sir John Eliot held or propounded, he would absolutely have dissented from him, and said that he is clearly of another opinion'. As Gardiner says: 'The falsehood was so unblushing that it can hardly be reckoned as a falsehood at all. He could never for an instant have expected to be believed.' John Selden was not released to return to his pen and books for many months to come. In the ensuing time he gained strength and forgot his momentary weakness to become a tenacious advocate of the just rights of himself and his fellow prisoners. Of them

---

[1] Rushworth, I, 662.

[2] *Ibid.*, 661.   [3] S.P.D., Chas. I, CXXXIX, nos. 6, 7.

[4] Add. MS. 30, 926, ff. 314–314v, also Harl. MS. 6846, f. 432v and Harl. MS. 2305, ff. 389–389v.

[5] *C.S.P.D., 1628–1629*, pp. 527, 543, 551, 555, give evidence that Coryton and Hayman were still in prison by the end of May. *Ibid., Addenda, 1625–1649*, p. 374, shows that Coryton (probably also Hayman) was released in June, 1629.

all Sir John Eliot was the solid rock against which Charles and his advisers might dash themselves in vain.[1]

To weaken such strength a commission was sent to Cornwall, as Sir John disclosed nearly a year later, to seize his property. Thanks to his foresight they found not a single acre of land in his name as owner or leaseholder and 'returned a *nihil*'.[2]

With rumour running rife in London of the possibility of another Parliament being summoned Charles issued a proclamation on March 27, in which he declared 'it presumption for any to prescribe any time unto us for Parliaments, the calling, continuing, and dissolving of which is always in our power'. In the same document he denounced Eliot and his activities of March 2 by declaring that rumours made it appear 'as if the scandalous and seditious proposition in the House of Commons, made by an outlawed man, desperate in mind and fortune, which was tumultuously taken up by some few, . . . had been the vote of the whole House, whereas the contrary is the truth'.[3] Doubtless Charles wanted to be sure that he could use the term outlaw in describing Eliot, so he had his legal advisers investigate the cases in which his enemy had been involved. The result has survived among the State Papers in a note dated March 25 which lists three outlawries against Sir John.[4]

I. BEFORE THE STAR CHAMBER

During April Charles and his Attorney-General, Heath, decided to prepare the way for proceedings in the Star Chamber against the nine prisoners. First the three chief justices were asked a series of questions. They gave their answers but desired the support of their colleagues on the bench. A few days later, on April 27 and 28, all twelve judges were asked similar questions by Heath and made their reply.[5] By means of the two sets of questions and their answers Charles and Heath hoped to

[1] S.P.D., Chas. I, CXXXVIII, no. 89; CXXXIX, no. 8; Gardiner, VII, 80.
[2] See above, p. 267.
[3] Thomas Rymer, *Foedera* (London, 1704–35), XIX, 62–3.
[4] They were for debt. S.P.D., Chas. I, CXXXIX, no. 53. For one of these see above, p. 177.
[5] For first set of questions and answers see S.P.D., Chas. I, CXLI, no. 44; J. Nalson, *An Impartial Collection, . . .* (London, 1682–3), II, 374–5; Cobbett, *State Trials* (London, 1816), III, 238, note. For the second set of questions and answers see S.P.D., Chas. I, CXLI, no. 52; Rushworth, I, 662–4; Cobbett, *State Trials* III, 236–8.

show that it was legal for the King to order an adjournment of the House of Commons whenever he pleased and to stop all further proceedings as soon as the order had been announced in the House. Furthermore, they wanted the judges to support the Crown's contention that Sir John Eliot and his friends, having acted criminally and contemptuously in the House of Commons and not having been punished by the Commons, could be tried for these actions outside of Parliament by the Court of Star Chamber. The King and his Attorney-General hoped the judges would say that Eliot and his colleagues had committed offences in tumultuously opposing the royal order for adjournment, in conspiring to arouse the people against the King and government by the written and spoken word, in attacking in the House of Commons Privy Councillors and judges by means of false and scandalous rumours[1] in order to arouse the people against them and bring the government into contempt, in making a protestation in the House of Commons against the levying and paying of tonnage and poundage without putting it to a vote or even putting the question, and in refusing to disclose matters of a treasonable nature against each other when being questioned. Charles believed that because of Eliot's unsavoury reputation the offences he was said to have committed might appear in a worse light than if they had been committed by somebody else. He wished Sir John to be called in person before the Court of Star Chamber where, if he refused to plead because of the privilege of Parliament, he could be overruled and censured for his refusal.

But the judges of the common law courts neither relished what Heath had prepared for them nor did they handle it with a proper subservient demeanour. They were extremely chary of opposing in any way the privileges and precedents of Parliament. They limited the King's power to adjourn by whatever precedents the two Houses could present on this point. They qualified the trial of a member for his actions in the House by an outside body with the proviso that these actions in no way had been covered by the privileges of Parliament. They declared the activities of members to be thus punishable offences only if they had not been done in a parliamentary way. They refused to define that phrase and went so far as to declare that under certain circumstances a tumultuous proceeding might be warranted by the privilege of the House of Commons. But they did declare without any reservation whatsoever that a member who by writing or speaking attempted

[1] See Eliot's speeches of Jan. 28 and March 2, above pp. 289, 311-12.

to stir the people against the King, government, or any part of it, not having been tried in Parliament, could be tried by an outside body. Finally they believed that Eliot should not be summoned to appear in person in the Court of Star Chamber but should be heard by counsel before he was overruled.

In spite of these limitations the opinions of the judges were considered to furnish a strong enough foundation on which to proceed in Star Chamber against the prisoners. On May 1 Heath 'informed this court that he had sent a messenger to serve the process of this court returnable immediately upon Sir John Eliot and the other members of the Commons' House . . . to appear in this court and answer an information there to be exhibited against them for very great offences'.[1] On May 7 the Attorney-General presented his 'Information'. This lengthy accusation consisted of three parts.[2] First Eliot was attacked for his speech of January 28 in which he accused Privy Councillors, judges, and other officials of conspiring to trample the liberties of the subject. Next Sir John was denounced for his conspiracy with the eight other members between February 25 and March 2 when they composed a paper containing 'divers false and scandalous assertions touching your Majesty's government'. Finally, all the proceedings of Eliot and his friends on March 2 composed the main body of Heath's charges. Though the Attorney denounced the opposition to the order for adjournment on March 2 and declared the activities of Eliot, Holles, and Valentine to be in contempt of his Majesty's command, he 'now waived the question of the King's right to enforce an adjournment which he had mooted in his private application to the judges'.[3] The 'Information' closed with a request that Eliot and his fellow prisoners be summoned before the Court of Star Chamber by writ of *subpoena*.

After several delays counsel for Sir John Eliot consisting of John Bramston,[4] William Holt, and Robert Mason[5] appeared before the court on May 22 to reply with a plea and demurrer.[6] The paramount point for Eliot in his demurrer (there was much more of a demurrer

---

[1] *C.S.P.D.*, *Addenda, 1625–1649*, p. 342, Harl. MS. 6846, f. 431.

[2] Rushworth, I, 665–70, S.P.D., Chas. I, CXLII, no. 36, CXLIII, no. 47.

[3] Gardiner, VII, 91.

[4] He was father of the autobiographer. *The Autobiography of Sir John Bramston* (Camden Soc., 1845), p. 7.

[5] One of the managers of the impeachment of Buckingham in 1626, and one who helped to frame the Petition of Right. *D.N.B.*

[6] S.P.D., Chas. I, CXLIII, nos. 4, 5.

than a plea in his arguments) was that as a member of Parliament he was not answerable to any other court for what he had said and done in the House of Commons. Never did he turn from this argument. It had great legal strength and represented his ideal, to safeguard at all costs the privileges of the House of Commons. As we have seen, the judges in their replies to Heath's questions always guarded against conflicting with the privileges of Parliament. Only if a member through speech and writing attempted to instigate sedition in the House did the judges hold him unprotected by these privileges. Heath should have concentrated on the point of sedition instead of spreading his net so widely. But the evidence with which to prove sedition against Sir John Eliot was extemely slim.

The document Eliot's attorneys compiled contained much more than the main argument cited above. They were masters in the art of finding flaws in the wording of Heath's 'Information'. For example, they discovered that it said nothing about Parliament's being prorogued, adjourned, or dissolved. Therefore, as far as the Court of Star Chamber and Sir John Eliot were concerned Parliament was still in session.

Under the circumstances, it was only natural that the Attorney-General should want to amend his 'Information' and that the defendants would request that they be permitted to alter their answers. To such motions the court agreed.[1] Heath made some corrections, and Eliot's lawyers combed the amended 'Information' for omissions and flaws in its wording. On June 1 Bramston, Mason and Henry Jones, possibly substituting for Holt, appeared before the Court of Star Chamber and read 'the further plea and demurrer of Sir John Eliot'.[2] They made good use of the mistakes and omissions they found. The clever arguments they concocted may have been good law; but Eliot's prestige was not advanced from the layman's point of view. To stand or fall by that part of the demurrer in which the jurisdiction of Star Chamber was repudiated because it conflicted with the privilege of Parliament was historically and constitutionally a far stronger position to take than any based on the accepted legal chicanery of that day. But for the lawyers, and no doubt for Eliot as well, it was necessary to construct a defence from every possible angle.

On June 6 when the Court of Star Chamber met to hear the views of the three chief judges on the case against Eliot and the eight other de-

---

[1] On May 29, C.S.P.D., 1628–1629, p. 558. See also C. and T. Chas. I, II, 16.
[2] S.P.D., Chas. I, CXLIV, no. 11, Bodleian, MS. Tanner LXXII, ff. 331–32v.

fendants nothing was done or determined. With the impatience of
Charles becoming obvious Lord Keeper Coventry 'very wisely and
seasonably advised the King that the point was so difficult, as the
opinion of all the judges in England needed to resolve and clear it'. The
point Coventry had in mind was whether to proceed in Star Chamber
with the trial of the nine members of the House. On the afternoon of
Tuesday, June 9, 'the judges were all sent for to Greenwich where the
King alone, without any of his Council being by, sent for them first one
by one commanding them to declare their opinion what he might do
in the Star Chamber business without either fear or flattery'. Of the
twelve judges seven advised dropping the case. The King accepted the
advice of the majority, and it was 'withdrawn out of the Star Chamber'.
Unquestionably the judges based their advice on the same difficulty
they had encountered in April—the privileges of Parliament. The other
defendants had all repudiated the jurisdiction of the Star Chamber.
Charles and Heath found that the combination of parliamentary privileges and judges who feared the law as much as they feared their King
was making it extremely difficult for them to bring that 'outlawed
man, desperate in mind and fortune' to justice.[1]

2. HABEAS CORPUS PROCEEDINGS

In the meantime legal proceedings of a slightly different nature involving six of the seven prisoners who remained in custody had been instituted. Coryton and Hayman did not participate. As has been seen,[2] they
were soon to be released. Strode, Long, Selden, Valentine, Holles and
Hobart sued out their writs of *Habeas Corpus*,[3] but Sir John Eliot did
not. Gardiner suggests that perhaps Eliot felt that if he took no part with
the rest, the judges might give a fairer consideration to the application
of the others. This is as good a reason as any with speculation as the
only key.

On May 6 application for the writ was made to the Court of King's
Bench. On the next day in a warrant for the detention of William
Strode the cause of his imprisonment was stated as sedition and contempt. Doubtless it was the same in the case of the others. Not until
early in June were the proceedings before the judges begun. The prin-

---

[1] Halliwell, J. O., *The Autobiography ... of Sir Simonds D'Ewes* (London, 1845), I, 413, 414
C. and T. Chas. I, II, 18.
[2] Above, p. 317, note 5.   [3] Gardiner, VII, 90.

cipal argument, furnished by John Selden for his counsel, was that the charges of sedition and contempt did not constitute treason and therefore should be no hindrance to the taking of bail in the ordinary course. The point was irrefutable and caused Heath, who was to reply for the government, so much concern that he requested a delay.

Now King Charles and his legal advisers produced political arguments, tricks, and excuses in such profusion that the judges were prevented from acting on the writs of the defendants. All through the Trinity term the six men failed to obtain their release on bail. But before the close of that term a change had occurred. In the list of applicants for bail the name of Sir John Eliot was added to those of his six friends. As has been suggested, he probably felt that he would no longer jeopardize the chances of his colleagues in obtaining their freedom. Therefore he wished to be associated with them in their new legal difficulties.[1]

Before the long vacation came to a close the government had made its decision on the *Habeas Corpus* proceedings. The offences committed were not capital, it was decided, therefore the prisoners were bailable by law. On September 9 Coventry, Manchester, Dorchester and Heath decided in conference that bail should be offered the seven imprisoned men.[2] In fact, it should be offered before October 9, the first day they could be brought before the Court of King's Bench in the Michaelmas term. But the government attached the vital condition that the seven must give security for their good behaviour while they were at liberty. On September 30 the judges accepted these terms. But Charles insisted that if the prisoners refused bail under the stipulated conditions, they should not be given another chance until they had asked pardon of the King.[3] A trap had been set which made it impossible for a man with the independence of Eliot to escape.

On October 3 each of the seven men were brought separately before Chief Justice Hyde in his chamber at Serjeants Inn.[4] Each was offered bail on condition that he give a bond of good behaviour. The request was an insult to the prisoners. It was perfectly legal to make it, but such a practice had rarely been employed. What was of paramount import-

---

[1] For the two above paragraphs see *State Trials* III, 240–87, Gardiner, VII, 92–6, Rushworth, I, 664, 680–81, Whitelocke, *Memorials*, I, 38, and *C. and T. Chas. I*, II, 22.

[2] Gardiner, VII, 109. S.P.D., Chas. I, CXLIX, no. 37.

[3] *C.S.P.D., 1629–1631*, pp. 68, 69.

[4] These proceedings are described in S.P.D., Chas. I, CL, no. 85. See also Gardiner, VII, 110–2.

ance to the prisoners was that 'for them to be bound to their good behaviour would argue and imply they had misbehaved themselves in Parliament, whereby they should betray their innocency and liberty'.[1] Six of the seven refused bail under the condition requested of them. Only Walter Long, the first to appear before Hyde, was tricked into accepting that condition and was released until the first day of the term, that is, for only six days. When he discovered that he had fallen into a trap Long was greatly dismayed. Without success he asked to be returned to prison with his friends.

At the opening of the Michaelmas term Walter Long succeeded in being restored to his friends in prison. His conscience was clear. Now all seven appeared before the judges of the court and were informed as a group of the hateful condition under which they would be released. Speaking for himself and his associates Selden argued that the privilege of Parliament would be put in jeopardy if they gave the bonds demanded. The judges replied that in the warrant the causes of their arrest were stated; but there was no mention of Parliament. Therefore, the contempt and sedition of which they were accused was against the government and had nothing to do with Parliament. In other words they refused to listen to any plea which had to do with the privileges of Parliament and thereby made it impossible for Selden and his colleagues to be set at liberty without giving bonds for their good behaviour. As they steadfastly refused to do this, they were all remanded back to prison with a warning from Hyde that they might stay there for seven years 'and withal intimated to them that they could have no more writs of *Habeas Corpus*'. The exception to this ruling was that Sir John Eliot was bailed '*per form*' so that he could 'sue out two writs of error against him, notwithstanding he had fully paid the debts and charges in law'. This legal respite, probably connected with the settlement of two of the three cases for which he was outlawed, had no material effect on Eliot's relationship with the other prisoners.[2]

The *Habeas Corpus* proceedings had reached an unfortunate end. Sir John Eliot and his six colleagues from the House of Commons were still prisoners. Charles had won the second round. But the tactics he had employed would hardly redound to his fame. With shoves and pushes from the King and his Attorney-General, Hyde and his puisne judges never broke the law; but they made use of every loophole at

[1] *C. and T. Chas. I*, II, 31.
[2] S.P.D., Chas. I, CL, no. 85.

their disposal in the interests of the Crown. The prisoners had gained in stature, while the King and his judges had shrunk to the level of tricksters. Before proceeding to deal with further legal actions taken against Eliot, let us see if it is possible to catch a more intimate glimpse of him during these nine months of imprisonment.

3. CONDITIONS SURROUNDING THE PRISONER

Sir John Eliot's confinement in the Tower on March 4 together with his friends was as a 'close' prisoner in contrast to 'safe'.[1] All visitors were excluded from such prisoners. As we have seen,[2] his study containing his trunks, cabinets, and papers had been sealed shortly after his arrest. As a 'close' prisoner Eliot could not possess books, paper, pen or ink.

Before the end of March, 1629, there already were reports of visitors appearing at the Tower to see the prisoners. According to surviving accounts none was successful in his quest. Some came to see each of the incarcerated parliament men. Friends and relatives of Denzil Holles called in considerable numbers. Of them all Eliot seems to have been the most popular. 'The Earl of Lincoln and others would have induced Sir Allen's son to have brought them to Sir John Eliot's lodging', wrote Sir Allen Apsley to Secretary Dorchester on March 20, 'which he refused, whereupon his Lordship went and "did adoration" at Mr Selden's window. Morton, a minister', Apsley continued, 'came near Sir John Eliot's window and called aloud to have spoken with him, but he did not answer him'.[3] Lord Rich and four or five others came to see Eliot and went to his window. Sir John opened it and began to speak, but his visitors were driven away by Eliot's keeper, Apsley reported in another account of his charges.[4] Others came, among them Sir Oliver Luke and Sir John Littleton, with no better results. On May 1 the Court of Star Chamber and on May 12 the Privy Council issued orders that counsel and solicitors be admitted to the prisoners.[5] Though these men were ordered to stick strictly to business, they unquestionably were able to act as messengers between their clients and friends on the outside.

For two months Eliot's active mind must have been sorely tried by his close confinement. Whether he employed some of his too great

[1] Privy Council Register, Chas. I, V, 119.   [2] See above, p. 315.
[3] C.S.P.D., 1628–1629, pp. 498–9.   [4] H.M.C. 12th Rept., App. Pt. I, 383–4.
[5] C.S.P.D., Addenda, 1625–1649, p. 342. Privy Council Register, Chas. I, V, 236, 244.

leisure in swinging dumb-bells and spinning a top, as Denzil Holles was reported to be doing,[1] is impossible to say. At least during May and early June, preparations for hearings and the hearings themselves in the Court of Star Chamber, as well as the *Habeas Corpus* proceedings, must have occupied much of the time and attention of Sir John and the others.

When Apsley was confronted with the prospect of keeping his prisoners in 'close' confinement during the long vacation, he thought another course might be advisable. Writing to Dorchester on June 23 he informed the Secretary that he had just received from other prisons the bodies of Hobart, Long, and Strode and desired to know whether they should be kept as close or safe prisoners. Apsley suggested that if they were 'safe' prisoners all who visited them would be known to his Majesty. Furthermore, the King would save £1,200 a year on their diet, as they would have to pay for their own food if held as 'safe' prisoners. Dorchester saw the wisdom of the Lieutenant's suggestion, and on the next day ordered that all seven prisoners be 'kept safely but not as close prisoners'.[2]

Immediately a change can be seen in the status of Eliot. On June 29 the Privy Council ordered its messenger to go to Sir John's chamber and 'to deliver out such clothes and linen and trunks of clothes and linen as he shall desire'.[3] Already on June 15 Eliot had written the first letter which has survived from this period of imprisonment.[4] He addressed it to his dear friend Richard Knightley of Northamptonshire[5] and disclosed that Knightley's servant had brought by this time a letter from his master to Eliot. Sir John told his friend nothing of the circumstances of his imprisonment, of his life in prison, or of his hopes for the future. All he disclosed was his state of mind, emphasizing his mental freedom and his communion with God. Of the few letters which have survived from June to November, 1629, there is only one which gives any hint of the condition of the seven prisoners. Writing again to Knightley on August 17 Sir John said there was no change in their status. They appeared to be forgotten, 'which cessation happily may settle the humours that were stirred, and then it may be all things will return unto their temper'. He also indicated that the prisoners saw nothing of each other, for it was Knightley's messenger who informed

---

[1] S.P.D., Chas. I, CXLII, no. 52.   [2] *C.S.P.D., 1628–1629*, pp. 587, 588.
[3] Privy Council Register, Chas. I, V, 329.   [4] *Letter Book*, pp. 52–5.
[5] M.P. for Northamptonshire in 1628. *O.R.*, I, 476.

Eliot of the good health of the six others whom he had visited separately.[1]

These hardships and sufferings of first the nine and then the seven members of the House of Commons were having an effect upon the nation as a whole. As early as April, 1629, William Lake wrote to Sir Henry Vane that 'business goes on *de mal en pis*, few or none paying duties, and those that pay do so under other men's names; so much are their tender consciences terrified at Sir John Eliot's *brutum fulmen*'. In July Sir Bernard Grenville wrote to Sir James Bagg about the discontent in Cornwall and spoke of 'the foulness of sundry ill dispositions, poisoned by that malcontent faction of Eliot, so much as all is out of order, the deputy lieutenants being either fearful or unwilling to do their duties'. On the last day of that month Viscount Grandison wrote to Sir Thomas Roe about 'the *Habeas Corpus* men' who were feeding themselves on popular applause and implied that they were becoming 'dangerous instruments' because men were hearkening after them. Obviously the government with its trickery and deceit in the *Habeas Corpus* proceedings had done itself no good. The prisoners were fast becoming martyrs in the eyes of many Englishmen.[2]

When these proceedings were reopened at the beginning of October, it appears that Eliot and his six companions were once more in 'close' instead of 'safe' custody. Apsley writing to Dorchester on the 2nd of that month spoke of bringing the bodies of the close prisoners to the Court of King's Bench. From a letter of Heath to Dorchester of October 13 it is clear that Apsley had been advocating that the prisoners should be given the liberty of the Tower to save the King the expense of their upkeep. Finally, on the 27th of that month Apsley indicated that the prisoners were about to have this liberty, if they did not already have it.[3]

Hardly had the point been settled when on October 29, at night, Eliot, Holles and Valentine were transferred from the Tower to the Marshalsea.[4] Walter Long had been committed there on October 9 when the rest were recommitted to the Tower. Selden, Strode, and Hobart were still in the custody of Sir Allen Apsley. One breach, how-

---

[1] *Letter Book*, p. 63.

[2] *C.S.P.D.*, *1628–1629*, p. 524, *ibid.*, *1629–1631*, pp. 15, 26.

[3] For this paragraph see *ibid.*, pp. 71, 72, 77, 83, and Egerton MS 2552, ff. 51–51v.

[4] Also called the King's Bench prison. Actually there were two prisons, one right next to the other. But contemporaries made no distinction and seemed to use the names interchangeably, as I am doing here.

ever, had been made among the seven. Denzil Holles 'was set at large, upon putting his bail for his good behaviour', on October 30. Theoretically Holles continued in the Marshalsea, actually he was out on bail.[1]

4. THE TRIAL IN THE COURT OF KING'S BENCH

The reason for moving Eliot and his two companions from the Tower to the Marshalsea was explained in a letter Heath wrote to Dorchester on October 13. He said: 'The clerk of the Crown states there is a necessity for those three against whom the information is prepared—Sir John Eliot, Denzil Holles, and Benjamin Valentine—to be sent to the King's Bench, otherwise they cannot be compelled to answer.' In other words, it had been decided to take action in the Court of King's Bench against the three most culpable for the seditious and contemptuous proceedings in the last session of Parliament. Just when this decision was reached it is difficult to decide. Bramston declared that 'all the judges and Barons in Trinity term last had resolved that an offence committed by a parliament man in Parliament, and not there punished, is punishable out of Parliament'. As has been seen,[2] on June 9 the judges advised dropping the case in Star Chamber. Possibly they advised at the same time that it should be tried in the Court of King's Bench. It is more likely that they did not give this advice until the end of the Trinity term or even during the long vacation.[3]

By the time the *Habeas Corpus* proceedings in Michaelmas term had been concluded, it was decided that Sir Robert Heath should present his information to the judges of the Court of King's Bench. This he did on November 4. But on the previous day the government had taken steps to make another careful survey of the papers of the prisoners. Though his papers were seized once again Sir John Eliot had a good deal more freedom in the Marshalsea than he had had in the Tower. He could read, write, and see his friends as well as leave his prison, presumably accompanied by a guard. Writing on December 10 to Knightley he speaks of 'the messenger meeting me on Thursday morning as I was going to the lecture at St Mary Overyes,[4] and his haste such as he could not stay an hour for my return'.[5]

[1] Gardiner, VII, 115, and *C. and T. Chas. I*, II, 36, 40.   [2] See above, p. 322.

[3] *C.S.P.D., 1629–1631*, p. 77, and *The Autobiography of Sir John Bramston*, p. 59.

[4] Now St Saviour's or Southwark Cathedral.

[5] *H.M.C. Rept. of the MSS. of the Duke of Buccleuch and Queensberry*, III, 344; Privy Council Register, Chas. I, V, 484; *Letter Book*, pp. 79–80.

Heath's information presented to Hyde and his three puisne judges on November 4 was fundamentally the same as that which had been brought before the Court of Star Chamber. Only now it was reduced to the offences committed by Eliot, Valentine and Holles. They were charged with sedition and conspiracy based on Sir John's speech of January 28 against the Council and judges, on Holles and Valentine's preventing the adjournment of Parliament by forcibly holding the Speaker in his chair, on Eliot's long speech of March 2, and Holles's re-capitulation of the chief points of that speech which were put into a resolution and presented to the House. On November 28, the last day of the Michaelmas term, after the defendants had refused to accept the jurisdiction of the court because (they said) the offences they had been accused of should be tried only in Parliament, the judges declined to hear the point argued and postponed it to the opening of the Hilary term. But each of the judges separately informed the counsel for the defendants that this case was triable in a court outside of Parliament and that that court was the King's Bench.[1]

By December, certainly by January, Selden, Strode and Hobart had been transferred to the Marshalsea. By that time Eliot and Valentine had made another request to be bailed but were refused unless they were willing 'to be bailed to their good behaviour'. Now Hobart, Strode and Selden were almost as free as was Denzil Holles out on bail. And Eliot and Valentine were by no means continuously confined within the four walls of their prison.[2]

On Monday, January 25, 1630, the first day of the Hilary term, Sir John Eliot, Benjamin Valentine and Denzil Holles appeared with their counsel before the judges of the Court of King's Bench. Eliot was repre-sented by the same three who had argued for him in the Star Chamber proceedings—Mason, Bramston and Holt. These three also represented Holles, while Valentine was defended by Mason and Calthorpe.[3] Gilbert Barrell is mentioned as another attorney for the defendants. Later in the proceedings presumably Holt deserted and William Lenthal, the future Speaker of the Long Parliament, was assigned as counsel in his place.[4]

---

[1] *State Trials*, III, 293–5; Rushworth, I, App. 44–5; *The Autobiography of Sir John Bram-ston* p. 59; *C. and T. Chas. I*, II, 44. I have put the remarks of the judges on November 28 rather than Jan. 26, as given by Forster, *Eliot*, II, 539, and Gardiner, VII, 115–6. Internal evidence of the sources used indicates the former rather than the latter date.

[2] *C. and T. Chas. I*, II, 44, and *Letter Book*, p. 83.

[3] See above, p. 320, for Eliot's counsel in the Star Chamber proceedings.

[4] For this paragraph see *C. and T. Chas. I*, II, 56, 57; *State Trials*, III, 309; *Letter Book*,

The case was opened on this Monday with the reading of the record followed by the argument of Mason in defence of Sir John Eliot. The issue before the judges was a simple one—did the Court of King's Bench have jurisdiction in the case? Though the judges had shown on the last day of the Michaelmas term that they were sure of their authority in the present instance, they had refused Heath's request to over-rule the plea of the defendants to the jurisdiction of the court. Counsel for the defence was thus confronted with the impossible. It must prove conclusively that the court had no jurisdiction and prove it to four judges who were already convinced that it had.[1]

In his argument[2] Mason defended Eliot first for his speech of January 28 in which he had accused 'some great peers of the realm' and others of conspiracy to trample the liberties of the subject. The lawyer insisted that the King can be informed of what is said in the House of Commons only by the House itself. Furthermore, he asserted that 'liberty of accusation has always been parliamentary'. And then he argued that 'words spoken in Parliament, which is a superior court, cannot be questioned in this court, which is inferior'.

Mason next opposed the charge that Eliot was in contempt to the King for resisting the adjournment of Parliament. 'The King himself may adjourn the House in person, or under the great seal, but not by verbal message,' he insisted. Therefore there was no contempt to the command of the King for adjournment, which had been delivered to the House on March 2 by a verbal message through the Speaker.

The third and last point of the counsel for the defence was that there was no conspiracy in detaining the Speaker in the chair. In fact, he claimed that the House had the privilege of detaining the Speaker in the chair if it be done only 'lightly' and 'softly'. Going further into the charge of conspiracy Mason declared that 'members of the House may advise of matters out of the House, for the House itself is not so much for consultation as for propositions of them'. Having concluded his argument Mason was informed by the court that 'the question is not now whether these matters be offences and whether true or false. But admitting them to be offences, the sole question is whether this court

---

pp. 89, 92, 93. To the five counsellors must be added a sixth whose name is unknown, for Eliot in his account of the proceedings indicates that that was the number of legal advisers retained by himself and his two colleagues.

[1] State Trials, III, 294–5; The Autobiography of Sir John Bramston, p. 59; Rushworth, I, App. 45.

[2] State Trials, III, 295–9, and P.E.MSS., 'Coll. by and con. Eliot', ff. 233–43v.

may punish them, so that a great part of your argument is nothing to the present.'[1]

The defence had not been strengthened by this argument, most of which was beside the point. The position of the three defendants was hopeless. They must first accept the jurisdiction of the court if they were to have any chance to refute the charges made in Heath's information. But by accepting this jurisdiction they would lose the main point of their defence, that what is said and done in Parliament can only be judged by Parliament. Eliot would never do this. The whole philosophy of his public life was at stake.

Hence Calthorpe, speaking on Tuesday, the 27th, in defence of Valentine, could do no good, even though he was careful to stick to the issue before the court.[2] He alleged that the defendant, not being accused of a capital offence but only of assault and conspiracy, was not examinable in the Court of King's Bench. If that were the case, he asserted, all acts of Parliament could be brought before an inferior court. With similar arguments and numerous precedents he strengthened his point, but all to no avail.

As soon as Calthorpe had concluded Heath replied.[3] He declared that though the offences were not capital they were criminal. Being criminal the Commons had no jurisdiction over them, especially as they had taken no action at the time. It would be impossible for a new Parliament to take cognizance of these offences, as the Commons were not a court of record and 'forbad their clerk to make entry of their speeches', the Attorney-General said. He admitted that the judges had frequently refused 'to give their judgment upon the privileges of Parliament'. But, he continued, if offences of a criminal nature were committed in Parliament, not punished there, and Parliament dissolved, that was quite a different matter. In such cases the Court of King's Bench did have jurisdiction.

The day was completed with a foregone conclusion. The judges declared that the Court of King's Bench had jurisdiction over the case even though the offences had been committed in Parliament. Therefore the prisoners should answer the charges brought against them. Each of the judges gave reasons for his opinions. Those of Hyde, Jones and Croke were not outstanding and were based on principles which al-

---

[1] *State Trials*, III, 299.
[2] *Ibid.*, 299–304.
[3] *Ibid.*, 304–5.

ready have been presented. But those of Justice Whitelocke were unique and to the point.[1]

The King is the supreme authority in the realm, he declared. His Majesty alone can question a subject for his words and actions. But, Whitelocke admitted, whatever a member of the House of Commons may do or say with the approval of the entire House may not be impugned by anybody, not even the King he implied. At the same time, when a member of the House by seditious words and actions, to which the House has not given its approval, becomes a malefactor, then that member has turned himself into a private person who can be questioned by the supreme authority in the state, the King. Will the privilege of Parliament protect this member? No, he answered by implication and declared that here in the Court of King's Bench the King was now questioning such private persons.

From the point of view of Law and precedents,[2] as understood in 1630, the reasoning of the judges, particularly that of Whitelocke, was entirely correct. The average contemporary who had any comprehension of the situation was bound to agree with their ruling. In the fight for freedom of speech and the liberties of Parliament the Commons had never before gone as far as Eliot and his colleagues did on March 2. Their words and actions[3] for the first time could be construed as crim-

---

[1] For this paragraph see *State Trials*, III, 305-9, and Gardiner, VII, 117-8.

[2] Among the various precedents mentioned by the defence only two need be discussed here. They are the cases of Thomas Haxey in 1397 and of Richard Strode in 1512. In the case of Haxey it is questionable that he was a member of the House of Commons. He had not spoken in Parliament but was merely responsible for a bill complaining of extravagance in the royal household. For this he was condemned by the Lords as a traitor. The reversal of this judgment in the first year of Henry IV had nothing to do with freedom of speech, for that was not one of the liberties of the Commons at this time. *Tudor Studies* (London, 1924), 'The Commons' Privilege of Free Speech in Parliament' by J. E. Neale, p. 259. W. R. Anson, *The Law and Custom of the Constitution*, I, 166.

In the case of Strode it is the act passed by Parliament which is vital. This prohibited legal proceedings by any court outside of Parliament 'for any bill speaking, reasoning, or declaring of any matter or matters concerning the Parliament'. On April 25, 1629, the judges declared this to be 'a particular act of Parliament, and extended only to Richard Strode'. Rushworth, I, 662. Though the defendants and their counsel might dispute this interpretation and declare the Strode act to be a general act and applicable to all similar cases in the future, there was at the time no organ of authority to uphold this interpretation. It was not until 1667 that the Commons by resolution interpreted the Strode act in this way.

[3] Neither side in the case separated the words from the actions as did the House of Lords in 1667 when it reversed the decision rendered by the Court of King's Bench in this case. As Holdsworth, VI, 98, says: 'One of the causes of error assigned was the fact that the speaking of seditious words and the assault on the Speaker were made the subject of one

inal. Though the House of Lords was, the House of Commons never had been, a court to try criminal offences, whether of members or outsiders. But the defendants never appealed to the jurisdiction of the Lords over that of King's Bench. To be sure, the definition of the offences committed in the last session of Parliament as criminal was questionable, to say the least. But that was not the point. Eliot, Valentine and Holles had been accused, rightly or wrongly, of such offences. Unquestionably the Court of King's Bench could handle this indictment, whoever the defendants were.[1]

But Whitelocke's reasoning went beyond this simple interpretation. He saw that the supreme authority in the state, that of the King, was being questioned by certain members of the House of Commons. Though Whitelocke does not say it, his argument leads directly to the conclusion that if Eliot and his friends had gained control of the House, that body as a whole would have challenged the supreme authority of the King. That was soon to be the issue of the century. Had Sir John Eliot been confronted with such an accusation, he would have been quick to repudiate it as an act of *lèse-majesté*. The ministers of the Crown, not its wearer, were still his enemies. But one cannot for ever be separating the King and his ministers, their policies and actions, particularly when the King and his officials, including his judges, refused to recognize such a separation. Unwillingly and unconsciously Eliot had been leading the Commons closer and closer to an attack upon the supreme authority of the King. Unconsciously he was preparing the ground for the open attack on the King twelve years later. Here was revolution in the making. By their stubborn stand against the Court of King's Bench, Eliot, Valentine and Holles finally succeeded in lighting the candle of freedom. In recent years matches had been struck repeatedly, only to flare up and burn out before the candle could be lit. But now it was being done. This candle of liberty and freedom of Parliament, which was burning brightly before the judges in Westminster Hall, though unseen by them as well as the defendants, would in time ignite a torch; that torch, clearly seen by all, would arouse thousands in the nation to fight with their lives against

judgment, when in fact there were two separate causes of action on which two separate judgments should have been given; because, even if the assault on the Speaker was cognizable by the court, the speaking of seditious words was not.' Holdsworth misdates this incident. See also *State Trials*, III, 332.

[1] Holdsworth, VI, 98, says: 'There is no doubt that, in so far as the court ruled that it had jurisdiction over crimes committed in the House, it was right.'

royal autocracy. This liberty and freedom of Parliament as proclaimed by Eliot and an ever-increasing number of his countrymen was to them gradually becoming synonymous with the liberty and freedom of Englishmen.

After the Court of King's Bench had formally declared on Tuesday, January 26, that the defendants were under its jurisdiction, Eliot, Valentine and Holles were face to face with the dilemma which had been overshadowing them ever since these proceedings began. How could they defend themselves against the charges brought before the court without repudiating their main contention that the House of Commons was the only body which had any jurisdiction over their past words and actions? The hopeless path, filled with hindrances, pitfalls and delays, which the defendants followed for over two weeks is graphically described by Eliot in a long letter without address dated February 15.[1]

It is a sad tale Sir John has too relate. Day after day progress was stopped either by the absence or the desertion of one or more of the six attorneys who were acting for the defendants. Clearly these lawyers did not have their hearts in the case. They showed no enthusiasm. They stayed away from meetings with their clients on any excuse. They saw that it was impossible to attain the objective of the defendants, that is, to give satisfaction to the court and at the same time maintain the privileges of Parliament. The case was hopeless. These attorneys were not idealists like Eliot. The liberties of Parliament still meant little to them. It is surprising that only one deserted. Coupled with this handicap there were two occasions when the defendants had their movements temporarily restricted by the court, so that even if the lawyers had been willing their clients could not have met them. The result of these situations was that the only thing Eliot, Valentine and Holles could do was to ask the court through their counsel for one delay after another. When on February 11 they requested that the case be postponed until the next term, the court refused and gave them until the next morning, the last day of the Hilary term, to present their argument. It was too late. Nothing could be prepared in so short a time.

But Eliot could not be present on that final Friday, February 12. He was ill. The strain of the last days had been too much for him. He gave as cause the cold and watching. We can imagine him chafing under temporary restraints in prison and waiting hour after hour in Serjeant

---

[1] *Letter Book*, pp. 89–95. It covers the period Jan. 26 to Feb. 12.

Bramston's chamber, pacing, standing, sitting, and always insisting that they must in no way endanger the privileges of his beloved House of Commons. More than likely worry as to how they were to surmount the insuperable barrier that confronted them contributed greatly to the break in his health.[1]

Before considering the judgment of the Court of King's Bench we must examine a paper prepared by Eliot and presumably intended for presentation to that body on the last day. Sir John must have realized some days before the end of the Hilary term that a *nihil dicit* would be the basis for the decision of the judges, 'which is held equivalent to a confession or pleading guilty', as Pory explained to Mead.[2] Under the circumstances of the case Eliot had been unable to defend or vindicate the position he had taken. He certainly did not consider himself guilty. Therefore he must justify himself before the judges and leave a record for posterity. The unfinished paper has survived.[3] Neither did he complete it nor have an opportunity to present it to the court. Probably it furnished a basis as well as a reason for writing not long afterwards his better-known justification, *An Apology for Socrates*, which will be discussed later.

Sir John begins by declaring that he is in a dilemma. If he submits to the court, his act will be considered 'a prejudice to posterity' and a danger to Parliament. If he does not, he will incur the censure of the Court of King's Bench. In this situation he wants it to be known that he has not been motivated by a sense of guilt, or by doubt that his past actions would be justified. The reason for his silence before the court is to show that his duty is to Parliament and that he has 'a fear of future censure in that court from which there is no appeal'.

The rest of the paper is composed chiefly of precedents through which he intended to show that the House of Commons is the body to try its members for their words or actions spoken or committed within its doors. But these precedents had had no influence on the Court of King's Bench. And when they are examined from the historical point of view they fail to support Eliot's stand.[4] But he made his stand. That

---

[1] Besides Eliot's letter of February 15 *C. and T. of Chas. I*, II, 56–57, throws light on the events of these two weeks.

[2] *C. and T. Chas. I*, II, 57, also *State Trials*, III, 309.

[3] P.E.MSS., 'Eliot, speeches, etc.', ff. 93–4.

[4] With the exception of the Strode case. This and the Haxey case, both cited by Eliot, have already been discussed (above, p. 332, note 2). The precedent of the reign of Henry IV where the King agreed not to accept information of the Commons from private

gave strength, actual and moral, to the new position the House of Commons seized a dozen years later and ultimately consolidated for all time.

When the Court of King's Bench met early on the morning of February 12, counsel for the defence gave excuses and asked for delay until the evening. The judges rejected the request. On the basis of a *nihil dicit* Justice Jones pronounced the defendants guilty of the charge brought against them in the information. The punishment he declared was that the three men were to be imprisoned during the King's pleasure. Eliot was to go to the Tower and the other two to other prisons. None of them could be freed until he had given security for his good behaviour and had made submission to the King and acknowledged his offence. Eliot, considered the ringleader, was fined £2,000, Holles 1,000 marks, and Valentine £500.[1]

The end of this legal wrangling had come. Both King Charles and Sir John Eliot had won. The King had won because Eliot was a prisoner until he acknowledged his offence. This he would never do. The prisoner had won because he had preserved the privileges and freedom of Parliament inviolate. As the trial had a strong personal flavour for Charles and his government, so it was entirely impersonal for the 'greatest offender' and his two companions in 'crime'. Individual liberty had been sacrificed to institutional freedom. But how did Eliot now regard the King? Could it be that he dissociated him completely from this trial? Could he have blamed only men like Weston and Heath for his present misfortune? It seems hardly possible, but it may have been true. Never did he mention the King in all these long proceedings. And for the few remaining years of his life he never in any form put the name of Charles I in writing. After months of study and contemplation in his prison we will find that Eliot could again express his faith in

---

sources had so many precedents to the contrary, particularly in the sixteenth century, that it had become worthless by the seventeenth century. The various precedents dealing with the judicial power of medieval Parliaments were in no way applicable to the House of Commons at any time in its history. That Parliament was the highest court of the realm during the middle ages was unquestioned, but the judges of that court were the peers of the realm and not the Commons. The peers still had their judicial powers by the seventeenth century, but the Commons had made no gains in this respect by that time. During the middle ages the Commons were of such insignificance in comparison with the peers, except in making money grants, that even at the end of the Lancastrian period they could hardly be said to have had any liberties or privileges of importance. It was not until the reign of Elizabeth that the fight for privileges really began and some progress was made by the Commons. But Eliot does not cite a single precedent from this reign. See Neale, 'The Commons' Privilege of Free Speech in Parliament', *Tudor Studies*, pp. 257–86.

[1] *State Trials*, III, 309–10, also *C. and T. Chas. I*, II, 57.

monarchy in general, if he had ever lost it. So often did he change his words to fit his moods. His inconsistencies were legion. But through them all ran two constant principles: never to denounce his Sovereign, and always to praise and defend the House of Commons.

The judgment of February, 1630, did not for long stand uncontested. In July, 1641, and again in November, 1667, the House of Commons by resolution declared it to be illegal and against the freedom and privilege of Parliament.[1] In December 1667, the House of Lords on a writ of error reversed the decision of Chief Justice Hyde and his puisne judges.[2] The highest court of the realm had finally spoken for Sir John Eliot and the House of Commons.

Before turning to Eliot's prison correspondence we must settle him in his allotted quarters. During the trial he had, of course, been confined to the King's Bench prison. But the court had ordered his return to the Tower. That return was made on February 27.[3] 'One Dudson, under-marshal of the King's Bench . . . when he delivered him at the Tower, made this formal speech: "Mr Lieutenant, I have brought you this worthy knight, whom I borrowed of you some few months ago and now do repay him again".'[4]

With Sir John lodged in the Tower for the rest of his life, the fate of his six companions who had not made their peace with the King must be briefly sketched. Walter Long was Eliot's companion, but he was in the Tower primarily because of his Star Chamber offence of having been returned a member of Parliament while serving as a sheriff.[5] Denzil Holles, on the other hand, was still out on bail. He had a fine of 1,000 marks to pay, 'which to avoid', as he reported to the Long Parliament, 'I made an escape and lived a banished man from this city, from my friends, and from my business . . . for the space of 7 or 8 years; and then at last was glad to pay my fine'.[6] But Selden, Hobart, Valentine and Strode moved between the Gatehouse and the King's

---

[1] *State Trials*, III, 310–5, Rushworth, I, App. 56–9.

[2] See above, p. 332, note 3, and below, p. 394.

[3] *C. and T. Chas. I*, II, 66. Mead writing to Stuteville on Feb. 27, *ibid*, 62, said: 'Concerning his (Eliot's) fine, my author heard him say that he had two cloaks, two suits, two pair of boots and gullasheer [galoshes], and a few books, and that was all his present substance; and if they could pick 2,000 out of that much good might it do them'. For the remaining comment on Eliot see above, p. 267. The circumstances of Eliot's change from the Marshalsea to the Tower are related by him in a letter to Sir Oliver Luke obviously misdated Feb. 3, for March 3. *Letter Book*, p. 96.

[4] *C. and T. Chas. I*, II, 66.   [5] *J.M.H.*, I, 372.

[6] Forster, *Eliot*, II, 562, note 2, quoting Sanford, *Studies of the Great Rebellion*, pp. 158–9.

Bench prisons for nearly a year with a good deal of freedom inter-
spersed. In the summer of 1630 to escape the plague in London they
visited friends in the country and were later reprimanded by the
Court of King's Bench for this 'vacation'. Early in March, 1631, Sir
Miles Hobart was released from the Gatehouse on a very small bail.
The first to fall by the wayside of those who remained loyal to Eliot's
ideal, Hobart was soon followed by Selden who was reported by Sir
John to be still on bail in October, 1631, and was virtually a free man by
January, 1632. But the exact changes in his status are almost impossible
to trace. Valentine and Strode, however, remained obdurate and therefore also remained in prison. But Valentine wandered freely from his
Gatehouse abode. Frequently he visited Eliot in the Tower, so frequently that in January, 1632, he was called to account and confined
with less freedom of movement to his prison. It was not until January,
1640, that King Charles released Valentine and Strode after ten years of
imprisonment for the cause believed in so strongly by Sir John Eliot.[1]

[1] The information about Selden, Hobart, Valentine, and Strode is to be found in *C. and
T. Chas. I*, II, 79, 88, 96, 103, 162, 163; *Letter Book*, pp. 155, 203; Gardiner, VII, 228, IX,
87.

CHAPTER XV

The Correspondence of a Prisoner

June, 1629, to March, 1632

IN studying the correspondence of a man one expects to learn much about him. He should unburden himself on paper to his intimate friends; his thoughts and feelings, his hopes and plans should all be there. He should disclose his temper to his enemies, his nature to his servants and subordinates. He should relate what he has done, dispense news of his surroundings, and correct mistaken information that has come to him. We approach the correspondence of Sir John Eliot, while a prisoner in the Tower, with the hope of being able to glean such a wealth of material. Unfortunately that is too much to expect from the letters to and from a political prisoner; moreover, many of them have been lost. Before we can look for the man, Eliot, in these letters, we must examine the nature of his correspondence.

Between June 25, 1629, and March 29, 1632, one hundred and twenty-nine letters written by Sir John Eliot and thirty-three received by him have survived.[1] These dates are taken because on the former Sir John was given pen and paper when he no longer was a 'close' prisoner in the Tower, while the latter is the date of his last surviving letter. Possibly because of ill-health he was too weak after that date to make

---

[1] Of these A. B. Grosart in his *Letter Book of Sir John Eliot* has printed ninety-six and twenty-four respectively. The rest are to be found for the most part in the ms. letter book at Port Eliot and have been printed, extracted, or paraphrased by Forster. One letter is to be found in the Dyce-Forster collection in the South Kensington Museum; two are among the Cotton MSS.; and two are to be found in the Additional MSS. Of these five Forster fails to mention or quote only one. This is the sole unpublished letter in the correspondence of Eliot I have discovered. It is Add. MS. 42, 711 D. As the page is torn at the bottom it contains no signature. But by comparing the handwriting with that in letters known to have been written by Bevil Grenville, it is obvious that he is the author of this one. The tone of the letter also fits him perfectly. At the top of the page is written 'to Sir John Eliot'. It is not dated but from internal evidence fits in March, 1632. Hereafter all letters cited from Grosart's *Letter Book* will be referred to only by the page in that book.

copies of the few letters he wrote during the last eight months of his life. It is highly improbable that he was unable to write any letters at all during this period. But had Eliot not made copies of his letters and preserved the first draft of a goodly number of them, few would now be available. That he wrote many more than are extant today is obvious on reading through his surviving correspondence. Either he did not make two drafts of every letter he wrote, or else the first drafts of a large number have been lost. At the same time it is clear that the thirty-three letters addressed to Sir John are only a small percentage of those he received. Consequently the gaps resulting from the missing letters on both sides frequently make it extremely difficult to understand Eliot from his correspondence.

Added to this difficulty is the fact that Sir John Eliot, being a political prisoner, had to be most careful about what he put down on paper. He could rarely give an opinion on any matter of political importance. And if he did, the opinion was couched in such obscure language that the modern reader is left completely in the dark. In addition Eliot was not gifted in the art of writing letters. A verbose, involved, and obscure style makes him difficult to read under normal circumstances. But when the letter he is answering is unavailable or when he has to prevent prying eyes from discovering anything vital in his words, then he becomes impossible to understand. Only now and then, either because of extreme care or because he loses himself in his subject, does Eliot display any art in his letters. When he does write well he is extremely good. John Hampden, on the other hand, never reached such heights or depths as a letter writer. In most of his letters he displayed a charm and grace frequently sprinkled with a strong sense of humour. Now and then there is a hint that a sense of humour was also one of Eliot's attributes. But it was too frequently blotted out or hidden under the gloom of his imprisonment, and only on occasion exhibited itself. Sir John, however, was a master at hiding a thought in a welter of words. Indeed there are times he gives the impression that he is writing only words without a thought behind them.

Another aspect of Eliot's correspondence which must be scrutinized is that it involved more than forty people.[1] Of these, five are outstanding. They are John Hampden, Sir Oliver Luke, Richard Knightley, Bevil Grenville and Thomas Godfrey. Of the letters in the hand of Sir

[1] He wrote letters to forty-five different men and women and received letters from fourteen different men.

John half were written to these five most intimate friends, while over half of those he received came from four of the five. Not a letter from Knightley has survived.

Outstanding of the five friends was John Hampden of Great Hampden in Buckinghamshire. Fifteen letters from Eliot to Hampden are available and nine[1] from Hampden to Sir John. The name of John Hampden is too well known to require any introduction. The two men were on the most intimate terms. Ready to advise on all subjects, to assist whenever aid was necessary, and to encourage when prospects were most dreary, Hampden showed himself to be the truest friend of all those who were attracted by Eliot's nature, personality, or ideals. Sir John, on the other hand, withheld nothing from the squire of Great Hampden and entrusted him with his writings, his deepest religious thoughts, and even with his sons.

Next to Hampden, if not equal to him in his friendship for Sir John, was Sir Oliver Luke of Woodend in Bedfordshire.[2] This typical country gentleman had represented his county in the last six Parliaments. Though not one of the prominent speakers, Luke loyally supported the 'country' party in the House of Commons. His puritanism was unquestioned and turned into Presbyterianism during the civil war. In his correspondence with Eliot left to us during this period the twenty letters written by Sir John and the three by Sir Oliver display an intimacy which, like that between Eliot and Hampden, had a stronger and firmer foundation than Eliot's fellowship with his remaining three particular friends.

Of these Richard Knightley of Fawsley in Northamptonshire is outstanding. This prominent puritan had inherited the family seat from his uncle, Sir Valentine Knightley, in 1618.[3] In fact, Sir Valentine's daughter, Elizabeth, was the wife of Sir Oliver Luke, while a cousin of Richard Knightley married Elizabeth, eldest daughter of John Hampden. The three men were bound together not only by their love of Eliot but also by ties of blood and marriage, relationships which interlinked the upper classes in these turbulent years of the seventeenth century.

---

[1] Eight of these have been printed by Lord Nugent in his *Some Memorials of John Hampden* (London, 1832), I, 160 *passim*.

[2] For facts about his life see Daniel and Samuel Lysons, *Magna Britania, Bedfordshire* (London, 1806), I, Pt. I, 71; W. M. Harvey, *The History and Antiquities of the Hundred of Willey in the County of Bedford* (1872–8), p. xix; *The Victoria County History of Bedfordshire* (London, 1904), II, 340.

[3] *D.N.B.*

Knightley, who was prominent in the opposition of four of the five last
Parliaments, had played his part in local government as sheriff and
deputy-lieutenant of Northamptonshire. Like Hampden he was interested in American colonization and trading companies. We have fifteen
letters Eliot wrote to Knightley but none from him to Sir John. These
letters of Eliot give the impression that his friendship for Knightley
lacked depth. They contain much elegance of phrase and expression of
love. But they frequently appear to be devoid of sincerity.

Bevil Grenville of Stow in Cornwall expressed his feelings for Eliot
in language similar to that used by Eliot in his letters to Knightley. Yet
one gets the impression that Grenville's love for Eliot was more sincere
than Eliot's love for Knightley. Bevil Grenville, a member of the last
five Parliaments, as we have seen,[1] broke with his father, Sir Bernard,
over his friendship with Eliot. Sir Bevil, as he later became, was not a
puritan and died fighting for his King.[2] Clarendon's opinion of him was
of the highest. 'He was a gallant and a sprightly gentleman, of the
greatest reputation and interest in Cornwall', he writes. On another
occasion he says that Grenville was 'the generally most loved man of
that county'.[3] There was nothing the gentle and courageous master of
Stow would refuse Sir John. Grenville seems to have worshipped him
more than did any of his other friends. On the other hand the dislike of
Sir John for Sir Bernard Grenville possibly served as a slight damper on
his friendship with Sir Bernard's son. In addition, Bevil Grenville,
though he had been an adherent, was not an ardent member of the
'country' party, if he can be called a party member at all. His four surviving letters to Eliot show him to be a blind supporter of Sir John.
Eliot's friendship for Grenville can be seen in the eight letters he wrote
to his Cornish admirer.

Finally, there is Thomas Godfrey of Grantham in Lincolnshire.
Godfrey, never a member of Parliament,[4] was the chief of Eliot's Lincolnshire friends. This group contained Sir William Armyne,[5] Sir
Edward Ayscough,[6] Thomas Hatcher,[7] and others. What the origin or
basis of the friendship between Eliot and these Lincolnshire gentry was
is difficult to say. We can suppose that they met in the House of Commons. They were mutually attracted. Eliot visited in Lincolnshire.

---

[1] See above, p. 159, note 3. [2] *D.N.B.*
[3] *History of the Rebellion* (Oxford, 1888), III, 82, note 1, II, 452.
[4] See above, p. 274, note 3.   [5] See above, p. 294, note 2.
[6] M.P. for the city of Lincoln in 1621 and 1628.
[7] M.P. for the city of Lincoln in 1624 and for Grantham in 1628.

There he met Godfrey, whom he found even more congenial than the others. Seven letters of Eliot to Godfrey and two from Godfrey to Eliot have survived. Only one to three letters to and from Eliot and any one of the other men of Lincolnshire are still available. Therefore, Thomas Godfrey appears to be Eliot's most intimate friend in this group. Certainly the tone of the letters between these two is that of much greater intimacy than is to be found in the six surviving letters to and from Hatcher and Eliot. Of Thomas Godfrey nothing of importance is known. His correspondence with Sir John is filled with friendly pleasantries and discloses little beyond talk about mutual friends.

Besides these friends there are two members of Sir John's family with whom he corresponded while in prison. His two eldest sons, John and Richard, were on the threshold of manhood when Eliot began his confinement.[1] During those last years before his death they entered Oxford University, left it, and went abroad. Of the two, Richard, as we shall see, gave his father a good deal of trouble for a brief period. To John, who was much more of a model son, four letters from his father have survived. To Richard only three were written by Sir John, while Eliot wrote one long epistle to both sons. It is a great pity that no letter from either son to his father has been preserved for posterity. Such a record might flash a new and different light on Sir John Eliot.

What sort of man do these numerous pages of correspondence portray? They show him grown older, wiser, and generally saner. Through many days and nights of leisure he had thought deeply. Deep thinking had mellowed him, had given him poise and assurance, had presented life to him in all its aspects. No longer can Eliot be thought of as a man who is liable to fly off the handle at a moment's notice. Now he can see both sides of every question and can weigh them against each other. And yet Sir John has not forsaken his ideals. If anything, they have become stronger. Even though he says nothing about the cause of liberty and freedom of Parliament—it was much too dangerous a subject to expound upon to his friends from behind the bars of his prison—yet it can be felt to be alive and running as an undercurrent through many of his letters. The freedom of his mind and heart, which he repeatedly mentions, is a reminder to one and all that he has not forgotten why he was being held in the Tower. What about his other ideal, his Sovereign? As he never mentioned by name or even by implication King Charles I, the impression left is that that particular Sovereign was not

[5] John was born in 1612 and Richard in 1614.

too popular with Sir John Eliot. But, as will be seen, the cause of monarchy had in no way suffered in his mind. The best and only government for England was by King and Parliament.

The relationship of Sir John to his fellow men is manifest in letter after letter. He was eager to help with his pen, influence, and all the means at his disposal friends of every degree, acquaintances, servants, or any man in trouble. He was kind-hearted to a fault, and his generosity was sometimes coloured by his impulsive nature.[1] Here are a few examples of the assistance he gave on so many occasions. Eliot made a careful study of the history of Lundy Island[2] and produced precedents of similar situations so that he could tell Bevil Grenville just what he as owner could do with this island.[3] He used his own credit to obtain at the mint a quantity of copper pence for Sir Oliver Luke.[4] He wrote to John Selden asking him to intervene on behalf of an official of the Marshalsea who, as a result of a quarrel, was losing his position there.[5] His pen was repeatedly employed in situations similar to the last example.

In dealing with his tenants through his steward, bailiff, and Maurice Hill, his chief servant, Sir John Eliot displayed an intimate knowledge of manorial affairs as well as justice and impartiality. At the same time he could be stern in his reprimand of some of these servants, if they had failed in their duties.[6] There were occasions when some of his friends placed him on a pedestal and even worshipped him. Eliot did not like it and refused to accept such adulation.[7] He was always modest and humble, though he had numerous opportunities to display the arrogance of a Wentworth. Where Sir John was a failure in human relations was with his son Richard. As we shall see, he did not understand the boy. He was either too similar in nature or too remote in age and outlook to know how to handle him.

Eliot wrote to only six women. Of the letters to the six there is one which gives us a totally different glimpse of the man than is to be found in the rest of his letters.[8] To Mrs Blount, who cannot be identified, he shows himself to be acting like a youthful lover, who is worried to

---

[1] Seen in exchange of letters with John Moyle over trouble one of Eliot's tenants had been giving Moyle and Sir John's solution in favour of Moyle. Pp. 143–5, 147–8.

[2] It was a small island in the Bristol Channel off the Devonshire coast and part of Grenville's estate.

[3] Pp. 192–4,   [4] P. 197.   [5] P. 101.

[6] Forster, *Eliot*, II, 634–5, P.E.MS. Letter Book.

[7] Pp. 209–11.   [8] Forster, *Eliot*, II, 647, P.E.MS. Letter Book.

death over her illness and is unable to eat or sleep until he has been assured of her good health. This isolated letter is most intriguing and makes one wonder whether love had not struck the heart of the melancholy prisoner in the Tower.

Eliot's religious views are so important that they will be discussed later at some length. There are, however, a great many letters in his correspondence, chiefly from Sir John, which contain no information or insight whatsoever. The prisoner had to be careful. Repeatedly he warned this or that friend that he could not write freely, or as he said to Luke: 'that I write not of particulars I presume you will excuse it who know the danger of the time'.[1] News he gave occasionally of events abroad, of the death of Apsley, of judicial and ecclesiastical advancements. The wanderings of his fellow prisoners, particularly of Benjamin Valentine, and their ultimate fate, as far as he knew, are topics which frequently appear in his letters. But there are certain subjects of major importance in Sir John Eliot's correspondence which need to be treated separately and at some length. In following them the character and personality of the man will repeatedly come to light.

I. ELIOT'S CHILDREN

The fortunes of his children, particularly of his two eldest sons, John and Richard, bulk large in his correspondence. These two, at school in Tiverton, received early in July, 1629, the first letter (a joint one) from their father after his imprisonment.[2] John, not seventeen, and Richard, two years younger, were subjected to a heavy barrage of Eliot's accumulated philosophy, religious and otherwise. He gave them only a word of admonition about improving their minds by study. Otherwise he wrote an essay for his sons on the advantages of introspection or 'observation of ourselves'. It must have been boring indeed to these two teen-agers. Possibly a serious-minded, contemplative boy of the seventeenth century could obtain pleasure and benefit from such a letter. But it is more logical to think that Eliot, having lost all contact with the lives and temperaments of his youthful but growing sons, missed his mark completely. Certainly Richard, because of his age and disposition which soon was to cause grief instead of joy in his father, must have been left cold by these weighty words. On the other hand, John, more

[1] P. 213.   [2] Pp. 55–61.

earnest and sober, may have profited by this excursion of his father into morals and religion.

From a letter Sir John wrote on August 15, 1629, to Mr Gedy, his father-in-law, we learn that John and Richard were to be sent to Oxford in the autumn and that their younger brother, Edward, was to take his place at school in Tiverton.[1] The other six children were living with their grandfather at Trebursey in Cornwall. The death of Gedy in September of that year was a severe blow to Eliot and his family.[2] Fortunately, the young brood fell under the watchful eye of Mrs Treise and supervision of their nurse, Sibill Polwheele, at Trebursey. Mrs Treise was the wife of Leonard, loyal friend of both Gedy and Eliot, who was the only one of half a dozen men to serve on all three groups of trustees established to administer the lands of Sir John and his father-in-law.[3] From his letter to Mrs Treise in October we also learn that Eliot expected his eldest daughter Elizabeth to come to London that winter.[4]

With the advent of Christmas John and Richard spent the holidays at Hampden House where they made an excellent impression on their host. To their father Hampden wrote: 'If ever you live to see a fruit answerable to the promise of the present blossoms, it will be a blessing of that weight as will turn the scale against all worldly afflictions and denominate your life happy'.[5] But during the winter these two young men spent at Lincoln College, Oxford, under the direction of Thomas Knightley, Fellow of that college and kinsman of Sir John's great friend, Richard Knightley,[6] all was not going well. According to reports received by his father Richard was the offender. He was spending far too much time with numerous friends carousing in the town of Oxford instead of studying diligently. Eliot wrote his son a touching sorrowful letter of reproof[7] in which he reminded him that everything, whether good or bad, he might do had an effect on his father whose love for Richard made him watch so carefully over him. He also called to his attention that at Oxford he was under special observation and that he was not an ordinary student, 'but your words, your actions, your conversations, your societies would be sifted there (if possible) to extract some scandal or advantage against me'. With burning words

---

[1] Pp. 64–5.   [2] P.E.MSS., Muniment Room, P. E. Title Deeds, no. 63.
[3] Will of Sir John Eliot. Forster, *Eliot* (2nd edit.), II, 369.
[4] Pp. 71–2.   [5] P. 85.   [6] See letter of Eliot to Richard Knightley, p. 111.
[7] On April 5, 1630. Pp. 102–5.

Eliot showed his son how his hopes of peace and tranquillity had been shattered. He did say that he would not judge him without hearing his side. If he was guilty, which he prays God he is not, 'let it be so no more'. With much more good advice he brought a long letter to a close.

In a most tactful letter written on the same day Sir John addressed the tutor of his sons.[1] He spoke about his great love for John and Richard and about his numerous enemies who could easily hurt him through his sons. Therefore, great caution was necessary, and they must not be permitted to be in the company of many people or make numerous friends. Not a word did he write of Richard's excesses. He hoped to see Thomas Knightley in London soon, where undoubtedly he would speak more freely.

Within ten days of these two letters Richard Eliot wrote his father. But what he wrote can be learned only indirectly through Eliot's reply of April 16.[2] The boy, it seems, had been very much upset by his father's letter. Richard was even afraid that he had lost his father's love. As to his misdeeds, they were apparently not as bad as Sir John had believed them to be. But he was not entirely innocent. Unquestionably promises of reform and correction filled the letter of the son to the father.

In writing to Richard, Eliot began with the assurance that the foundation of his love for him was as solid as a rock. All he had wanted to do in his last letter was to show him the evils he was approaching. In other words he wanted to give him a good scare and temporarily, at least, had succeeded. Sir John mentioned various types of evils which Richard seemed anxious to avoid. 'In this endeavour,' he concluded, 'you compose my satisfaction, and my hopes are great. Strive to give it a perfection and you gain me, as my affection and love are constantly your own.'

In a note to John written also on April 16[3] the father suggested that he buy material for clothes suitable to mourning, which he wished him to continue to wear, undoubtedly in memory of his grandfather. He also spoke of his sister, Bess, who was well at Stepney and had been to see her father yesterday.

In May John and Richard in the company of their tutor visited Sir John at the Tower for the Whitsun holidays. But the greater part of these holidays they were to spend with the Hampdens where 'they

[1] Pp. 105-7.   [2] Pp. 107-8.   [3] Pp. 108-9.

should again have the happiness to kiss your hands and be directed by your counsel', Eliot wrote to Hampden.[1] Elizabeth, on the other hand, went to visit the Lukes in Bedfordshire in June.[2] There she appears to have spent the summer, for Sir John writing to Luke on August 10[3] heartily agreed with the suggestion that Bess be taught music. Her father was willing to pay anything for a teacher and also to purchase an instrument for his daughter. About a week later Hampden, who had been visiting the Lukes, wrote to Eliot[4] to say that both he and Lady Luke were opposed to Bess's returning to the school in Stepney. 'In my judgment,' he said, 'there is much more danger in such a nursery than in a school for boys, for though an ill tincture be dangerous in either, yet it is perfectly recoverable in these, hardly or never in the other.' From appearances Bess Eliot did not return to her school in Stepney but remained indefinitely as a guest at Woodend in Bedfordshire. There is no further mention of her in the correspondence of her father.

A word must be said about the younger Eliots. On July 2, 1630, Sir John wrote an enigmatic letter to his cousin Mrs Langworthy,[5] in whose 'view' he wanted the children to remain. But whether they were to be sent to Cuddenbeak or remain at Trebursey and whether they should continue under the supervision of their nurse Polwheele, it is impossible to say. The important point of the letter is that the children had been ill and that one of their number had died. Eliot displayed no grief or dismay at the death of Thomas,[6] his eighth child and fourth son.[7] The supposition is that he died a short time before this letter was written. But that is all that is known or can be surmised.

In the autumn of 1630 John and Richard Eliot returned to Oxford accompanied by their father's prayers, from which he hoped that Richard in particular would benefit. Sir John waited for a long time for a letter from his second son. When it finally came he sat down on November 7 and composed a long and careful reply.[8] It seems that Eliot was far from satisfied with the conduct of this difficult son of his. Again he lectured him and appealed to his better nature. He and his brother John, their father declared, must be models for the rest of the family. Their goodness must be perfect. It was not enough for Richard

---

[1] P. 112. [2] Pp. 116–8. [3] Pp. 126–7.
[4] The only source for this letter is Forster, *Eliot*, II, 602–3, 574. He says that it is a ms. letter in his possession 'which had not been preserved among the Port Eliot MSS'. I was unable to find it among Forster's papers preserved in the Dyce-Forster Collection.
[5] Pp. 118–9. [6] Will of Sir John Eliot, Forster, *Eliot* (2nd edit.), II, 371.
[7] He was born in Sept. 1626. [8] Pp. 139–42.

to abandon some of his acquaintances; he must leave them all and 're-tire wholly to' himself. And then he launched into a philosophical essay on virtue. In closing in language of the orator of the House of Commons he appealed to Richard to mend his ways. It is doubtful that such words would have a lasting effect on Richard Eliot. His nature, much like that of his paternal grandfather and even of his father, was too gay and sociable, too desirous of companionship and entertainment to adhere strictly to studies and to gain pleasure from books. For over a year Sir John Eliot had been obtaining strength and virtue from his confinement and privacy. He now was reading, studying, and thinking as he never had before, certainly far more than when he attended Oxford as a youth. He had forgotten those days and believed that an impulsive lad of sixteen could and should act like a man close to forty who was forced to be virtuous, studious and reflective. John, but not his brother Richard, had a personality and character which fitted him much better into the academic life of Oxford and enabled him to understand his father's wishes and philosophy.

On the eve of the Christmas holidays of the year 1630 the prisoner in the Tower had planned to send his eldest sons for a brief visit to the Lukes at Woodend. But that was made impossible when John and Richard were suddenly held at Oxford at the order of the government. From a note to Luke[1] and two letters to Hampden early in the new year[2], it is possible to deduce from the secretive and cryptic language of Sir John that his sons were probably detained to punish him for his refusal to change his attitude towards the charges on which he was imprisoned. Possibly the restrictions were ordered to prevent the father from having a happy Christmas and not to cause any real harm. In his letter of January 7 to Hampden, Eliot implied that the order detaining John and Richard had already been revoked, but that it was too late for them to appear at Hampden House. Obviously, it had been planned that the two young men come to London, then go to Woodend, and spend the remainder of their holidays with the Hampdens.

Poor Richard Eliot! He could not be a model son, not even a good boy. In March of 1631 he again was involved in an escapade, and this time it was serious. There is not the slightest hint in Eliot's letter to John Hampden what the trouble was about.[3] But Sir John was deeply hurt. 'I confess it makes me in an agony,' he told Hampden, 'and, as I

[1] Dec. 31, 1630, p. 150.   [2] Jan. 7 and 13, pp. 151–3.
[3] Pp. 156–8.

grieve, there has been such occasion I could wish it were forgotten.' He admitted that nothing could be done about it, for a thorough investigation would only 'make the wounds the larger'. Sir John did not think too well of those concerned in the affair, but he was not curious as to what each one was doing, 'who were the actors in this scene', and 'what plots may be suspected'. What he was certain of is that 'it was the folly of the patient, and I hope by God appointed to instruct him for the future'. Eliot did wonder, however, that Poole, the master of the college,[1] had not ascertained all the facts and somehow brought them to his attention. His plans for the present were, unless Hampden advised otherwise, quietly 'to withdraw my charge from thence, and a while retain it near me, if it may be, to work some new impressions'. Eliot expected to send a servant to Oxford to bring Richard to London. On their way to London Richard would visit Hampden House where Sir John hoped his friend would give his wayward son some sound advice.

It appears that John Eliot did not want to stay alone at Oxford, so both arrived at the Hampdens'. There John Hampden had a talk with Richard and gave him 'a taste of those apprehensions he is like to find with you, which, I tell him, future obedience to your pleasure rather than justification of past passages must remove'.[2] Hampden declared that Richard promised to mend his ways, 'but', he continued, 'you know virtuous actions flow not infallibly from the flexiblest dispositions'. He was unwilling as yet to advise what course to follow with Richard, but he did think that John could be safely returned to Oxford. It seems that John was involved in another incident. But as Hampden wrote, it was manifest what 'good satisfaction he received at the vice-chancellor's fair carriage towards him'.

By April 19 when Eliot wrote to Sir Oliver Luke[3] it had been decided by their father that both sons should not return to Oxford and that they should go abroad. Sir John told Sir Oliver that he intended to send Richard to the Low Countries to serve under Sir Edward Harwood[4] while John was to travel in France. Undoubtedly, Richard was far better suited to be a soldier than a student. But being barely sixteen years old, he appears to modern eyes to be extremely young to

---

[1] This is what Forster, *Eliot*, II, 582, calls him. But I have been unable to find any Poole (under variant spellings) who could be identified as the master of Lincoln College at this time.

[2] Hampden to Eliot, April 4, pp. 158–60.

[3] Pp. 160–1.   [4] He had recently commanded a regiment in the campaign in the Netherlands and had also taken part in the actions of Cadiz and Rhé. Forster, *Eliot*, II, 585.

enter upon such a strenuous life. John, on the other hand, at the age of eighteen was ready to spend some years in travel. When Sir John wrote the same news to Hampden a week later[1] he gave more details and said this about Richard's prospects as a soldier in the Netherlands: 'I hope he shall have such direction and advice as may better the University for his manners, and not be without some advantage for his letters.' Why John did not return to Oxford he explained by saying: 'the elder knowing this resolution for his brother, I find not desirous to return from whence he came, it being as he takes it a degree behind the other. And I confess my judgment is not otherwise.' Eliot hoped that Richard would be off within the week, while John, for whom he had obtained his licence to leave the country, was only waiting for the first opportunity to cross the Channel.

When Sir John on the next day wrote Thomas Knightley,[2] the tutor of the boys, he told him that he had acted on his advice and was taking them both out of Oxford. But he did not tell him what his plans for them were. And then on the last day of April he wrote a polite, helpful little note of introduction for Richard to Sir Edward Harwood.[3] The two young men were now set for adventures in foreign lands. Battle should tame down the exuberance of Richard. Travel should broaden and educate John.

These steps had all been taken by Sir John Eliot without the advice of his friends, particularly that of John Hampden. The impression one gets is that Eliot was eager for Hampden's suggestions and would consider them seriously. When they came it was too late. The young men had left England. In an over-tactful letter Hampden showed that he did not approve of what Sir John had done.[4] He had other plans for Richard and John. Delicately he suggested that the younger might have combined action in the field during the summer with contemplation and study during the winter. Just how this was to be done he did not say. And then in a postscript he said: 'Do not think by what I say that I am fully satisfied of your younger son's course intended, for I have a crotchet out of the ordinary way, which I would have acquainted you with if I had spoken with you before he had gone but am almost ashamed to communicate.' What did he mean by his 'crotchet'? It is most intriguing. As to John he was more explicit. He did not think that France was a good place for so young and inexperienced a man to go to, where the people 'make it their religion to be superstitious in

[1] Pp. 161–4.   [2] Pp. 164–5.   [3] P. 165.   [4] On May 11, pp. 167–9.

impiety and their behaviour to be affected in ill manners'. Hampden would have sent him 'to visit Cambridge as a free man for variety and delight'. Of course, it was out of the question for Sir John to recall his sons and follow the advice of John Hampden.

Early in July the Oxford careers of John and Richard Eliot were closed by an exchange of letters between Thomas Knightley and Sir John Eliot.[1] The letters concern themselves chiefly with settling the college expenses of the boys and with disposing of their personal effects. But Knightley did have something to say about what had happened to his charges. He was pleased that Richard had seen the last of his college days. Yet he wished that John's withdrawal had not been so 'speedy'. He explained that 'had I received but the least intimation of this your resolution, I should have taken a little more pains in furnishing him with some other grounds of learning which he wants. But my hope is that his own industry by God's blessing will supply that defect.' Sir John made no reply to this statement. But we do learn from his letter that he paid the tutor £6 per person for an academic year and was not sure that it was enough.

Three letters of Eliot from the summer of 1631 to his eldest son have survived.[2] After that there is silence. They were written a month apart and were replies to letters from John which are no longer available. None of the correspondence between Richard and his father is in existence today. But from remarks to John we know that Eliot had heard from his second son, though he did not write as frequently as his brother.

In the first of the three letters Eliot expounded at length upon his son's finances. The £100 per year he had allowed him seemed not to have been enough, so Sir John doubled it. But he gave him a good lecture on economy and reminded him of the rising expense of educating his younger brothers and sisters. At the same time he admitted that John must not neglect his studies and exercises 'which are for the ornament and ability both of the mind and body and a main part of the intention which you travel for'. Eliot was not at all enthusiastic that his son spend money learning to ride horseback, particularly according to the French fashion. Riding, he felt, was only for pleasure in England, as it could be of no use in the army which was composed at that time essentially of infantry. But he left it up to his son and declared 'therein let you own liking guide you'.

[1] Knightley wrote to Eliot on June 6 and Sir John replied on July 9, pp. 170-2, 181-2.
[2] June 30, Aug. 1, Sept. 1, pp. 180-1, 188-9, 190-2.

The second letter contained a strong comment on John's poor penmanship and a request that he try to improve it. He also advised his son on how to treat Sir Isaac Wake, English ambassador in Paris recently transferred from Savoy, who had snubbed the young man. It was simply that, as he did not require the services of Sir Isaac, he should ignore him.

There is much interesting advice in the third letter of Sir John Eliot to his eldest son. That young man had asked permission to travel immediately into Italy with some titled friends. Eliot first warned him against associating with titled people unless they were really worthy and virtuous. Then he admitted that the opportunity to travel in good company was an excellent reason for such a journey, 'but the time I doubt not yet seasonable to answer it'. The trouble was as Sir John saw it that an Italian autumn with its fruits and 'the corruption of [its] air through the strife of heat and moisture' made it most dangerous to the health of strangers. Furthermore, he felt that the plague was still a danger in many Italian towns until the first frost had removed it. There could be no more sensible advice than to stay away from Italy at that time of the year.

But John had also argued that a trip to Italy would help him in his study of languages, particularly Italian. To this his father replied that just the opposite was true. Without a good knowledge of French it would be much more difficult and less pleasant for him to learn Italian. To attempt to master Italian without knowing French, Eliot argued, would postpone the study of the more important language to a time when John was liable to have less leisure for it. 'Whereas,' he continued, 'if you shall yet gain some perfection in the French and then pass into Italy, what you there lose will be regained again at your returning homeward and you become a master in the tongue.' Sir John wanted his son to spend the winter in France and go to Italy in the spring. Taking for granted that John would go to Italy as he had suggested, Eliot advised him where to travel: 'The territories of the Church I hope you will avoid (those I confess are dangerous as all Spain, which by no means I can allow you once to enter). But other parts are free and peaceable as in England where with discretion you may as much retain your safety.' The Protestant who was not afraid to let his son travel in Catholic France or most of Italy drew the line at the citadel of the Papacy and the land of its chief defender. Eliot closed with a sensible religious and moral exhortation: 'Be careful in your religion.

M

Make your devotions frequent. Seek your blessing from above. Draw your imitation to good patterns. Let not vain pageantries deceive you. Prepare your estimation by your virtue which your own carriage and example must acquire.'

One other child of Sir John Eliot is mentioned in his correspondence. On October 9, 1631, he asked Maurice Hill to bring his eleven-year-old daughter Bridget to London.[1] There she was to go to school, possibly at the one attended by Elizabeth in Stepney. He ignored the dislike Lady Luke and John Hampden had expressed for girls' schools.[2] But with no wife to educate his daughters, Eliot was forced to depend on such institutions, whatever his opinion of them may have been. Of course, he could not impose on friends for the education of four daughters.

The children of Sir John Eliot fade out of his correspondence with a postscript to a letter from Hampden to Eliot dated March 21, 1632.[3] He asked to be remembered to his soldier, 'if not gone to his colours'. Richard was back in England on furlough. But the prisoner in the Tower was ill. Where was John? Was he returning to England, or about to take off for Italy after a winter in Paris?

2. ELIOT'S RELIGIOUS VIEWS

In order to understand the religious views of Sir John Eliot while a prisoner in the Tower, a word must be described and defined. That word is puritanism, one of the most elusive terms whether used by people of the sixteenth and seventeenth centuries or by their historians.

From the accession of Edward VI to the Restoration period puritanism was rarely static. But with the rise of Thomas Cartwright to prominence at Cambridge University, ten to a dozen years after the accession of Queen Elizabeth, the puritan movement gained much in doctrinal and spiritual uniformity and also gained an objective. To change the Church of England into a Presbyterian Church was that objective. Unfortunately from the puritan point of view, the governments of Elizabeth, James I, and Charles I until the fifth decade of the seventeenth century made it impossible for puritans even to approach this ideal of church organization. Instead the followers of Cartwright,

---

[1] Forster, *Eliot*, II, 598. P.E.MS. Letter Book.
[2] See above, p. 348.
[3] Add MS. *5016. 1, f. 1. Forster, *Eliot*, II, 717.

preachers ever growing in numbers with each decade and mostly
trained at Cambridge, temporarily lost sight of their ideal and concentrated on bringing as many people as possible into the doctrinal and
spiritual fold of their religion. Their cardinal doctrine was the corner-
stone of Calvinism, predestination, which was coupled with salvation by
faith. They preached universal sin but joined to it equality of all men
before God. Any man could be saved by receiving Christ into his spirit
and by believing in Him. 'The manifestation of grace in the elect was
faith' in Christ. To these preachers, most of whom managed to stay
within the Church of England until the sixteen-thirties, 'the will of
God was revealed in the Bible, in the human heart and in nature'. This
they proclaimed in lectures and from their pulpits to an ever-growing
number of puritan Englishmen, who, however, remained a distinct
minority in the nation. Men must be saved; men must commune with
God; men must 'trust in nothing but God and the spirit within themselves'. They must 'trust in Jesus Christ and put on the whole armour of
God'. Such was the puritan spirit of the early seventeenth century. But
at the same time the movement was on the attack, it was negative and
denunciatory. The bishops of the Church of England were assailed, the
ceremonies of the Church were decried, the policies of the Stuart governments were denounced, and the way of life of most Englishmen
was disapproved of. And then when the Church of England began to
fall under the influence of men like Richard Neile and William Laud
with their insistence on elaborate ceremonies and episcopal authority,
when Arminianism began to take control, the puritans became more
bitter in their attack, denounced the Church as papistical and showed
themselves to be strongly anti-clerical. Many moderate Anglicans, believing in the Church of England as established by law in the reign of
Elizabeth, joined the puritans in their attack. And many such Anglicans
turned into puritans spiritually and doctrinally.[1]

Sir John Eliot had been one of those moderate Anglicans who believed strongly in the Elizabethan establishment. Soon after the accession of Charles, Arminianism began to trouble Eliot. At the same time
he seems to have fallen under the influence of such puritans as Richard
Knightley, Sir Oliver Luke and John Hampden. In his great speech on
religion delivered on January 29, 1629,[2] Sir John showed that he had

---

[1] William Haller, *The Rise of Puritanism* (New York, 1938), particularly pp. 51, 83, 87,
88, 173, and M. M. Knappen, *Two Elizabethan Puritan Diaries* (Chicago, 1933), p. 4.
[2] See above, pp. 280-2.

already accepted two puritan characteristics, anti-ceremonialism and anti-clericalism. He was soon on the road to accepting puritanism in all its aspects. Unfortunately Eliot has left no evidence of the spiritual side of his development until he became a prisoner in the Tower. During the first four months of his 'close' confinement he had ample leisure to search his soul and seek his God. Writing his first letter to Richard Knightley on June 25, 1629,[1] he described his religious ecstasy in the following words:

'No day has seemed too long; no night has once been tedious; no fears, no terrors, no opposed power or greatness has affrighted me; no outward crosses or losses have been troublesome; no grief, no sadness, no melancholy has oppressed me; but a continual pleasure and joy in the Almighty has still comforted me. The influence of His graces has enriched me; His power, His greatness has secured me; His all sufficiency has given me both boldness and confidence in Him, that no attempt could move it.'

He rushed on to express his joy in God and presumed that his friend had been in competition with him for His blessings. Here is an example of spiritual meditation of which the most ardent puritan could be proud. Knightley is known to have been such a puritan. He must have been delighted to accept Eliot into the fold.

A week later Sir John had to disclose to his youthful sons his newly acquired religious fervour.[2] In line after line he described to John and Richard the joys of communion with his God. When by December, 1629, Eliot was enjoying the comparative freedom of the Marshalsea, John Hampden was afraid that his easier, pleasanter life might dampen his religious zeal. He hoped 'that God may find you as much His, now you enjoy the benefit of secondary helps, as you found Him yours while by deprivation of all others you were cast upon His immediate support'.[3] The confirmed puritan feared that the convert might lose his ardour and revert to the old forms of worship. In reply two days later Sir John made no comment about his friend's remarks. But we have seen how at this time he went to a lecture at St Mary Overyes.[4] His remark sounds as though he were in the habit of attending lectures. They were conducted by puritan preachers who exhorted their audiences to seek

[1] Pp. 52–5.   [2] Pp. 55–61.   [3] P. 76.   [4] See above, p. 328.

God's salvation. If Eliot attended them regularly, they must have helped to keep him on the straight and narrow path.

That Eliot was a puritan neophyte is confirmed by his remarks to Luke on religion in a letter of March 3, 1630. He told Sir Oliver that 'the support I have still found does still follow me. The experience it has given me denies me not to doubt it, my confidence and tranquillity in all degrees and places having the same meridian'.[1] Whether Sir John can be said to have joined permanently the puritan ranks is difficult to say. Only occasionally in his surviving correspondence did he mention religion. In the summer of 1630 he expounded to Mrs Corbet on the blessings and power of God.[2] Nearly a year later finding nothing much to write about, he elaborated to Knightley on the mutations of God's love.[3] Not until his health began to break down was he continually seeking the aid of God.

In December, 1631, Eliot was forced into new lodgings which would endanger his health.[4] Immediately he began to dwell upon God and His ways. Writing to Hampden[5] and to Knightley[6] he showed that he was depending more and more on the assistance of the Almighty, not on the Church with her services and ceremonies. Early in 1632 Sir Oliver Luke throws some light on to the spiritual path Sir John was following.[7] He wrote his friend that he was overjoyed at the revival of his religious faith and commented on the glories and blessings of God. The prisoner in the Tower had obviously been slipping in his zeal for the Deity. Now Luke admitted he was again as one with his puritan brethren. That this was true may be seen from four of the last five surviving letters of his correspondence, all written in March, 1632, two to Knightley and two to Hampden.[8] In the last of these to his closest friend Sir John Eliot reached a climax of devotional passion. He wrote:

'Oh the infinite mercy of our Master! Dear friend, how it abounds to us that are unworthy of His service! How broken! How imperfect! How perverse and crooked are our ways in obedience to Him! How exactly straight the line of His providence unto us drawn out through all occurrents and particulars to the whole length and measure of our

---

[1] P. 96. [2] Pp. 130–2. She was the widow of Sir John Corbet bart. of Norfolk whose son inherited the title. G.E.C., *Complete Baronetage*.

[3] June 27, 1631, pp. 176–7. [4] See below, p. 363. [5] P. 211–2.

[6] Pp. 213–4. [7] Pp. 214–5. [8] Written between March 15 and 29, pp. 224–32. The fifth is a note to Luke dated March 21 in which he does not mention religion.

time! How perfect is His love that has given His Son unto us and with him has promised likewise to give us all things!'

On and on he went in this vein. What a magnificent preacher the puritan churches lost in the death of this idealistic orator.

3. ELIOT'S READING AND WRITING

As the new zeal for religion began to develop, it is logical that Eliot should have become an ardent reader of the Bible. He may have read it every day, for all we know, although there is not the slightest hint in his entire correspondence that he ever looked at the Bible. From his writings it can be seen that he knew it well, but the works of the great classical authors he knew even better. Friends frequently wrote that they were sending him books, and Eliot often thanked them for such favours. Rarely were authors and titles given. To be sure, Richard James, Sir Robert Cotton's librarian,[1] said that he was sending him the *de Constantia* of Lipsius and a book by Jerome Cardan, the sixteenth century Italian physician.[2] But this is the exception rather than the rule.

Among the reading matter at Sir John's disposal in the Tower was a manuscript pamphlet called 'General Observations for the Plantations of New England'.[3] How he got possession of it is not disclosed. He loaned it to Hampden at his friend's request with the comment that he did not think much of it.[4] With that the pamphlet disappears from the prisoner's correspondence. It is the only contact he is known to have had with the colonies, or with projects for colonization.

While Sir John Eliot was in the Tower he wrote two treatises, *The Monarchy of Man* and *De JureMaiestatis*, an essay he called *An Apology for Socrates*, and the first part of a major historical work entitled *Negotium Posterorum*. The nature of these writings will be discussed in the next chapter. Here their mention in his correspondence will be examined to see, if possible, when each was begun and to learn the criticism Eliot's friends gave of them. A major difficulty is that in no instance was a title

---

[1] For a description of him see *The Autobiography . . . of Sir Simonds D'Ewes, Bart.*, II, 39.

[2] Pp. 66-7.

[3] Written either by John Winthrop or John White. Massachusetts Historical Society, *Proceedings* (1st Ser., 1864-5), VIII, 417-27, and same soc. *Winthrop Papers* (Spec. Pub. no. 20), II, 106-45.

[4] Hampden to Eliot, Dec. 8, 1629, and Eliot to Hampden, Dec. 10, pp. 76, 78-9.

given. And frequently the identification of a work is well-nigh impossible.

There are a number of hints in several letters Sir John Eliot wrote to John Hampden between May, 1630, and January, 1631, that he was engaged in writing a treatise, undoubtedly *The Monarchy of Man*, which he was anxious that Hampden should read and criticize.[1] But it was not until April, 1631, that Hampden indicated in a letter to Eliot that he had received the first part of *The Monarchy of Man*.[2] Of course, he did not mention its title then or at any other time. To avoid confusion the title will be used whenever internal evidence leaves little doubt which work is under consideration by Sir John or his correspondents. Hampden asked Eliot to send him the second part of *The Monarchy of Man* as soon as he had finished it. Then he hoped to give his opinion of both parts. In the meantime he ventured to give some of his views on the first part. He called it 'an exquisite nosegay composed of curious flowers bound together with as fine a thread'. But, he continued, 'I must in the end expect honey from my friend, somewhat out of those flowers digested, made his own, and giving a true taste of his own sweetness'. This flowery language meant simply that Eliot had presented an array of examples and precedents from which Hampden hoped he would draw his own conclusions.

To this expression of his friend's estimate Eliot replied on April 26 that 'the work was done in haste as a recreation not a business in the midst of things more serious (which one day may be honoured by your view), whereof this took but the times of intermission, as an interjection of the fancy for entertainment and delight'.[3] By 'things more serious' Sir John could only have meant the history of his times, his *Negotium Posterorum*. He said nothing about Hampden's criticism. But he was anxious to get the second part of *The Monarchy of Man* into his hands, so that he could receive Hampden's view on it.

Those views were not put on paper until June 29.[4] Eliot was told by his Buckinghamshire friend that the second part of the treatise had been read only once and that hurriedly. Therefore, Hampden hesitated to give his opinion. In typical language he first praised the picture of the government of England presented by Eliot. Then with great tact he began his strictures. Again he objected to the superabundance of examples and precedents. 'Would not a less model have given a full repre-

---

[1] Pp. 112, 124, 153.   [2] P. 159.
[3] Pp. 162–3.   [4] Pp. 178–9.

sentation of that subject, not by diminution but by contraction of parts?' he asked. 'I desire to learn, I dare not say.' To soften even this criticism he admitted that if he were asked what part to omit he could not tell and might say, none.

When Sir John replied on July 19 he disclosed that the first part of *The Monarchy of Man* had already been returned to him.[1] He asked that a second be sent back as soon as possible, as another friend was eager to see it. His objection to the impressions of Hampden was that there were not enough of them, that they were not detailed enough, and that they were accompanied by too much praise. He did say that if he applied Hampden's advice and eliminated examples and precedents in the first part of his treatise, 'I may pervert your meaning, having no rule to warrant it'. He reminded his friend that the first part dealt solely with politics 'whose property it is, as I take it, to be handled by authorities. And I remember not amongst the later writers where I have seen it otherwise'. In fact, the book Hampden had just sent him, Eliot said, employed this method. He concluded his remarks about his writings by saying that some of the examples which were 'obnoxious to my sense' he had discarded already. As to the rest Hampden must give a 'better indication of your reason, wherein you must deal freely and particularly'. Sir John was perfectly justified in treating his friend's too tactful criticism in this fashion. He was not willing to read between the lines of Hampden's letter. That gentleman must come into the open with his strictures and justify them and any proposed alterations.

The reply to this letter is most disappointing.[2] Dated July 27, Hampden said in his letter that Eliot had commanded him to give satisfaction far beyond his ability. But when they should meet in London, he would not refuse to be of service, even to betraying his ignorance. As so often happened, the thread of Eliot's correspondence was broken by the visit of one or another of his friends to the Tower.

The next person to see *The Monarchy of Man* was Thomas Hatcher of Lincolnshire. While Hampden had seen it all, but one part at a time, Hatcher was sent the entire treatise at once. Again Sir John told this friend that it was written for recreation while he was undertaking a much more serious work. Again he was eager for criticism. But between September 1, 1631, and December 17, when five letters were exchanged between the two men,[3] Eliot could get nothing but the most

[1] Pp. 184–6.   [2] Pp. 187–8.
[3] Forster, *Eliot*, II, 653–9. P.E. MS. Letter Book.

saccharine praise from his Lincolnshire friend. He did promise to have more to say when he came to London. One point of interest Hatcher made. By implication he suggested the publication of this treatise, but at the same time acknowledged that it would be a difficult and dangerous thing to do.

Sir John Eliot was still working on *The Monarchy of Man*, probably revising it and making copies, as late as December 26, 1631, according to a letter to Hampden.[1] He asked his friend for comment on those translations 'you excepted at'. Copies of the treatise were being sent to one friend after another. One was in the hands of Richard James,[2] and another was being read by Sir Oliver Luke in January, 1632.[3] Richard James was the second to suggest, openly this time, that *The Monarchy of Man* be published; but it should be done anonymously. Later in January James sent a list of ten minor factual corrections but gave no general criticism.[4]

That Sir John was working on his *Negotium Posterorum* is attested by a letter he wrote to Sir William Courtney on February 20, 1632,[5] in which he asked that soldier for detailed information and any records he might have on the expedition to Cadiz. Either his request was never filled, or more likely illness prevented him from using what Courtney sent. The *Negotium Posterorum* ends with a description of Sir Edward Cecil, the leader of the expedition to Cadiz, without a word about the expedition itself.

The first hint of the existence of the other treatise, the *De Jure Maiestatis*, is in the last surviving letter Eliot wrote to Sir Oliver Luke on March 21st.[6] Sir John informed his friend that he could not return 'the book', as he had not yet copied it. 'In the meantime I have herewith sent to entertain you another of less trouble to be read. And this likewise is all of it I have, for which I must pray you when you are weary of it to render it me again.' This is indeed a very slight hint. Usually when he referred to his writings he spoke of 'those papers'. This was a book. But it was not complete and therefore it must have been in manuscript. Consequently, it may be part of a 'book' Eliot had written rather than one he had copied in part. If this was a work of Eliot's it could not have been *The Monarchy of Man*, as Luke had seen that in January. It certainly would not be the *Negotium Posterorum*, as that could hardly be said to be 'less trouble to read'. Yes, it might be the *Apology for Socrates*, but one gets the impression that that essay never

[1] P. 212.   [2] P. 215.   [3] P. 218.   [4] P. 216.   [5] Pp. 221-2.   [6] P. 226.

lay behind 'those papers' in the correspondence of the prisoner in the Tower.

Eliot's last reference to papers of any kind was in his letter to Hampden of March 22, 1632.[1] He wished his friend to send him as soon as possible 'certain papers'. What were they? We can only speculate.

The picture this correspondence presents is that most of Eliot's friends saw *The Monarchy of Man*. Of them all only Hampden gave criticism of any value. One gets the feeling that his friends were either too much in awe of him to pass an honest judgment on the work of so great a man, or else they were afraid to speak their thoughts freely because they knew that Eliot was not good at taking criticism. It is probable that a few friends saw the *De Jure Maiestatis*, but hardly likely that any of them laid eyes on the *Negotium Posterorum*.

When did Eliot begin his original writing in the Tower? The presumption is that *An Apology for Socrates*, so closely related to the trial in King's Bench, was the first begun and completed. But there is no evidence of any kind that he ever showed it to his friends. Having finished the *Apology* rather quickly he began to think of devoting himself to his history of the times. But before he could start putting it down on paper, he would have to do a lot of research. To keep his mind and pen active he decided to record for his friends the nature of an ideal government suitable for his country. By April, 1630, he had already begun to work on the *Negotium* and at the same time he was reading for as well as putting on paper the first part of *The Monarchy*. It is useless to assume anything more about the *Negotium Posterorum* or the *De Jure Maiestatis*. That fragment of history and the treatise were probably completed by the end of March, 1632. To any man reading and writing letters or essays, treatises or histories, health is imperative. The prisoner in the Tower was no exception in this respect.

4. ELIOT'S HEALTH

The first evidence we have that Sir John Eliot was not too robust was his illness which made it impossible for him to attend the court on February 12, 1630, when the judges of King's Bench gave their judgment.[2] He appears, however, to have recovered completely from the cold he contracted during the strain of the trial. On July 5 of that year

[1] P. 228.   [2] See above, p. 337.

he wrote to Richard Knightley that he was in good health.[1] But by March 22, 1631, Sir John was troubled by a stomach ailment. He wrote to Luke that 'I am now in physic, and so far, as I hope God will bless it, towards recovery of my health. The disaffection of my stomach is repaired, and I now cleanse a little to take off all remainders'.[2] This frank exposition is the only reference available to the health of the prisoner during 1631.

By January, 1632, Luke had become apprehensive. 'All I can think of is to desire your care of your health,' he wrote, 'which is the sole danger I apprehend in this, assuring myself all else will be returned with advantage.'[3] And yet on January 12 Pory wrote to Puckering that 'this other day Sir John Eliot's attorney-at-law[4] told me he had been with him long since his removal into his new lodging and found him the same cheerful, healthful, undaunted man that ever he was'.[5]

Here is mentioned Sir John's change of lodging. It seems that by December, 1631, too many rumours and reports were circulating about the prisoner and too many visitors were crowding into his quarters. On the 21st of that month the Privy Council ordered Eliot put under close surveillance[6] and a few days later on a warrant from the King he was removed to 'where candle light may be suffered but scarce fire', he wrote to Hampden.[7] 'None but my servants, hardly my son, may have admittance to me. My friends I must desire for their own sakes to forbear coming to the Tower.' What a delightful Christmas present Charles had given his prisoner! A room where he could not have a fire in the middle of winter augurs ill for the health of a man already weakened by eighteen months of confinement. No wonder that Luke, a week or so later, was worried about his health.

Before the end of January another change of lodging had taken place. This is known from a letter Eliot wrote to Sir Oliver.[8] But he said nothing about the nature of his new quarters, whether they were better or worse than those he had just left. In a letter Pory wrote to Puckering on January 26 he gave his correspondent the information that 'I hear Sir John Eliot is to remove out of his dark smoky lodging into a better'.[9] That he had already moved, according to the above letter Eliot wrote to Luke two days earlier, does not weaken Pory's news. But that his room was much better than the old one is doubtful, otherwise he would

---

[1] P. 120.　[2] P. 155.　[3] P. 215.　[4] Robert Mason.　[5] C. and T. Chas. I, II, 158.
[6] Privy Council Register, Chas. I, VII, 330–1.
[7] On Dec. 26, pp. 211–2.　[8] Jan. 24, pp. 217–8.　[9] C. and T. Chas. I, II, 163.

have mentioned it to Luke. In other words, Sir John's health was still in jeopardy because of the conditions under which he was living.

Within less than a month the evidence is too clear that Eliot had been ill again. Writing to Sir Edward Ayscough on February 21[1] he said that the prescriptions he had sent him, for which he was most grateful, had restored his health. In spite of the figurative language used by Sir John, it can be seen that a respiratory disease had again taken hold of him. And the hold, though it appears to have been relaxed, was permanent. That can be seen in Eliot's letter to Knightley of March 15.[2] Without his usual colourful but confusing language he described his illness in words which could leave no doubt about their meaning. For more than two weeks, he wrote, illness had incapacitated him. He had had a cold for a long time, he said, and its symptoms were becoming dangerous. He had no appetite and his whole system had been weakened. 'Some doubt there is of a consumption.' But they were applying remedies to prevent it. That Sir John Eliot was in the first stages of tuberculosis and that little could be done to save him unless his quarters were changed is all too obvious. By March 21 he wrote to Luke that his health was 'amending' and that he had only hoarseness and a bit of a cough left.[3] He was hopeful of complete recovery. In his letter to Knightley of the next day Sir John did not seem as hopeful and was resigned to leaving his fate in the hands of God.[4] Strangely enough it was not until this day, March 22, that Eliot wrote a detailed account of his illness, much the same as he had written to Knightley on the 15th, to John Hampden.[5] He did add that 'I find myself bettered, though not well'.

At this point Bevil Grenville's undated letter fits perfectly[6]. His opening sentence shows the state of mind he was in: 'Such and so great is my agony and distraction at the reports which fly abroad and strike mine ears, as I cannot express it nor well tell what I would say.' He said that he had heard rumours that Eliot was dead, sick, and well again. He could not believe any of them but was afraid that either of the first two might be true. Grenville was terribly worried, 'wholly from myself', as he said. He begged Sir John to give him speedy news of his health, or else he did not know what he would do with himself. One report he had heard was that Eliot's physicians had said that country air would be a great help to his recovery. Here Grenville declared that he had been

[1] P. 223. [2] P. 224-5.
[3] P. 226. [4] P. 227. [5] P. 228. [6] See above, p. 339, note 1.

informed that Sir John might have his liberty if he would but ask for it. For the sake of his friends, children, and country Grenville besought him to seek his liberty, 'if it may be had on any honourable terms. I will not desire you to abandon a good cause. But if a little bending may prevent a breaking, yield a little unto it, it may render you the stronger to serve your country hereafter'. In these impassioned words spoke a great lover of life and mankind. Bevil Grenville was also an idealist, but his ideals were different from those of Sir John Eliot. To him man was more precious than his ideas. Therefore, he could advocate that Eliot meet the King half way at least. But half way, as we shall see, was just as bad as going the whole way for Sir John. Even to suggest that he might be slightly in the wrong was impossible for him. That would destroy his ideal, liberty and freedom of the House of Commons. It is to be hoped, though, that Eliot informed his friend of the status of his health with speed and precision.

One more description of the progress of Sir John's ailment is to be found in the last surviving letter written to John Hampden on March 29, 1632.[1] For the last three days he had been out of doors, he wrote, so he had not been continuously confined to his dreary chamber. But each time he returned to his quarters he 'brought in new impressions of the cold'. On the other hand, this activity had improved his appetite and his strength. He explained that cold was the cause of his sickness, but in time 'heat and tenderness by close keeping in my chamber has since increased my weakness'. His doctors had told him that air and exercise were his best medicine.

The correspondence of Sir John Eliot had come to a close. Unquestionably he received many and wrote some letters between April 1 and November 28, 1632. But none have been left to us. His damp and dreary chamber in the Tower slowly became his tomb, as racked and weakened by consumption he carried on existence.

[1] P. 229.

CHAPTER XVI

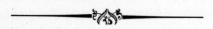

The Philosopher of the Tower

1629 to 1632

THE writings of Sir John Eliot on philosophy and history when compared with those of his great contemporaries such as Bacon and Hobbes
are of little significance. But they are of great importance in giving us a
picture of the man, in throwing light and shade on his character and
personality. Hence they must be examined in some detail.

To historians his most valuable work and to Eliot his most important
legacy to posterity was the history of his own time, the *Negotium
Posterorum*. The work remained a fragment because of his tragic death.
It has been made the basis of an earlier chapter[1] and therefore can be
ignored here.

I. AN APOLOGY FOR SOCRATES

As has been suggested, the first of his writings to be begun and completed was his ten thousand word essay, which he called *An Apology for
Socrates*.[2] Eliot had planned, it will be recalled, to present on February
12, 1630, to the Court of King's Bench a paper in which he justified
and explained his refusal to plead to the jurisdiction of the court.[3] Due
to a cold he had been unable both to complete and present this paper.
Therefore, as soon as he had regained his health, he must have decided
to record for posterity the same reasons for his actions and the principles behind them. He changed only the form and the setting. The
result was *An Apology for Socrates*.

[1] See above, Chap. V.
[2] See above, p. 362. P.E. MSS., 'Parliamentary and Unspoken Speeches', ff. 104-30,
is the only manuscript copy of this work in existence. Grosart has printed it with acceptable care and accuracy at the beginning of his first volume of the *Negotium Posterorum*.
[3] See above, p. 335.

Eliot had been a prisoner for a year. Of this time four months had been spent in close confinement when he saw none of his friends. In many other ways he had suffered during that year, and of much he had been deprived. At the conclusion of the trial he believed he would be, as a result of the condition imposed by the court, a prisoner for life. In other words, he was already dead. Consequently, transporting himself into antiquity, he could write of Socrates recently dead that, while he yet lived, he had

'suffered in his fortune, . . . in his person, in his liberty, in his life; to be made poor and naked, to be imprisoned and restrained, nay not to be at all, not to have the proper use of anything, not to have knowledge of society, not to have being and existence, his faculties confiscated, his friends debarred his presence, himself deprived the world.'[1]

This picture fits perfectly the misfortunes of Sir John during the first year of his imprisonment.

But why did he choose Socrates as his prototype? Because, like Socrates, Eliot was searching for the truth, truth in government, truth in the state and its ministers. Because, like Socrates, he might be accused of having corrupted the youth of the state when his leadership in Parliament had directed men against the government of the King. Because, like Socrates accused of having acted impiously against the gods, Sir John had denounced the accepted religious policy of the state. And, like Socrates, he drank the cup of hemlock when he refused to plead in court, with the result that he suffered imprisonment equal to death.

More important still, the Athenian state of the day of Socrates was a setting which fitted perfectly the mind of Eliot at this time. In comparing himself to Socrates, a senator, and the English Parliament to the Athenian senate,[2] he could find no parallel in the Athenian state to the English King. Consequently monarchy was simply ignored. No doubt it was during the first year or more of his imprisonment that Sir John had drifted further away from his belief in kingship than at any other time in his life. As a result of intensive reading and speculation he gradually regained faith in monarchy. But in the spring of 1630 the less he thought about that institution the better for his peace of mind. Hence he

---

[1] *Apology*, p. 30.
[2] Here Eliot has confused the government of Athens with that of Rome. There was no senate in Athens. Socrates was condemned by a jury in an Athenian court.

chose the Athenian senate as the setting for his own vindication. Sir John is extremely careful to avoid all suggestion of monarchy and adhere strictly to the terminology of republican government. Knowing his ability to mix his history and politics, one suspects it was more than by chance that he stuck so consistently to his setting in his *Apology*. This is all the more remarkable when it is remembered that the precedents he employs to vindicate Socrates before the Athenian senate naturally all stem from the English monarchy.

This essay we are considering was according to its form and nature an address, an oration to the citizens of Athens. It is the greatest speech Eliot ever wrote. It is his swan song to the House of Commons, the justification of his actions and himself to the Parliaments of the future, to the people of England. Written in the first person and repeatedly addressing the Athenians, he defends Socrates for his silence when various accusations were made against him in the Senate. He was accused of having spoken against Melitus, later his judge (Chief Justice Hyde), against Anytus, the prosecutor (Attorney-General Heath), and against Lyco, the informer (Speaker Finch).[1] Hyde, Heath and Finch are named as both the cause for Eliot's offence and the means of punishing him for it.

In his defence of Socrates for refusing to plead before Melitus, Sir John presents the old arguments that those who had offended in the Senate should be punished only in that place, and that nobody should be arrested or tried 'for matters and agitations in that sphere'.[2] And then he makes great use of precedents worded to fit the setting of the Athenian senate with their sources in English history clearly indicated in marginal notes. Once again he turns to the Haxey case, the Strode case, and the resolution on freedom of speech in 1621 as well as the Lancastrian precedents of 2 Henry IV and 27 and 31 Henry VI.[3] The case of Socrates, he says, was not merely his own case but that of the senate and the Athenians themselves. Therefore, Socrates, by refusing to plead in a lower court, is not guilty of breaking the law, as the accusation against him reads. Another charge against Socrates was that in refusing to plead he was contemptuous of the law, especially as the judges had made a ruling on this point. To this Eliot replies that a legal process is a

[1] *Apology*, pp. 7–8.   [2] *Ibid.*, p. 10.

[3] For the Haxey and Strode cases see above, p. 332, note 2. For the Lancastrian precedents see A. B. White and Wallace Notestein, *Source Problems in English History* (New York, 1915), pp. 165, 194, note 4.

legal writ and therefore superior to the ruling of the judges. He goes
so far as to say that 'judgments may err' and that 'the sentence of the
judges cannot be more valid than the authority of the law'.[1] In concluding his reply to this charge the defender of Socrates writes that in
preserving the liberties of his country the great Athenian surely cannot
be considered guilty of an offence in refusing to plead before the judges.

Along similar lines Eliot continues his defence of his own innocence
in the name of Socrates based upon his silence and refusal to plead. By
this policy, he concludes, Socrates received the judgment against himself and thereby preserved the privileges of the Senate and the liberties
of the Athenians. Hiding behind the dead Socrates and behind the great
constitutional principle he had been defending, Sir John Eliot throws
modesty to the winds and praises the 'unmatched, unparalleled, un-
exampled virtues, piety and integrity of Socrates'.[2]

In this oration we find Eliot at his best, equal to the best while active
in Parliament. As he wrote his imagination and his love for the House
of Commons carried him to heights far above those he later reached in
defending monarchy with his pen in his prison quarters.

2. 'THE MONARCHY OF MAN'

The Monarchy of Man,[3] which Sir John probably completed within a
year after writing his Apology, is divided into two parts. The first deals
with politics and runs to over a third of the seventy thousand word
composition. The second is a discourse on ethics.

Sir John Eliot begins his work by declaring that the monarchy of
man, being modelled on that of God, is the best of all governments and
is in all respects perfect. 'Man,' Eliot says, '[is] to be the governor of
himself, an exact monarchy within him, in the composition of which
state nothing without him may have interest but all stand as subservient
to his use, he only to his Maker's.'[4] He then enumerates the various or-
gans and senses of man's body and relates them to the government of a
monarchy. Thereupon Sir John declares that God is responsible for this
monarchy, for all power comes from God.

---

[1] Apology, p. 21.   [2] Ibid., p. 29.

[3] The Grosart edition is taken from B. M. Harl. 2228 which is probably the 'fair copy'
Eliot finally made of this work. At Port Eliot there is another copy of this treatise which
is not as complete or as legible as the Harleian copy. See Monarchy of Man, I, 136.

[4] Ibid., II, 10.

After this introduction Eliot enters upon an exposition of an actual monarchy and explains his method of handling that subject. He declares that first the outcome or end of monarchy must be discovered. This is twofold: it must work towards the glory of God, it must aim at the welfare and preservation of the people. A monarchy is directed to these ends by feeding and protecting the people as well as by instructing and guiding them through pastors, governors, officers and ministers.

Sir John has thus launched on a dissertation of politics in which he employs a detailed comparison of handling of a ship with that of a state. Likewise he compares the unselfishness of a physician with that of a prince. A prince must always act in the interest of his subjects and not in his own. He rules the state by means of his supreme judicature for the good and welfare of the subject.

Examining the nature of princes Eliot finds that though they were at first perfect, in time they degenerated. Therefore, because princes 'have lost that perfection', it is necessary that laws be prescribed 'by the wisdom of a council'.[1] By implication he admits that the Stuarts, particularly Charles I, are not perfect and must be assisted by a Parliament—for by a council he means a Parliament—in making laws. In fact, he goes even further when he asserts that princes are subject to the law, subject to laws made by themselves and their predecessors.[2] Of course he means laws made by a prince and his council or Parliament. He gives a great many examples from classical antiquity to show that princes are bound by and under the law; and he comes to the conclusion that submission to the law is no dishonour to a prince.

Sir John admits, however, that there are features of government which do not involve law, such as war, peace, seditions, leagues, treaties, etc. These must be handled by the prince for the ultimate welfare of the state, in which he must be guided by virtue. Again he reminds his reader that a prince rules for the common good and not for a private interest. The object of government is to preserve the whole and maintain harmony among the parts. Thus laws, if excellent and not too numerous, and constitutions preserve the whole; and a Parliament helps to keep harmony among the parts.

Without a break of any kind Sir John Eliot turns from politics to ethics, the second part of *The Monarchy of Man*. He declares that the

---

[1] *Monarchy of Man*, II, 42.   [2] See *ibid.*, II, 44-5, for subtle reference to his own relations with Charles I.

chief supports of monarchy are religion and virtue, which lead to the public or supreme good. Everything and everybody in the state are working for that supreme good which is happiness.

He then defines happiness at great length and comes to the conclusion that it is a state of mind coming from God in which knowledge combines feelings and actions in conformity with reason. This supreme state of happiness is to be found in oneself, so that the highest and lowest can attain it, can be kings. He, a prisoner, can reach this supreme state of mind, can be a king, in spite of all the efforts to the contrary of Charles and his government, Eliot implies.

At this point Sir John devotes much space to a discussion of the evil forces opposed to happiness and the means which must be employed to overcome them. In the end he believes that man can attain happiness when the passions are guided and directed by the virtues in accordance with reason. Through the entire account the man Eliot appears time and time again. How right Richard James was when he wrote: 'Your treatise is a very good account of yourself.'[1]

In concluding *The Monarchy of Man* Sir John proposes to answer the question of how to obtain the virtues. If this has been done supreme happiness has been obtained. Using the term virtue rather loosely, he says that it consists of action and contemplation. But action is composed of doing and saying, and the former means doing good first to everybody and then to oneself. When it comes to speech, only reason can dictate its limits. Expounding on the bane of loquacity he asserts that too much talking is one of the greatest evils of man. Could it be that Sir John Eliot had learned a lesson?

Contemplation, on the other hand, is the true form of a perfect soul and mind, and it depends essentially on wisdom. Being given the opportunity Eliot expounds at length on wisdom and contemplation. He comes to the conclusion that the mind is king and commands all. To have an all-powerful, limitless mind is the perfection of man. That is 'the true end and object of this monarchy of man'.[2]

Such is the argument of *The Monarchy of Man*. It contains nothing new, no startling ideas, and no profound wisdom. But its homely truths will find a response in the mind and heart of every reader. To be sure, all men will not agree with all of Eliot's ethics. His evils, as he defines them, seem bad and his virtues good. Yet few will agree that fear,

[1] *Letter Book*, p. 215.
[2] *Monarchy*, II, 227.

desire, pleasure, and sorrow are man's worst enemies. Similarly some philosophers might dispute the interaction of the evils and the virtues and the parts played by the mind and reason, as they are presented by Eliot. It must not be forgotten, however, that Sir John was using himself as a model, and that, as he told his friends, the composition of this treatise gave him pleasure and was a relaxation from more serious writing. Eliot glossed over the harder and more disagreeable facts of life. Idealism is a constant note in this treatise. It is particularly manifest in the first part where he deals with politics and where he disseminates many of the ideas he developed during his House of Commons days. Good government to him still meant the harmonious working of King and Parliament. King Charles and Sir Thomas Wentworth could find no fault here. Sir John gives no hint that revolution in government played any part in his political philosophy.

Besides being a philosopher of some ability Eliot shows himself to be an intimate student and lover of the classics. *The Monarchy of Man* is overloaded with citations from and references to Greek and Roman, as well as a few more modern, authorities. His pages are filled with Latin quotations which sometimes are far from accurate as to spelling and exact wording. He gives no evidence of knowing Greek[1] and undoubtedly had read his Aristotle and Plato in Latin translations. In most cases he cites in the margin his authorities, frequently giving the particular work and at times even the page from which he is quoting. Obviously books were not lacking to Sir John in his Tower study. Close to fifty different works are cited by him, and his knowledge of many of them was clearly intimate. He gives over four hundred citations from or references to classical authorities. More than eighty times does he refer to the works of Plato and over seventy times to those of Seneca. Cicero, a great favourite, appears in one form or another well over sixty times, while Aristotle, Tacitus, and Plutarch are continually mentioned. A great many of the works of these authors he must have read over and over again. And some of them he must have had at hand while he was writing. It would have been impossible for Eliot to have obtained all these references and quotations from some compendium or to have found them in the works of a few modern writers, such as Jean Bodin. Undoubtedly he did pick up in this way a goodly number of references to lesser authorities, both modern and classical.

What is noteworthy is the dearth of Christian authorities in *The*

[1] As will be seen below, p. 380, in his *De Jure Maiestatis*, he knew a few words of Greek.

Monarchy of Man. Hardly thirty references are there from the books of the Bible, and the majority of these are from the Old Testament. Of the Church fathers, St. Augustine and St. Jerome are each referred to twice. And that is the extent of the list. The universal God or even the pagan gods are called upon far more frequently than the God Eliot referred to in the puritan exhortations of his letters. And there is barely a mention of Jesus Christ in all this learning about how man should live. Unquestionably pagan authorities were uppermost in the mind of Eliot at the time he wrote *The Monarchy of Man*. Deeply religious he was. But his religion at the time of writing his treatise was of the world in all its antiquity. As we have seen, there were moments—and probably many more than have been recorded—when Sir John was stirred to his depths by Christian religious fervour, when his puritanism brought him into closer touch with his God than was the lot of most men of his day. To Eliot, as to the majority of men of the seventeenth or even the twentieth centuries, religious speculation was a matter of mood and feeling rather than an ever-present force which impelled him day by day throughout his life. The mood of *The Monarchy of Man* was essentially Greek and Roman paganism ruled by a universal Deity. Sir John was a true child of his age which still thrilled to the classicism engendered by the Renaissance of the two previous centuries.

There were also modern writers to whom Sir John Eliot referred in his treatise. The Frenchman Jean Bodin was a great favourite as was the Italian Jerome Cardan. Machiavelli is cited occasionally as are Philippe de Comines, Sir John Fortescue, Henningus Arnisaeus, and Justus Lipsius. Of his own day only Sir Thomas Overbury and Sir Walter Raleigh could serve the purpose of the moralist. He quotes from a poem by Overbury on the weakness of carnal beauty,[1] and praises the strength of Raleigh awaiting death on the scaffold.[2]

To the modern reader there is much to be desired in the style of *The Monarchy of Man*. It is a combination of that of a pedant, classicist and orator. Now it drags with an overabundance of classical references and quotations. Now it is heavy with archaic and stilted words. Now it soars to heights better suited to the House of Commons than to the reader looking for instruction and entertainment. To be sure, there are on occasion brilliant passages, but they are like oases in a desert. As Hampden suggested, there is too much in *The Monarchy of Man*. It could have been cut in half and made far more readable, instructive and

---

[1] *Monarchy*, II, 169.   [2] See above, p. 31.

entertaining. In the end, what has the philosopher of the Tower to offer? This: monarchy is an ideal of government best suited to man; but man harassed by certain evils, must live according to a few simple idealistic rules of life guided by the principles of wisdom and virtue. That is Eliot's contribution to philosophy. It isn't much, but it has tremendous value in giving us a picture of Sir John Eliot in the Tower. It parades before us his thoughts and ideals and shows us a man attacked and punished time and again by his King and government still loyal to monarchy with all its trappings and powers.

3. 'DE JURE MAIESTATIS'

But the views of Eliot on monarchy, that is, on the power of a king, are far better and more carefully displayed in his *De Jure Maiestatis*.[1] Before analysing this work, it would be well to examine the connection between Sir John Eliot, writer, philosopher, and prisoner in the Tower to Sir John Eliot, prominent west-countryman, vice-admiral of Devon, and a leader of the opposition in the House of Commons. The relation, as far as the *De Jure* is concerned, is very tenuous. The only common bond is that both Eliots were idealists. That is an obvious discovery one makes on reading the *De Jure*. On the other hand, virtually none of the ideas Sir John was developing between 1625 and 1629 are to be found in this treatise. The only link between his speeches of this period and the thought of his dissertation is his idealization of kingship. In the period when he was writing the *De Jure* he completely forgot the immediate past. Kingship, yes, divine right kingship,[2] which Eliot describes in his treatise, is based on books of history and politics, none of which come down to his own day and most of which deal with classical or medieval times.

Sir John becomes a scholar to whom the present is of no importance or significance. Only rarely does he think of his own day, and then his thoughts have nothing to do with the political theories he had enunciated in the House of Commons. But it must be remembered that Eliot, like other leaders of the Commons, was denouncing and attack-

---

[1] The only ms. copy of this treatise in existence is that at Port Eliot. It consists of 121 folios which Grosart has printed with care and general accuracy. See *De Jure*, pp. xix–xx.

[2] As Professor Margaret Judson in her *The Crisis of the Constitution*, p. 177, shows, all Englishmen in the early seventeenth century believed in the divine right of kings without any assistance given them by the political philosophy of James I.

ing the government of Charles I, his ministers, and particularly the Duke of Buckingham. To him the King could do no wrong. Hence it was not difficult for Sir John to develop an ideal kingship based upon his historical and political reading which was classical in its conception and medieval in its powers.

The treatise which resembles the *De Jure Maiestatis* most closely is *The True Law of Free Monarchies*[1] by James I. Practically every word Eliot wrote in his work would have received the enthusiastic approbation of the first Stuart King of England. The two authors agree on almost every point. What is strange in the light of Sir John Eliot's love of the House of Commons, in the light of the political theory he stated in *The Monarchy of Man*, is that the word Parliament or any synonym of it rarely appears in the *De Jure*. The reason for this extraordinary neglect is that the kings about whom Sir John read and wrote had little to do with Parliaments, councils, or assemblies. The king and his people, the king and his country, is the monarch and his interests with which Eliot is chiefly concerned. Therefore, in analysing his ideas on this subject we must forget completely the immediate past, just as he did, and accept what he has written for what it is worth in the light of universal monarchy.

If we only knew when and why this transition in thought took place in the mind of Eliot while residing in the Tower. Though not extreme, there definitely is a break between the political thought expressed by Sir John in *The Monarchy of Man* and that expressed in the *De Jure*. Had we the comment of just one friend on this treatise we might obtain some slight insight on the above questions.

The *De Jure Maiestatis* is divided into three books of which the first two are arranged in seven chapters each, while the third, a brief one, contains no chapter divisions. Eliot declares that his first book 'is of majesty in general', of which the initial chapter deals with definition. 'Majesty,' he writes, 'properly taken is chief power in any estate which binds all others under it within laws but is not holden itself by any laws but of God and nature.'[2]

In his next chapter Sir John devotes his attention to denying that either the Emperor or the Pope have power over kings. He insists that every king has absolute power in his own kingdom, though he admits that the Emperor has precedence over all kings.

[1] C. H. McIlwain, *The Political Works of James I*, pp. 53–70.
[2] *De Jure*, p. 4.

Eliot really enters into his subject in his third chapter when he analyses the power of a king in his own country. There must be one single, supreme power in every state, he asserts. Such power or majesty is above the law, and a ruler fully endowed with it is under no authority but that of God. An absolute king, to be sure, must govern according to law and reason. Yet if he does not, he cannot be judged by human law. Only God can punish a king for breaking the law, but God's punishment is very severe. Therefore, evil kings should consider the punishment that awaits them from God who sees all and from whom there is no appeal, writes Eliot. He has described the divine right king of James I.

In his fourth chapter Sir John shows that it is no dishonour to a king to give precedence to the Emperor or even to the Pope. At the same time he takes this opportunity to denounce the temporal powers of the Pope, particularly the papal assumption to depose kings. Surely the ghost of James was guiding the hand of the prisoner in the Tower.

This discussion leads Eliot into the feudal relationships of kings, which is the subject of his next chapter. After a survey of medieval feudal obligations, particularly in England, and a further condemnation of the temporal power of the papacy, he declares that a king who is a vassal to another for a fief outside his own kingdom does not lose majesty. But he is not at all sure of this point. Weighing contradictory theories against each other Eliot finally convinces himself that 'the person of that king which hath done homage to another doth not retain majesty untainted'.[1] While arguing that a king should not be both a king and a vassal, there comes to his mind the thought that one king should not be king over several states unless he can join them into a 'league'. As a result Eliot becomes an advocate of the union of England and Scotland with one Parliament for both countries. How delighted King James would have been over this point.

The subject of the feudal oath turns Eliot's mind to other royal oaths with which he deals at length in his sixth chapter. The oaths a king may take, however, are of little value in the eyes of Sir John.

Finally in the last chapter of the first book Eliot deals with the question of whether a king should keep the laws of his predecessor. This he answers simply by saying 'that a prince which hath majesty is not bound by the decrees of his antecessor, . . . but only so far forth as the public good and the laws of God and nature do require'.[2]

[1] *De Jure*, p. 50.   [2] *Ibid.*, p. 85.

The second book of Eliot's *De Jure Maiestatis* is more easily organized than was the first. It deals with the powers of majesty which, after considerable effort, Sir John boils down to five. He calls these powers major as opposed to those that are minor with which he deals in his third book.

But first he discusses the powers of majesty in general. He defends royal prerogatives or royalties, as he prefers to call them, from various angles. Then in a second chapter he denies that subjects can share the powers of majesty with a king. Finally in his third chapter he begins to analyse his five major powers of majesty which he has listed as 'creating magistrates, making laws, decreeing of war and peace, coining of money, [and] authority of establishing and maintaining of religion'.[1]

The first of the major powers Eliot discusses is that of making laws. Throughout this chapter he clearly demonstrates that a king must have the power to make and enforce law in order to be able to rule. At the same time he has the power to break them, but only civil laws, not divine or natural laws.

In his fourth chapter Sir John couples the power of appointing magistrates with the subject of final appeal. In the first he confuses the creation of an office with the naming of the holder of that office. In the second he speaks of the power of the English King to pardon in criminal cases and shows that appeal in English civil cases is carried to the Lord Chancellor on a writ of error. He closes his chapter by discussing briefly the general power of a king to transfer all offices on being crowned, to ennoble subjects, and to summon assemblies.

In discussing the royal power of making peace and war in his next chapter, Sir John Eliot changes the main emphasis to power over arms. In the first chapter of this book he has already spoken briefly and conventionally on the powers of a king over peace and war. Here he is primarily interested in the control and use of arms at home, for he says that kings should keep the manufacture of arms in their own hands. In fact, subjects should not be permitted to keep, bear, or use arms, not even small daggers. Eliot believes that arms should be kept in public arsenals and should be distributed to soldiers when the time comes for their use. On the same basis he asserts that the right to fortify cities and build castles belongs to majesty. Working through a denunciation of private warfare and the right of a subject to treat for peace, he concludes by declaring that majesty has the power to send ambassadors to foreign countries.

[1] *De Jure*, p. 98.

After summarizing the points of the preceding chapters and indicating what is to follow, Eliot begins his sixth chapter on 'the right that majesty hath over church and in causes ecclesiastical'. Forgetting that he had ever said in Parliament that the Commons should have much to say about religion, he now asserts that the king 'must have the charge of religion to whose care and guidance the . . . state is committed'.[1] Kings have the power to make laws for ecclesiastical discipline as well as to confer benefices and elect bishops. Kings have the power to call church assemblies and strengthen church laws, though they must do this with the assistance of their clergy. But he admits that kings must employ the clergy assembled in synods to establish the true faith. At every opportunity in this chapter Sir John attacks the Papacy. He continually diverts his thoughts to this enemy and goes so far as to assert that kings, not popes, should summon national and even general councils of the Church. Not a word does our prisoner write against the Arminians. His sources know nothing about them.

Finally Sir John turns to his fifth and last major power of majesty which is that over money. In his exposition of this subject he shows only a very rudimentary understanding of the principles underlying the use of money. His prime interest is to keep the value of money stable. The power and duty of a king is to maintain a stable currency whose weight and value must not fluctuate. He admits that a king has the power to alter the value of money for his own benefit and to the harm of his subjects. But a prince should not do this, as it is against the law of nature. Eliot takes it for granted that all kings have a plentiful supply of money because of their power to coin it. Having completed his five major powers Sir John can now turn to the minor powers of majesty which are the subject of his third book.

At the beginning of this last book of the *De Jure* Sir John Eliot declares that the lesser powers are privileges rather than rights of majesty. He lists among others the wearing of purple by the Roman Emperors, the use of yellow wax in French royal seals, and the wearing of long hair by the Merovingian Kings. From a mention of these privileges he turns to the fiscal rights of kings, which is the real subject of this book.

A king, Sir John says, like each of his subjects, has his own property and goods. A king neither possesses nor has rights over the goods of his subjects. A king is the guardian of the state and of the goods and property of his subjects. As all things belong to God, though He has given

[1] *De Jure*, p. 135.

every person proprietary rights, so a king is lord of all the land, though his subjects possess their own property. In England, Eliot asserts, all tenures are from the King. So majesty maintains public safety in order to preserve private property. But a king may on occasion be forced to take private property for the sake of public good. Indeed a prince may even seize the person as well as the property of a subject but only 'when necessity urges for the safety of the state, as of a sudden the cutting of a traitor or person pestilent and dangerous to the state by violence when it cannot be done by ordinary course of justice'.[1] After expounding at some length on the morals of the king's seizing the person and property of his subjects Eliot declares that in an emergency a king may tax his subjects for the good of the nation. But he adds that if it is possible such taxes should be repaid. There is no other mention of the taxing powers of a king. Sir John clearly believes in the well-accepted medieval theory that a king should live of his own and tax his subjects only in case of a crisis. Finally, he closes his treatise with the assertion that a king may not alienate any part of his kingdom without the consent of his subjects who have the same interest in property as the king has in sovereignty.

As Sir John wrote he seems to wander further and further from reality and from events and ideas of his own day. Dozens of historical examples from all ages and all countries of the known world he combines to illustrate his points without much regard for historical synthesis or truth. In the third book of his De Jure Maiestatis as well as in his entire treatise Sir John Eliot has created powers for a king which fit his own moral principles, his own ideals, but do not fit any particular king, country, or age, least of all England in the early seventeenth century.

What impresses the reader in this treatise is the amount of antiquarian research which is displayed on every page. No one can doubt that Eliot read widely. But that he read the works of every one of the hundred and twenty or more authorities he cites is highly questionable. Undoubtedly he made good use of references in the books he read as well as of compendiums and epitomes, which were commonly employed in his day. He must have read many of the works of the more than twenty authors each of whom he cites or quotes at least five times. The History of Rome by the third century Roman historian, Dion Cassius, to whom there are over twenty references, obviously had a favoured place on his table. Some of the works of Livy, Plutarch, Tacitus, Angelo Baldeschi or Baldus, Valerious Maximous, Caius Sue-

[1] De Jure, p. 168.

tonius, Jean Bodin, and Aristotle, all of whom he cites at least ten times, must have been in his prison study. As in *The Monarchy of Man* he gives marginal references, most of which are too general to be of any value. Of course the Bible is a favourite with Sir John, from which he gives more than sixty citations, and, as is to be expected, there are three times as many from the Old Testament as from the New. Quotations in Latin are numerous, too numerous in the *De Jure*. On a few occasions one or two words in Greek appear which give the impression that Eliot had little if any knowledge of that language. Practically all his quotations from his Greek authorities are in Latin.

There is evidence of a good deal of original thought in this treatise. But one gains the impression that it emanates from the mind of a neophyte in the fields of history and political theory. At the same time Eliot gives the impression of having worked hard at being a scholar; his learning did not sit lightly on him. To be sure, it was the fashion of the day, as Sir John told Hampden,[1] to quote one authority after another. This has the result of hiding any originality under a mountain of learning. But the greatest lack Sir John displays in his *De Jure* is in historical judgment as well as in what might be called orderliness, something closely akin to organization. In every chapter he wanders back and forth over his points and frequently repeats himself. He cites one author after another without displaying any knowledge of their comparative value or of the correct bearing of the quotation to the matter in hand. Anything that has the least appearance of substantiating the point he is making is grist for his mill. As in the case of *The Monarchy of Man*, he could have improved his *De Jure Maiestatis* a hundredfold by re-writing it and by eliminating many of his illustrations from history.

The style of the *De Jure* is an improvement over that of the earlier treatise. It is less oratorical and a bit less pedantic. Undoubtedly his subject helped him, as it is more historical or even factual and much less philosophical than that of *The Monarchy of Man*. But the two treatises could never become part of the living literature of the seventeenth century; they bear the unmistakable stamp of Sir John Eliot. As a writer he was too erratic and too stilted to be rated highly. Brilliant he was at times; moving are some of his passages. But the strong idealistic strain in him prevented him from thinking clearly, sent his head into the clouds, and kept his feet from moving at an even pace upon the ground. Sir John was an orator but not a writer. The House of Com-

---

[1] See above, p. 360.

mons frequently inspired him; and burning issues brought out the best in him. But in the quiet of a prison cell midst the works of his classical favourites his pen could be induced to reach similar heights only on rare occasions. The *De Jure Maiestatis* in so many respects is out of tune with the Sir John Eliot depicted in these pages that one wonders what lay behind it. Could Sir John have thought of dedicating it to Charles I? Could he have intended it as a bid for release from prison?

That he had some expectation of being released can be seen from the draft of a speech he wrote while in the Tower. It was to his beloved Commons. During the last two years of his imprisonment there were occasional rumours that Charles was about to summon a Parliament. The evidence we have is that Eliot never seemed to believe in such rumours. But on one occasion at least, he must have had more than a hope that Parliament would meet, for he wrote his speech.[1] Instances have been given when Sir John Eliot prepared speeches in anticipation of delivery. This is the last and clearest instance of what might be called a characteristic of Sir John. In this last speech he presents with his old eloquence and much elaboration the oft-told story of the importance and value of the liberties and privileges of the Commons. Kings in the past were successful as long as they co-operated with Parliament, but as soon as they depended on favourites disaster came to them and the nation. No blame is cast upon the King except for listening to the advice of favourites instead of that of Parliament. Kingship still remains inviolate. The suffering during years of imprisonment at the hands of Charles I and his judges is brushed aside. A favourite, whoever he may now be, is again the evil genius. Reading and meditating, dreaming and writing Eliot could not forget those days when Parliament had sat. Only his body, growing feebler month by month, refused in the end to let that active mind find a way to reconcile the King with the House of Commons.

---

[1] P.E. MSS., 'Eliot, speeches, etc.', ff. 100-3v, also Forster, *Eliot*, II, 700-4 (2nd edit., 445-8). From internal evidence it is obvious that the speech was written while Eliot was in the Tower, probably during the last four months of 1631 when rumours of a Parliament were strongest.

CHAPTER XVII

Property Bequeathed

December 20, 1630

IN spite of the fact that Sir John Eliot was still relatively a young man when he began his residence in the Tower as a prisoner of the King, the conditions of his imprisonment soon made it imperative that he prepare his last will and testament. And this he did some time before he was seized with his fatal illness. His will is dated December 20, 1630.[1]

Before discussing Eliot's will some mention must be made of that of Richard Gedy who died on September 17, 1629.[2] It will be remembered that Sir John was already at that time a prisoner in the Tower. Moreover, his children were all minors and the property of Gedy was bequeathed to those children. To be sure, the lion's share of this estate went to John Eliot, the prisoner's eldest son. But the burdens of Sir John were greatly increased by the fact that he was made the administrator of the will of his father-in-law. There were numerous debts to be paid. Otherwise he could do very little until at least his eldest son had come of age. In the meantime the extensive Gedy lands were being administered by five trustees until the will could be executed.[3]

Where Eliot ran into difficulties was when he decided to make his own will. Then he had to take that of his father-in-law into considera-

---

[1] The original is at Somerset House in London. This has been compared with a copy to be found among the P.E. MSS., Munim. Room, P.E. Title Deeds, no. 27. They are exactly the same except for the signatures. The copy contains the two codicils as well as the administration granted the executors when the will was proved in the Prerogative Court of Canterbury on Dec. 11, 1632. The will is not printed by Forster in the 1st edit. of his *Eliot*, but it is to be found in the 2nd edit., II, 369–72. With spelling and punctuation modernized the Forster version of the will is fairly accurate. Its chief weakness is that it omits the two codicils.

[2] See above, p. 346.

[3] His property consisted of several manors and a goodly number of other parcels of land. The five trustees were Hugh Boscawen, John Trefuses, John Norleigh, esqs., and Peter Mayowe and Leonard Treise, gents. Forster, *Eliot*, 2nd edit., II, 369–70.

tion and virtually incorporate it into his own. The resulting document was far from simple. Of course Sir John did not draft it himself. On December 13 he wrote to Robert Mason, his friend and legal adviser.[1] With the letter he enclosed a rough draft of his will which he asked Mason to 'digest to the best advantage of your judgment'. In the finished document, dated a week later, Robert Mason esq. of Lincoln's Inn was named one of the six executors. The other five were Bevil Grenville esq., Sir Dudley Digges, John Arundel esq., William Scawen gent., and Maurice Hill gent. This list immediately raises the questions why were neither Hampden nor Luke included and what was the reason for making Digges an executor. Why Eliot did not include these two most intimate friends among the executors of his will, he alone can answer. Why he included Sir Dudley Digges is another matter.

We have seen how Eliot and Digges were close associates in the second Parliament of the reign of Charles I, how they gradually drifted apart during the third, and how Digges finally became a supporter of the government of Charles when the Duke of Buckingham had been eliminated. Politically they were not on speaking terms, though privately they may have had some contacts even though no letter to or from Digges has survived in the correspondence of the prisoner in the Tower. But Eliot must have known that Sir Dudley Digges had received in 1630 a grant of the reversion of the Mastership of the Rolls expectant on the death of Sir Julius Caesar.[2] Could it be the prisoner thought this old friend of his, though politically on the wrong side, might, if properly treated, some day be willing to assist his heirs? It would have been better for Eliot had the office been the Mastership of the Court of Wards and Liveries. Vassal of the King for Port Eliot, Sir John must have realized that this court might have a good deal to say about the inheritance of his children, especially were they under age at the time of his death. But that inheritance might just as easily fall into the clutches of the Court of Chancery. To have as Master of the Rolls an old friend and particularly an executor of his will should help his heirs in any suit brought before this judge. Such a reason must at least be seriously considered, with no other plausible one at hand, why Eliot named Sir Dudney Digges one of the executors of his will.

To return to that will, Robert Mason besides receiving as an executor

[1] Forster, *Eliot*, 1st edit., II, 598, note, misdated Dec. 15. P.E. MSS., Letter Book.
[2] *D.N.B.*

a gold ring worth forty shillings engraved with the motto *Armore et Confidentia*, was left an annuity of £5 'for his counsel and advice in the managing and disposing of my estate according to my will'. Mason received his fee for services he had already performed as well as for those to be performed. Unquestionably the generosity of this bequest was caused by the fact that the lawyer was more than just the counsel of the testator and his testament. He was an old friend and co-defender of the liberties of Parliament, a man who had stuck to Eliot and his cause through thick and thin. And in December, 1630, between the 13th and 20th, Robert Mason was undoubtedly responsible for the final phrasing of Sir John Eliot's will. He worded the difficult property contracts which compose the greater part of this document.

As has been said, what made this will so complex was that it was a combination of two wills, that of Gedy and that of Eliot. It was necessary for Sir John to create one large estate of his property and Gedy's for the benefit of the creditors and legatees of the two men as well as of the four surviving Eliot boys. This estate was first of all to provide funds for raising and educating the six younger children. Next it was to pay all the debts of the two men and provide for the legacies in the two wills. Finally, the lands of the estate were to be divided among the sons of Sir John Eliot as provided by the two wills, but in particular by the will of Sir John which somewhat modified that of Richard Gedy in this respect.

In the case of his four daughters, Eliot provided that they 'shall have convenient allowance and maintenance for their several and respective breeding and education at the discretion of' his executors. But as soon as they were married, or unmarried reached the age of 24, they were to receive the legacies left them by their father and grandfather. The legacies from both amounted to £1,500 for Elizabeth and £1,200 each for Bridget, Radigund, and Susan.[1] In a codicil dated November 21, 1632, Sir John added £500 to the portion of his daughter Elizabeth. As to Eliot's younger sons, Edward and Nicholas (Thomas having died since Gedy made his will), they were to have 'such convenient and fitting maintenance for their breeding and education as to my executors shall seem meet until my executors shall think fit to send them severally to the University'. On entering Oxford the two young men were to be given £50 a year each until at the age of 21 they were to receive the lands bequeathed to them by their grandfather. Richard Eliot, on the

---

[1] Gedy had left £1,200 to Elizabeth and £1,000 each to the other three.

other hand, was to have £100 a year on the death of his father until the lands willed to him were put in his possession. But Eliot made it quite clear and repeated the point several times in his will that all the debts and legacies of himself and his father-in-law must be paid before any of the lands were to be conveyed to his sons. The money to provide for these debts and legacies was to be raised by the sale of the personal property of Gedy and Eliot and by means of copyhold leases on the lands of the combined estates. Sir John, however, did specify that the demesne lands of Cuddenbeak should be leased only year by year, so that they could be acquired by his eldest son, John, as soon as he came of age. At no place in his will did Eliot leave any of his own land to his younger sons. All his real property, after providing for his debts and legacies, was to go to John Eliot.[1] But, as has been mentioned, John was also to receive the greater part of the Gedy lands.[2] Richard, Edward and Nicholas were to inherit proportionately smaller amounts of land from their grandfather. As Thomas Eliot, now dead, had received his share by the will of his grandfather, Sir John provided that that portion of land should all go to Nicholas and not be shared with the other three. Obviously this might be a source of trouble in the future. But it was doubtless a fair division, for the lands which Nicholas finally inherited probably did not amount to much more than those of Edward Eliot.

[1] His chief holdings were the manor of Port Eliot held of the King for a 1/50 of a knight's fee, the manor of Cuddenbeak leased of the Bishop of Exeter for three lives, the Borough of St. Germans held of the King in socage, and the manor of Hatch in Devon.

[2] Richard Gedy was a much wealthier landholder than Sir John Eliot. When in 1635 John Eliot made a request for a special livery of his father's lands, they were valued at the extremely low figure of £49 a year to avoid paying heavy fees to the Court of Wards and Liveries. For a basis of comparison there exists a similar request from John Eliot for the lands he had inherited from Gedy in which their annual value was declared to be £74 8s. This excluded the Gedy lands which went to the younger sons of Eliot. P.E. MSS., Muniment Room, P.E. Title Deeds, nos. 29 and 30.

Fortunately there are preserved at Port Eliot accounts which give us the true value of at least the greater part of the combined estates of Gedy and Eliot. They are the reckoning of Maurice Hill, 'Receiver etc., for the demesnes, rectories, mills, rents, fines and profits, and other dues' for the two years 1631 and 1632, each ending at Michaelmas. These accounts include all the Eliot lands but, according to Sir John's will, only part of the Gedy lands. The income from rents each year amounted to about £950. To this was added each year £1,000 to £1,500 from the other items mentioned in the above title. Rents from the manor and barton of Cuddenbeak, which are two separate items, amounted to around £270 a year, while the barton of Port Eliot produced only £66. On the other hand, the barton of Wisewandra, which was part of the Gedy lands, payed a rent of around £500 a year. These are a few of the chief items and give some idea of the real value of the property left to the children of Sir John, particularly to his eldest son. P.E. MSS., Muniment Room, Manor of Cuddenbeak, Title Deeds, Bundle LXIX.

There were a number of people outside of his immediate family who were granted legacies by Sir John Eliot. The annuity to Robert Mason has already been mentioned. Maurice Hill was particularly favoured. He was given an annuity of £20 until the lease on certain copyhold lands had become void. Then he was to hold these lands for life. Leonard Treise, close friend and favoured trustee of Eliot and Gedy lands, was left £100. To Thomas Dix, former minister of St. Germans and Eliot's tutor, was bequeathed £10. Though he had left St. Germans in 1625 for another parish, he had administered the church of St. Germans during Sir John's youth and had laid the foundation of his education. Finally, nurse Polwheele and George Heywood, Eliot's servant, received £5 each.

Of all his goods and chattels Sir John left only a few to his eldest son and none to any of his other children. His books and papers, his best horse and arms, and his best 'silver bason and ewer with the flagons and sugar box suitable thereunto' were to go to John Eliot. The rest of his goods as well as those of Gedy he left to his executors to be used to help defray the debts and legacies of himself and his father-in-law.

Of the two codicils he added, one has already been mentioned. On the 27th of November, 1632, less than twenty-four hours before he died, he added a second codicil. In it he besought and entreated the Master of the Court of Wards and Liveries to grant the wardship of his son and heir, John Eliot, to his two kinsmen, John Trefuses and Hugh Boscawen, and to Maurice Hill. John was still a minor, though he lacked only a little more than ten months before reaching his twenty-first birthday.

Though John Eliot made formal request for livery of his father's and grandfather's lands in 1635, he did not receive them until 1640.[1] Like many others he suffered during the civil wars. Being a supporter of the parliamentary side his lands were sequestered for four years by the royalists in Cornwall. In a petition he presented to Parliament in the autumn of 1647 John Eliot disclosed that the debts and legacies of his father and grandfather had saddled him with a financial burden of more than £17,000.[2] The implication he left was that much, if not all, of this large sum was still unpaid. It must have been a goodly number of years, if ever, before the heir of Sir John Eliot could live as comfortably and prosperously as had been hoped and desired by his father and grandfather.

[1] P.E. MSS., Munim. Room, P.E. Title Deeds, nos. 29, 30, 31, 32.
[2] P.E. MSS., 'Coll. by and con. Eliot', ff. 272–5.

CHAPTER XVIII

'Buried in the Church of that Parish where he died'

November 28, 1632

SEVEN of the last eight months of the life of Sir John Eliot are a complete blank for the historian. It is only during the thirty days preceding his death that light is shed upon a life which was rapidly ebbing. Despite the location of his chamber in the Tower, despite walks within the precincts of his prison, his lungs, attacked by disease, were growing weaker day by day.

The first recorded news of the prisoner comes from the pen of Mr Pory writing from London to Lord Brooke on October 25, 1632.[1] He said that Mason had made a motion to the Court of King's Bench for the release of Sir John Eliot in order that he might regain his health. Lord Chief Justice Richardson replied, according to Pory, that, though Sir John Eliot had been brought low in body, 'yet was he as high and lofty in mind as ever'. The bench, as stated in this letter, suggested that Eliot petition the King. A few days later Sir John acted on the suggestion of the court and petitioned: 'I humbly beseech your Majesty you will command your judges to set me at liberty that for recovery of my health I may take some fresh air.' On receiving this petition by the hands of the Lieutenant of the Tower, Charles replied that 'it was not humble enough'. Again Eliot approached the King, this time through his son, with a petition in which he said: 'I am heartily sorry to have displeased your Majesty, and . . . do humbly beseech you once again to command your judges to set me at liberty that when I have recovered my health I may return back to my prison.' The only effect this petition had was to arouse the anger of the Lieutenant who told Eliot that he, the Lieutenant, not Sir John's son or anybody else, should be the bearer of a petition from a prisoner in the Tower to the King. He in-

[1] *C. and T. Chas. I*, II, 185.

formed Eliot that if in a third petition he 'would humble himself to his Majesty in acknowledging his fault and craving pardon, he would willingly deliver it, and made no doubt but he should obtain his liberty'. To this offer the prisoner replied by thanking his keeper for his friendly advice. 'My spirits are grown feeble and faint,' he said, 'which, when it shall please God to restore unto their former vigour, I will take it farther into my consideration.'[1] Even with death staring him in the face Eliot would not budge from the stand he had taken for fear of endangering the liberties of the House of Commons.

These incidents occurred early in November. By that time it was clear to Eliot that he had not many days to live. This is confirmed by Mr Pory who, shortly before the middle of that month, met Sir John's attorney in St. Paul's Churchyard who told him 'he had been that morning with Sir John in the Tower and found him so far spent with his consumption as not like to live a week longer'.[2]

In the short time left to him Eliot had much to do. Persuaded by his friends, no doubt, he called in a portrait painter.[3] The resulting record for posterity is most interesting but not exactly pleasing. Dishevelled and wasted the dying man stands dressed in a beautiful nightgown or dressing gown trimmed and patterned with bands of finest lace. But the face, though emaciated and partially disguised by his straggly hair, is unmistakably that of Sir John Eliot. The black eyes, made more striking by the bags beneath them, have lost their wistful look and with a distinct bulge stare into space. The prominent and distinguished nose together with the high cheek bones could only be made more angular, more striking by approaching death. But the artist refused to depict the extreme ravages of disease, gave the face a sallow pallor, but left it with its normal wedge-shape running from the broad, high forehead, now partially covered by strands of unkempt hair, to the pointed beard, deprived of its fullness and neat trim. In the long, fine fingers of his left hand Eliot holds a comb. He seems to be waiting to use it, if the artist will give him time; or else he has just combed out his hair which has become matted from days of lying on his bed. In his weakened condition every motion must have been an effort. That he was able to pose for any length of time standing on his feet seems hard to believe.

---

[1] These petitions are described in a letter Pory wrote from London on Dec. 13. He admits that the wording of the petitions and Eliot's final comment are merely 'to this effect'. C. and T. Chas. I, II, 209.

[2] Ibid., 195, Nov. 15.   [3] His name is unknown.

SIR JOHN ELIOT IN HIS NIGHTGOWN

Painted a few days before he died in the Tower, November, 1632

From the portrait at Port Eliot
reproduced by permission of the Earl of St. Germans

It was his last physical ordeal for the sake of friends, family, and posterity. In the bookery at Port Eliot this portrait has hung for centuries, a grim reminder to Eliot's descendants and their friends that he suffered and died for liberty. Two other portraits of the man also hang in the halls of that family seat. Both were painted by an unknown artist in 1628 when Sir John was at the height of his career. The sadness that seems to emerge from the fine eyes and the firm, straight mouth makes one wonder whether he was not posing for these pictures during the months following the death of his wife. Of course we know that a great deal of the time he took life and himself very seriously. A display of gaiety and a sense of humour were exceptions rather than the rule. Hence the artist in 1628 was probably portraying the man as he normally looked and not necessarily as a sorrowing widower. Only the finest portrait painter can depict the difference between gravity and sorrow; and Eliot's artist, though good, was far from being exceptional.

These are the portraits of a man who in his youth had been gay, impetuous, and often thoughtless. On reaching maturity he had proved to be an able and loyal servant of the Lord Admiral. By that time idealism began to dominate his thinking. His love of King and country were paramount. His King was perfect and must be implicitly trusted and obeyed. His country must be governed to perfection, by King and Parliament. On entering Parliament he was impressed by that assembly, by the House of Commons. The more he saw of the Commons the more he believed in them. The rights, privileges and liberties of the House of Commons must be defended. That quickly became a policy which had to be supported at all costs. Soon the idealist saw that all was not perfect. The liberties of Parliament were being endangered. The government of England was far from good. Who was to blame? Not the King. Not Parliament. But the ministers, a minister, of the King. They were at fault, were endangering the liberties of the Commons and also subordinating the good of the country to their own selfish ends. Thus argued Sir John Eliot, the champion of both King and Commons.

And now his fame as an orator began to grow as his attack and defence became more bitter and impassioned. He had shown that he was an able speaker early in his parliamentary career. But his great gift of oratory came to light in his denunciation of the Duke of Buckingham. Not always was Eliot the orator, not always could he move the Commons. At times he was so impetuous in his attack or defence that the Commons were not ready to follow him. Only after mature deliberation could they accept his point of view. At other times his words had no effect whatsoever on his listeners. He talked a great deal, too much in fact. He found it difficult to listen to others. Indeed, there were a number of occasions when Sir John Eliot was considered a bore by his colleagues. And then suddenly he would be inspired and his words would move the members of the House to an outburst of applause. Eliot was at his best in the session of 1626 and during June of 1628 when he was hot on the trail of the royal favourite. But he was also good, very good, in defending parliamentary liberties and the Church of England, as he understood it, during the short session of 1629. These were the times when he was the leader, when he was followed by a majority of the House of Commons.

The ideas and policies behind the words of the orator were at times excellent. But he was not alone in presenting them to the Commons, and his were by no means always the best. Contrary to what has frequently been asserted, Sir John Eliot was not the brains of the opposition at all times and under all circumstances between 1625 and 1629.[1] Sir Thomas Wentworth, Sir Robert Phelips, Sir Edward Coke, even Sir Dudley Digges, and still others demonstrated on numerous occasions that they were the mental superiors of Eliot and often prepared and even presented projects which later Sir John, the orator, induced the Commons to accept.

Sir John Eliot's fame rests to a certain extent on his ability, on his oratory, but above all it rests on his defence of the liberties of the House of Commons, on his defence of freedom of speech for which he sacrificed his life.

But for several years before that life came to an end there must have been a doubt in the man's mind about the perfection of his Sovereign. One feels that at the end of his parliamentary career and when he was thrown into prison for the last time. But his months of contemplation in the Tower enabled him to regain his faith in government by King and Parliament. Whether he was also able to recapture his old faith in Charles I is doubtful. Eliot had the ability to put the personal and the theoretical into separate compartments. At the same time he had a mind which rarely was able to think an abstract subject through from beginning to end. His thoughts so often seemed to be distracted.

---

[1] Of course, by Forster. Recently Esme Wingfield-Stratford in his *Charles, King of England, 1600–1637* (London, 1949). Pt. IV, presents Eliot as the brains of the evil opposition which was planning revolution.

By the middle of November, 1632, the thoughts of this ailing man could only have been on death. But before the end came there was one more thing for Eliot to do. That was to find a wife for his son John. Sir Oliver Luke had been consulting with the prisoner on this matter for some days. On November 24 Luke informed Sir Daniel Norton of Southwicke, Hants, that Eliot desired the marriage of his son to Sir Daniel's daughter Honora. On the 26th Norton visited Sir John in the Tower. The match was agreed upon. Honora's marriage portion was to be £3,000 provided John Eliot's estate amounted to £1,500 per annum, of which £700 would be settled on his wife for her jointure. The prospective bride and groom met each other for the first time, presumably in Hants, on November 27. Shortly before this the bride's mother had applied to the Court of Wards and Liveries for a royal licence to enable her daughter to marry the son, a minor, of a vassal of the King. That all concerned in this marriage knew on November 27 that Sir John Eliot had only a day or so, if not a few hours, to live is self-evident. They also knew that if the marriage was not performed before the death of Sir John, his son would become the ward of the King, and the whole affair would be involved in red tape and expense in the Court of Wards. Therefore, it was decided to consummate the marriage before the licence had arrived. This was done on the morning of November 28 at West Burrant, Hants. But death had defeated the purpose of the 'conspirators'. Nine hours earlier at two o'clock in the morning of November 28, unknown to his son and to the Nortons in Hampshire, Sir John Eliot died in the Tower. In due course the Court of Wards had its say, fined all concerned in the affair, and doubled the marriage fee to be paid by the ward of the King from £2,000 to £4,000 because no licence had been obtained.[1]

Sir John Eliot was dead. With the help of disease Charles I had conquered. But the spirit of political liberty brought to life by the Petition of Right was immeasurably strengthened by the martyrdom of Eliot. He had died for a cause which was understood by only a few Englishmen at the time, freedom of speech in the House of Commons. Within ten years that cause had been expanded into freedom from royal tyranny into revolution, and was being proclaimed throughout the land. The memory of Eliot's death inspired thousands of his countrymen. Throughout the succeeding centuries this liberty which Eliot did so much to bring before the nation was gradually extended to all men.

[1] For this affair see 'Inventory', pp. vi-viii.

That same spirit which Sir John Eliot helped to engender in Englishmen of the seventeenth century carried them to victory over foreign tyranny in the twentieth.

Though we do not know what the feelings of Eliot towards Charles were at the time of his death, we do know that the King hated him bitterly. Even death could not destroy this feeling. John Eliot petitioned the King to be permitted to take his father's body into Cornwall for burial among his ancestors. But the only answer he received from his Sovereign was the infamous reply: 'Let Sir John Eliot's body be buried in the church of that parish where he died.'[1] Thus the Tower of London, a monument to the power of monarchy, became the shrine of the martyr to political liberty in England.

In bringing the life of Sir John Eliot to a close we must follow the fortunes of his memory in the House of Commons and Parliament. The debt the lower House owed for the inspiration aroused by the great idealistic orator could not be paid for by acts and resolutions. Though they were passed, Eliot received his true reward when Parliament in succeeding decades put into execution the principles for which he had fought and died.

Five days after the opening of the Short Parliament, on April 18, 1640, it was ordered by the Commons that the records and proceedings in the Courts of Star Chamber and King's Bench concerning Sir John Eliot and the other members, who had been questioned for their words and actions in the last Parliament, should be sent for immediately.[2] On that day there was also some discussion of the activities of March 2, 1629, particularly in respect to the part Mr Speaker had played. But no action was taken on this matter. On April 21 the records requested by the House were presented.[3] Nothing was done about them. That is the last heard of this subject in the Short Parliament which had so many more serious grievances to discuss.

The Long Parliament did not forget Sir John Eliot. On July 8, 1641, the Commons resolved 'that the exhibiting of the information against Mr Holles, Sir John Eliot and Mr Valentine in the King's Bench, being members of the Parliament, for matter done in Parliament, was a breach of the privilege of Parliament'.[4] And then on December 1, 1641, in that great indictment of the reign of Charles I, the Grand Remonstrance, Eliot, though his name was not mentioned, was given a mar-

---

[1] C. and T. Chas. I, II, 209.
[2] C. J., II, 6.   [3] Ibid., 8.   [4] Ibid., 200.

tyr's crown. Denouncing the arrest and mistreatment of the nine members after the third Parliament of the reign, it says in its 15th article:

'of whom one died by the cruelty and harshness of his imprisonment, which would admit of no relaxation, notwithstanding the imminent danger of his life did sufficiently appear by the declaration of his physician; and his release, or at least his refreshment, was sought by many humble petitions; and his blood still cried either for vengeance or repentance of those ministers of state who have at once obstructed the course both of his Majesty's justice and mercy.'[1]

The strenuous days preceding the outbreak of the civil war and during the war itself diverted attention from any action on behalf of Eliot. It was not until January 18, 1647, that the Commons again displayed an interest in Sir John and his more fortunate sufferers for the cause. On that day it was resolved

'that the sum of five thousand pounds be assigned for the damages, losses, imprisonments, and sufferings sustained and undergone by Sir John Eliot for his service done to the commonwealth in the Parliament of *tertio Caroli*, to be disposed of in such manner as this House shall appoint.'[2]

But that was not all. It was also resolved on that day that two thousand pounds be paid to Mr Eliot being 'part of four thousand pounds paid into the late Court of Wards and Liveries by the heirs of Sir John Eliot, by reason of his marriage with Sir Daniel Norton's daughter'. As there was no further action taken on either of these resolutions, it can readily be seen why Sir John's son complained of not having received any of this money.[3] Finally, the Commons on this January 18, 1647, ordered that the decree of the late Court of Wards and Liveries against Eliot's heir should be examined by a committee with a report to the House and also

'that it be referred to the committee of the Tower to examine after what manner Sir John Eliot came to his death, his usage in the Tower,

---

[1] Gardiner, *Constitutional Documents*, p. 210, Rushworth, IV, 440.
[2] *C. J.*, V, 55. [3] In the petition he presented to Parliament in 1647. See above, p. 386.

and to view the rooms and places where he was imprisoned and where he died, and to report the same to the House'.[1]

But no report was made by either of these committees. The case of Sir John Eliot does not appear again in the records of the Long Parliament or any of the Cromwellian Parliaments.

It was the 'Cavalier' Parliament of Charles II which completely vindicated the stand taken by Sir John Eliot and his co-defendants in 1630. On November 23, 1667, the House of Commons resolved 'that the judgment given 5 Car. I against Sir John Eliot, Denzil Holles, and Benjamin Valentine Esquires, in the King's Bench was an illegal judgment and against the freedom of privileges of Parliament'.[2] On December 11 of that year the House of Lords declared that judgment 'to be erroneous'.[3]

Of the privileges of Parliament that of freedom of speech was by far the most important. Victory against direct royal interference with freedom of speech in the House of Commons had been won to all intents and purposes in the last Parliament of James I. Opposition to the interference of a royal court of lower rank than Parliament with this privilege had sent Eliot to his martyr's death. To prevent for all time such interference the Bill of Rights in 1689 declared 'that the freedom of speech and debates or proceedings in Parliament ought not to be impeached or questioned in any court or place out of Parliament'. Sir John Eliot had not died in vain.

---

[1] C. J., V, 55.　　[2] Ibid., IX, 25.　　[3] L. J., XII, 166.

BIBLIOGRAPHY

PORT ELIOT MANUSCRIPTS

A life of Sir John Eliot cannot be written without an extensive use of his letters, papers and documents at Port Eliot in St. Germans, Cornwall. In the church of St. Germans I found the parish register which contains the births and deaths of the members of the Eliot family. At Port Eliot Sir John's papers are to be found in the bookery, a small library adjacent to the main library of the house, and in the muniment room. The letters and papers in the bookery were arranged and bound under the direction of John Forster, as the *Historical Manuscripts Commission, 1st Report* (London, 1870) Appendix, p. 42, tells us. These manuscripts are in ten volumes handsomely bound in morocco but not numbered. On the backs of the volumes are the following titles for which Forster is undoubtedly responsible:

ABBREVIATIONS	
[P.E. MSS., Eliot, speeches, etc.]	*Miscellaneous Papers of Sir John Eliot, Letters, Treatises, etc., Collected or Transcribed*
[P.E. MSS., Eliot, speeches, etc.]	*Original Manuscripts by Sir John Eliot, Parliamentary and Unspoken Speeches, Collections of Precedents, Philosophical Fragments, etc.*
[P.E. MSS., Eliot and Bucks]	*Sir John Eliot and the Duke of Buckingham, Papers Written or Collected by Eliot*
[E.P.N. 1626(1), E.P.N. 1626(2)]	*First and Second Parliaments of Charles I, 1625–1626, Eliot's Notes and Extracts from Journals*
[P.E. MSS., Coll. by and con. Eliot]	*Collections by and concerning Sir John Eliot, 1622–1629, and His Eldest Son, 1646–1659*
	Journals, Letters and Papers Relating to Spain, 1604–1629
	Arguments Concerning the Liberty of the Person, 3 Car. 1628
[Letter Book]	*The Letter Book of Sir John Eliot*
	The Negotium Posterorum
	De Jure Maiestatis

There is also in the bookery a modern filing box which contains a few assorted papers from the seventeenth and later centuries. One of these is a nineteenth century copy of the apology of John Eliot to John Moyle.

Finally I found in the bookery a beautifully bound manuscript, 'Catalogue of the Ancient Deeds and Papers in the Muniment Room at Port Eliot Arranged and Compiled with Notes on the Family of Eliot' by Charles Henderson. It is dated New Year's Day, 1928, and contains abstracts or brief descriptions of most of the manuscripts Mr Henderson found in the muniment room.

The manuscripts in the muniment room are preserved in a large black box or trunk. They have been classified and tied into bundles by Mr Henderson. The most important classifications are:

> Port Eliot, Title Deeds
> Manor Cuddenbeak, Title Deeds
> St. Germans Borough, Title Deeds.

For some unknown reason John Forster never saw the manuscripts in the muniment room. There is no mention of any of them in his *Sir John Eliot*.

ABBREVIATIONS The most important writings of Eliot have been edited and published by Alexander B. Grosart. They are:

[*Monarchy*] *The Monarchy of Man by Sir John Eliot*
2 vols., Priv. Printed, 1879
Grosart used Eliot's draft of this work which is now Harleian MS. 2228 in the British Museum.

[*Apology*] *An Apology for Socrates and Negotium Posterorum by*
[*Neg. Post.*] *Sir John Eliot*
2 vols., Priv. Printed, 1881
To each of these two volumes Grosart has added a Supplement in which he has printed a total of fifteen speeches or fragments of speeches written by Eliot. He found these speeches in the bound volumes of papers in the bookery at Port Eliot.

[*De Jure*] *De Jure Maiestatis or Political Treatise of Government (1628–*
[*Letter Book*] *1630) and The Letter Book of Sir John Eliot.*
2 vols., Priv. Printed, 1882.
The Letter Book is by no means complete and contains only the most important letters in the manuscript Letter Book.

PARLIAMENTARY DIARIES

Fully as important for a life of Eliot as his own papers are the parliamentary diaries of five of the six Parliaments or sessions of which he was a member. Most of the diaries are unpublished and have been used in typescript form. They are for the Parliament of 1624.

[Nicholas] Edward Nicholas's Parliamentary Note Book, Feb. 19 to May 29, 1624.
State Papers, Domestic Series, James I, CLXVI.

[Holland]   The Diary of Sir Thomas Holland for 1624
                 Bodleian Library: Feb. 25 to April 9 in Tanner 392,
                 April 10 to May 15 in Rawlinson, D., 1100.

[Holles]   The Diary of John Holles for 1624
                 Harleian MS. 6383.

[Earle]   The Diary of Sir Walter Earle for the Parliament of 1624
                 Additional MS. 18597.

[Gurney]   The Gurney Diary for 1624
                 At Keswick Hall near Norwich belonging to the Gurney
                 family.

[Pym]   The Diary of John Pym for 1624
                 Additional MS. 26639.

[Harl. 159]   A Diary for 1624
                 Harleian MS. 159.

             Parliament of 1625
             A Diary of the Parliament of 1625
[Calthorpe]   In the Lady Anstruther-Gough-Calthorpe Collection at
                 Elvetham, Hartley-Wintney, in Hampshire near Basing-
                 stoke.
             Gardiner, S. R., edit.
[C.D.]   *Debates in the House of Commons in 1625*
                 Camden Society, Second Series, 1873.

             Parliament of 1626
[Whitelocke] Bulstrode Whitelocke's Journal of the Parliament of 1626.
                 Cambridge University Library, D.D. 12, 20–22
[Rich]   Sir Nathaniel Rich's Diary of the Parliament of 1626.
                 Duke of Manchester's MSS. at Kimbolton Castle,
                 St Neots, Huntingdonshire.
[Grosvenor]   Sir Richard Grosvenor's Diary of the Parliament of 1626
                 Dublin, Trinity College Library, 611.

             Parliament of 1628
[Borlase]   The Borlase Manuscript
                 Stowe MS. 366.
[Grosvenor(2)] Notes of Proceedings taken by Sir Richard Grosvenor, 1628
                 Dublin, Trinity College Library.
[Nicholas(2)] Notes of Sir Edward Nicholas for 1628
                 State Papers, Domestic Series, Charles I, XCVII.
[Mass. MS.]   The True Relation
                 Manuscript in the possession of the Massachusetts
                 Historical Society.
             Notes by ——

[Harl. 2313]   Harleian MSS. 2313, 5324.
[Harl. 5324]

                         Notes by ——
[Harl. 1601]   Harleian MS. 1601.

                         Notes of Mr Lowther
[*Lowther*]   *Historical Manuscripts Commission, 13th Report*, Appendix
                         VII, pp. 33–60.

                    The Session of 1629
                         Notestein, Wallace and Relf, Frances H.
[*C.D. 1629*]   *Commons Debates for 1629.*
                         University of Minnesota Press, 1921.

PUBLIC RECORD OFFICE MANUSCRIPTS

State Papers, Domestic Series, James I and Charles I; Crown Office Docquet
Book; Crown Office Entry Book; Patent Roll, vols. 19, 20; Privy Council
Register of Charles I, vols. II, III, IV, V, VII; High Court of Admiralty, Act
Books, Miscellanea, Oyer et Terminer.

BRITISH MUSEUM MANUSCRIPTS

A goodly number in the Additional and Harleian Collections as well as one to
three in each of the following collections: Cotton, Egerton, Hargrave, Lans-
downe, Sloane and Stowe.

BODLEIAN LIBRARY MANUSCRIPTS

Several in each of the following: Ashmole, English history, Perrott, Rawlinson,
Tanner and Browne Willis.

THE DYCE–FORSTER COLLECTION

This is in the South Kensington Museum, London. These papers of John
Forster contain only one of the numerous lost Eliot manuscripts and shed no
new light on the life of Sir John Eliot.

PRINTED COLLECTIONS

These include such standard collections as the *Acts of the Privy Council, 1621 to
1628*, in 6 vols.; 9 vols. of the *Calendar of State Papers, Domestic Series*; 10 of the
Reports of the *Historical Manuscripts Commission*; Thomas Rymer's *Foedera;*
Robert Steele's *Tudor and Stuart Proclamations.*

Among the dozen or more well-known parliamentary collections are *The
Journals of the House of Commons; The Journals of the House of Lords;* Thomas
Fuller, *Ephemeris Parliamentaria* (London, 1654); John Rushworth, *Historical
Collections;* William Cobbett, *The Parliamentary History of England; The Parlia-
mentary or Constitutional History of England* (London, 1751–62); *Statutes of the
Realm;* and others. Mention should be made of *Journals of the House of Commons*

from *21st of June to 5th of July, 1625, in the first year of the Reign of King Charles the First* (London, N.D.). 'These Journals were discovered in the Archives of the House of Lords in the year 1877 and are supposed to have been compiled in the year 1625 by the son of the Clerk of the House of Commons, who was first appointed in 1620 to act as the Deputy of his Father during his sickness ...'

GENERAL PRINTED PRIMARY SOURCES

These are numerous and include such items as Thomas Birch, *The Court and Times of Charles the First*, 2 vols. (London, 1849); *The Autobiography of Sir John Bramston* (Camden Society, 1845); John Hacket, *Scrinia Reserata*, 2 vols. (London, 1693); J. O. Halliwell, *The Autobiography and Correspondence of Sir Simonds D'Ewes, Bart.*, 2 vols. (London, 1845); William Knowler, *The Earl of Strafforde's Letters and Dispatches*, 2 vols. (London, 1739); N. E. McClure, *Letters of John Chamberlain*, 2 vols. (Philadelphia, 1939); and R. G. Marsden, *Select Pleas in the Court of Admiralty*, Vol. II (Selden Society, 1897).

SECONDARY WORKS

These include many standard reference works, histories, general and local, biographies, articles, and numerous monographs. They are all listed in the footnotes. Outstanding among them is S. R. Gardiner, *The History of England, 1603–1642*, 10 vols.

INDEX

portant speeches: August 1, 85–6;
August 6, 88–9; the Cotton
speech, 92; **MP 1626**, 104–49;
speech on February 10, 105–6;
case of the *St Peter*, 108–11;
organizes attack on Buckingham,
111–15; blames Buckingham, 116;
speech of March 27, 117–20;
speech of March 29, 122–3;
epilogue in Buckingham's impeachment, 135–8; imprisoned
with Digges, 139–45; suspended
as vice-admiral, 154; imprisoned
for refusing to lend, 158; inquiry
against, 159–65; petition from the
Gatehouse, 166–9; Cornish election, 173–81; **MP 1628**, 184–265;
important speeches: March 20
(not delivered), 186–7; March 22,
189–90; April 21 (not delivered),
212n; proposes bill of rights, 216;
dispute with Wentworth over
Lords, 233–5; speech of June 3,
243–5; stopped in middle of
speech of June 5, 249–50; death
of wife, 264–5; lands in hands of
trustees, 266–7; second wife proposed for, 268–71; Christmas with
Warwick, 276; **MP 1629**, 278–
315; speech of January 29, 280–2;
correspondence of winter 1629,
301–7; leader of radicals on
March 2, 307–15; speech, 311–13;
imprisoned in Tower, 315; questioned by Privy Council, 317;
brought before Star Chamber,
320–1; sues out writ of *habeas
corpus*, 323–4; visited in the Tower,
325; tried in Court of King's
Bench, 329–34; condemned, 336;
correspondence from Tower with
intimate friends, 339–45; his
letters from Tower to two eldest
sons, 345–54; his religious views
as seen in correspondence, 355–8;
discusses writings with friends in
correspondence, 358–62; his health

as seen in his correspondence,
362–5; analysis of his writings,
366–81; *An Apology for Scorates*,
366–9; *The Monarchy of Man*,
369–74; *De Jure Maiestatis*, 374–
81; his will, 382–6; last days in
the Tower, 387–91; his death, 391
Eliot, John, eldest son of Sir John,
22, 24, 24n, 26, 266, 270, 274, 302,
343, 343n; letters to, from Sir
John, showing Oxford career and
travels, 345–52, 354, 356; property left in will of father to, 382,
386–7; marriage, 391; refused
burial of father in Cornwall, 392,
393
Eliot, Katherine, daughter of Daniel
Eliot, 18n
Eliot, Lady Radigund, wife of Sir
John, marriage, 23, 24–6; death,
264–5, 266–8, 302, 389
Eliot, Nicholas, fifth son of Sir
John, 18n, 24, 24n, 264, 384–5
Eliot, Radigund, third daughter of
Sir John, 24n, 384
Eliot, Richard, father of Sir John,
17n, 18–21; died, 22, 23n, 23–5
Eliot, Richard, second son of Sir
John, 22, 24n, 266, 270, 274, 343n;
letters to, from Sir John, showing
Oxford and army career, 343–52,
354, 356; property received in
father's will, 384–5
Eliot, Susan, fourth daughter of Sir
John, 24n, 62, 384
Eliot, Thomas, fourth son of Sir
John, 24n, 348, 384–5
Elizabeth, Princess, of the Palatinate,
Queen of Bohemia, 208, 280n
Elizabeth I, Queen of England,
18–19, 21, 43, 54, 72, 77n, 106,
119, 148, 237, 244, 281, 304, 336n,
354–5
Ely, Bishop of (William Long-
champ), time of Richard I, 137
Emperor, Holy Roman, 76, 375–6;
Roman, 378

F

G

GEORGE ALLEN & UNWIN LTD

London: 40 Museum Street, W.C.1

Auckland: 24 Wyndham Street
Bombay: 15 Graham Road, Ballard Estate, Bombay, 1
Calcutta: 17 Chittaranjan Avenue, Calcutta 13
Cape Town: 109 Long Street
Karachi: 254 Ingle Road
New Delhi: 13–14 Ajmeri Gate Extension, New Delhi 1
São Paulo: Avenida 9 de Jullo 1138–Ap. 51
Sydney, N.S.W.: Bradbury House, 55 York Street
Toronto: 91 Wellington Street West

**NOTICE - A fine of
10¢ per day is due
when book is overdue.**